*The Audubon* ...

ALSO BY FRANK GRAHAM, JR.

*Disaster by Default:*
*Politics and Water Pollution* (1966)

*Since Silent Spring* (1970)

*Man's Dominion:*
*The Story of Conservation in America* (1971)

*Where the Place Called Morning Lies* (1973)

*Gulls: A Social History* (1975)

*Potomac: The Nation's River* (1976)

*The Adirondack Park* (1978)

*A Farewell to Heroes* (1981)

*The Dragon Hunters* (1984)

# The Audubon Ark

## A HISTORY OF THE NATIONAL AUDUBON SOCIETY

### by Frank Graham, Jr.

WITH CARL W. BUCHHEISTER

UNIVERSITY OF TEXAS PRESS

AUSTIN

Printed in the United States of America
First University of Texas Press edition, 1992
Published by arrangement with Alfred A. Knopf, Inc.

Grateful acknowledgment is made to the following for permission to reprint
previously published and unpublished material:

FRANCES COLLIN, TRUSTEE: Excerpt from letter of Rachel Carson to Marie Rodell.
Reprinted by permission of Frances Collin, Trustee u.w.o. Rachel Carson.

DUTTON: Excerpt from *Adventures in Bird Protection* by T. Gilbert Pearson.
Copyright 1937 by D. Appleton-Century, Inc. Reprinted by permission of Dutton,
an imprint of New American Library, a division of Penguin Books USA Inc.

FALES LIBRARY, NEW YORK UNIVERSITY: Excerpt from "Boy Meets Bulfinch"
by Geoffrey T. Hellman, originally published in *The New Yorker* (March 4, 1939).
Geoffrey T. Hellman Papers, Fales Library, New York University.
Reprinted by permission.

∞ The paper used in this publication meets the minimum requirements of American
National Standard for Information Sciences—Permanence of Paper for
Printed Library Materials, ANSI Z39.48–1984.

Library of Congress Cataloging–in–Publication Data

Graham, Frank, [date]
    The Audubon ark : a history of the National Audubon Society / by Frank Graham, Jr.
with Carl W. Buchheister. — 1st University of Texas Press ed.
    p.   cm.
    Originally published: New York : Knopf, 1990.
    Includes bibliographical references and index.
    ISBN 0–292–70440–2 (alk. paper)
    1. National Audubon Society—History.   I. Buchheister, Carl W., d. 1986.
QL671.G7   1992
598'.06073—dc20                                                                91–43864
                                                                                    CIP

What better comfort have we, or what other
        Profit in living
Than to feed, sobered by the truth of Nature,
Awhile upon her bounty and her beauty,
And hand her torch of gladness to the ages
        Following after?

                    SANTAYANA, *Ode*

# Audubon: Today and Tomorrow

## BY PETER A. A. BERLE

*President, National Audubon Society*

You are about to embark on a colorful and inspiriting adventure. This book tells the story of a movement, uniquely American, that began with a handful of men and women determined to stop the slaughter of birds for commercial enterprise. It evolved, through a series of dramatic and sometimes turbulent events, into the National Audubon Society. Today the Society, with a professional staff of 350 and a membership close to 600,000, grapples with local issues across the land and complex environmental problems that threaten the biological and political stability of our planet.

The founders had a vision. They saw their embryonic organization as a moral force that could sway public opinion and push government toward what they believed ought to be a national goal—to make a secure place for the wild birds and other animals that *their* ancestors had taken for granted. They wanted their countrymen to view wildlife not as a commodity to be exploited and used up but as a part of America's heritage, to be managed wisely and sustained for future generations. They were totally committed to the conservation of natural resources. This book shows that many of the goals they fought for have been reached.

In our era, which has generated threats to life far more pervasive than anything our predecessors foresaw, does the Audubon movement still hold a vision of similar intensity? I believe it does. Audubon remains based on the democratic notion that an organization of individuals, from a diversity of backgrounds yet acting from shared convictions, can effect the fundamental changes in society that government is not capable of initiating itself (as recent experience amply demonstrates). Audubon stands as a positive alternative for all those who feel powerless when confronted with society's indifference to values they hold precious.

But individuals, or groups of them, can be most effective when backed by hard science. Audubon's science division, engaged in policy, ecosystem, and ornithological research, gives the organization special capability and credibility. In addition, all Audubon sanctuaries, which now number more than eighty, are laboratories, or potential laboratories, that can support research and enable us to show the public the importance of specific ecosystems.

The key to Audubon's future role as an instrument of change, as a means of truly enfranchising large numbers of Americans, is its chapter system. We have a network of more than five hundred local chapters—individual Audubon Societies, if you will, yet bonded into a single organization that reaches from Maine to Hawaii and Guam, and southward through Mexico and the Caribbean to Central and South America. When our members join the National Audubon Society, they automatically become members of the chapters in their communities and a portion of their dues is allocated to the local groups. This network is the model on which we hope to build the National Audubon Society of the future. The strategy hinges on the integration of all the traditional Audubon elements into a Society in which they work together seamlessly, with the Society in turn forging ties with other organizations and institutions that profess compatible goals.

Each of the Audubon chapters has its own priorities. To be effective, the chapter activists—men and women from a variety of backgrounds and occupations—are already moving toward professionalism in the environmental field. With the aid of publications and specific training designed by the Audubon staff, chapter members are well versed in local and national issues, as well as adept in the techniques of lobbying, publicity, and other tools for effecting change. The chapters will play an increasingly important role in distributing educational materials and integrating our sanctuaries' activities into the local communities. Through its chapters, Audubon has the potential to articulate the environmental conscience of America. The chapter also provides the mechanism by which major national battles are waged. When members of Congress return home from Washington, they are met by Audubon constituents who are advocates for positions articulated by the professional team of lobbyists in Audubon's governmental affairs office in the capital.

It is fitting that we hold a vision of the specific steps by which Audubon can make a difference. If, for instance, the Society is to represent America's environmental conscience, it ought to reflect hopes and values across a broad spectrum of the country. Like other environmental organizations, we have become more aggressive and imaginative in attracting people of all ages and ethnic backgrounds. But we still must prove to a wider range of Americans that Audubon is relevant to their concerns for the future.

The importance of education has been stressed throughout most of the Society's history. We continue to reach out to our membership, and beyond it, with a blend of traditional tools and modern technology. Our splendid magazine, *Audubon,* and our children's educational program, *Audubon Adventures*, represent a continuum, publications and programs under various names that have carried the Audubon message to both adults and children since early in this century. *American Birds* addresses serious birders and *The Audubon Activist* keeps individual activists current with environmental issues.

We have embraced the technology that defines modern communication. Our *World of Audubon* television specials bring the Audubon name and an environmental perspective into millions of households. The Society is producing award-winning educational computer software and interactive computer video material that give a new dimension to education.

National Audubon broadens its base by reaching out to form coalitions with organizations whose interests were not always seen as compatible with our own. A list of current and potential allies includes environmental and conservation groups throughout the world; religious organizations; school systems; minority organizations; labor organizations; and groups formed to work for ecologically sound agricultural practices, safety in the workplace, and the development of renewable energy systems. It will be a major step forward for American conservation as alliances are forged with industries and other corporations to help protect the environment on which each of us depends.

Audubon's interest in wildlife remains as strong as ever. But, in keeping with new threats and challenges, we are involved in specific projects that no one in the Society dreamed of a few years ago. We are working earnestly with business leaders to establish a set of principles by which corporations and their shareholders will assume a more direct responsibility for the environment. We have taken part in the development of a bilateral Soviet–American "Citizens' Treaty on Ecological Security." And we have helped to brief government representatives on their way to attend summit meetings of world leaders.

Audubon's future relevance must be demonstrated by the way it responds to emerging issues that affect both wildlife and people—among them biotechnology, the threats posed by global warming, and the need to set a sensible balance between population and natural resources. Governments have generally failed to provide appropriate leadership in addressing the environmental problems that we can go on sidestepping only at great peril. It rests with citizen activists, working together in private organizations like the National Audubon Society, to confront these complex issues with all the imagination we can summon up as we head into the twenty-first century.

# *Preface*

This book was planned more than two decades ago by Carl W. Buchheister after he retired as president of the National Audubon Society. It was fortunate he began work as early as he did, for he was able to talk to a number of men and women who were active in the Society during earlier eras but have now passed on. He assembled the notes and documents and transcripts of interviews that form the basis for many episodes in this book.

In January 1973, he and I collaborated on an article in *Audubon*, "From the Swamps and Back: A Concise History of the Audubon Movement," that summarized the results of his research to that date. Carl hoped to spend his retirement writing that history in full.

Age and illness, however, kept him from making more than a tentative start on the manuscript. Finally, in the fall of 1985, he wrote to me from his retirement home in Chapel Hill, North Carolina, asking me to take over the writing, with the added request that his part in the book's preparation be acknowledged upon publication.

I soon began to realize the magnitude of the project that lay ahead. There was no such entity as an Audubon Archives. Many of the essential documents were widely scattered—in the files of various departments in New York; at the headquarters of the Society's field research department in Tavernier, Florida; in an old barn at the Miles Wildlife Sanctuary in Sharon, Connecticut; and in the Rare Books and Manuscripts Division of the New York Public Library. Much of the material was not catalogued. Other important papers had been lost in a flood at Audubon House in the early 1960s.

I visited Carl and Harriet Buchheister that fall and again in the spring of 1986, drawing them out in conversation about the years in which he had played a leading role in Audubon affairs. Carl had remained a "gentleman of the old school"; even during his last illness, he never failed to put on a coat and tie before coming in to dinner. His memory was clear, and as the evening wore on he would invariably drop his reserve and, doubling over with laughter (which I knew often brought on pain or discomfort), give some revealing picture of the past which it would never have occurred to him to put into a book; accompanying each story was the reminder, "Now, you can't *print* this," an admonition I am afraid I have not always observed.

In the early summer of 1986, Carl bundled up the material he had not already turned over to me and shipped it in two large boxes to my home in Maine. On July 25, as prominent "Auduboners" of past and present were assembling on Hog Island for the Fiftieth Anniversary Celebration of the Audubon Camp in Maine (of which he had been director for twenty-five years before and after becoming Audubon president), Carl Buchheister died in Chapel Hill at the age of eighty-five.

My job was just beginning. To supplement the material left by Carl, I rechecked the depositories of material he had investigated, talked to many of the men and women active in Audubon affairs since Carl's retirement, and read through all of the issues of the Society's official publication, which from 1899 to the present has gone through several identities as *Bird-Lore, Audubon Magazine,* and *Audubon.* I also drew heavily on my own past writings, including a thirty-thousand-word article on the history of the Society's sanctuary system, "The Audubon Ark" (*Audubon,* January 1978), and two books, *Man's Dominion: The Story of Conservation in America* (M. Evans, 1971) and *Gulls: A Social History* (Random House, 1975).

Because many of the actors in the Audubon drama wrote and talked so articulately of their work, Carl and I had decided to give them free rein, letting them tell the story wherever possible in words drawn from their reports and other writings, or from our interviews with them. Their reminiscences summon up a sense of *place,* which in part is what the Audubon story is all about. What we humans call "landscape" is, after all, simply the habitat of the wild creatures around us.

This book is also about a unique institution, the men and women who created and maintained it, and what the naturalist Henry Beston called those "other nations, caught with ourselves in the net of life and time," for whose survival the National Audubon Society came into being. The gulls, egrets, cranes, flamingos, and condors receive special attention here. But I hope that the book makes plain the fact that the Audubon movement is ultimately concerned with the survival of *all* life on Earth.

Because I have reviewed each of the documents Carl uncovered, the errors of fact or interpretation found here are mine. The inspiration and the spirit behind the book remain his.

FRANK GRAHAM, JR.
*Milbridge, Maine*

# *Acknowledgments*

It isn't easy to single out the many men and women who helped to pull the threads of this story together. My debt to Carl Buchheister is noted above. If he had lived to share in the writing of this book, he would also have expressed his gratitude for the invaluable help of his wife, Harriet Buchheister, who shared his plans and travels as he pursued his labor of love; I acknowledge that debt for him here.

In my own case, there are four people who must be mentioned at once. Charles H. Callison, a former executive vice president of the National Audubon Society, brought me into the movement in the first place and then was responsible for bringing me together again with Carl Buchheister when it became apparent that Carl's health would prevent him from going on with his work. Les Line, editor of *Audubon,* generously gave me the time away from my duties as a field editor of the magazine to write the book and remained a source of strength and much-needed help throughout. Peter A. A. Berle, president of the Society, assured me of the complete freedom to write the story as I saw fit, never attempting to get me to put a pleasant face on controversial events even during some trying times at Audubon. And Barbara Linton, the Society's librarian, was the glue that held the project together, finding material and dispatching it to me in Maine from the vantage point of her office in New York.

To all the members of the "Audubon family," past and present, who gave me an insight into the story and helped directly or indirectly while I was writing this book, I extend my deepest gratitude: John M. "Frosty" Anderson, Marie Aull, David Blankinship, John Borneman, Mary Joy Breton, B. Bartram Cadbury, Marshal T. Case, Noel Chandler, Roderick Chandler, Roland C. Clement, Susan Roney Drennan, Mike Dudek, Michael Duever, Frank Dunstan, Brock Evans, Joseph J. Hickey, Martha Hill, John and Mary Johansen, William Kolodnicki, Stephen W. Kress, George Laycock, Susan Parker Martin, J. P. Myers, Donal C. O'Brien, Jr., John Ogden, Glenn Olson, Christopher Palmer, Richard T. Paul,

Roger Tory Peterson, Russell L. Peterson, Olin Sewall Pettingill, Jr., the late Richard L. Plunkett, Walt Pomeroy, Jean Porter, Richard H. Pough, George Powell, Elizabeth Raisbeck, Nathaniel P. Reed, Scott Reed, Philip Schaeffer, Gene Setzer, Wayne Short, Donna Slattery, Gary Soucie, Alexander "Sandy" Sprunt IV, Elvis T. Stahr, Larry Thompson, Ruth Troscianiec, Robert K. Turner, Barbara Wightman, Chris Wille, and Karen Witte.

I also thank Richard K. Walton for letting me see parts of his history of the Massachusetts Audubon Society before publication; William H. Drury, Jr., for added information on "Mass Audubon"; the staff of the Bangor Public Library for the usual courtesy and efficiency; and Barbara K. Bristol, my editor at Alfred A. Knopf, for her patience, perseverance, and guidance during the long delays in getting this manuscript into print.

Finally, I want to express my gratitude to Ada Graham, who shared my travels and research, and whose constructive suggestions helped to shape this book.

# The Audubon Ark

*1*

The first Audubon Society was the ephemeral creation in 1886 of a man now remembered mainly (if at all) as a big game hunter and the proprietor of *Forest and Stream,* then the most prestigious hunting and fishing journal in the United States. This Audubon Society functioned for a time only in the pages of *Forest and Stream.* It collected no dues, owned no property, lobbied no legislatures, sued no malefactors. After a year it emerged as a separate publication called *The Audubon Magazine,* still an organization wholly on paper, and it finally expired in 1888. Throughout its existence, the society remained essentially a pamphlet.

This characterization is not a slight. American democracy was forged and sustained by the eloquence of generations of thick-skinned pamphleteers—cranks and fanatics as well as philosophers and philanthropists—and its founder designed the new society in that noble tradition. It had a cause and a target, and its adherents were dispensed a mixture of fact, entertainment, and exhortation that brought forth an enthusiastic response, if not any very effective action.

"Within the past few years, the destruction of our birds has increased at a rate which is alarming," the first issue of *The Audubon Magazine* reported. "This destruction now takes place on such a large scale as to seriously threaten the existence of a number of our most useful species. It is carried on chiefly by men and boys who sell the skins or plumage to be used for ornamental purposes—principally for the trimming of women's hats, bonnets and clothing."

The founder of the aborted movement to stop the slaughter of birds was not the flamboyant painter of American birdlife, John James Audubon (who had died in 1851), but a man named George Bird Grinnell, who tended to hide his own remarkable achievements under the proverbial bushel. The connection between the two men was indirect but tangible.

George Bird Grinnell,
who started it all. COURTESY OF
YALE UNIVERSITY LIBRARY

Grinnell's father owned an investment business in New York City. In 1857 the family moved to Audubon Park, the site along the Hudson River in upper Manhattan to which the painter had retired near the end of his life; there, in his ruined mind, Audubon had pursued (like Orion in Hades) the phantoms of beasts he had once hunted across the hills. Lucy Audubon, the painter's widow, still lived amid the dreams and mementos in the house on this rural estate. The property had recently been subdivided and new houses sold or rented to prosperous families from the growing city, which yet lay six or eight miles to the south.

Lucy Audubon assumed a large role in Grinnell's life. She conducted the most convenient schoolhouse in that outlying region, gathering her grandchildren and the other young scholars in the neighborhood into her second-floor bedroom overlooking the river, where she held her classes. Not "Mrs. Audubon," but "Grandma," was the name the children, neighbors as well as relatives, gave to the woman in the invariable black dress and white snood. Perhaps of even more lasting impact on the young Grinnell than the daily lessons were the artifacts of the dead painter and naturalist: antlers and muzzle-loaders and powder flasks hung here and there in the house, and in an old loft where Grinnell played stood piles of the red muslin-bound copies of Audubon's *Ornithological Biography* and boxes of bird skins brought back from expeditions that are now the stuff of legend. A portrait of Audubon with his gun and dog in the wilderness, made by his son, John Woodhouse Audubon, hung in the dining room. In spring, the thoughts of boys in Lucy Audubon's class turned to the woods and the great river outside, and much free time was spent trying to bring down wild creatures with gun or bow-and-arrow. (Passenger pigeons were a favorite target because of their abundance during migration.) "My present impression is that the little boys of Audubon Park—all of them—ought to have been sent to some reform school," Grinnell was to write years later.

Apparently destined to carry on the family investment business, Grinnell attended Yale University; but, like those of his idol Audubon, his interests lay almost wholly in wild places. For most adventurous American men of Grinnell's generation, the West became synonymous with those wild places, and he spent his summers pursuing fossils and big game animals on the far side of the Mississippi. The year 1874 was decisive in his life. He dissolved the family business, to his father's chagrin, and returned to Yale to study vertebrate paleontology under Othniel C. Marsh, the most celebrated and imposing of the nineteenth-century "bone hunters" in the United States. As he worked toward a doctorate in osteology and paleontology, Grinnell completed his dissertation on "The Osteology of *Geococcyx californianus*," which is the scientific name for that eccentric cuckoo we usually call the roadrunner. Then, having taken part in several expeditions to the West with his mentor, Professor Marsh, he was invited by Marsh's friend General George Armstrong Custer, to join his expedition in 1874 as a scientist to explore the Black Hills in the Department of the Dakota. (Because of his work at Yale, Grinnell was forced to turn down an invitation from Custer to explore the Big Horn Mountains with him in the summer of 1876, and thus escaped the massacre at Little Big Horn.)

Meanwhile, Grinnell had been contributing articles about big game hunting to *Forest and Stream*. As it turned out, his contribution to the infant weekly journal that was then struggling under an inattentive editor amounted to more than prose; the Grinnells, father and son, were methodically buying up shares in the Forest and Stream Publishing Company. Soon young George Bird Grinnell was the magazine's editor, established in an office at 40 Park Row (the old *Times* building in lower Manhattan). While straightening out its finances, he maintained *Forest and Stream*'s original approach as a "hook-and-bullet" publication with a conscience. Among the articles and the notes of entertainment and advice for sportsmen, it carried hard-hitting editorials about what came to be called "game-hogs" (a term coined by a rival magazine's editor, G. O. Shields). Grinnell was particularly incensed by the practice of killing wild game for sale to restaurants, hotels, and wholesale suppliers of meat.

"The game supply which makes possible the general indulgence in field sports is of incalculable advantage to individuals and the nation," he once wrote in *Forest and Stream.* "But a game supply which makes possible the traffic in game as a luxury has no such importance. If this be granted, public policy demands that the traffic in game be abolished."

Grinnell was to be a leader in the campaign that outlawed market hunting, as he was to be in so many other pioneer reforms in wildlife conservation. (In 1894, he issued an early warning about lead poisoning in waterfowl caused by the eating of spent shotgun pellets, a problem that is still very much alive nearly a century later.) There seemed no end to his interest in a wild America that was at the vanishing point. He explored little-known corners of the West, took part in the hunts and ceremonies of his friends the Pawnee Indians, and chronicled the decline of the bison herds. But early in his editorial career he became particularly moved by a phenomenon that was affecting Americans almost anywhere they lived—the widespread destruction of common birds.

In their search for relief, those men and women who deplored the killing of wild birds could expect little help from state or federal agencies—notwithstanding a school of conservation historians that contends the beginning of reform sprang from a dedicated bureaucracy. This premise is based on a narrow concept of what conservation is, and even allowing that concept, a hard look at bureaucratic achievement in this field discloses that the initiative of government agencies in large matters of conservation is rare and generally overstated; inertia is the rule. When relief appeared for the nation's hard-pressed wild birds, it came (just as it has during so many other environmental crises) from private individuals working through organizations of their own.

The first concrete step (aside from some mainly ineffective state laws) toward bird protection was taken in 1883 with the formation of the American Ornithologists' Union at the American Museum of Natural History in New York. The impetus for this organization came from three professional ornithologists, Elliott Coues, J. A. Allen, and William Brewster. That all three men were closely identified with New England was not a coincidence, for the birds of farm and garden were an integral part of a New Englander's memory and cultural heritage, as well as the subject of reams of immortal or indifferent verse.

The AOU's primary concerns, because of the nature of its membership, were professional and addressed such questions as the economic importance of birds as well as their distribution and migration patterns. Soon, through the lobbying of influential members in Washington, a section on economic ornithology was created within the federal government; this agency eventually evolved into the Bureau of the Biological Survey.

What modern ecologists call "the Mother Goose Syndrome" ruled mankind's approach to the animal kingdom (just as it often does today): animals of all kinds were designated "good" or "bad," depending on how they were viewed to affect human interests. The good were sentimentalized, the bad summarily executed. Even more advanced ornithologists of the time, who realized that farmers needed to be educated in the facts of animal life, ironically were themselves relentless in their persecution of such carnivores as hawks and owls, not realizing that those birds preyed mainly on rodents and other herbivores that were harmful to agriculture.

Meanwhile, a number of AOU members, including Grinnell, pressed for action against the unrestricted slaughter of birds. The organization created a Committee on the Protection of North American Birds, which, in 1886, issued a bulletin containing one of the most important documents in the history of wildlife conservation. It was referred to as the "Model Law," which the committee hoped would form a basis for legislation in each of the states. Quite specific in its various proposals, it distinguished between game and nongame birds and classified only the ducks and geese; rails and coots; shorebirds; and turkey, grouse, pheasants, and quail among the former. All other birds were to be strictly protected under this law with the exception of the English sparrow (whose iniquities are discussed below). Going further, the law proposed to prohibit anyone from taking or destroying the eggs or nest of any bird whatsoever except, of course, the English sparrow. Other sections, as might be expected from the document's authorship, exempted scientific collectors from those prohibitions.

The AOU's Model Law was to be a battleground for years to come. Although the committee had hoped to forestall organized opposition to the proposed legislation by specifically omitting the traditional game birds from its protective umbrella, the fact that all other native birds and their eggs were to be put off-limits brought forth a general outcry. A familiar sentiment of the time was that all animal life was fair game. Hadn't the Bible given man dominion over "the fish of the sea and over the fowl of the air"? Even nongame birds were resources for the pot in many nineteenth-century homes. Taxidermists complained that such legislation would ruin their trade. Some leading ornithologists were opposed too, fearing that the Model Law might restrict scientific collecting.

"I don't protect birds," the ornithologist Charles B. Cory said. "I kill them."

The successive reports issued by the AOU Committee on Bird Protection form an impressive document on what can be called the "age of extermination." The bison herds were being decimated by a generation of Buffalo Bills, shot from horseback as part of the genocide campaign against the Plains Indians, and even "just for fun" from the windows of railroad cars. The same mentality that ravaged American forests with saw and fire soon shot the passenger pigeon and the Carolina parakeet to extinction.

But, in general, the birds suffering most were those whose nature kept them close to the water during the breeding season or on migration. The first North American bird to disappear after the arrival of the Europeans was the great auk, a large, flightless seabird closely related to the puffins. The great auk was doomed as soon as the fishermen began going ashore on its nesting islands in the North Atlantic, where it was easily killed with sticks, then salted away in barrels to be used on long voyages as food or bait.

Shorebirds, a large and diverse group that includes the plovers and sandpipers, were threatened *en masse*. Most of these birds nest in the far north among the grasses, icy pools, and briefly blooming wildflowers of the tundra. On the way to or from the tundra they traverse the thousands of miles connecting it with their winter homes, which may be anywhere from the Gulf Coast of the United States to Mexico and South America. Under the best of circumstances during the last century, the shorebirds were forced twice each year to run the gauntlet of guns fired by those who were out for sport or food.

The hunting of shorebirds became big business. Market gunners scoured the coast for these birds, selling bagfuls of them to restaurants, hotels, or wholesalers. An economy of scale was at work here. The shorebirds fly in large flocks, and at high tide crowd together on rocks and beaches, giving the impression from a little distance of tightly massed vegetation. A gunner was able to kill dozens of the smaller birds with a single "blaze at the feathers." A lighthouse keeper, describing the hunting of "peeps," or small sandpipers, on an island off the coast of Maine, wrote:

"They form in flocks and sit on the shore. Gunners come here and slaughter them awfully, for it is no trick to fire into a big flock of them and wound a large number. After the gunners have been here, my children bring in many wounded ones, some with broken wings or legs shot off, or eyes shot out, in all shapes. The gunners don't get half they shoot down."

But reports were most dramatic from Florida, which had become the chief hunting grounds of the millinery gunners who supplied a large part of the ornamental plumes for the American fashion industry. There, in a state still sparsely settled by humans, the change from abundant birdlife to scarcity and in some cases extirpation had occurred with incredible speed. No one noted the decline more precisely than the ornithologist W. E. D. Scott of Princeton University, who had made his first visit to Florida in 1876. Around the Oklawaha River and nearby lakes he found great numbers of birds, including roseate spoonbills, Carolina parakeets, snail kites, and limpkins. He reported that he returned to Princeton with a load of specimens that had required a six-ox team to haul out to Silver Springs. When Scott visited Florida again in 1879, birds were still abundant on the Gulf Coast. By 1886, however, it was apparent that others besides himself were removing birds by the wagonload, and he was amazed at their scarcity. Scott wrote a series of articles for *The Auk,* the AOU's journal, describing the plume hunters and their methods.

"I have spent the past four winters and two summers in Florida," he wrote. "My old hunting grounds have all been faithfully traversed, some of them many times, and the roseate spoonbill is almost as great a stranger to me as to my fellow workers who live the year-round in Massachusetts."

State laws to protect birds were few and weak, and even those few were seldom enforced. As George Shiras III, a congressman and noted nature photographer, later observed, "The attitude at that time in all the states may be expressed as favoring 'an open season on migrant game birds when they are within the state and a closed season during their absence.'"

It was against this overwhelming tide of greed, folly, and indifference that the advocates of reform worked in the middle 1880s. The scholarly Grinnell began to believe that neither government restrictions nor professional diligence was sufficient to counter the tide. He knew that in Great Britain, where similar destruction was carried on, a long literary tradition of admiration for birds and their qualities was beginning to stir outrage about their disappearance. Private individuals there had formed several protective organizations, including the Selborne Society. (The Royal Society for the Protection of Birds was created in 1889.)

Grinnell began his campaign for a private movement in this country in an editorial for *Forest and Stream* on February 11, 1886:

"We propose the formation of an Association for the protection of wild birds and their eggs, which shall be called the Audubon Society. Its membership is to be free to everyone who is willing to lend a helping hand in forwarding the objects for which it is formed. These objects will be to prevent, so far as possible, (1) the killing of any wild birds not used for food; (2) the destruction of nests or eggs of any wild bird; and (3) the wearing of feathers as ornaments or trimming for dress."

The name for the new society was foreordained from the days when young Grinnell had explored the rooms and loft of the great bird painter's old home. At first glance, however, there might seem a certain irony in calling a society to protect birds after John James Audubon. His writings reverberate as often with the crack of rifles as with the song of birds. In his *Ornithological Biography*, he wrote about hunting Canada geese: "We continued to shoot until the number of geese obtained would seem to you so very large that I shall not specify it," and then lamented, "Oh, that we had more guns!" After describing a great slaughter of pelicans in which he took enthusiastic part in the Florida Keys, he went on:

"Over those enormous mud-flats, a foot or two of water is quite sufficient to drive all the birds ashore, even the tallest Heron or Flamingo, and the tide seems to flow at once over the whole expanse. Each of us, provided with a gun, posted himself behind a bush, and no sooner had the water forced the winged creatures to approach the shore than the work of destruction commenced. When it at length ceased, the collected mass of birds of different kinds looked not unlike a small haycock."

Yet elsewhere in his work, Audubon condemned the senseless killing. Of his trip to Labrador in 1833, he recalled:

"We talked of the country where we were, of the beings best fitted to live and prosper here, not only of our species, but of all species, and also of the enormous destruction of everything here, except the rocks. . . . We are often told rum kills the Indian; I think not; it is oftener the want of food, the loss of hope as he loses sight of all that was once abundant, before the white man intruded on his land and killed off the wild quadrupeds and birds with which he has fed and clothed himself since his creation. Nature herself seems perishing."

Audubon set out to represent the wild things of his adopted land in their natural habitats, alive and moving. The 430-odd watercolors for *The Birds of America* exist as tangible proof that he succeeded. But there is yet a more durable heritage. Audubon's idea of a bird, of *birdness* itself, passed into the nation's consciousness and, already in Grinnell's time, influenced the way Americans looked at the natural world. They see the physical organism, composed of feathers, bone, and flesh, of course, but even the drabbest plumage seems simply a sheath for that something wild and inexpressible with which Audubon infused his birds. Watchers utterly innocent of ornithology often feel this primitive emotional pull. Audubon, through his paintings, passed on a way of seeing

George Bird Grinnell's *Audubon Magazine* represented the
first stage of the bird protection movement. NAS

to later generations of Americans and implied that in learning about birds they might also open themselves to the poetry of their lives.

Now, in addressing a potential audience as "president pro tem" of the new society, Grinnell reached beyond the sportsmen (and perhaps the game-hogs) who were his regular readers to the women who wore plumes on their hats and the small boys who stalked songbirds with guns and slingshots. The way to effect a change of heart, Grinnell believed, was through articulate persuasion, or, as he wrote, "the education of our whole people to an understanding of the usefulness of the birds and the folly of permitting their wholesale destruction." Compulsory measures were not necessary, for if the destruction of birds could be brought home to the public, the wearing of feathers would go out of fashion and small boys would lay aside their slingshots. The society furnished pledges on request and, simply by signing, one became a member—with a certificate to boot.

The response to Grinnell's manifesto must have surprised and encouraged him. Besides thousands of signed pledges, he received letters of support from a number of notable personages of the time, including Oliver Wendell Holmes and the Reverend Henry Ward Beecher. Charles Dudley Warner, who had collaborated with Mark Twain on the novel *The Gilded Age,* congratulated Grinnell for founding the society, adding, "a dead bird does not help the appearance of an ugly woman, and a pretty woman needs no such adornment." Not quite so pithy were the remarks of the society's most revered member, John Greenleaf Whittier, who wrote only three days after Grinnell's first announcement:

"I heartily approve of the proposed Audubon Society. . . . I could almost wish that the shooters of the birds, the taxidermists who prepare their skins, and the fashionable wearers of their feathers might share the penalty which was visited upon the Ancient Mariner who shot the Albatross."

By 1887, the society had been incorporated in New York State and boasted a membership of 39,000 men, women, and children who pledged not to molest the birds. Grinnell's pamphleteering instincts were at their highest. To reach a wider audience, he determined to set the infant society on its own, and in February of that year he published the first issue of *The Audubon Magazine.* The price was six cents a copy, or fifty cents for an annual subscription. The cover, graced by a portrait of John James Audubon surrounded by birds hovering above leafy ornamental branches, gave the organization's full name as the *Audubon Society for the Protection of Birds.*

Although Grinnell, in an unsigned notice, apologized that the "great amount of official and explanatory matter" had necessarily crowded out the lighter and more entertaining features that were to be staples of future issues, there was fare for all the family: Part One of a breezy biography of Audubon, several inspirational articles on the society's work, a life history of the Baltimore oriole, a story by a man in Atlanta, Georgia, about his pet parrot, and a fairy story about two little princesses who cared only for each other and, after rejecting their many suitors, "lived all their life together, two happy old maids." But by far the most memorable item, reprinted and circulated often in the years ahead, was Celia Thaxter's "Woman's Heartlessness," a vitriolic attack on fashionable women who refused to give up wearing plumes. The well-known poet recounted her argument with a typical cultivated but heartless woman.

"It was merely a waste of breath," Celia Thaxter concluded, "and she went her way, a charnel house of beaks and claws and bones and feathers and glass eyes upon her fatuous head."

This Audubon Society's rapid success was, in part, its undoing. Grinnell had neither the time nor the staff at *Forest and Stream* to keep up with the added correspondence and administrative details. Nor was the ardor of the membership sufficient to overcome even the willfulness of Celia Thaxter's society matrons. The slaughter continued and, with the close of the magazine's second volume in December 1888, Grinnell threw in the towel, and his Audubon Society ceased to exist. Grinnell, however, took a parting shot.

"Fashion decrees feathers; and feathers it is," he wrote. "This condition of affairs must be something of a shock to the leaders of the Audubon Society, who were sanguine enough to believe that the moral idea represented by their movement would be efficacious to influence society at large."

## 2

*O*n one of those damply chill mornings in early January that turn the thoughts of New Englanders to sunnier regions, Mrs. Augustus Hemenway sat in her comfortable home at 273 Clarendon Street in Boston and mused on a special aspect of Florida life. The year was 1896. She had been reading an account of the destruction of heronries throughout the South. Perhaps it was the sort of vivid picture that the ornithologist T. Gilbert Pearson was to sketch later on from his own experiences in a southern swamp:

"In the tall bushes, growing in a secluded pond in a swamp, a small colony of herons had their nesting home. I accompanied a squirrel hunter one day to the spot, and the scene which met our eyes was not a pleasant one. I had expected to see some of the beautiful herons about their nest, or standing on the trees nearby, but not a living one could be found, while here and there in the mud lay the lifeless forms of eight of the birds. They had been shot down and the skin bearing the plumes stripped from their backs. Flies were busily at work, and they swarmed up with hideous buzzings as we approached each spot where a victim lay.

"This was not the worst; in four of the nests young orphan birds could be seen who were clamoring piteously for food which their dead parents would never again bring to them. A little one was discovered lying with its head and neck hanging out of the nest, happily now past suffering. On higher ground the embers of a fire gave evidence of the plume hunters' camp.

"The next spring I visited the nesting site, but found only the old nests fast falling to decay."

Harriet Hemenway's response was energetic and direct. Her family background, indeed, was dominated by action and public service, for she was a Lawrence by birth, and her paternal grandfather had founded one of the great mercantile firms in Massachusetts. Cotton mills in Lawrence and Lowell still testified to the family's wealth and influence. Her father, Amos Lawrence, had been active in the antislavery movement as a young man; later, he was a candidate for governor of Massachusetts and served in the prestigious position of treasurer of Harvard College. Harriet's husband, Augustus Hemenway, came from an equally powerful family with its wealth rooted in South American silver and nitrate mines, and Augustus himself had served in the state legislature, had given money to build the Hemenway Gymnasium at Harvard and a library in Canton, and had become a trustee of the Boston Museum of Fine Arts. Harriet and Augustus Hemenway shared a love for the outdoors, and on their thousand-acre farm in Canton or on their other properties in New Hampshire and on Cape Cod often hiked and watched the local birds.

On this day Harriet Hemenway took down from a shelf her copy of *The Boston Blue Book* and, with her cousin Minna B. Hall, went carefully through its pages.

"We marked the ladies of fashion who would be likely to wear aigrettes on their hats or in their hair," Minna Hall later recalled. "We then set out circulars asking the women to join a society for the protection of birds, especially the egret. Some women joined and some who preferred to wear the feathers would not join."

Although Harriet Hemenway knew where the strings of power lay, she preferred to work them behind the scenes. She was aware that if a society to protect birds were to be successful, it would need to reach people far beyond her own circle. As a result, when she called an organizational meeting at her home on February 10 of that year, the participants included, besides a Lowell and a Cabot, two prominent naturalists of the day, Outram Bangs and Charles S. Minot. The latter had worked at Harvard with Louis Agassiz (the most influential biologist in nineteenth-century America) and was president of the American Society of Naturalists. Accordingly, the participants reached for the name already made synonymous with bird protection by George Bird Grinnell and called their new organization the Massachusetts Audubon Society. They elected Minot as chairman of its board of directors. The current Audubon movement dates directly to that late afternoon on Clarendon Street.

The membership was broadened further at a meeting the following week, to which William Brewster was invited and at which he was elected president of the society. The addition of Brewster in a dominant role was something of a coup for the society. He had been a co-founder of the Nuttall Ornithological Club, the first such organization in the United States, and of the American Ornithologists' Union. He was recognized as the outstanding field ornithologist of his time. And, like nearly all of the other men who played vital roles in this movement, he was as familiar with guns as were any of the professional hunters of the day.

Brewster's position as Curator of the Museum of Comparative Zoology at Harvard provided him with an ideal base from which to function as a scientific arbiter. Though he published little during his lifetime, he was an indefatigable observer and correspondent; in his notebooks and journals, meticulously maintained, he created the scholarly bedrock from which later ornithologists stepped up into print.

Like other naturalists and sportsmen of his day, Brewster sometimes rivaled the game-hogs in his depredations. He took part as a young man in trapshooting contests in which passenger pigeons, netted in the wild for the purpose, were the living targets. Thousands of these birds, then within a few decades of their total extinction, were destroyed during each trapshooting contest.

And yet, at a time when primitive optical aids left shotguns as the most certain means of scientific identification of birds, Brewster could not be described as trigger-happy. When puzzled about what sort of food an adult flicker was feeding its young one day, he remained unenlightened, concluding, "I could not bring myself to kill one of the latter and settle the point in that way."

Thus the Massachusetts Audubon Society was composed of the city's conscionable ladies of fashion and a group of men who were interested in both ornithology and the field sports; the little old lady in tennis shoes is as mythical as the basilisk. The ties of Brewster and Minot to national organizations lent prestige to the new society, while Harriet Hemenway in the background (she did not even appear on the board of directors until 1910) provided infusions of cash whenever and wherever needed. Among its vice presidents the society numbered Sarah Orne Jewett, Charles Francis Adams, and Mrs. Louis Agassiz. By the end of its first year it had 1,284 members, 358 of whom were schoolchildren.

The organization's goal was stated in its bylaws: "to discourage the buying and wearing, for ornamental purposes, of the feathers of any wild birds except ducks and game birds, and to otherwise further the protection of native birds." After some discussion in subsequent board meetings, and perhaps over the opposition of the sportsmen present, the qualifying phrase "except ducks and game birds" was stricken from the bylaws.

One of the weaknesses of Grinnell's original Audubon Society was its failure to work for the passage of the Model Law or other protective legislation. The Massachusetts Audubon Society took a step forward in that respect at its second meeting when it invited George Mackay to join the board of directors. Mackay was a sportsman who did most of his waterfowl shooting on the islands off the Massachusetts shore, especially Muskeget and Penikese, and he had become acutely aware that gulls and terns were rapidly disappearing along the New England coast.

(Edward Sturtevant, an ornithologist in Rhode Island, reported that he did not see a herring gull there for four summers during the 1870s, and a modern ecologist, William H. Drury, has pointed out that in a series of photographs of Cape Cod and the Provincetown fishing fleet taken near the turn of the century, not a single gull is visible in the background.) Mackay became a self-appointed warden of the Massachusetts islands, brandishing copies of an 1886 state law that imposed a fine of ten dollars on anyone who killed gulls and terns or pilfered their eggs. He was apparently the only person, in or out of state government, who thought to enforce the law. He brooked no violations, regardless of the perpetrator, and shot several short-eared owls that persisted in capturing the seabirds.

Mackay had also acquired experience in legislative matters, having frequently appeared at the State House to lobby for stronger protective laws. Now he went there regularly to represent the Massachusetts Audubon Society. Although the spring shooting of shorebirds had been abolished in the state, they were killed for the market in many western and southern states as they passed through on their way to their breeding grounds in the far north. Thousands of those birds, including golden plovers, Eskimo curlews, and upland sandpipers (then called Bartramian sandpipers), showed up in Boston's markets and restaurants every spring.

"These birds are permitted to be sold in Massachusetts during the closed season provided *they have been taken out of the state,*" Mackay reported. "I have tried very hard to prevent such sale *here* but without success."

Strong national legislation, as well as networks of sanctuaries, was still to come. In the meantime, the Massachusetts Audubon Society worked on the local level, using Grinnell's plan of basing reform on a caring, well-informed public. The pamphlet was the primary weapon in this campaign for hearts and minds, and the society issued a steady stream of printed matter that included didactic tracts ("Ostrich Feathers," "How Birds Affect the Farm and Garden," and a reprint of Celia Thaxter's popular "Woman's Heartlessness") as well as instructional leaflets ("Hints to Bird Students" and "The Baltimore Oriole").

The society sold Audubon calendars, with illustrations and descriptive text on birds, for fifty cents apiece. Again, taking a leaf from Grinnell's work, the new society actively recruited junior members, supporting a Bird Day in the schools by sending appropriate literature to teachers and enrolling youngsters at no cost, provided they signed a pledge card that read: "I promise not to harm our birds or their eggs, and to protect them both whenever I am able." The society also produced a poster-size bird chart based on one distributed by the Society for the Protection of Birds in Germany. The Massachusetts version displayed portraits of twenty-six New England birds on a cloth backing, distributed with a roller for classroom use.

In an attempt to blanket the state with its message, the society also recruited adult volunteers to proselytize on the local level. The volunteers, called local secretaries, signed up new members, distributed pamphlets, and kept the board of directors informed of developments in their regions. One of those volunteers noted that more people were feeding the birds in the winter, "but the women will not give up wearing feathers." And another went beyond the call of duty in sticking up for her feathered charges. "I have also entertained birds who come about my house by placing food and water and bird houses for them," she wrote from Brighton. "And last, but not least, I killed our handsome cat because she killed more birds than two or three ladies could wear on their hats."

This time the Audubon idea was to endure. The Pennsylvania Audubon Society was founded later in 1896. During the following year, Audubon societies sprang up in New York, New Hampshire, Illinois, Maine, Wisconsin, New Jersey, Rhode Island, Connecticut, and the District of Columbia. In the nation's capital, as in Boston and other areas, a prominent woman was the central figure around whom the local society was organized; the Audubon Society of the District of Columbia had its beginnings in the home of Mrs. John Dewhurst Patten of Georgetown, in cooperation with the American Ornithologists' Union, with its avowed purpose "The protection and study of birds." Its first president was George Miller Sternberg, Surgeon-General, United States Army, while Assistant Secretary of the Navy Theodore Roosevelt soon became one of its honorary vice presidents. Frank M. Chapman came to Washington from the American Museum of Natural History to deliver the society's first public lecture, speaking on the theme, "Woman as a Bird Enemy."

The movement kept spreading westward, and in 1898 Audubon societies were formed in Ohio, Indiana, Tennessee, Minnesota, Texas, and California. Pamphlets and bird charts spread the good word from one state to another, while the wearers of plumes took the brunt of the assault. As in any new movement made up of relatively small numbers of passionate believers, there was a cultish sense of solidarity, with occasional outbreaks of self-righteousness. Squabbling was generally muted, though in 1902 the secretary of the Massachusetts Audubon Society "was instructed to write the Oklahoma Society congratulating them on the organization of a state society and asking for an explanation of their use of the seal of the Massachusetts Society."

Arkansas hunters bagged these 110 ducks in two hours. NAS

Although the killing of birds for the plume trade was widespread, with particular trouble spots in Florida, Maine, and Virginia, most of the Audubon leaders were aware that the heart of the problem lay in New York City, the center of the millinery industry. If bird destruction was to be fought as a national evil with many interlocking strands, those strands could be most effectively cut at the center. The struggle required great energy and a national vision, and they too were to be found in New York, in the person of William Dutcher.

Dutcher, who had been born in 1846 in Stelton, New Jersey, was a general agent of the Prudential Life Insurance Company. Turn-of-the-century photographs show him as a prosperous businessman—bearded and spectacled, his gray head of hair lengthening into full sideburns. In a letter to a legislator during the bird-protection struggle, he deprecated his ability as a public speaker and added, "I had to commence to work when I was a little over 13 years of age, and had very little schooling before that time." Nevertheless, he more than made up for any lack of formal training by what everyone recognized as extraordinary personal qualities. At Dutcher's death, the ornithologist T. S. Palmer noted that "Energy, sincerity, sympathy and a remarkable tenacity of purpose were some of the characteristics which enabled him to overcome obstacles that would have disheartened a less determined man and made it possible to score success under conditions that seemed to invite nothing but failure."

Like so many of the other leaders of the early Audubon movement, Dutcher enjoyed hunting birds. He combined this recreation with a taste for science. He amassed an important collection of birds along the Long Island and New Jersey shores and, in the spirit of the dedicated amateurs who contributed so weightily to late-nineteenth-century botany, entomology, and ornithology, wrote a number of scientific papers about birdlife in his area. At the AOU's founding, he was elected an associate member and soon became the most enterprising member of its Committee on the Protection of North American Birds. There he played a part in the dissemination of the Model Law and, with George Bird Grinnell, in the launching of the first Audubon Society. For sixteen years he served as the AOU's treasurer and worked actively through the 1890s for the passage of bird-protection legislation in several states.

Dutcher also cooperated with the various state Audubon societies, beginning with that in Massachusetts. He hesitated to portray as prime villains the "heartless" woman of fashion or the backwoods plume hunter, but made his main targets the leaders of the millinery industry who exploited them both. Only national legislation that effectively banished the feathers of wild birds from commerce, he believed, would effectively change the fashion business. Until then, a holding action was needed to protect the birds on their breeding grounds where they were most vulnerable. Dutcher especially admired the work of George Mackay in Massachusetts, who had operated on the assumption that bird-protection laws were worthless without a means of enforcing them. Flourishing seabird colonies on the islands off Massachusetts existed as testimony to his success. The sanctuary and warden system that the National Audubon Society brought to its highest expression had its origin in 1900 as William Dutcher began to build on Mackay's early protection work.

Dutcher added to his duties with the AOU the position of treasurer. "This protection work will ruin my regular business if I do not give it up soon," he wrote to a friend early in 1900. In fact, he was to become more involved in it than ever. In the same year Abbott H. Thayer, a Boston-born AOU member in New Hampshire, then living near Mount Monadnock, provided Dutcher with the means to take forceful action. Thayer himself was a remarkable man—a painter of animals and landscapes as well as of idealized figures of women (one of his most popular paintings was called "The Virgin," and many of his pictures went into leading museums). Later, with his son, Gerald, he wrote a book about protective coloration in animals which served as the inspiration for the new art of military camouflage during World War I.

Now, in 1900, Thayer offered to raise money to hire wardens and protect the most critical seabird nesting colonies. Dutcher, almost alone

William Dutcher
almost singlehandedly
pulled the Audubon
movement together early
in this century. NAS

Abbott H. Thayer,
shown here in a painting
by his daughter,
Gladys Thayer Reasoner,
raised the money
that sustained the early
Audubon warden
system. COURTESY OF
ABBOTT T. FENN

among AOU members, had faith in Thayer's plan. He accepted the offer enthusiastically and agreed to find suitable men to staff the new warden system. The public contributed $1,400 to the Thayer Fund that year.

Dutcher and his allies received another boost at this time in the form of one of the landmark conservation laws. The Lacey Act was brought about by a curious mixture of arguments, conflicting passions, and legal ingenuity.

In 1898 Senator George F. Hoar of Massachusetts (who was one of the authors of the Sherman Anti-Trust Act) had started the process by introducing a bill in Congress to prohibit the importation, sale, or ship-ment of millinery plumes in the United States. Hoar aroused wide sym-pathy for his legislation by circulating a petition, supposed to have been signed by a number of wild birds, asking men and women to spare their lives. *The Millinery Trade Review* called on its members to crush "this most iniquitous and childish measure." The bill failed to win enough votes in Congress, a circumstance that Audubon leaders later attributed to the AOU, which did not lend its prestige to the bill's support.

The AOU's defection in this case was an indication of the unease among many ornithologists, as well as sportsmen, about what they felt to be the overzealous approach of the new bird-protection movement. Early in 1900, protective legislation in New York State ran into a flood of alarming rumors about its ultimate impact on legitimate scientists as well as on sportsmen. (Although New York had already passed a bird-protection law of sorts, gulls and terns were classed among "web-footed wildfowl," and thus remained fair game.)

While protective legislation was slowly making its way through var-ious state legislatures, the emphasis for the moment was back on Wash-ington, where Congressman John F. Lacey of Iowa had introduced a bill similar to Senator Hoar's. Lacey's bill invoked the "commerce clause" of the Constitution (which gives the federal government the authority to regulate interstate traffic in goods) to prohibit the shipment from one state to another of birds and other animals killed in violation of state laws. Thus, if Massachusetts had a strong law prohibiting the killing of birds, no parts of those birds, including their feathers, could be shipped out of the state to be processed in New York or any other state.

Of almost equal importance in winning the support of certain un-sentimental parties was a prohibition in the bill against the importation of any animals from abroad without government permits. It was well noted at the time that this provision included the English sparrow (now generally called the house sparrow), which had been imported to the United States during the nineteenth century under the impression that it would consume enormous numbers of insect pests. This aggressive, prolific, and adaptable Old World species, which is only very distantly related to the three dozen or so species of attractive native American sparrows, was soon regarded as a pest in its own right. Freed in its new environment from the enemies and diseases that kept its numbers in harmony with its native surroundings, and finding ample food in the droppings of grain-eating horses that thronged city parks and streets, the new arrival transformed those areas into what one observer (perhaps a suppressed xenophobe) called "avian ghettos crammed with greedy, filthy, bickering clouds of a single alien species."

Moreover, these sparrows revealed a fondness for the farmer's grains and fruits and a hankering for the nesting places of native species such as bluebirds. As the sparrows appropriated prime nesting holes and boxes before the bluebirds returned from their migrations, what Thoreau had called "the plaintive spring-restoring peep of the bluebird" was becoming absent from many localities. The alien birds had their defenders, just as our city pigeons do today. But the AOU had joined the campaign to destroy English sparrows and their nests "on sight," and Lacey's bill won many adherents simply by the promise it gave of preventing such unfortunate importations in the future.

Congress passed the Lacey Act in 1900. Freight agents soon began to ask searching questions about the origins of packages that contained bird plumes and thus put a crimp in the milliners' shipping plans. The legislation had a glaring loophole in that it did not apply when birds were killed in states that had no protective laws. (By 1900, only five states had passed legislation based on the AOU's Model Law.) But Dutcher and the Audubon societies now held a club with which they occasionally exacted some satisfaction. They could begin to concentrate on the specific sources of millinery plumes.

3

The use of feathers for personal ornament was not a creation of the Victorian Age. Dignitaries of the ancient world, medieval crusaders, Renaissance dandies, and aborigines throughout the Americas adorned their heads or headgear with plumes of differing shapes and colors; "panache" is a word derived from the Latin for feather, *pinna,* and is suggestive of the dash and swagger we associate with such embellishments.

But the use of feathers in earlier times was on a small scale and likely to cause little grief among bird populations. Even during the eighteenth century, when feathers became an important item of fashion among women, their use was pretty well restricted to the nobility and *demimonde.* Madame de Pompadour added, among other ornaments, the feathers of exotic birds to her innovative coiffure and set a new pace in fashion. Shipments of bird skins made their way to French ports from all over the world, ultimately to gild the natural charms of grand ladies. One such shipment from French Guiana, seized by a British warship, was found to contain a species new to science; the ornithologist George Edwards, perhaps with ironic gallantry, named this gorgeous little reddish-lavender bird the Pompadour cotinga after the lady for whom its plumage had supposedly been intended.

But, as the nineteenth century progressed, more and more families raised themselves economically above the subsistence level and entered the middle class. By 1850, the desire of women to adorn themselves with feathers swept the United States and Western Europe. The millinery industry, detecting a good thing, was in part responsible for creating the fashion and did its best to sustain it. (*Milliner* is an English corruption of "Milaner," after the inhabitants of the Italian city from which women's finery was long exported to England.) Magazines such as *Harper's Bazaar* and *Godey's Lady's Book and Magazine* (the latter had a circulation of more than 100,000 copies before the Civil War) were extremely influential in stimulating the new styles.

The result of this craving for flamboyant plumes was a daily fashion parade, on the streets and in the ballrooms, depressing to humanitarians and ornithologists alike. The top of a woman's hat became transformed into a grisly *nature morte* of chiffon lace and taffeta ribbons mingled with plumes, wings, and indeed the entire bodies of birds (the grotesqueness heightened if the specimen happened to be any of the long-billed shore-birds).

The society page of a contemporary newspaper observed that "Miss ———looked extremely well in white, with a whole nest of sparkling, scintillating birds in her hair, which it would have puzzled an ornithologist to classify." In fact, only an ornithologist was able to appreciate the variety of which *les fantasies* were composed. Frank M. Chapman of the American Museum of Natural History, during two strolls through the shopping districts of Manhattan in 1896, counted, with a birdwatcher's incomparable zeal, 700 hats, 542 of which were decorated with feathers. Most of the unadorned hats belonged to "ladies in mourning or elderly ladies." Chapman recognized forty different species of birds, including Wilson's warblers, pileated woodpeckers, "Acadian" owls, bluebirds, pine grosbeaks, and a northern shrike, or "butcher-bird."

As Robert Henry Welker points out in his book, *Birds and Men,* the plumage fad was not an isolated phenomenon but one extravagant stroke among many that created what came to be called the Gilded Age. Hats, coiffures, and derrières, like furniture and "cottages," grew massive and, in the eyes of later commentators, vulgar and ostentatious. Ornateness became the criterion of the desirable.

The toll on birdlife all around the world was incalculable. The AOU estimated as early as 1886 that five million North American birds of about fifty species were killed annually "for fashion." Bulky bales of plumes flowed unendingly into New York, Paris, and London. Two years later, *The Auk* noted that a public sale advertised by one London firm was thought to involve more birds than were contained in all of the ornithological collections in the United States; a British dealer admitted that during the past year he had sold two million small birds "of every kind and color."

Some shorebirds were shot for the millinery trade, especially the long-billed species whose prepared heads added a bizarre touch to a hat, but generally their drab rock-and-sand grays and browns were not in demand. And, among the more flamboyant colors, the pinks and carmines of, for instance, the roseate spoonbills tended to fade rather quickly. White remained fashion's preference. The birds most eagerly sought by the millinery gunners in the United States were the two white egrets (sometimes called herons)—the great egret and the snowy egret.

It was the widespread
use of feathers, and even
entire birds, for
millinery purposes in the late
nineteenth century
that prompted the creation
of the first Audubon
societies. NAS

The latter provided the highly prized "aigrettes," or long plumes, that grow only in the breeding season from between the shoulders and extend to or beyond the tail. When the snowy egret's plumes are in good condition, they are gracefully recurved at the tips. As public disapproval of plume-hunting mounted, the milliners attempted to obscure some of the details of their trade.

"Dealers often state the aigrettes are manufactured," William Dutcher once wrote, "but this is not so; man has never yet been able to imitate successfully these beautiful plumes; all that are offered for sale have been torn from the backs of the smaller white Herons. Even the stiff plumes, or 'stubs,' are not manufactured but are the plumes of the larger species of white Herons. Herons' plumes are often sold as 'ospreys'; that is simply another trade name used to disguise the fact that they are Herons' plumes. The Osprey of science is the Fish Hawk, which produces no plumes of any kind."

For many Americans the appearance of feathers on a hat or gown became like the red flag to the bull, a symbol of defiance and challenge, a mark of arrogant cruelty. Because of the ostentatious character of the fashion, the plume became the standard around which the Audubon leaders could most easily rally the public to push for bird protection. As the new century opened, the slaughtering grounds of the herons and egrets lay chiefly in the remote southern swamps or the marshes of the Far West. Dutcher, impatient to put to work the resources of the Thayer Fund, decided to concentrate first on the islands off the coast of Maine, which were of much easier access. He had already established contacts there and consequently had certain knowledge of the widespread destruction of another family of birds—the gulls and terns.

At this distance, it is not easy to appreciate the extent to which gulls were used by humans a century or more ago. The English settlers brought from the old country a taste for these birds and their eggs. Gulls were often part of the fare at banquets in the big houses of England, and during the seventeenth century the chicks were collected on their breeding grounds and fattened in "gull houses" on country estates. Noble ladies sent gulls as gifts for the tables of neighboring houses, just as later generations might send a ham or a brace of pheasants.

The adaptable herring gulls, which had so far withstood the raids of the eggers (coastal people fond of eating the gulls' eggs) much better than other species by retreating to the outer islands off Maine, were suddenly attacked by the millinery industry's gunners around 1875. This added blow was almost too much for them, and by the end of the century they seldom nested anywhere on the Atlantic Coast south of Penobscot Bay. As they became increasingly scarce, dealers paid forty cents apiece for the white-plumaged adults and twenty cents for the brown immature birds.

In early February 1900, Dutcher was in Bangor, where he learned that milliners were supplying Maine Indians with guns and large amounts of ammunition to kill gulls and their smaller relatives, the terns.

"There is no law protecting the gulls along our Maine coast, and they may be shot anywhere, even in the harbor of Bangor where they come fall and spring," he wrote to Thayer. "The fishermen shoot hundreds of all the gulls that occur by using a sneak boat which is disguised to resemble a lot of drift stuff, and by gradually skulling this up to a flock of gulls can secure a number ere they take aloft."

Dutcher and Thayer remained in extremely close touch during this period, orchestrating the bird-protection movement; the businessman attended to the myriad details while the artist came up with the money. That winter, besides dunning his well-to-do friends for contributions for the protection work, Thayer prepared a general appeal for funds which was sent out by the AOU to more than two thousand potential contributors as well as to all members of Congress. Thayer's name led the list of signatures on the appeal, though it was supported by those of other leaders in the AOU, including William Brewster, J. A. Allen, Frank M. Chapman, and, of course, Dutcher. To attract the professional audience at which the appeal was primarily aimed, Thayer stressed the utility of gulls, pointing out the quantities of garbage customarily dumped in American rivers and bays and the capacity of gulls as scavengers.

With money in hand to hire wardens to patrol the Maine islands, Dutcher still lacked a legal basis to stop the killing. He was already at work laying the groundwork for the passage of the AOU Model Law in the state legislature, but in the meantime he determined to slow down the plume hunters by invoking the laws of trespass. Accordingly, he used his contacts within the federal government to exact promises from the Light House Department to forbid landing of eggers and plume hunters on the many islands where lighthouses then stood. He also began a search for the owners of other critical nesting islands and asked their permission to post signs warning against trespass. Finally, he set about building a dependable warden system.

One of Dutcher's correspondents in Maine directed him to William Grant, keeper of the lighthouse at Matinicus Rock. Dutcher wrote to Grant, asking about the birds that nested on the rock and whether he would agree to protect them in exchange for a small sum of money at the end of the breeding season. On April 6, Grant replied that "I will do my best to protect the birds and do not want any compensation," thus becoming the first wildlife warden on the Maine coast.

The romantic aura of Matinicus Rock matches its historic place in the history of wildlife conservation. The most remote speck of land in the remote Matinicus Archipelago (which includes Matinicus Island, Wooden Ball, and Seal Island), it consists of twenty-nine acres of rock and turf, twenty-three miles south of Rockland. A lighthouse was established there by order of President John Quincy Adams in 1827. Although gulls no longer nested there at the turn of the century, it retained an important colony of Arctic terns.

Dutcher, who had expressed an interest in visiting Matinicus Rock, was assured by Grant that there was no great risk of landing on the rock in fair weather and that, if the sea should turn nasty, he would find a good harbor nearby at Matinicus Island. It must have come as something of a jolt to Dutcher shortly afterward to receive the following letter from Matinicus Island.

"I regret exceedingly to state that William G. Grant joined the 'Great Majority' this past week," another of Dutcher's correspondents wrote. "He was a thorough gentleman and spoke very pleasantly of his hope of entertaining you on your Eastern trip. It is expected the first assistant keeper will succeed him. Mr. James Hall is the finest shot in these parts and also a fine fellow."

Dutcher kept building his corps of wardens, recruited mainly from among lighthouse keepers who in most cases agreed to guard their own islands and any others with nesting birds nearby. Most of them were enthusiastic and agreed to accept the assignment for the season in return for as little as twenty-five or thirty dollars. Part of their duties was to post the No Trespass signs, printed on muslin, that Dutcher mailed to each of them. That the assignment was not without risk is evident from a letter he received after the middle of May from William F. Stanley, the lightkeeper on Great Duck Island off Mount Desert:

"We have two thousand gulls mated and building nests. On the 16th inst. two canoes with Indians landed here. My man went to their camp with one of your posters and read it to them. When the poster was read the Indians laughed at him and talked to him badly. They all had guns and said they had come to the island to kill gulls and get what eggs they can.

"I went to them on the 17th inst. and tried to explain to them they would not listen to me and we have had some words. I told them I would dog their tracks. While I was over there I see another canoe with three Indians in it landing here. They are bound to get the gulls by gun torch or snare. A boy is now letting me [know?] that the Indians are firing guns. But their work is in the night. I cannot learn their names. If I had a Kodak I could get their faces or catch them in the act. But I had rather shoot them. Posters don't count."

Dutcher sent off telegrams to the owners of the island, asking permission for a lawyer representing the AOU in Maine to enforce no-trespassing statutes and stop the Indians' depredations: . . . I WILL PAY YOU FIFTY DOLLARS TO PREVENT THEM FROM DOING SO THIS BREEDING SEASON. ACTION MUST BE TAKEN AT ONCE. ANSWER AT MY EXPENSE. Apparently a number of gulls were killed before the Indians could be induced to leave the island.

That summer Dutcher paid a visit to the bird islands off the Maine coast. He traveled part of the way on one of the big steamers that once plied the coast, walking the promenade deck and catching glimpses of passing gulls and terns. On the boat he struck up an acquaintance with an Indian who worked for most of the year as a mason around Bar Harbor but who took time off occasionally to shoot gulls when the milliners' prices were high. He was able to earn more money shooting gulls, he told Dutcher, than he could as a mason. At least ten thousand large gulls had been killed during 1899 along the Maine coast and on nearby Canadian islands, the Indian said. Dutcher dutifully recorded the details of the conversation in his notebook:

"The price went from about $5 per dozen to $12. A dozen consists of two wings and 3 pieces, two of the breast and one back. It takes about 4 gulls to make a dozen. The pieces are stripped from the dead bird and are then washed and cured. Some of the birds are shot, some are snared on or about the nests, and some are caught on trawl lines that are baited. This season the demand is not so great, and the price has gone down to $4 per dozen."

The island in which Dutcher was most interested was No Man's Land, the site of the largest herring gull colony in the United States. He left the steamer at Rockland and went by tug to Matinicus Island, a trip of about eighteen miles. There he was introduced to "Uncle Mark" Young, the owner of No Man's Land and an elderly bachelor whom Dutcher considered eccentric but extremely entertaining. Young had given up fishing and now ran a general store on Matinicus, opening it at four o'clock every afternoon "to do a little trading with the people." Dutcher agreed to pay him fifty dollars to watch the birds that summer.

Early on the morning after his arrival, Dutcher arranged for Young to take him to the island. The old man met him at the wharf with a large dory, and the two of them took turns rowing the mile or more through a rough sea to the gull colony. At their approach the gulls rose from the island's rocks and spruces, circling and screaming overhead. Dutcher, on his first visit to a large gull colony, was greatly moved. He estimated the birds' numbers at nearly four thousand. Young, guiding his dory over the moving, toppling crests of surf and avoiding the outpost rocks, landed Dutcher among the boulders on No Man's Land's shore. They walked past Young's grazing sheep to the higher part of the twelve-acre island.

"I commenced to see the young gulls," Dutcher wrote afterward in his notebook. "Some were as big as hens and from that down to little ones just out of the shell. It was a novel experience for me to see these young birds. The very small ones would try to hide as soon as I came near them. If they hid their head in the grass or under a stump they thought that the whole body was hidden. The larger ones would run just as soon as I came near them so it was almost impossible to photograph them."

Young told Dutcher that he had kept gunners from shooting the birds with the aid of the No Trespassing posters. The only troublemakers, he reported, were "fishermen who do not live on Matinicus." The colony, Dutcher concluded, was in excellent condition, and his experience there strengthened his belief in the value of a warden system.

The following winter brought no diminution in Dutcher's activity. Early in the year he traveled to Albany, where he helped to lobby for strengthening amendments to New York's bird-protection law and saw them safely through the legislative process. Then, accompanied by a state game warden, he visited the shops selling caged birds in New York City. Whenever he found protected native species on sale, he warned the dealer of the violations and, if confronted by unrepentance, took the dealer to court. He also visited department stores and retail milliners in the city to distribute copies of the new federal and state laws.

At the same time, Dutcher redoubled his efforts to have sound legislation passed in other states. Here he worked closely with T. S. Palmer of the United States Biological Survey, a member of the AOU and an authority on game laws. The two men studied the results of prosecutions brought against violators of game laws and found better ways to strengthen their cases. Palmer was so successful in his surveys of millinery shops in Washington that, when he found violations of the Lacey Act, bales of plumage were often hastily returned to wholesalers in New York. And Dutcher, his hand also strengthened by the Lacey Act, sent the authorities to a warehouse in Baltimore where twenty-six thousand gull skins were seized.

At the beginning of 1901, Dutcher (having won over Maine's fish and game commissioner with his letters and literature) traveled with Palmer to Augusta to lobby the state legislature. They gave an illustrated talk before a legislative committee, assisted by a Bowdoin College professor who provided and operated a lantern to project glass slides made from photographs of various seabirds.

The Model Law passed the Maine legislature and in February the governor signed it into law. In all, eleven states, including New Hampshire, Massachusetts, Connecticut, New York, New Jersey, Delaware, Florida, Wisconsin, and Wyoming, passed new laws or strengthening amendments to existing laws.

Dutcher was already at work lining up wardens for the coming breeding season. He was to engage twenty-seven during 1901, eleven in Maine and eight in Virginia. Abbott Thayer diligently wrote to those on his list of likely prospects, collecting nearly seventeen hundred dollars for the season's work. Dutcher sent each warden a booklet of printed forms, asking him to provide certain information, including the answers to such questions as: What birds are you protecting? When did each kind of bird arrive in the spring, and how many of each kind? and What success did the birds have? Under "Remarks," Uncle Markie Young noted in his tremulous handwriting: "Wea have sum hard harted Followes that would like to sute Birds if thear was aloud to But they Well no the pennltys."

In Virginia, where other hard-hearted fellows were apt to molest the birds, Dutcher had hired the captains at federal "life-saving establishments" along the coast to guard terns, laughing gulls, black skim-

A government agent displays whistling swans
killed illegally early in this century. NAS

mers, and other seabirds. J. R. Andrews stood watch for forty dollars at
Cobb Island, where boatmen tended to "eat the young skimmers." But,
later in the summer, he wrote to Dutcher fairly panting with pride and
satisfaction:

"I caught three men the best you ever see. I was in my lookout and
I see the boat and I was satisfied what they were after. So I let myself
go up the beach and hid in the grass about where I thought they would
land. And they did land a brest of me with three baskets and chunks to
kill the young birds with. And as soon as they landed I see what they
were up to and I raised up right in front of them with my gun. I ask
them what they were after. They first said nothing but I made them own
that they came to kill the young birds and they promised me if I would
let them off that they would never come after young birds a gaine. And
I told them if they ever did I would shoot them and I have not seen a
man on the beach since. The birds are all flying around now and there
is a mess of them here. They have more than double since last season."

That summer Dutcher kept a long-distance watch from New York
on the Maine colonies. Reports from wardens and his other correspondents filled in the picture. He estimated that Great Duck Island was the
site of the largest herring gull colony in the United States. That island

and Little Duck Island nearby apparently fledged about three thousand young gulls during the summer, while Mark Young reported complete protection on No Man's Land and the production of twenty-five hundred young birds. Likewise, James Hall, keeper of the Matinicus Rock Lighthouse, reported a successful season for the nesting terns and black guillemots. Hall's report is of special interest to modern ornithologists. It did not mention gulls, indicating that those birds had been driven off the rock at some previous time, but it did mention that two pairs of sea parrots, or puffins, "raised young during the season." Until the 1970s, Matinicus Rock remained the only breeding site of the Atlantic puffin in the United States.

There was already a change in the atmosphere of the bird-protection movement. With increasing success, there were signs of foot-dragging within the movement; whereas the various state Audubon societies were on the point of uniting in a close association of their own to advance the cause of bird protection, the AOU was quietly backing off. Thayer, writing from Monadnock to Dutcher in September, referred to opposition within the AOU to the 1901 appeal for funds and let his bitterness run away with him:

"Nothing but death or ill health will stop me from going on drumming up the funds, inexplicable as it is to me that the whole A.O.U. contains no other man willing to even do this. . . . If I couldn't have found a Dutcher who knows what I could have done—I dream I should have given my own time two months a year, but *you* have a *head* as well as a *heart* and I'm sure I don't know how your business gets on. My own life work is art, and but for the fact that a change of occupation partly refreshes my painting powers I could scarcely get on with both."

Dutcher, in fact, was soon eased off the AOU's Bird Protection Committee, and the "protectionists" in that organization went into eclipse. T. Gilbert Pearson, who was eventually to carry on Dutcher's work, looked back on that period from a calmer vantage point after a lapse of many years.

"The explanation given at the time," he wrote in his book, *Adventures in Bird Protection,* "was that the newly formed Audubon Association alone was sufficient to look out for bird protection, but many of us believe that this was not the real motive of the action. Dr. A. K. Fisher was appointed to succeed Dutcher as Chairman of the union's Bird Protection Committee and retained this position for eighteen years. During this period, the committee seldom functioned, very rarely even making any report to the union. Nearly every active ornithologist at that time was engaged in collecting birds, and the use of the opera-glass in making identifications was in little vogue. Most 'sight records' were looked upon as questionable evidence. . . . Fisher was frankly hostile and said that if the [Audubon] association did not actually advocate the stopping of scientific collecting it at least was to blame for what was taking place, because it was arousing interest all over the country in birds, which reacted against collectors."

## 4

*I*nspiration and information through the printed word, which had been the means for creating the original Audubon Society, now brought the new Audubon movement together. By 1901, there were thirty-six Audubon societies scattered across a continent not yet unified by radio and television, aircraft and interstate highways, or ready access to the telephone. One's message needed to be set in type if it was to reach the wished-for audience.

While bird protection was still mainly directed by the American Ornithologists' Union, its official journal, *The Auk,* served to spread the word by publishing the reports prepared by its Bird Protection Committee. But the ties had loosened between that scientific organization and the "protectionists." Fortunately for the infant Audubon movement, there was close at hand to its leaders an infant publication called *Bird-Lore,* the brainchild of Frank M. Chapman.

Chapman was to people interested in birds in the first part of this century what Roger Tory Peterson was to become three or four decades later—their first teacher and their perennial guide. He had come to the American Museum of Natural History in 1887 as a volunteer assistant to J. A. Allen and later succeeded him as curator of birds. From that citadel he would set out on a variety of expeditions to study the bird-life of the Americas and the Caribbean and write a number of popular books (mostly in longhand) about his expeditions, including *Camps and Cruises of an Ornithologist* and *Bird Studies with a Camera.* His *Handbook of Birds of Eastern North America* instructed a couple of generations in the fundamentals of field ornithology. A man of many parts, he found his avocation in music; friends marveled at his accomplished whistling and his "perfect mimicry of birds." (His son, Frank, Jr., became a Metropolitan Opera baritone and married the celebrated soprano Gladys Swarthout.) Precocity was a part of his makeup too, and very early in his career he had made a name for himself in the scientific arena.

"Dr. Chapman's greatest contribution to museology has been the introduction of the habitat idea in exhibitions," wrote Geoffrey Hellman in his profile of this popular scientist in *The New Yorker* in 1939. "Fifty years ago an American museum's concept of a bird exhibit consisted of a lot of stuffed specimens arranged in a manner reminiscent of the grill of a college club. Around 1900, John L. Cadwalader, an early patron of the Museum, gave Dr. Chapman $1,200 and asked him to get up a bird group with a background that would make sense. Dr. Chapman produced a Cobb's Island, Virginia, group, which contained black skimmers and other indigenous birds against a setting of beach composed of actual sand and artificial seaweed, which merged with a painted background of ocean, sky, and birds. Nesting birds were placed on the beach. A good many of the people in the Museum thought this was too informal and that the painted background verged on the sensational, but President [Morris K.] Jesup proclaimed it beautiful. . . . The habitat idea has been applied to all the other departments in the Museum and has been taken up by museums all over the world."

Still earlier, Chapman financed and launched the bimonthly magazine *Bird-Lore*. The first issue, selling for twenty cents a copy (or one dollar for a year's subscription) and with the admonitory motto "A bird in the bush is worth two in the hand," appeared in February 1899. This publication evolved into *Audubon* more than forty years later. Then, as in its present manifestation, it bound the Audubon movement together with a mix of articles, illustrations, and editorials that attracted a readership among people interested in birds and the outdoors.

Under Chapman's direction the magazine was an independent, profit-making venture. He and his wife, Fannie, sent out the first nine issues from their home in Englewood, New Jersey. But, wearying under the burden as circulation increased, Chapman transferred that end of the operation to Harrisburg, Pennsylvania, where first the Macmillan Company and later a printing firm took on the chore of mailing and distribution.

Chapman, in promoting the new magazine to potential readers, had promised to publish articles by the most prominent contemporary writers on birds, and he fulfilled that commitment. The very first issue had as its lead article "In Warbler Time," by the "Sage of Slabsides," John Burroughs. In recognition of what was then an extremely primitive art form, there was also an article on photography as a tool in bird study by Thomas S. Roberts, who later wrote the two-volume *Birds of Minnesota*. Chapman had also promised to deliver the finest photographs of wild birds ever published in America, though the state of the art still left something to be desired. A later naturalist, Edwin Way Teale, once examined the first two years of *Bird-Lore* and counted eighty-eight photo-

Frank M. Chapman at work. AMERICAN MUSEUM OF NATURAL HISTORY

graphs of stuffed birds to only seventy-six of living birds; several of the latter had been taken in zoos.

Of more immediate importance to the readers of *Bird-Lore* was a long feature in every issue on news from the various state societies. This Audubon Department was prepared by Mabel Osgood Wright, one of the ablest of the group of women writers near the turn of the century whose books (often anthropomorphic in tone) had helped to arouse widespread sympathy for an interest in native birds. Two of Wright's books, *The Friendship of Nature* (1894) and *Birdcraft* (1895) were warmly praised by Frank Chapman himself. Later she collaborated with the prestigious Elliott Coues on another popular book, *Citizen Bird,* which was illustrated by the man who was to become the premier painter of birds in the next generation, Louis Agassiz Fuertes. Moreover, Wright was well fitted for her *Bird-Lore* assignment by a background in the bird-protection movement—as a founder and first president of the Connecticut Audubon Society, a member of the AOU, and the guiding hand behind one of the earliest bird sanctuaries, Birdcraft, in Fairfield, Connecticut.

"It was quite true that some of the material in earlier issues verged on 'corn,' especially the verse," Roger Tory Peterson once wrote. "The funniest, undoubtedly, were several stanzas by T. Gilbert Pearson that began: 'Which would you choose for life's short whirl, the girl with the gun or the camera girl?' The poem was illustrated by a wash drawing of a young lady with a box camera and another with a shotgun, shooting quail."

Even those lines can be forgiven in the light of *Bird-Lore*'s many contributions to the cause of bird protection, including the origination of the annual Christmas Bird Count. Chapman suggested the event in the issue of December 1900:

"It is not many years ago that sportsmen were accustomed to meet on Christmas Day, 'choose sides,' and then . . . hie themselves to the fields and woods on the cheerful mission of killing practically everything in fur or feathers that crossed their path. . . . Now *Bird-Lore* proposes a new kind of Christmas side hunt in the form of a Christmas Bird Census, and we hope that all our readers who have the opportunity would aid in making it a success by spending a portion of Christmas Day with the birds, and sending a report of their 'hunt' to *Bird-Lore* before they retire that night."

Twenty-seven people in twenty-five localities accepted the challenge and went out on that Christmas to count birds. (The idea caught on and, under the National Audubon Society's sponsorship, the count has grown yearly. At Christmas 1988, 42,671 men, women, and children took part in 1,563 Christmas Bird Counts from Alaska and the Yukon Territory to Panama and the Amazon. The total number of species seen ranged from a high of 341 in Panama's Atlantic Canal Area to one [15 ravens] in Prudhoe Bay, Alaska. The event has become more than simply a game, for it has created a wide interest in birds and their protection while providing scientists with an unparalleled source of raw data over time and space.)

With its growth in readership, *Bird-Lore* also enjoyed a modest surge in advertising as the handful of ads for bird books in the first issue were joined by those for a variety of products, including cameras whose prices were pegged between five and ten dollars. That the publication had been accepted as the voice of the Audubon movement by all the state societies was reflected in the news items it reproduced. One suggested that at least a part of the enemy forces was in retreat, for *Bird-Lore* reprinted an ad that had been placed in another publication in 1902 by a millinery wholesaler in Lindenhurst, Long Island. The milliner offered for sale "a variety of Fancy Feathers, Wings, Aigrettes and Birds for apparel," then concluded with this conciliatory note: "To our kind and feeling friends who are prejudiced against the wearing of birds, besides such as are protected by law, we respectfully offer a fine selection of *Fish* of different breeds, which are the latest Parisian creation."

In reality, contacts between the two warring elements were tentative and likely to break down at any juncture. The protectionists tried to promote a line of millinery called "Audubonnets," decorated with ribbons and other nonplumage items, but without much success. And an early olive branch offered by the millinery industry was received with mixed feelings by the Audubon societies and finally rejected.

This offer came about in 1900 when the Millinery Merchants Protective Association approached the Audubon leaders and the AOU with an alluring pledge "not to kill or buy any more North American birds from hunters or such people who make it a business to destroy North American birds." The milliners reserved the right to sell all of the North American birds and their plumage then in storage. But, after agreeing to police the industry, the milliners presented what was to be the sticking point:

"In return for this pledge, we expect the Audubon Society and the Ornithological Union to pledge themselves to do all in their power to prevent laws being enacted in Congress, or in any of the states, which shall interfere with the manufacturing or selling of plumage or skins from barnyard fowl, edible birds and game birds killed in their season and all birds which are not North American birds."

Many of the leading ornithologists were inclined to accept the agreement. In an editorial in *Bird-Lore,* Frank Chapman urged his colleagues to give the milliners' offer a fair hearing, writing that "We cannot hope to abolish the trade in feathers, but if, by a concession, we can so control it that our native birds shall be exempt from its demands, we shall have afforded them a measure of protection we had not expected to secure in this generation nor the next."

Dutcher and the AOU's Joel A. Allen concurred. But the hinterlands were yet to be heard from and, when they were, the proposed agreement was dead. William Brewster promised to use all the influence he had to defeat it in the AOU. "It does not seem to me to be so much a question of expediency as of absolute right and wrong," he wrote. "No such compromise is possible." Mabel Osgood Wright was even more scathing, damning the proposal from a political as well as an ethical standpoint. She used her "department" in *Bird-Lore* to skewer the proposal point by point, reminding her readers that the Audubon movement was being asked to prevent enactment of the very laws it was formed to campaign for, and asked who was to determine a bird's citizenship or edibility. And she concluded:

"No Audubon Society that is true in spirit, as well as in letter, to its platform and constituents can sign this agreement; for to do so is literally saying to its members, 'We will not interfere with you even if you cover your hats with birds so long as they are marked *killed in Europe*'!"

Most of the other state societies agreed with their colleagues in Massachusetts and Connecticut. Three years later, in April 1903, the milliners came forth with another proposal, agreeing to refrain from importing and selling gulls, terns, grebes, egrets, herons, hummingbirds, and songbirds regardless of their country of origin. In return, the Audubon societies agreed to refrain from sending game wardens to "interfere" with milliners operating in a legal manner and to stop pushing for legislation "that has for its object restrictions against the importation, manufacture or sale of fancy feathers obtained from domesticated fowls or . . . of foreign birds, other than those specifically mentioned above."

This time Mabel Osgood Wright urged her readers to accept the agreement so as not to "imperil our influence as logical bird protectors." Not all of the state societies went along, but enough did to keep the agreement alive for three years. Dutcher even served for a time as a representative of the U.S. Department of Agriculture, "to aid officers of the collector of customs or importers by advice or by inspection of samples submitted to you for the purpose regarding the importation of plumage for millinery purposes." But eventually the milliners took offense at what they regarded as sniping from *Bird-Lore* at the wearers of feathers.

"Give these people an inch and they will take an ell," fumed *The Millinery Trade Review* as the spirit of cooperation succumbed.

# 5

$\mathscr{A}$s reports from around the country arrived on William Dutcher's desk in New York, he became increasingly aware of the bird-protection movement's erratic progress. Some of the Audubon societies were large and active, as in Massachusetts, where the society established strong ties with the state government. George W. Field, who taught at the Massachusetts Institute of Technology, served as a state commissioner of fish and game and also joined the board of directors of the Massachusetts Audubon Society. In other states, the Audubon movement was weak and largely ineffective.

Thus Dutcher urged some sort of a union through which the Audubon societies could work together to present a strong national front. Members of a number of these societies had met briefly while attending the AOU meeting in Cambridge in 1900 and formed a committee to consider Dutcher's recommendations for a joining of forces. The response was favorable, and in 1901 another meeting took place, this time in New York, at which the various state representatives formed a loose federation called the National Committee of the Audubon Societies of America. They agreed that each society was to appoint one member to the committee, that an annual conference be held, and that the members of the committee "may be empowered to represent the Societies whenever concerted action on the part of the Societies be deemed by the Committee expedient." The members elected Dutcher as chairman.

However, the very first provision of the agreement stated clearly that "the several Societies retain their individuality." They wanted no part of a merger at this point in which they might lose their separate identities. This note has endured throughout the history of the Audubon movement and, as we shall see, persists to the present day.

By the end of 1903, there were thirty-seven state societies, most of which belonged to the national committee. The best of them had organized a variety of projects: lobbying the state legislatures for stronger laws; tacking up signs in post offices, railroad stations, and other public places warning against the killing and shipping of birds; distributing educational leaflets and the Massachusetts Audubon Society bird charts to schools; presenting slide lectures; and admonishing women through lectures and the newspapers to desist from wearing wild bird plumage.

In that year Abbott Thayer raised $4,000 for the warden fund—the highest in any year to date. Dutcher continued to secure earnest wardens, still concentrating on the colonies in Maine and Virginia, but beginning to cast an eye toward the Deep South, where small birds such as robins and bobolinks were shot regularly for food and could be seen for sale in the shops, "strung up like onions." His most effective ally there was a young college instructor in biology at the State Normal and Industrial College in North Carolina, T. Gilbert Pearson. Pearson's work quickly catapulted that state into a position of leadership in protective legislation and was to lead him to New York and into the role of Dutcher's aide and eventual successor.

The national nature of the Audubon movement and the rising enthusiasm induced Dutcher to reach further afield for new blood. He became acquainted with William L. Finley, who had grown up in Portland, Oregon, become interested in birds, and emerged as a leader in Audubon work on the West Coast about 1903. He was a pioneer in bird photography, and his pictures of birdlife in the marshes around Klamath and Malheur lakes created an interest in bird protection in the Far West. His work, in fact, reached even farther—all the way to the White House, where President Roosevelt lent a sympathetic ear to Finley's message and eventually established two marshes in Oregon as federal wildlife refuges, one of them, south of Corvallis, named in Finley's honor.

Roosevelt, who became President of the United States upon William McKinley's assassination in 1901, was in on the ground floor of the movement because of his early association with the Audubon Society of the District of Columbia. In 1908, he arranged to have the first motion pictures ever taken of wild birds shown in the East Room of the White House, an event which he shared with local Audubon members as well as other friends and cabinet officials. Lucy Warner Maynard, the author of *The Birds of Washington and Vicinity,* later described the evening:

"The President was in the best of spirits and awaited the 'movie' (though not called that in those days) as eagerly as any of us. Mr. [Richard] Kearton [an Englishman who had brought the film to Washington] first showed pictures of a make-believe cow and a sheep, which he and his brother had built, and which were so natural that, he said, dogs barked at them. The sheep held a camera and the cow both camera and man, and they moved about in the vicinity of the nests, so that they got perfectly natural and charming pictures."

Roosevelt later made a list of the fifty-six species of birds he had

The unmistakable figure of Theodore Roosevelt, striding through a royal
tern colony on Grand Cochere Island, Louisiana, in 1915. NAS

seen on the White House grounds. In fact, his ties to ornithology can
be traced all the way back to his boyhood, when he searched local markets in New York City for specimens for the "museum of natural history" he and his cousins put together for themselves. Those ties were
strengthened during his days at Harvard, when he joined the Nuttall
Ornithological Club, and during vacations in the Adirondacks, when he
and a friend compiled and published a detailed list of the birds of
Franklin County, New York. Roosevelt was an outspoken foe of the
English sparrow and while still in college contributed to the literature
on that heated topic by writing that he had seen mobs of English sparrows "assault" other small birds, and actually kill a sapsucker. A sparrow enthusiast retorted that Roosevelt was "sophomoric."

He became acquainted with most of the prominent members of the
bird-protection movement, notably George Bird Grinnell. The two men
had much in common, both being part-time ranchers and big game
hunters in the West and later conservationists who were responsible for
the prestigious Boone and Crockett Club; Grinnell originated the idea
for the club, and Roosevelt was the host at a dinner party that brought
the founding members together. Roosevelt and Grinnell campaigned for
stronger game laws, collaborated in the editing of three books on big
game hunting, and remained friends for the rest of their lives.

Dutcher and Frank Chapman took advantage of Roosevelt's interest in birds at every opportunity. Their most notable success with him was in the matter of Pelican Island. This island in the Indian River on the east coast of Florida consisted of four acres covered, before the Civil War, by a thick mangrove growth; a colony of herons, ibises, and roseate spoonbills nested there in the vegetation, their numbers splashing the sky with color. An overabundance of nesting birds and a severe frost in 1886 killed the mangroves, about the same time that the plume hunters were cleaning up the birds.

When Chapman visited the island on his honeymoon in 1898, it was a treeless mudflat taken over by nesting brown pelicans. He collected a few pelicans as specimens and with his bride, Fannie, settled down to prepare their skins. Later he was to call Pelican Island "by far the most fascinating place it has ever been my fortune to see in the world of birds," an estimate colored, perhaps, by his own state of mind at the time. Chapman issued a plea for the preservation of the pelican colony, noting that it was the only breeding site of those birds on the Atlantic coast of Florida and that it was accessible not only to plume hunters, but also to local fishermen who believed themselves to be in competition with every fish-eating bird.

Chapman's plea aroused enough interest among Audubon members to raise money with which to buy the island from the government. When the offer became bogged down in the General Land Office, Chapman and Dutcher went to the White House. Roosevelt was unable to skirt the difficulties in putting federal property up for sale, but he did the next best thing. On March 14, 1903, he issued an executive order: "It is hereby ordered that Pelican Island in Indian River . . . be, and it is hereby, reserved and set apart for the use of the Department of Agriculture as a preserve and breeding ground for native birds."

It was the first of fifty-three sanctuaries for birds and other wildlife that Roosevelt was to create on federal property before he left office in 1909, and it set a significant precedent. Aside from the national parks, no federal wildlife refuge existed before then anywhere in the continental United States. Because Pelican Island and the refuges that followed were set aside by executive order, Congress did not appropriate any money for enforcing their protection. For some years afterward, the system of federal refuges was guarded by wardens paid for by the Audubon societies, which, under Dutcher's direction, had assumed the management of the Thayer Fund.

Paul Kroegel, the warden hired at seven dollars a month to guard Pelican Island, erected a large sign in the colony, proclaiming the birds to be "wards of the government" and warning hunters away. But when Chapman visited there the next spring, he "found to my surprise and disgust that with a uniformity of action which left no doubt as to their attitude," the birds had deserted the island. For the first time within memory not a bird nested there.

Chapman was perplexed, especially when he found pelicans nesting on two small islands nearby. Kroegel suggested that the pelicans had been made uneasy by the large sign. Although Chapman was dubious, he ordered Kroegel to replace it with several small signs, and the birds returned to the island's unrelieved silhouette the next season.

While Chapman was working for the cause in Florida, Dutcher had solidified the Audubon movement in New York. For some time he had been concerned about the day-to-day nature of the movement, darting from crisis to crisis but without either the structure or the staff to carry out the long-term crusade that bird protection had become. He remembered the fleeting existence of Grinnell's Audubon Society. From his own experience he had found the objectives of the AOU's Bird Protection Committee to be unstable, dependent on the waxing and waning enthusiasm of that organization's leaders, whose interests were chiefly scientific. Even the National Committee of Audubon Societies was a will-o'-the-wisp, simply an agreement for the separate societies to work together in a common cause, and dependent on the strength and capacity of those widely scattered units.

The next step, Dutcher had felt, was to incorporate the organization, thus attaining a semblance of permanence as well as legal and financial security. In the fall of 1904 his hand was forced. "You will recall in September that I wrote to you that a stranger, who had been attracted to and was interested in our work, called and gave me a check for $400," Dutcher said in a note to Abbott Thayer on November 22. "One day last week he called me up on the phone and told me that he had just made a new will in which he had left a legacy of $100,000 to our Society, provided we would incorporate at once."

The beneficent stranger was Albert Willcox, a wealthy New Yorker who, in tendering his gift, had asked Dutcher for anonymity during his lifetime. His father had operated a small insurance business in Manhattan and a farm on Staten Island, where Albert grew up. The young man eventually took over the firm which, under the name A. W. Willcox and Company, earned him a great deal of money in fire and marine insurance. (His brother, David, became president of the Delaware and Hudson Railway.) But Albert Willcox was not inclined to devote his life utterly to the pursuit of money. He felt very strongly about the persecution of animals of all kinds.

Acting on this sympathy, Willcox expressed his hope that the Audubon societies would broaden their scope to include the protection of all wild animals. And he told Dutcher that a national society, once formed and incorporated, must have at the outset a paid secretary, or financial agent, who would solicit memberships and contributions. To make this possible, he agreed to give the new society $3,000 a year for the next two years to employ a suitable person on a half-time basis.

Dutcher already had such a person in mind—T. Gilbert Pearson, the young college professor who had accomplished a great deal in his home state as the founder and president of the North Carolina Audubon Society. Dutcher asked Pearson to come to New York to meet Willcox, and the two men formed a liking for each other.

"I met him in his office in Nassau Street," Pearson wrote many years later. "He said that he was deeply concerned about two great evils which existed in our country, one the terrible destruction of birds and game animals; the other, the abuses being heaped upon the Negroes of the Southern States. I did not talk much about the second point, but had something to say about bird and game protection. After luncheon he said, 'Now, we will go and see Mr. Dutcher.' "

In Dutcher's office the agreement was made for Pearson to spend at least half of his time working for the new corporation, in New York or wherever else Dutcher felt his services were needed. At the same time, Willcox told Dutcher that, if he were convinced that the men and women who agreed to serve as board members "are of a class that will faithfully carry out the present purposes and plans of your Society I may not limit the sum [of his bequest] to $100,000."

With this offer in hand, Dutcher wrote to a number of prominent members of the Audubon movement, including Grinnell, William Brewster, and John E. Thayer in Massachusetts, and Mrs. Kingsmill Marrs of the Florida Audubon Society, and found all of them in favor of the incorporation of a national Audubon organization supported by paying members.

Dutcher had already obtained a lawyer, Samuel T. Carter of New York, to prepare for the incorporation. Carter drew up a constitution, by-laws, and a certificate of incorporation which was filed in the office of the Secretary of State of New York. These steps brought into existence, on January 5, 1905, the National Association of Audubon Societies for the Protection of Wild Birds and Animals.

Dutcher called a meeting at the American Museum of Natural History on January 30 to organize the new association. Present besides Dutcher were Frank Chapman, J. A. Allen, Samuel Carter, Hermon C. Bumpus, Mabel Osgood Wright, and Mrs. C. B. Davenport. They promptly voted to adopt the constitution and by-laws and then adjourned. These incorporators gathered later on the same afternoon to hold the first meeting of the board of directors. They elected William Dutcher as president of the National Association, John E. Thayer as first vice president, Theodore S. Palmer second vice president, T. Gilbert

Pearson as secretary, and Frank Chapman as treasurer. In keeping with the notion that the new organization was to be chiefly a federation, the constitution provided for a board of thirty directors, twenty of whom were to be named by the state societies. All of the societies remained as independent organizations, with their own officers and dues-paying members.

In line with the hopes of Albert Willcox, the board of directors included many of the most prominent men and women identified with bird protection in every part of the country, among them all of the elected officers—and George Bird Grinnell. As Willcox had stipulated, the new organization's objectives were to be carried out by the support of dues-paying members and contributors, diligently sought out by Pearson. Thus, the Thayer Fund was discontinued.

The new Audubon Association immediately set up shop at 141 Broadway in lower Manhattan. Although its objectives had been set forth in the constitution in a series of legal phrases, they were stated more aptly shortly afterward by Dutcher in the pages of *Bird-Lore*:

"The object of this organization is to be a barrier between wild birds and animals and a very large unthinking class, and a smaller but more harmful class of selfish people. The unthinking, or, in plain English, the ignorant class, we hope to reach through educational channels, while the selfish people we shall control through the enforcement of wise laws, reservations or bird refuges, and the warden system."

Willcox kept his promise to Dutcher. When he died in the summer of 1906, the National Association of Audubon Societies received a bequest of $100,000 to establish a substantial interest-bearing endowment fund. As the board of directors and the association's objectives apparently had met with the benefactor's approval, he also left the National Association one half of his residual estate (the other half going to the Tuskegee Normal and Industrial Institute), to be paid upon the death of his brother. After calculating that David Willcox was apparently hale and hearty and had a life expectancy of another sixteen years, the board agreed to take its share immediately and settled for a total bequest of $331,072.

"With one stroke of his pen," Dutcher wrote later, "he [Willcox] perpetuated the work of animal and bird protection in this country."

*6*

*T*he Everglades is a broad river of grass, the water seeping southward along a front nearly seventy miles wide from Okeechobee, the vast
shallow lake in central Florida. But the ripple on the river's surface is
not of water but of grass; more precisely, of a sedge called sawgrass.
Spears of sawgrass, their knifelike edges grating on each other in the
wind to create a fierce, exciting music all their own, rise from the creep-
ing river as a prairie that looks to the traveler as broad as Asia. Here
and there bayheads of tangled trees and vines rise on slight elevations
of the land like tiny islands in the grassy river.

On the rim of the Everglades, separating it from the open sea yet
part of both land and sea, grow thickets of mangroves. These small trees,
standing tiptoe as it were on arched and labyrinthine roots, restrain the
surging seawater from overwhelming the sweet flow that moves inexo-
rably from Okeechobee toward Florida Bay. Just as the Nile lays down
the fertile strip that gives life to Egypt, so the immense and intricate
expanse of brackish water at the tip of Florida produces a unique community of trees and sedges, reptiles and fishes, mammals and birds.

This teeming world remained almost free of white settlers until long
after much of the rest of the country had given way to them. The Civil
War began to change the region's isolation. Deserters from both sides
made their way into the sanctuary of the Everglades; other settlers, impelled by the economic and social disasters that were the aftermath of
war, followed the deserters into the region.

"It wasn't a force of numbers, however, that spelled doom to wildlife
as much as the pioneer aspect of these settlers," Robert Porter Allen
wrote in *The Roseate Spoonbill*. "Everyone carried a gun, an ax and a
determination to wrest a living from the wilderness. And most of them
did, whether they grew tomatoes on land cleared with their own hands
or shot plume birds."

The plume hunters were a mixed bag of humanity. Some were ignorant and desperate men who shot a few long-legged birds, made a

quick slit down their backs with a rusty knife, and peeled away the feathers on the backs and tails; there was always a dealer around to hand them whiskey money for a clump of plumes. Others, like Alfred LeChevalier (known simply as Chevalier, or "the Old Frenchman"), were wandering adventurers whose motivation was partly trade and partly science. LeChevalier had acquired a reputation as an eccentric, perhaps because of his inability to handle the English language with the colloquial expertise of the resident Crackers. A shooting accident had blown away two fingers and a part of his hand, but he learned to shoot again, propping the gun on his right elbow to fire. He and his assistants roamed both coasts, collecting bird skins for both science and the millinery trade. They dealt in high-quality plumes, taking all the skin off the bird's body and out to the first joint of the wing, then rubbing the skin with corn meal and stretching it with small sticks to dry. For a while the Chevalier party kept a base at Boca Ciega Bay near Tampa where it took them, one traveler to the area said, "five breeding seasons to break up, by killing and frightening the birds away, this once incomparable breeding resort" of the plume birds.

And finally there were men like J. H. Batty, who had owned a taxidermist's shop in New York City for many years, only to give it up for the adventurous life of shooting plume birds in the Everglades. W. E. D. Scott, writing in *The Auk* about his trip to Florida in 1886, reported that Batty employed at least sixty gunners, and that in May of that year they were shooting knots, sanderlings, and ruddy turnstones over decoys, as well as least terns and Wilson's plovers. Elsewhere, they were shooting everything from barred owls to songbirds for northern millinery firms. One of the gunners told Scott that "Mr. Batty was constantly purchasing and trading with native and other gunners for plumes and round and flat skins of all the desirable birds of the region."

Before the end of the century, Batty underwent a change of heart and resolved to earn an honest living by collecting birds and mammals selectively for the American Museum of Natural History. After he was killed by the accidental discharge of his own gun while collecting in Mexico, a fellow ornithologist eulogized him as "a man of the most kindly nature, trustful, and thoroughly conscientious in his work."

William Dutcher, armed with the fund provided by Abbott Thayer and a version of the Model Law passed by Florida in 1901, finally took action. A small but eager Florida Audubon Society was already in place. Trouble spots were located and wardens recommended. Dutcher's grasp, in fact, extended beyond the Florida Keys all the way to the Dry Tortugas, a spatter of small islands about sixty-five miles west of Key West, which was the site of a U.S. Marine installation as well as of the largest breeding colonies of noddy and sooty terns in the United States. John

James Audubon had visited the Tortugas in 1840 and gave a dramatic account of the vast numbers of birds there on Bird Key and the destruction of adults, as well as the young, by eggers. The egging and the killing of the terns for the plume trade (often by Key West fishermen or the marines stationed at Fort Jefferson) had continued into the present century.

In 1902, Dutcher succeeded in gaining the cooperation of the military authorities, as he had of the Lighthouse Board on the Maine islands, and soon sent a warden there. He also hired as a warden the keeper of the Sand Key Lighthouse, closer to Key West. The correspondence between Dutcher and Frank Chapman, who regularly spent part of each winter in Florida, emphasized the differences in their approach to the warden system. Dutcher believed in hounding malefactors wherever they operated; Chapman saw the system not so much as a police force but rather as an instrument of education and public relations. He wrote to Dutcher in 1904 from south Florida, expressing his belief that sending a warden to the Tortugas was a waste of money.

"To my mind, one of the most important features of the warden system is not so much the birds it protects as the people it educates," Chapman wrote. "The mere fact that it is *someone's business* to protect birds is in itself an eloquent lesson of the importance of bird protection. I believe also that our limited funds should be expended where the results will be observable. The Tortugas birds visit the extreme edge of the United States only to breed, and they pass the winter south of our limits. No people receive any benefit from the existence of this colony, whereas if you could have a warden at the north end of Indian River in the Oak Hill district where the birds are now nesting abundantly, several rookeries might be established under protection. . . . The region is infested with tourists in the winter, and a warden's work would become widely known."

Chapman closed this letter to Dutcher with a paragraph about a warden that, in the light of his previous comments and the events of the year to come, can be seen as deeply ironic. This warden's value in terms of conservation education was to be immeasurable.

"I was favorably impressed with Bradley, and believe he is doing the best he can," Chapman wrote of his warden-guide to rookeries in south Florida. "He is somewhat inclined to talk about himself and his work and the risks he runs in the performance of his duties, but he has, I think, a pride in his office and an enmity for law breakers which would lead him to convict them, if possible. He seems especially outraged by the looting of the Cuthbert Rookery and obviously would be glad to get the offenders."

Guy Bradley had grown up in southern Florida and as a boy hunted

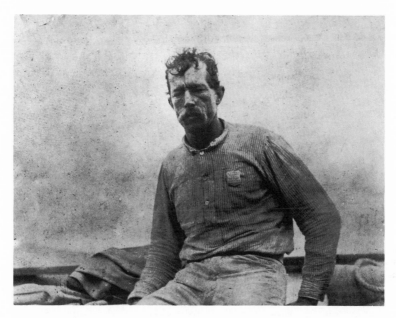

Guy Bradley, whose murder in 1905 gave impetus
to the new Audubon movement. NAS

plume birds in the Everglades, selling them at one time to "the Old
Frenchman." There were land-development schemes for south Florida
even in those days; promoters envisioned draining the Everglades to
plant vegetables and fruit trees, and building a railroad from Cape Sable,
at the tip, to Key West. As a part of one of those schemes, free land
was offered to families that would settle in the isolated community of
Flamingo near Cape Sable. Bradley's father had moved there as an agent
for one of the land companies. Guy married in Flamingo and fathered
two sons of his own, supporting his family by farming and working as
a surveyor for a land company. At the time of Chapman's visit, he was
thirty-five years old, strong, deeply tanned, with thinning curly hair and
a mustache.

The course of his life merged with the bird-protection movement in
1902 when Kirk Munroe, an active member of the Florida Audubon
Society, made an extended cruise among the Keys and along the state's
southern coast. On his return to Coconut Grove, Munroe wrote to the
society's president, Mrs. Kingsmill Marrs, about the destruction of birdlife in that region. "At Cape Sable I found the paradise of plume hunters
and the purgatory of birds," he told her. In particular, he mentioned
the frequent shooting in a large inland rookery that was said to be one
of the last refuges in the state for the plume birds, and he urged the

prompt appointment of a warden to try to put a stop to the slaughter. And then Munroe became specific:

"The game warden to deal with this situation must be a resident, well acquainted with local conditions, a strong, fearless man and one fully alive to the value of bird protection. Fortunately for the birds and for us, I found residing at Cape Sable a man who combines in himself all these requirements. He is Mr. Guy Bradley, a young, recently married man, brought up from earliest childhood on the east coast of Florida, a thorough woodsman, a plume hunter by occupation before the passage of the present law, since which time, as I have ample testimony, he has not killed a bird. . . . I have known these Bradley boys for many years and can honestly say that I know of no better man for game warden in the whole state of Florida than Guy."

Mrs. Marrs, who was regularly in touch with Dutcher to report on the Florida Audubon Society's membership and educational campaigns (she also knew of Dutcher's work on the Maine coast, where she spent her summers at Prout's Neck), sent Munroe's letter to him in New York. Dutcher immediately put the letter to use to spur the collection of funds for the warden system. Satisfied that he had the right man, Dutcher wrote to Bradley at Flamingo on May 20, 1902, informing him that he was to be hired at thirty-five dollars a month as a warden representing the American Ornithologists' Union. (Bradley did not become an "Audubon warden" until the National Association of Audubon Societies was incorporated.) Dutcher told him that he would be expected to protect all of the birds in his region, except those considered fair game under Florida's laws; he enumerated those falling outside the protective legislation as "English sparrow, sharp-shinned hawk, Cooper's hawk, great-horned owl, crow, ricebird [bobolink], meadow-lark, jackdaw [grackle], butcher-bird [shrike] and game birds in their season." He also asked Bradley to send him the names of some of the local plume hunters as well as the firms with which they did business in New York.

Bradley wrote back, accepting the position and informing Dutcher that the height of the plume-hunting season was from the middle of January to the middle of May, when the birds were breeding and in their nuptial plumage. During the rest of the year, he said, the heaviest shooting was done by those who killed the birds, especially ibises and roseate spoonbills, for food. Most of the plume-hunting, he said, was carried on by men who came in from the Ten Thousand Islands and other localities, so that he would not be able to supply their names until he had caught them in the act.

"I will certainly do all that I can to find out who are the New York buyers," Bradley wrote. "I believe Sterns Bros. are still in the business. They used to buy heavily some years ago when I used to hunt plume birds, but since the game laws were passed, I have not killed a plume bird for it is a cruel and hard calling notwithstanding being unlawful. I make this statement upon honor and can give you as reference a member of your own Society Mr. Kirk Munroe, whom I have known for years."

That Bradley was no bumpkin is clear from the letters and reports he sent to Dutcher. Here he is responding to a request for written evidence of the involvement of New York millinery dealers with Florida's plume hunters, in this case a circular announcing that a firm was ready to buy plumes and bird skins.

"Enclosed please find the first piece of evidence I have been able to get my hands on," Bradley wrote. "I hope it will be of some good to the cause and if such letters are any service to you I would like to be allowed to make a suggestion, namely, that before acting on this letter or circular, that I be given a little time to get more of them for you before putting such firms on their guard. If you could give me the names of other firms that deal in feathers—I could get them to send price lists such as the one I have. I only make this suggestion, and I hope you will not think it is too forward or 'cheeky.' "

Dutcher had used this ploy in the past, particularly on the Maine coast, where he had asked wardens to write decoy letters to New York dealers. Now, in the summer of 1902, he sent Bradley a list of firms in New York that he believed were handling feathers in violation of the Lacey Act. "Please ask them if they will buy plume birds from you," he wrote, "and also what kinds of birds, and how many they will take, and the price they will give you. I note the inquiry from Louis Stern & Co., and shall take some steps to see whether they can be punished."

From the beginning, there was a sense that Guy Bradley was in danger. Florida Audubon's Mrs. Kingsmill Marrs advised Dutcher that Fort Myers was a hotbed of plume hunters. One dealer alone, she reported, employed between forty and sixty hunters. She was concerned about trumpeting the news that a warden had been hired to protect south Florida's birds through the efforts of Audubon groups, "because it might bring harm to Bradley." But Bradley was already on patrol. To ease his long trips over open water, the Florida Audubon Society eventually bought him a motor launch, fueled by naphtha, called the *Audubon*.

Word that a few spectacular colonies of the large wading birds still existed in the depths of the Everglades stirred excitement among northern ornithologists. Several of them, including Frank Chapman, met Bradley on their visits to see the birds and were impressed by his dedication. Two ornithologists who made the pilgrimage in 1903 were Herbert K. Job, a naturalist and photographer, and Arthur Cleveland Bent, whose *Life Histories of North American Birds* (issued by the Smithsonian Institution in twenty-one numbers and reprinted in twenty-six volumes) is one of America's ornithological classics. The most detailed account of Bradley at work was left by Job in his book *Wild Wings* and in the report he and Bent wrote for Dutcher after their trip.

Job and Bent were met by Bradley at Miami, then the terminus of the Florida East Coast Railroad, and went with him by sloop through the Keys to Flamingo. Tormented by mosquitoes and hordes of horseflies that the locals referred to sardonically as "sharpshooters,"and worried by a lack of fresh water, the two ornithologists nevertheless followed their guide into the heart of the Everglades. Bradley pushed ahead of them through the maze of mangrove roots and subtropical jungle, alternately shoving and carrying a fifty-pound canoe. Job marveled at their guide's endurance and resourcefulness. (Job himself must have had considerable endurance too, for he plodded along behind, carrying his bulky camera and glass photographic plates; he tumbled several times into "deceitful" mudholes and became ill after succumbing to the temptation to drink the brackish water.)

But the ornithologists' reward came as they penetrated to remote bayous and found the surviving colonies of plume birds—roseate spoonbills, snowy egrets, and Louisiana (now called tri-colored) herons. Job felt he had "reached the high water mark of spectacular sights in the bird world."

But there was more to come. The ultimate object of their journey was Cuthbert Lake, a name that reverberates as hauntingly in the history of plume-hunting as that of Little Big Horn in the Indian wars. It was named for a plume hunter who had heard rumors of a great rookery in the interior of the 'Glades. Cuthbert searched for days, so the story went, picking up a clue from a white feather floating toward him through the mangroves and climbing scraggly trees to puzzle out the prevailing direction of the birds in flight. When he found the rookery at last, he moved in with his small Flobert rifle and took an enormous toll of the confused birds.

Bradley had located the Cuthbert Rookery in the course of his duties as an Audubon warden. The colony had somewhat recovered, and Job, upon his arrival there after an arduous trip, found the sign warning away plume hunters that his guide had erected a few months before. Job estimated that three thousand pairs of various wading birds were nesting there at the time. He photographed as many of the birds as he could reach, struggling through the tangled mangroves and mashing, quite by accident, quantities of mosquitoes between the films in packing his plates away. He even found the time to reflect on the superiority of his way of treating birds to that of Audubon, when "he and John Bachman visited an egret rookery and killed forty-six of the birds. He quaintly comments in his great book that 'many more of them might have been killed, but we became tired of shooting them.' No wonder! But those were unenlightened times and there was no camera hunting."

Job and Bent, after such a trip, had nothing but praise for Bradley and his brother-in-law, Bill Burton, whom they also met. The enormous extent of the wardens' territory (it was about seventy miles by small boat to Key West in the south, and another sixty miles to the border of Lee County in the northwest), as well as the obstacles to travel in the 'Glades, made their work daunting. The two northern ornithologists also noted the other hazards.

"The native conchs [poor whites] and negroes," they wrote, "many of whom are desperate characters, can, by watching the wardens' movements, visit the rookeries with impunity and make wholesale depredations on the young herons, ibises and even cormorants for food. Several expeditions of this kind have already been broken up by the judicious employment of negro spies, who have kept the wardens informed." But, so great was the admiration of Job and Bent for these wardens that they added: "The Bradleys have the reputation of being the best rifle shots in that vicinity and they would not hesitate to shoot when necessary. The Bradleys and Burton together would be more than a match for any party they are likely to meet."

Guy Bradley made other trips to Cuthbert Lake, keeping watch over the rookery, but plume hunters kept watch over Bradley too. Often they observed his movements and went in to ply their destructive trade after he had gone away. In 1904 Bradley contracted to escort Frank Chapman to Cuthbert Lake, but brought bad news instead to their meeting place. The plume hunters had recently "shot it out," killing or driving away all of the nesting birds.

"You could've walked right around the rookery on those birds' bodies—between four and five hundred of them," Bradley said.

Then he mentioned something to Chapman that he had told him on earlier occasions. He expected an attempt to be made on his life.

There was good reason for Bradley's anxiety. He had made enemies among the gunners, especially a Flamingo man and Civil War veteran named Walter Smith, whose son he is said to have arrested twice for killing birds. Smith had told his neighbors that if Bradley ever again tried to arrest any member of his family he would kill him. In the spring of 1905, Dutcher had again used his contacts in Florida, this time to have Bradley appointed game warden of Monroe County, an appointment gladly made by the state because the recently incorporated National Association of Audubon Societies was paying his salary. (Walter Smith, hoping to replace Bradley, had tried to secure the appointment

Herbert K. Job, who
accompanied Guy Bradley
into the Everglades. NAS

through friends in Key West.) The new title, Dutcher hoped, would
make Bradley's duties more explicit to the local courts.

On Saturday, July 8, of that year, Bradley was in his cottage at
Flamingo. From the little porch on the cottage he could look out across
the wide, calm sweep of Florida Bay. Stepping outside, he caught sight
of a sail on the horizon. He watched curiously as the sail moved toward
a small island called Oyster Key, where a few plume birds occasionally
gathered. Bradley probably was aware that the schooner belonged to
Walter Smith. According to witnesses, he pushed his own small boat
into the water and rowed the two miles under a warm sun to Oyster
Key. A few minutes later Bradley was shot and killed.

Isolation and official indifference obscured the details of the crime
for some time. The first public announcement of the shooting did not
occur on the mainland until the following Friday, when the *Daily Miami*

*Metropolis* published a story on page eight under the headline "Guy Bradley Was Wounded." The details of the story seemed to have been supplied by Walter Smith, who asserted he was "turtling" near Flamingo when Bradley came alongside in a skiff, said he had come to arrest Smith's son, and demanded to board the schooner. Smith refused, whereupon Bradley (well known to be a crack shot) fired at close range— and missed. Smith said he returned the fire and Bradley fell back into his boat. Not sure whether his victim was dead or alive, Smith sailed away to Key West, as the small boat drifted toward Cape Sable.

The following day, July 15, the *Metropolis* reported in a front page story that Bradley had died instantly. His mother and father, who were in Miami at the time, had not known of the shooting until they read it in the paper. The elder Bradley told the *Metropolis* that his son "had had considerable trouble with violators," of the game laws and that "Smith was in the habit of breaking these laws."

Dutcher, in New York, was stunned by the news. He immediately arranged for legal assistance to see that justice was done, retaining State Senator Lewis A. Harris of Key West and Colonel James T. Sanders of Miami to work with the prosecution. Details of the killing then began to filter in to Dutcher.

It was known that the boat carrying Bradley's body drifted to East Cape Sable, where a couple of residents, curious about the turkey vultures wheeling overhead, rowed out to make the discovery. Smith was taken before a coroner's jury, which heard testimony and then lodged a charge of murder against him. Smith went to jail, in lieu of $5,000 bail, and awaited grand jury action; two men who were with him in the schooner were charged as accessories to the murder. The most authoritative account of events on that fatal day survive in Sanders' report to Dutcher, based on his interviews with witnesses and a review of subsequent testimony:

"Smith, his son, and two smaller sons, aged seven and eleven years, and another young man; also two friends, one Ethridge, and one Alonzo Sawyer, on board of Smith's schooner boat, sailed up to the rookery, directly opposite and about two miles distant from Bradley's house, and anchored. Young Smith and his friend went ashore onto the island where the rookery was located, and there began shooting the egrets. . . .

"Knowing Bradley and his boat, and seeing him on the way to the schooner, [Smith] fired his rifle as a signal to the boy and the other young man, to return to the schooner, which they did, having their birds already killed, in the boat with them, and arriving at the schooner at about the time Bradley arrived.

"Smith asked Bradley what he wanted, and Bradley informed him that he wanted his son, and his son's companion, under a charge of violating the law by shooting plume-birds. Smith said, 'Well, if you want him, you have got to have a warrant.' Bradley informed Smith that where he found parties in the act of perpetrating a crime, a warrant was not necessary. Smith then said, 'Well, if you want him you have to come aboard of this boat and take him,' at the same time picking up his rifle. Bradley said, 'Put down that rifle, and I will come aboard.' "

What took place immediately afterward was reported only in Smith's testimony. The others said that they were below and, after the words between Smith and Bradley, they heard two shots, a pistol and a rifle fired almost simultaneously. Smith's story was that the warden fired first, the bullet embedding itself in the mast. Smith then shot Bradley.

Shortly afterward, relatives of Bradley's widow went to Flamingo and burned Smith's house. But the authorities in Key West were not similarly stirred to action. Until Sanders arrived no one had bothered to summon witnesses to Key West. He managed to import at least one important witness from the mainland and gave what he believed to be convincing proof to the authorities that Bradley had not fired at Smith: Bradley's pistol showed no powder marks in the barrel, nor was the cylinder under the pistol's hammer in the position it should have been had he fired. Smith retained the local prosecutor to defend him. The grand jury did not return an indictment against him, and he was released from jail. Dutcher, of course, was outraged.

"A home broken up," he wrote in *Bird-Lore,* "children left fatherless, a woman widowed and sorrowing, a faithful and devoted warden, who was a young and sturdy man, cut off in a moment, and for what? That a few more plume birds might be secured to adorn heartless women's bonnets. Heretofore the price has been the life of the birds, now is added human blood."

The incident had touched the public's consciousness. Women's clubs forswore the use of plumes and encouraged others to do the same. There was a generous response to the Audubon Association's drive to raise money and build a home for the widow in Key West. Herbert Job wrote an article for *Collier's* called "Bird Protection's First Martyr," and donated the magazine's check for $225 to the fund. (Job later told Dutcher, in a writer's timeless lament, that the magazine's editors had emasculated the article and tucked it away among the advertisements.) And to Dutcher at the association's office came a message from the White House:

"Permit me on behalf of both Mrs. Roosevelt and myself to say how heartily we sympathize not only with the work of the Audubon Societies generally, but particularly in their efforts to stop the sale and use of the so-called 'Aigrettes'—the plumes of the white herons. If anything, Mrs. Roosevelt feels more strongly than I do in the matter."

Bradley lies buried at Cape Sable, on a ridge of snow-white shells overlooking the sea. A stone was erected there in his memory:

GUY M. BRADLEY
1870–1905
FAITHFUL UNTO DEATH

AS GAME WARDEN OF MONROE COUNTY
HE GAVE HIS LIFE FOR THE CAUSE
TO WHICH HE WAS PLEDGED

*7*

"T he surest way to send a wild bird into oblivion is to set a price on its head," wrote T. Gilbert Pearson, who spent forty years of a peripatetic life trying to remove the dollar sign from wildlife. The world in which he grew up could not have supplied him with a great deal of optimism about his eventual success.

Yet William Dutcher knew what he was about when he summoned Pearson to New York, puffed him up, groomed him as his successor in the Audubon Association, and turned him loose in an unfamiliar world of big-city politicians and shady merchants. Dutcher, straight as a lance, relentlessly efficient, idealistic, and uncompromising, found in this pragmatic and nimble-witted young man an appropriate complement to his own abilities. If the bird-protection movement was to make headway in the twentieth century, it required the full-time services of more than one crusader.

Gilbert Pearson, like Guy Bradley, was a product of backwoods Florida. His parents, who were Quakers and Midwesterners, had set up housekeeping in a log cabin among the pinelands that surrounded the town of Archer near Gainesville, and young Gilbert grew up eating grits, corn bread, and white salt pork with the farmers and alligator hunters of the region. Hunting wild things for the market and the pot was also a way of life. Gunfire, rather than birdsong, was the customary sound in the piney woods.

Tales of the feather trade supplied part of the background to Pearson's youth during the 1880s. When he was thirteen and had saved enough money to buy a gun, his first victim was a grackle, a trophy of which he was so proud that he took it with him to bed. "It proved to be covered with parasites which promptly swarmed over the bed, filling me with discomfort and my mother with dismay," he wrote years afterward. Pearson buried it, but not before he had cut off the wings to tack on the wall of his room. One evening he noticed they were missing. "Later I discovered them adorning one of my sister's hats," he wrote.

Soon Pearson was in the grip of one of those adolescent passions that consume every hour squeezed from the daily routine. He began a collection of the eggs of wild birds, ransacking the neighborhood for nests with a young friend and, in the process, acquiring a good deal of knowledge about their proprietors. He and his friend also shot birds, which they mounted with the aid of a pamphlet on the *Art of Taxidermy*, and young Pearson traded all of his duplicate sets of eggs for a copy of Elliott Coues's *Key to North American Birds*. He wrote articles for the leading egg collectors' journal, *The Oologist*.

But, unlike most adolescent passions, this one contributed materially to the boy's prospects in life. He was an indefatigable correspondent in his teens (he exchanged notes and eggs with other collectors and even tried to drum up a little business with milliners in New York) and, in 1891, he wrote to various colleges to offer his ornithological collection in return for an education. Pearson received no encouraging replies for some time. Then he struck a deal with Guilford College, a small Quaker school in North Carolina, which offered him two years of board and tuition if he would bring along his collection of eggs and mounted birds and maintain the "college cabinet," or rudimentary museum.

Pearson, from the first, was dedicated to self-improvement. Ill prepared for a liberal education when he arrived, he applied himself to mastering everything from social etiquette to the English language. (He meticulously noted later that he read one hundred and five books at Guilford.) Although biology was the main course of study, he already possessed a foundation of its practical aspects before he came to Guilford, and it may have been that his most valuable achievement there was fitting himself for public speaking. He became the leading member of the college debating team. His increasing skill as an orator happened to coincide with his dawning realization of the plight of those birds in which he had been interested since childhood.

When some tracts on birds, perhaps as a by-product of Grinnell's *Audubon Magazine,* fell into his hands, Pearson prepared for a school function an oration on "The Destruction of American Birds." Evening after evening he retired to a secluded place near the campus and declaimed his flowery phrases to the pine thickets. On the appointed night, he impressed even his fellow students with his fervor and eloquence as he concluded his speech by stepping forward on stage with outstretched arms and lifted eyes to utter: "O fashion, O women of America, how many crimes are committed in your name!"

Pearson's eloquence also came into play when he persuaded college board members to let him finish his education at Guilford under his original agreement with the school. Still using the art of persuasion, he went on to pursue his education at the University of North Carolina while working in the office of the state geologist. Afterward he taught biology at Guilford and then at the State Normal and Industrial College, a school for women in Greensboro. Birds, however, continued to be his chief interest. He was astonished that his students, most of whom were headed for careers as teachers, spent much of their time in biology classes drawing cross sections of a fern's stem, and the ligaments from a bullfrog's neck as revealed through a microscope, but had not the faintest idea of how to identify by sight or sound the common birds on campus.

"These girls should learn to know the birds so they can tell their pupils about them—their correct names, where they migrate, and of what value they are on the farms and in the orchards," Pearson insisted. "They should be given the opportunity to acquire that intelligent appreciation of nature that can come only from study of the outdoor life in the woods and fields."

This was an expression of the philosophy that would guide him in later years as he put into place a system of education on a far wider scale. He had, in fact, a wider audience already in view. The notes he compiled from his lectures and field trips around the Greensboro area became the basis of a small book, *Stories of Bird Life,* that he wrote and published in 1901. Inevitably the book came to the unflagging attention of William Dutcher, who wrote to Pearson from New York in December of that year. Would Pearson help to have the Model Law passed in North Carolina? And would he be interested in organizing a state Audubon Society?

Pearson at first was doubtful. He had read some bird-protection literature and been unfavorably impressed by its inaccuracies and exaggerations. "The statements that birds designed for the millinery trade were skinned alive so their feathers would not fade," he recalled, "that the bird life of Connecticut had been reduced 75 percent during the past fifteen years, and that all species of American birds soon would become exterminated, indicated the presence of extremists in the field of bird protection, whose writings could serve to mislead the uninformed, and would hurt our cause with thinking people."

But, on pressing Dutcher for more information, Pearson became satisfied that the movement was now in good hands. He judged the literature distributed by the Audubon societies through the new National Committee to be an accurate reflection of the unrestrained killing of birds, and he accepted the challenge. In March 1902, he called a meeting of 200 interested people in the chapel at the University of North Carolina in Chapel Hill, spoke to them about the glories and value of birds, and before the evening was over had enrolled 148 of them as paying members in the Audubon Society of North Carolina. In a short time, he was traveling to and fro in the state, lecturing and enrolling new

T. Gilbert Pearson, who led the young National Association
of Audubon Societies to a number of major triumphs.

members with all the fervor of a Bible-thumping preacher (though all
his life he seems to have regarded organized religion as a benighted and
troublemaking force).

"Gentleman hunters and their families were my main supporters,"
he wrote later. "They loved the out-of-doors and wanted market-shooting
and plume-hunting brought to an end; while men who did not hunt
seemed to take no interest in laws to protect wild life."

Even Pearson's marriage to Elsie Weatherly, an aspiring violinist whom he had admired for several years, did not slow him down. He began to travel widely, going north for Audubon and AOU meetings. Soon he was added to both the National Committee of Audubon Societies and the AOU's Bird Protection Committee. His bride, Elsie, took over his classes in Greensboro while he attended these meetings. In Washington, he addressed a meeting of the Audubon Committee and gave an inspirational talk that impressed Frank Chapman and others present.

In 1903, Pearson carried his crusade to the North Carolina legislature (or General Assembly). He knew that the most bitter opposition to any protective bill would arise in the coastal counties, where both the locals and visitors carried on the intensive shooting of ducks, geese, shorebirds, gulls, and terns all year round. To gather information for the coming debate in the legislature, he made a tour of the coast, stopping first in Norfolk, Virginia, to visit the city markets, where barrels of birds and other game were on sale.

From there he traveled southward by sailboats and horse carts toward Cape Hatteras. He chatted with market shooters, plume hunters, and wealthy northerners in their duck clubs.

"I examined the storage houses of local shippers where hung countless ducks, geese and occasionally swan, and saw dozens of barrels of these birds loaded on boats to be transferred to the railroad for shipment," he wrote. "I visited sheds where quantities of terns had been skinned for the feather trade. I saw men shooting wild fowl from blinds and sink boxes, and at night watched the moving lights that gleamed from the prows of boats as hunters in the darkness silently rowed to the rafts of sleeping redheads and canvas-backs and fired broadsides into them at point-blank range."

When he went to the General Assembly in Raleigh, Pearson was well prepared for struggle. Through earlier contacts with both legislators and the governor he had arranged for the Model Law to be introduced with considerable support. Pearson was nothing if not audacious. Aware that even the strongest law required enforcement, especially in regions where the people were accustomed to shoot at anything they were willing to spend a bullet on, he had written into the bill a provision for a warden system. The wardens were to be chosen and organized by the Audubon Society of North Carolina, but paid for by a new fee on nonresident hunting licenses. In what may have been the boldest step of all, Pearson arranged to have himself invited to address the entire General Assembly.

Perhaps the Assembly was stunned by the daring nature of the proposal, which in effect asked that a private organization be invested with the authority of a department of the state and its enterprise funded by state license fees. There were, of course, some expressions of dissent and ridicule from the floor. ("If we have nothing better to do than listen to a man talk about jaybirds and sparrows, we had better go home," a legislator fumed.) But finally the Assembly settled down as Pearson began to explain the nature of his bill, using every art practiced by southern orators of the day.

"It was absolutely essential to hold the attention of those Assemblymen, and I sought earnestly to prevent them from anticipating the outcome of a single paragraph or even a sentence," he recalled. "I had been taught that a speaker must keep a bow-shot ahead of the thoughts of his listeners lest they weary, and he lose their attention. I spoke with rapidity but with careful distinction, striving never to slur a word, never to repeat an idea, and never to allow my voice to fall at the end of a sentence. I knew positively that every man in that legislative hall heard distinctly, and clearly understood every word I uttered."

The General Assembly agreed to consider the bill. There were rough moments ahead, but Pearson was relentless, confronting legislators in corridors or hotel lobbies and urging Audubon members around the state to make their voices heard. Opponents argued that the bill was an infringement on personal liberties, or, because it imposed fees on non-residents, a lapse in "Southern hospitality." But the Audubon side prevailed. The General Assembly passed that year the first law ever enacted in any South Atlantic or Gulf Coast state to provide for a statewide game warden system. Pearson (who, in effect, had become the South's first game commissioner) immediately received applications for positions as wardens, many of them from men who apparently believed that a substantial salary went with the job.

"One offered to divide his salary," Pearson reported, "and reminded me that the more I paid him the more he could give me."

The new law was not, of course, universally popular in North Carolina. Some citizens were outraged because Audubon wardens arrested violators of the game laws without reference to race or social position. In Burlington, "one of the most wealthy and influential citizens" was arrested for killing dozens of chimney swifts, a holocaust he consummated by setting fire to his chimney with straw after covering it with a screen, and thus roasting the trapped swifts. One of the culprit's neighbors expressed indignation over his arrest in a letter to the *Raleigh News and Observer*: "If the Honorable T. Gilbert Pearson and his legion of women and children backers think that they can compel intelligent people to put up with a nuisance like this, he is mistaken."

There was a determined effort in the state to control the killing of game for the northern markets. Pearson and one of his wardens received a tip that a market hunter was shipping quail out of the state in crates ostensibly packed with eggs. They located the contraband at the railroad station in Greensboro. Two newspaper reporters, learning that the quail had been seized, asked the warden how he had guessed that the egg crates had contained illegal game.

"There was no guesswork about it," the warden replied. "That dog of mine pointed the box for us." Then he leaned over and patted the head of a small, short-haired black dog which generally tagged along with him on his enforcement work. The story was duly printed, North Carolinians marveled at the dog's uncanny pointing ability, and the shipping of game dropped off in the Greensboro region.

There seemed to be no such local sympathy for the preservation of plume birds, which presented neither a challenge for the sportsman nor an attraction for the gourmet. A plume hunter Pearson spoke to defended the unceasing barrage that had nearly eliminated the terns from parts of the North Carolina coast.

"Pore folks have as good a right to live as city people," the gunner said. "The good Lord put us here and the Good Book says, 'Man shall have dominion over all creatures.' They're our'n to use."

This was the young man whom Dutcher brought to New York in 1905 to become the first salaried, full-time Audubon executive. As yet, Gilbert Pearson was not a permanent New Yorker, because he served as secretary of the Audubon Society of North Carolina and special agent of the National Association of Audubon Societies as well as the latter's secretary. Dutcher apparently was delighted with his new aide. He dispatched him regularly throughout most of the eastern United States to lobby in legislatures and to lecture against the wearing of the aigrette, which the two men now referred to as "The White Badge of Cruelty." (Apparently there was an attempt at the time by more febrile minds to frighten women away from the aigrette by labeling it "the badge of the harlot," but the idea never quite caught on.) To a reporter who inquired about a lecture by Pearson to the New Jersey Federation of Women's Clubs, Dutcher remarked that "Professor Pearson rarely has any notes, speaking quite extemporaneously as he is so thoroughly posted on this subject."

That extemporaneous voice would remain a force in the American conservation movement for the next thirty years.

*8*

The first five years of the Audubon Association were especially stormy. A backlash against the movement sprang up in many places. In Florida, the atmosphere remained so charged that Dutcher and the local Audubon leaders did not appoint a successor to Guy Bradley. In North Carolina, a game warden was struck in the face, hands, and body by birdshot when he attempted to arrest a man he had discovered hunting ducks illegally at night. The warden was able to recognize his assailant, but no conviction came of the incident. Another Audubon warden, Columbus G. MacLeod, was killed in Charlotte Harbor, Florida, while on patrol, apparently by plume hunters, in 1908, and a third, L. P. Reeves, was murdered the same year by "fish pirates" near Branchville, South Carolina. No one was ever convicted of those crimes, either.

A report by the secretary of the South Carolina Audubon Society in 1909, which speaks of the rising local interest in bird protection, gives the flavor of the times:

"One immediate effect was the trial and conviction of Arthur Lambert, notorious poacher and plume hunter. Lambert had shot up the rookery of American egrets photographed by F. M. Chapman, and when hotly pursued by wardens with warrants, had sprung overboard in Sampit River and swum ashore, escaping into the swamps of Georgetown County, with which he was perfectly familiar. Some two weeks afterward he was captured in Georgetown, secreted in a trunk, by deputy Jack Ward.

"Lambert was carried to McClellanville, Charleston County, tried before Magistrate G. W. Ward, and convicted both of trespass and killing nongame birds. He was accompanied by one Palmer, notorious 'blind tiger' or illicit whiskey dealer, of Georgetown, who has been acting as a broker in buying plumes."

Dutcher, while maintaining his firm belief that education and legislation must eventually turn the tide in favor of bird protection, relied in the meantime on the warden system. He was clear-eyed when confronting human depravity. In Massachusetts, there were rumors that Penikese Island, long the site of an important tern colony, was to be converted by the state into a home for lepers.

"As there are only six of them in Massachusetts," Dutcher wrote to a colleague, "it would not be a bad thing for the terns as the lepers would keep people away more effectively than laws or wardens."

This gloomy cast of mind was not typical of Dutcher, who elsewhere seized every chance to carry out his plan to save America's birds. In 1905, the Audubon Association's first year of operation, more than two thousand dollars was spent on wardens, lawyers for the Bradley case, and "detective work." Among the culprits bagged that year was Lewis Mitchell, the chief of Maine's Passamaquoddy tribe, who was arrested while trying to sell gulls' plumage in Massachusetts. Mitchell contended that, as an Indian, he had certain treaty rights permitting him to kill birds, and that therefore the game laws did not apply to him. The Massachusetts court convicted him, confiscated the plumes, fined him fifty dollars, and sent him to jail for two days. Maine's courts also went after Mitchell, denying him special privileges to kill birds, while courts in Florida upheld the game laws against a similar claim by the Seminoles.

Dutcher was constantly looking for people of talent to serve in the Audubon movement. Funds from the Willcox legacy made it possible for the Audubon Association to employ as an agent the distinguished ornithologist Edward Howe Forbush to work with the legislature in Massachusetts. Although Forbush was unable to push through a bill to stop the spring shooting of wild ducks, he was in part responsible for legislation that protected eagles, loons, the larger gulls, and "useful hawks and owls." (Species such as the sharp-shinned and Cooper's hawks and the peregrine falcon were still considered "varmints" and thus liable to be shot on sight.) The heath hen, already on its way to extinction, was given a momentary respite by the authorization of a state reservation on Martha's Vineyard, and the Audubon Association contributed money for its development.

The Willcox legacy also provided for a field agent in Oregon, where William L. Finley kept an eye on the legislature as well as on the huge wildfowl areas in the Klamath and Tule marshes. When a bill passed the legislature that enabled fruit growers to kill the varied thrush, Lewis's woodpecker, and any other birds they considered harmful, Finley persuaded the governor to veto the measure. And, perhaps going beyond the call of duty, he accosted a prostitute in Portland and dashed her plumed hat into the gutter.

These and other agents for whom the Audubon Association contracted more or less regularly suggest the expanding nature of the New

York office. The old National Committee had been superseded by an incorporated association, or federation, of the state societies guided ostensibly by a board of thirty members. Now even that mechanism was seen to be cumbersome. Most of those board members, scattered across the country, were not able to attend the board meetings, which were always held in New York City, so that the meetings proceeded without representation at all proportionate to the general membership.

As a prelude, then, to the annual meeting to be held at the American Museum of Natural History on October 17, 1908, the core of the Audubon leadership (which included Dutcher, Pearson, Chapman, and attorney Samuel T. Carter, who had prepared the articles of incorporation for the Audubon Association in 1905) proposed a change in the organization's constitution. The board of directors was to be reduced from thirty to eleven members. Those who were not able to attend regularly would submit their resignations and immediately join a new entity called the Advisory Board. The reconstituted board of eleven members would be formed mainly from the remaining members of the old board and would then carry on the Audubon Association's business in a more efficient manner. The change was approved at the meeting, and the National Association of Audubon Societies took a giant step toward what it has become today—not a federation of state societies but a unified national organization with a variety of chapters and affiliates.

The move to strengthen the Audubon Association by consolidating in one office the power to act on a national scale did little to brighten the bird-protection campaign in the various states. In fact, by 1908, the picture was deteriorating. All of the reforms the Audubon societies had worked for most strenuously—the abolition of plume and market hunting as well as of the spring shooting of wildfowl on migration—seemed no closer to going into effect, and almost everywhere the Model Law was in danger of being gutted. There was a succession of firefights in which Dutcher, Pearson, T. S. Palmer, and other Audubon stalwarts rushed to state capitals or sent financial aid to beleaguered state societies to try to fend off harmful legislation.

In Michigan, bills were introduced to provide bounties on kingfishers, great blue herons, "chicken hawks," and English sparrows, but after a lively skirmish only the bounty on the detested sparrow passed the legislature. In Maine, an attempt to exclude gulls from protection (because they ate drying fish or fish scraps scattered on farms as fertilizer) was beaten back. In California, the legislature was persuaded to reduce the daily bag limit on ducks from fifty to thirty-five, but it took protection away from all fish-eating birds except "gulls and blue and white cranes." (In that state, the Audubon movement was weak, and Dutcher encouraged the Cooper Ornithological Society to take the lead.)

The Audubon Association mustered all of its forces, including Dutcher, Pearson, and Forbush, to counter a drive in Congress to deprive the Bureau of the Biological Survey of its funding. According to Pearson, "this movement emanated from powerful cold-storage interests as the Survey's influence was being felt in the efforts being made to break up the extensive business of keeping game in cold storage throughout the year." Such a move would have undermined the federal government's cooperation with the Audubon societies in enforcing certain state game laws that were affected by the Lacey Act. Pearson, through his friends in North Carolina, even had himself appointed a delegate to the Southern Cotton Grower's Association, where he argued persuasively on the role of the Biological Survey in studying the efficacy of birds in controlling the boll weevil and gained that association's support for the Survey. The Biological Survey retained its funding.

The most discouraging setback, especially for Pearson, came in North Carolina. Under great pressure from the market-hunting interests on the coast, the legislature voted to remove a number of counties throughout the state from the warden system organized by the Audubon Society. Thus those counties lost their game wardens, and the killing of birds resumed unchecked. Game protection in North Carolina quickly fell into disarray as each county opted for measures of its own. As Pearson pointed out, legislatures in the United States and Canada passed a total of two hundred and twenty game laws in 1909.

"Of these North Carolina alone enacted sixty-nine, all but one being local county measures," Pearson wrote. "The United States government, which every year publishes a sheet showing the open seasons for hunting in the various states of the Union, and the Provinces of Canada, is now forced to publish two of equal size, the second one containing only the game-laws of North Carolina."

Foremost on William Dutcher's mind, however, was still the opposition to the plume trade that had brought the modern Audubon movement into being. The front lines of that struggle still lay in New York. (The field of battle usually determines the combatants' headquarters and, though Audubon has chosen to remain in New York City, most national conservation organizations formed since that time have opened their main offices close to the sources of political power in Washington, D.C.) Dutcher had looked to the rise of ostrich farming to provide alternatives to the killing of wild herons and egrets. As he once wrote, "taking plumes from an ostrich is no more painful to the bird than shearing is to a sheep," and at their meetings local Audubon societies had displayed "Audubon millinery," consisting of hats adorned with ribbons and ostrich plumes.

The idea of farming ostriches for their plumes was an old one, in both Europe and North America. South Africa, which had a large population of wild ostriches, was the first country to make a success of raising the birds for the feather trade and by the early twentieth century had a foreign market worth about six million dollars. Ostriches from South Africa had been imported to Anaheim, California, as early as 1882. Other ostrich farms sprang up in California, Arizona, Florida, Arkansas, and even North Carolina, so that by 1900 there were about three thousand ostriches in America.

Dutcher had hoped to see the industry expand even more. This was desirable from the milliners' point of view, for the plumes of domesticated birds were considered far superior to those of wild ones. And, of course, it was desirable from the bird protectors' point of view, for no blood was drawn, and the birds soon grew another crop of feathers.

"Plucking is done by putting the ostrich in a V-shaped corral just large enough to admit its body, with room for the workman," Dutcher explained to Audubon members. "A hood, shaped like a long stocking, is placed over the head of the ostrich when it becomes perfectly docile. The workman then raises the wings and clips the feathers that are fully ripe . . . the large feathers are cut off, and in two months' time, when the quill is dried up, it is pulled out."

But the American industry never supplied enough feathers to make much of a difference, and the Boer War (1899–1902) put a crimp in South Africa's production. The wholesale milliners went on doing business as usual, buying aigrettes from plume hunters while contending that only nonnative birds were killed. Because the plumage of native white herons is almost indistinguishable from that of their African and Asian relatives, no one was likely to prove them wrong. Birds killed illegally in one state and shipped to another (a violation of the Lacey Act) were palmed off as "foreign birds." Nor did the Lacey Act apply to plume birds killed in the states where they were not protected.

Dutcher had been trying for some time to promote legislation that would strike at the heart of the millinery industry in New York. Early in 1910, he sent Pearson to Albany to work on the passage of what became known as the Audubon Plumage Bill. Its key provision was a ban on the sale or possession of the plumage from birds in the *same family* with any species protected in New York State, where herons and egrets, as well as gulls, terns, and songbirds, were already protected. As millinery plumage consisted to a great extent of native birds in those groups or their relatives in other states, or countries, the use of plumes in American millinery would be badly crippled.

Gilbert Pearson looked forward to his assignment in Albany with some anxiety. Most of his lobbying experience had been in southern legislatures, and he was still a bit awed by Yankees. He was a good mixer, however, and made a point of striking up conversations with legislators in Albany's Kenmore and Ten Eyck hotels. Apparently they found his anecdotes of life in the South, told in various dialects, excruciatingly funny. Thus, though Pearson never quite overcame his distaste for beer, he managed to become one of the boys and soon was a familiar and well-liked figure in Albany's legislative circles.

The milliners had responded to the Audubon Plumage Bill with a great show of force in the capital, where their chief spokesman in the legislature was Assemblyman Alfred E. Smith. The future governor of the state and presidential candidate accepted the milliners' contention that thousands of New Yorkers would be thrown out of work by the passage of the bill and the industry itself destroyed. The milliners also argued that not a single native songbird was then used in the millinery trade. Pearson was equal to the occasion. Before attending a legislative hearing, he scoured the shops and came up with a number of "Chanticleer Bows," which were on sale in Albany's department stores. This item was made of a pretty ribbon onto which had been sewn the head of a skylark, a European bird enjoying a short-lived existence around New York City after its introduction there by local admirers of birds and English poetry.

Pearson also pressed on legislators that old standby of the reformer—a flood of judiciously selected pamphlets extolling the merits of his cause. One of his ablest supporters in the state senate was Franklin D. Roosevelt. On the debit side were a hostile editorial in *The New York Times* (which called the bill "piffling legislation") and a spate of sarcasm by an attorney for the milliners, who had dredged up confessions of lusty bird-shooting expeditions by John James Audubon himself. An article in *Outlook,* a popular magazine of the day, which asserted that herons and egrets were injurious to fish and other natural resources and should not be conserved, added to the pressure against the bill.

But public sentiment was on the Audubon side. Letters flowed in to the legislators from their constituents urging them to vote in the affirmative. After the Audubon Plumage Bill was amended to allow milliners a year in which to dispose of their stocks of feathers, it was passed by the legislature and signed into law by Governor Charles Evans Hughes on May 7, 1910.

"It was William Dutcher who planned and executed the feather fight in Albany," Pearson wrote many years later. "He was responsible for all that took place in winning the struggle and his was the ever-present worry about the money to finance the campaign. I always have been grateful to him for allowing me the privilege of serving as his field marshal, and I cherish in my memory certain generous words which in the moment of triumph he said to me when our opponents had been driven from the field."

Pearson's tribute (in which he artfully reminded the reader of his own substantial part in the triumph) points to the culmination of Dutcher's long career in bird protection. He was already beginning to hand on much of his burden to the younger man. He was in failing health, and the death of his only child, Mary, came as an added blow. After the passage of the Audubon Plumage Bill, he sailed for Europe, where he attended the Fifth International Ornithological Congress in Berlin. There he spoke on the international exploitation of wild birds in the millinery, food, and pet industries. Upon his return to the United States, his friends presented him with a check for more than six thousand dollars, which they had raised as a special endowment for the Audubon Association under the Mary Dutcher Memorial Fund. It was the only check he ever accepted for his Audubon work.

On October 19, 1910, William Dutcher suffered a stroke that left him paralyzed and helpless. He lived on for another ten years, deprived of the power of speech, even of the ability to express himself in writing. Although he retained the title of president, Gilbert Pearson succeeded him as the chief executive officer of the Audubon Association.

# 9

The illness that ended William Dutcher's career transformed T. Gilbert Pearson's life as well. For some years, Pearson had been essentially an itinerant, rushing from one legislative battle to another, occupying an office in New York City mainly when Dutcher was absent, and functioning as the Audubon Association's secretary from Greensboro, which he continued to look on as home. Suddenly he was called to Manhattan to lead what was then the only large private organization in the United States devoted primarily to wildlife protection.

These two early Audubon leaders, though they shared a common vision, were in many respects contrasting personalities. Dutcher was the more sophisticated of the two, a successful businessman in New York, and in ornithology an example of the expert amateur; the precision of his notebooks and the papers he contributed to professional journals such as *The Auk* reveal a genuinely scientific turn of mind. While circumstances prodded him into a policy of deficit spending, he was nevertheless the great innovator in all of the areas that became the core of Audubon's programs: a warden and sanctuary system, nature education for children, political action, and a close working relationship with biologists in the federal government.

Pearson, in some ways, never outgrew the image of a small-town booster. He was comfortable with rural politicians, could spin yarns and ethnic jokes with the best of them, and always eyed with some suspicion the pleasures of big-city life. Although he wrote widely about birds for popular consumption, there was less of the scientist about him than the pamphleteer, the evangelist, and the entrepreneur. Dutcher, from the first, recognized Pearson's organizational ability and his indefatigable attention to detail; Pearson was what we would call today a workaholic. Once he had arrived in New York, he learned to cultivate the powerful and the wealthy, to Audubon's lasting benefit. The perfect pupil, he carried through on all of Dutcher's innovations, adjusting them to the times.

If Gilbert Pearson looms inordinately large in any retelling of the Audubon story, it is not hard to find the reasons. He worked mainly at a time when the staff of the Audubon Association was small and the state societies (aside from those in Massachusetts and one or two other places) impoverished and without strong leadership, so that often the Audubon movement seemed to be a one-man operation. His tenure in a position of leadership—three decades—was far longer than that of any other person in Audubon history. Finally, he was the only Audubon leader to write a book devoted to his experiences in the movement; *Adventures in Bird Protection* remains the most important primary source on the subject.

If his arrival in New York was a time of turbulence for the thirty-seven-year-old Pearson, he experienced other sensations as well after closing his office on lower Broadway at the end of each working day. Much of his salary was sent to Greensboro, where Elsie Pearson and the three children were to remain for another year until he found a home for them in the North. Meanwhile, he took his work back with him in the evenings to the room he had rented in a hotel on the upper West Side, or he walked off his loneliness on garish streets where every face was that of a stranger.

When daylight came, Pearson was back in battle, and in some senses this also was a lonely exercise. All through its history, the Audubon movement has fluctuated between grass-roots strength and increased centralization. By 1911, the first full year of Pearson's administration, the National Association of Audubon Societies had become less an association than a dynamic central office. With Dutcher gone from the scene, the dynamism originated mostly in Pearson, who maintained the office at 141 Broadway with a chief clerk (Beecher S. Bowdish), a bookkeeper, two stenographers, and an office boy. (The combined salaries of Pearson's staff amounted to $3,271.15.) This office serviced the organization's 1,250 or so life and sustaining members.

Besides his New York staff, Pearson could count on three part-time field agents: Edward Howe Forbush in New England, Captain M. B. Davis in Texas, and William L. Finley in Oregon. Although there were then thirty-nine state Audubon societies in existence, they remained separate organizations with their own policies and budgets, and only four of them even held membership in the National Association. A few societies, including those in Massachusetts and the Carolinas, had adequate budgets and programs. "Many, however, were 'State' societies in name only and most people did not even know of their existence," Pearson wrote later. "I recall that from one Commonwealth I received letters from two groups of people both calling themselves the State Audubon Society. Inquiry revealed that neither group had heard of the other, although one had enjoyed a paper existence for several years."

The National Association's board of directors in 1911 was composed solely of males and restricted to the familiar Boston–New York–Washington, D.C. axis. (Both circumstances were reflections of the time—the first, of social restraints, and the second, partly, of the difficulties of long-distance travel in an era before commercial air service was available.) All of these eleven members, who included William Brewster, Frank M. Chapman, George Bird Grinnell, and Theodore S. Palmer, were scientists, and most of them were also members of the American Ornithologists' Union. A brief check by the economy-oriented Pearson disclosed that five of the board members had not paid their Audubon dues for 1911, but since he was grateful for the advice and support of such personages, he did not bring up the matter.

In January of that year, the board met as usual at the American Museum and elected one of their own, J. A. Allen of Harvard, as acting president of the Audubon Association. (The board refused to name a new president as long as Dutcher was alive; T. S. Palmer, still with the Bureau of the Biological Survey in Washington, succeeded Allen in 1912, and then the following year Frederic A. Lucas, the director of the American Museum, became acting president and served in that office until Dutcher's death at the end of the decade.) The board designated Pearson as general executive officer. Within months, the Audubon Association found larger quarters uptown at 1974 Broadway, near Sixty-sixth street.

Pearson, already feeling personally isolated in a Yankee city, was further discomfited by overt hostility among groups from which he had expected a measure of support. Many professional ornithologists now looked on the Audubon societies as a radical organization that, if given enough encouragement, might campaign to stop the shooting of birds even by scientific collectors. The AOU's Bird Protection Committee, chaired by A. K. Fisher, had stopped functioning almost completely.

"Some of the strongest dislike of the Association which I inherited centered in Washington," Pearson recalled. "I went to see Doctor E. W. Nelson [chief] of the Biological Survey, to have a frank discussion about the matter, but he refused to talk with me. He said it would be a waste of time to enter into the matter. I tried to talk to a brillant young naturalist named Alexander Wetmore [later curator of ornithology at the Smithsonian Institution, and a member of the Audubon Association's board of directors]. He knew who I was, but when I spoke to him he replied that he believed he had not met me, and turned abruptly away."

If that was the reaction to the work of the Audubon societies among scientists, it can be imagined what the hunters thought! Indeed, Pearson felt that many Audubon members went too far in condemning the hunting of birds for sport, for he had been a hunter himself and liked to point out the part that other hunters such as Grinnell, Brewster, Chapman, Dutcher, Forbush, and Theodore Roosevelt had played in the Audubon movement. The antihunting brigade, he believed, had made no similar contributions to the cause of wildlife protection.

But, before Pearson had a chance to begin mending fences, his new administration was faced with a critical challenge. The Democrats having taken control of the New York state legislature, the new Assembly leader was Alfred E. Smith, who had led the unsuccessful fight against the Audubon Plumage Bill in the previous session. A bill to repeal the law was introduced in the Assembly in February 1911. Once again, bitter words were launched on both sides from pamphlets, editorials, and legislative statements. The bird protectionists received a lift that spring when Governor Woodrow Wilson of New Jersey signed into law a plumage bill passed by that state's legislature.

An even greater blow to the milliners was Pearson's debunking of their story that herons and egrets need not be killed to collect their plumes. According to the milliners, they bought their plumes from Venezuelans who gathered them under the trees in which herons and egrets retired to molt. "Everywhere on the ground," wrote the milliners' authority, "as well as on the tree branches and on the bushes and thickets, they leave their feathers which at that moment must form the happiness of the natives and of the workmen busy with the harvest thereof."

Pearson, in turn, produced an American who had worked as a plume hunter in Venezuela for ten years. He proved to be an arresting and effective witness, pointing out that the few plumes, called "dead feathers," that were picked up from the ground were damaged and far less valuable than those torn from the bodies of birds that had been shot. "The natives of the country, who do virtually all of the hunting, are not provident in their nature and their practices are of a most cruel and brutal nature," he testified. "I have seen them frequently pull the plumes from wounded birds, leaving the crippled birds to die of starvation, unable to respond to the hungry cries of their young in the nests above. I have known these people to tie and prop up wounded egrets on the marsh where they would attract the attention of other birds flying by. These decoys they leave in this position until they die of their wounds or from the attacks of insects. I have seen the terrible red ants of that country actually eating out the eyes of these wounded, helpless birds."

The reformed plume hunter's testimony was extremely effective. With the outspoken help of Franklin D. Roosevelt, the chairman of the state senate's Committee on Forest, Fish and Game, the Audubon forces held their ground, and the plumage bill survived.

Crackdowns on feather dealers by the police followed almost immediately in New York City. In an effort to carry on their traffic in the plumes of wild birds, some of the milliners moved to Philadelphia. But Pearson assigned the National Association's chief clerk, Beecher Bowdish, to follow them to the City of Brotherly Love, where he expended $2,000 and relentless effort in lobbying, and in 1913 Pennsylvania passed its own plumage bill.

Meanwhile, within weeks of its legislative victory in New York, the bird-preservation side was back in Albany, this time to push through the campaign Grinnell had begun two decades earlier in *Forest and Stream* to stop the sale of wild game. Nineteen states had passed laws to that effect in the intervening years, but loopholes abounded. New York's law, for instance, prohibited the sale of grouse, quail, and woodcock killed in *that* state, but the wholesalers in game maintained a flourishing business by asserting that the birds had been shipped to them from other states.

It is appropriate here to glance at the relationship (often tumultuous) between the National Association and the man who joined Pearson and Grinnell in 1911 to fight for a bill against the sale of wild game. William Temple Hornaday's concern for the preservation of endangered species, coupled with a notable lack of concern for the feelings of those who did not agree with him, brought him fame and a measure of success far beyond that of most of the other conservationists of his time.

"Fully ten percent of the human race consists of people who will lie, steal, throw rubbish in parks, and destroy wildlife whenever and wherever they can do so without being stopped by a policeman and a club," he wrote in his popular book *Our Vanishing Wildlife* in 1913.

Those words were written in a spirit of comparative good will, before further experiences with sportsmen and fellow conservationists dampened Hornaday's cautious enthusiasm about the human animal. Like most of his colleagues in the movement, he had learned about wildlife by roaming the woods and fields as a boy and shooting at everything he saw.

But, while a student at Iowa State College, he began to feel there was something senseless about killing an animal and then throwing most of it away. His biology courses convinced him that taxidermy might be a justification of the hunt. Hornaday went on to Ward's Natural Science Establishment in Rochester, New York, where he mastered the taxidermist's trade, and from there journeyed to the wild places of Africa, Asia, and the American West. He shot crocodiles along muddy streams, elephants in bamboo thickets, tigers at jungle watering holes, and buffaloes on the Great Plains. In Borneo he visited headhunting Dyaks to observe the trophies hung about their houses and noted, with a young scientist's objective wit, that "none of the skulls is labelled with locality, date, sex, and species, as crania always should be, to be valuable."

Back in the United States, Hornaday pioneered in the creation of lifelike animal groups for several museums and became the first superintendent of the National Zoological Park in Washington, which he had been instrumental in creating. After a row over the zoo's physical layout, he retreated in a huff to Buffalo, New York, where he wrote a novel and a manual of taxidermy. His absence from center stage was brief. He came to New York as the first director of the Bronx Zoo and from that position, by dealing alternately in persuasion and anathema, rallied the devotees of wildlife preservation for several decades.

Wherever he looked, Hornaday could detect no such concern for wildlife as that which burned in his own breast. He was particularly bothered by the technological strides of the gun manufacturers, who made the slaughter of game all too simple even for indifferent marksmen. Modern communications, rapid transportation, skilled hunting dogs, and automatic weapons increased the efficiency with which urban people could locate, pursue, and bag their prey. By 1910, Hornaday was calling for tight restrictions on hunters, having read that one dealer in New York sold more than a million game birds a year. That fall, Hornaday received a visit at the Bronx Zoo from a "good sportsman."

"The market gunners of Long Island and the game dealers of New York have formed three strong organizations," he quoted the sportsman as telling him, "and they say they are going to wipe off our statute books all the laws for the protection of feathered game. They are going to send a man to the legislature expressly to do whatever they tell him about game."

"Well, damn their souls," Hornaday claimed to have replied (and probably did), "we will give them the fight of their lives. We will introduce a bill to stop the sale of game, and carry the war right into the enemy's camp."

Hornaday gathered facts and raised funds for the kind of dramatic confrontation he relished. The bill, which he ordered drawn up by a lawyer, was named for Howard R. Bayne of Staten Island, chairman of the Senate Judiciary Committee, who lent his prestige to the campaign in Albany. Grinnell and Pearson enthusiastically joined the battle, though there was not unanimity within the Audubon ranks. In later years, Pearson wrote that William Brewster, the first president of the Massachusetts Audubon Society, resigned from the National Association's board of directors because he thought banning the sale of game was too radical a measure. After a sharp skirmish with the restaurant and hotel interests in the New York legislature during the spring of 1911, the proponents of the "Bayne Bill" accepted a compromise to a complete ban on the sale of game: the state would permit traffic in certain European deer and game birds, as well as pheasants, mallards, and black ducks raised on American game farms. The signing of this bill into law in June of that year, and of similar bills a year later in Massachusetts and California, virtually ended the large-scale traffic in native wild game in the United States.

Despite the victories in several states, the gaps in legislation on the national level as well as the abundance of milliners, merchants, and hunters who evaded the law, continued to frustrate the bird-protection forces. Several of the shorebirds, including the Eskimo curlew, seemed to be on their way to extinction. The Carolina parakeet was already gone. The passenger pigeon, whose enormous flocks once seemed to dominate American forests, had disappeared from the wild; in June 1910, the last male of the species died in captivity, leaving only an old female called Martha in the Cincinnati Zoo. A pigeon enthusiast that year offered a $300 reward to anyone finding a nest of the species, but no one ever claimed the money, and Martha died in her cage in 1913. With hardly a thought about the matter, mankind had consigned the pigeons' galelike uproar to the eerie silence of extinction.

The egrets hit their low point in numbers about 1910. The Audubon Association conducted explorations for rookeries in four southern states but located only ten (one each in Florida, Georgia, and North Carolina, and seven in South Carolina), and estimated that they contained 1,400 great egrets and 250 snowy egrets. Pearson arranged for those rookeries to be guarded by wardens or local Audubon members. A report filed in 1912 by James Henry Rice, Jr., an Audubon field agent in South Carolina, suggested that a warden's life was constantly at risk, though local laws gave him some reasons for optimism:

"Early this year, Arthur Lambert, formerly fined three times for shooting up a rookery on the preserve of the Santee Gun Club, near McClellanville, was indicted before the United States District Court at Spartanburg, charged with trespass and violating a court order. He was convicted and sentenced to eight months in jail. This kept him out of mischief until the plume season was over."

A singular example of private enterprise in bird protection was being carried on at the time in Louisiana by E. A. McIlhenny of the family which produced Tabasco Sauce. Over a period of years he had captured some young egrets near his estate, raised them on Avery Island, which he owned, and gave them sufficient protection so that they returned to nest each year. By 1909 there were several thousand nesting egrets of various species on Avery Island, and McIlhenny arranged to release some in southern Florida to give the local population there a boost.

Encouraged by these and other successes on the local level, Pearson and William Hornaday took their act to Washington. They hoped to prod Congress into legislation that would close the remaining loopholes through which shady milliners and game dealers carried on their trade in wild birds. The two conservation leaders timed their visit to coincide with the opening of debate in Congress on the Underwood Tariff Bill, sponsored by President Woodrow Wilson's administration; the plan they hatched was to have a clause tacked on to the bill banning the importation of all wild birds' plumage.

In addition to their usual assault on legislators by pamphlet and direct testimony, Pearson and Hornaday resorted to the most modern technology. They obtained a film, made in Louisiana, showing the invasion of a heronry by plume hunters, the shooting of birds, the distress of the chicks remaining in the nests, and the eventual "skinning" of the slaughtered herons. In a hall they rented near the Capitol, they ran the film continuously one afternoon and evening (interspersed with their own remarks) for the benefit of the congressmen and their families invited for the occasion.

Hornaday, predictably, went for broke. He submitted to the House Ways and Means Committee a clause that would ban the import of plumes or other parts of any wild birds whatsoever (except for scientific or educational purposes). It is not clear whether the two men disagreed at this point or whether, as Pearson later maintained, they schemed to offer an alternative in the event "we could not have the whole loaf"; but at any rate Pearson submitted a clause that would ban only the plumage of American species known to migrate to foreign countries, and of birds "indistinguishable" from American species.

The milliners had been caught napping by the conservationists' backdoor tactics. Only when Hornaday's "whole-loaf" clause slipped through the House with hardly a dissenting vote did the milliners rush to the Senate to try to undo the damage. Working around the clock, they persuaded the Senate Finance Committee to amend Hornaday's clause so that the plumage of any bird commonly recognized as "edible or pestiferous" could be imported. As Pearson pointed out, such a phrase would render the entire clause meaningless. It would be difficult to find a bird that is not "commonly" thought to be edible somewhere in the world, and even herons and egrets were universally considered pestiferous by the operators of fish hatcheries.

Among the legislators not swayed by either the rhetoric or the film of the bird protectionists was Senator James A. Reed of Missouri. His attack on the plumage clause is still considered a classic exposition of the anticonservation position:

"I really want to know," Reed asked his colleagues, "why there should be any sympathy or sentiment about a long-legged, long-necked bird that lives in swamps, and eats tadpoles and fish and crawfish and things of that kind; why we should worry ourselves into a frenzy because some lady adorns her hat with one of its feathers, which appears to be the only use it has? . . . If the young are then left to starve, it would seem to me the proper idea would be to establish a foundling asylum for the young, but still let humanity utilize this bird for the only purpose that evidently the Lord made it for, namely so that we could get aigrettes for bonnets of our beautiful ladies."

In the end, the milliners could not muster enough men of Reed's sensibilities in the Senate, and the plumage clause remained intact. On October 3, 1913, President Wilson signed the bill into law. Within a few days, fashionable women, stepping off ocean liners on their return from buying sprees in Paris and London, were met by customs inspectors who relieved them of their millinery adornments. Eight years after Guy Bradley's murder, the traffic in wild birds' plumage went wholly underground.

# 10

It was ironic that the dream long held by both Dutcher and Pearson—of the National Association of Audubon Societies functioning on a truly national scale—began turning into a reality not through the warden system or political action but through an educational program. By enrolling *millions* of children in Junior Audubon clubs, the Audubon movement effectively spread its name and influence into every state in the nation.

George Bird Grinnell had been the first to recognize the value of children to the bird-protection movement. By taking advantage of a youngster's natural sympathy for wild animals in trouble, he enrolled thousands of them as members in his short-lived Audubon Society. One of the first campaigns of the Massachusetts Audubon Society and other state organizations was to enlist children and their teachers in the cause. In fact, the bird charts published by Massachusetts Audubon became a prominent feature of the National Association's educational program, once it found a place in the schools.

Dutcher had insisted as early as 1902 that educational programs, especially for children, were essential to the Audubon movement's eventual success. He wrote the first of his educational leaflets the following year for the National Committee of Audubon Societies, and continued to write them until his catastrophic illness. Each leaflet, composed of four pages of text and relevant illustrations, was devoted to a single bird and described its haunts, habits, and food. The latter was particularly important to Dutcher and other early leaders of the bird-protection movement, as they liked to stress (and sometimes overstressed) the value of birds to agriculture as destroyers of rodents and insects.

Many of the early leaflets were illustrated by the man who was rapidly becoming the foremost painter of American birdlife in that era, Louis Agassiz Fuertes. One of Dutcher's most effective leaflets described the life and death of "The Snowy Heron," or snowy egret, combining the bird's natural history with a graphic account of its slaughter by plume hunters. At the end of each leaflet was a feature outlining "study points" for teachers and pupils. The National Committee subsidized their bulk sale to schools and interested groups, while arranging to have some of them reprinted in *Bird-Lore.*

But, just as Grinnell's Audubon movement never got beyond the production of a magazine, Dutcher's school program seemed destined never to evolve much beyond a series of leaflets. The press of warden assignments, legislative struggles and, perhaps most restricting, a lack of money kept him from organizing the "children's bird clubs" that he had envisioned. Then, in 1910, there appeared on the scene a woman who was to have a profound influence on the future of the Audubon movement.

Margaret Olivia Slocum Sage was the widow of Russell Sage, a prominent financier and an associate of Jay Gould in gaining control of railroads and the Western Union Telegraph Company. A year after Sage's death in 1906, his widow established the Russell Sage Foundation in New York to work with various social agencies for "the improvement of social and living conditions" in the United States. Because of her interest in birds, Mrs. Sage had been horrified by the indiscriminate shooting of American robins which she had observed on trips to the South; she was later to buy Marsh Island in the Gulf of Mexico to give to the state of Louisiana as a bird sanctuary. Gilbert Pearson, guessing that she was a potential contributor to the Audubon societies, had been in touch with her for some time. In 1910, she made her first substantial contribution, a check for $500 with which Pearson produced a series of pamphlets designed to create sympathy for the robin, a bird that was then under great pressure as an item of food and sport in the southern states. Pearson approached Mrs. Sage again a few months afterward with a wider object in view.

"This resulted a little later in a talk with her attorney, Robert W. deForest, who asked me to tell him about the Audubon Association's accomplishments, and how we handled our money," Pearson recalled. "When my explanations were finished, he asked me what we would do with $5,000 if such an amount would be given to us. I at once told him that we would use it for educational work in the southern states, especially in the schools. His next statement pleased me greatly, and I made a record of his words upon returning to the office. He said, 'You have made the impression on me that I hoped you would and I am authorized by Mrs. Russell Sage to say that she will give to the Audubon Association $5,000 a year for three years to be used for your educational work in the South.' "

Pearson, as usual, lost no time in putting together a project, and Dutcher had the satisfaction of seeing an announcement of the proposed

Forty boys and girls show off their prize-winning birdhouses in 1917. NAS

"Junior Audubon Classes" in *Bird-Lore* shortly before he became ill. The program, as Pearson designed it in the fall of 1910, remained substantially the same for almost sixty years. Each child paid ten cents a year to become a Junior Audubon member, in turn receiving a set of colored pictures, bird leaflets, and an "Audubon button" bearing the likeness of a mockingbird. The classroom teacher received, free of charge, a subscription to *Bird-Lore* in return for teaching at least one lesson a month about bird life.

Although the materials cost the Audubon Association twice what the children paid for them, its leaders have always thought that what became known as the Junior Audubon clubs were well worth the investment. The psychological impact on members seems to have been considerable. Before the modern media broke down regional barriers, children were lifted out of purely local programs into a national effort symbolized by buttons and leaflets shipped to them from New York, while the dues they were required to pay gave them a sense of direct participation in the campaign to protect birds. The members became "news" in a national publication after Frank Chapman created a "School Department" in *Bird-Lore* under the editorship of Alice Hall Walker of Rhode Island;

this feature included information about projects helpful to both teachers and junior members, as well as letters from the children, accounts of their activities, and even photographs of their classes.

Moreover, when Pearson invited the teachers to become an important element in this program (acting on an old vision held by Dutcher of teachers as "Audubon Auxiliaries"), he widened the Audubon influence. The teachers became, as Joseph Kastner has phrased it in his book, *A World of Watchers,* "imbuers"; in the future, thousands of naturalists and other adults would testify to how they were "imbued" with a love for nature by those dedicated women during Audubon programs back in grammar school.

The Sage Fund, consisting mainly of the philanthropist's annual donations, allowed Pearson to hire additional field agents in the South, notably Katherine H. Stuart in Virginia. With her help, the Virginia Audubon Society won the first major legislative victory for Margaret Sage's favorite cause, the protection of the robin.

"When the bill came up for consideration in the [Virginia] Senate," Pearson wrote, "a battalion of school-children appeared and their leaders were permitted to march up the aisle to the presiding officer and present a petition bearing 10,000 names, asking that man's friend, the harbinger of spring, should be accorded the protection it deserved. The plea was greeted with applause and the bill passed by a large majority."

The hope to expand the Junior Audubon clubs outside the South was thwarted for the first couple of years by a shortage of money. But in 1912 a godfather appeared in Pearson's office to more than equal the Margaret Sage contribution. He was William P. Wharton of Groton, Massachusetts, whose only stipulation in making a donation of $5,000 was that the money be directed toward expanding nature education in the rest of the country and that he be given complete anonymity. (Although Wharton was to make increasingly generous gifts to Audubon's educational programs, totaling more than four hundred thousand dollars in the next decade alone, he always remained "the anonymous benefactor.")

The program was immensely successful from the start. *Bird-Lore* promoted, besides leaflets on individual birds, a series of large glass slides of 134 species, taken from illustrations by popular artists and colored by hand, appropriate for projection by the stereopticon machines of the day. A correspondent of that publication, writing about the schoolchildren in South Berwick, Maine, near the New Hampshire border, pointed out the new sense of responsibility provided by the program:

"One small pupil discovered some New Hampshire boys climbing to one of the robins' nests near his home, and endeavored to drive them away. Not succeeding in this, the plucky little one went promptly for a policeman, who gave the intruders convincing proof that it is not safe to violate our Maine laws for the protection of birds."

The program grew at a rate not even Pearson had imagined. By 1915, there were 152,164 children enrolled in 7,728 Junior Audubon classes throughout the United States and Canada.

Meanwhile, if children were to be attracted by colored pictures and moral persuasion to the Audubon cause, other threats to American bird-life were to be dealt with more harshly. Two of Pearson's bugbears were foreigners and cats. In his crusade against depredations by pothunters of southern European origin, he was joined by Chapman, Forbush, and Hornaday, all of whom protested loud and often against the penchant of Italians and other immigrants for shooting little birds and putting them into the cooking pot. As early as 1905, the Audubon Association had urged its members to "do all they can to suppress the alien gunner and bring him to justice," and had succeeded in pushing a law through the New York legislature prohibiting aliens from carrying firearms in "public places." The campaign, reflecting an age-old animosity toward newcomers, was carried on for some years in the pages of *Bird-Lore;* one of its photographs showed a litter of dead songbirds, which the caption described as "the contents of an Italian hunter's game bag."

Free-roaming cats caused an even greater gnashing of teeth, and there were repeated calls in *Bird-Lore* and from state societies to curb this everyday menace. Letters frequently described the toll of birds taken by cats, and one promising plan (though it was never put into effect) involved the destruction of stray cats and a tax on those with homes, a dollar for a male and three dollars for a female.

"If a nuisance cannot be eaten, tax it," an Audubon member wrote.

A sign of the Audubon Association's increasing influence in wildlife matters was a startling proposition made in 1911 by a well-known American corporation. Pearson was called on in his office by two representatives of the Winchester Repeating Arms Company. One of them, H. S. Leonard, told him they were going to start an organization to put some controls on the killing of game birds and mammals, because "as the game decreases our business grows less."

"Mr. Leonard asked if I would accept the job of running such an Association," Pearson wrote. "He then said his company would provide $5,000 or $10,000 as a fund to start the work and that their sales-agents would enroll members whose fees would help keep the organization growing."

Pearson, though apparently flattered by the offer, thought that Winchester was not thinking in big enough terms. He pointed out that what was good for Winchester ought to be good for the other gun and ammunition companies, and suggested that they pool their resources and pledge at least $25,000 a year for five years, "if they expected to build a going organization of a national scope."

Leonard returned to New York with the pledges made by various companies and renewed his proposition. Pearson, however, had by then seen an even greater opportunity and suggested that the arms manufacturers simply give the money to the Audubon Association to finance a game-protection department of its own.

"He went away and soon sent me a letter formally inviting me to become President of an American Game Protective Association, which would at once be incorporated," Pearson recalled. "Or, if I preferred, the money would be given to the Audubon Association, provided it would be used for game protection and that I should be the one to direct the work. The letter stated that if the money went to the Association the donors would ask for no representation on its Board of Directors; nor would they seek in any way to control or to influence its policies. As such a gift would about double the Association's income they said it would be agreeable with them if half my salary should come from this fund, and they thought the salary should be raised from $3,000 to $6,000 a year."

Pearson took the proposition to the Association's board, which held a special meeting to consider it. Although there was opposition among the members, a majority voted to accept the offer and devote the money to wildlife protection.

"Instantly there was a cry that the Audubon Association had sold out to the gun people who wanted to kill all the birds of the country," Pearson wrote. "This came chiefly from men who had no connection with our organization. Some of it was from a man who, we had reason to believe, was chagrined because the money had not been given to him to spend."

Pearson did not identify that man, but it may be noted that the most piercing outcry against this accommodation came from the Bronx Zoo, where the formidable Hornaday held sway and was soliciting money from Mrs. Russell Sage, Henry Ford, George Eastman, and Andrew Carnegie for his own very successful wildlife projects. In any event, the board of directors hastily reconsidered and came to the conclusion that accepting the money would leave the Association vulnerable to the attacks of its "enemies." Pearson bowed out of any further direct dealings with the arms companies, which proceeded to form their own organization, The American Game Protective Association, as originally planned. On George Bird Grinnell's recommendation, they appointed as its president John B. Burnham, a well-known sportsman who had once worked for him at *Forest and Stream.*

Burnham and the new organization joined hands with the Audubon Association in some of the big propaganda and legislative battles for wildlife in the following years. Hornaday, however, detested the thought of working hand in glove with the gunmakers and resented Pearson's easy friendship with people like Burnham. When Burnham's name was later proposed for membership in the Boone and Crockett Club, which Grinnell and Theodore Roosevelt had helped to found, Hornaday worked relentlessly behind the scenes and blocked his acceptance for nearly four years. Grinnell was greatly annoyed.

"I am not crying down or disposed to quarrel with Hornaday, whom I like," he wrote to another club member. "He is a good fellow, and a useful man so long as he works in his own job. It is when he goes outside of his own job that he . . . stirs up trouble—not for himself, for he delights in a row, but for others including his employers, who may not like a row so much."

But by then events had been set in motion to bring all of the parties, including Pearson, Grinnell, Burnham, and Hornaday, into a collaboration that was to culminate in the single most important victory ever achieved by the bird-protection movement.

# 11

*G*ilbert Pearson, a grass-roots activist in every sense of the word, was caught in the nightmare of trying to preserve wildlife through the crazy-quilt pattern of local laws. He had been one of the earliest successful organizers of Audubon action on the state level. He had sharpened his lobbying skills in a variety of state legislatures. But he knew better than anyone else that bird protection under the piecemeal conditions that then prevailed was a never-ending struggle, demanding a constant rushing about to plug loopholes in one state capital (or even county seat) while preparing to move on and repair the damage done in another.

The nineteenth century had witnessed a constant strengthening of the legal principle that wildlife regulation belonged solely in the hands of the individual states. The final peg in that framework seemed to have been set in place by the United States Supreme Court in 1896. A man named Geer had been convicted in Connecticut for trying to ship game birds out of the state, though the birds had been killed legally in Connecticut. Geer appealed his conviction on the grounds that the statute improperly interfered with the power of Congress to regulate interstate commerce.

The Supreme Court, in *Geer* v. *Connecticut,* decided in favor of the state and in doing so summarized a general theory of state "ownership" of wildlife. Justice Edward White, writing the majority opinion, traced the history of government control over the taking of wildlife from antiquity through American independence, and concluded that the states had received the "right to control and regulate the common property in game" directly from the British King and Parliament. The court rejected the argument that the federal concern with interstate commerce was relevant in that case.

The Lacey Act of 1900, which had been vital to the development of the early Audubon movement, did not affect the decision in *Geer* v. *Connecticut.* By prohibiting the interstate shipment of animals killed in violation of state laws, it did in fact throw its weight behind the enforcement of those laws. In the years immediately following the passage of the Lacey Act, some courts took the view that Congress had relinquished any claim to regulate interstate traffic in game.

Still, among thoughtful people there lingered the heretical notion that migratory birds did not even belong to a nation, much less to a smaller political entity. The first man to challenge the theory of state ownership of wild birds was George Shiras III, perhaps the outstanding wildlife photographer of his time. Shiras came from a family of distinguished public servants in Pennsylvania, and early in this century he was prevailed upon by friends interested in wildlife to run for Congress. During his brief service in Washington, Shiras concentrated on what would become known later as environmental legislation. It occurred to him, while he was working on a public health measure to protect the public against polluted water served on railroad trains, that if the federal government was able to eradicate "germs" in interstate traffic, it ought to be able to protect game birds that flew from one state to another.

In 1904 Shiras introduced a bill in Congress providing "that all wild geese, wild swans, brant, wild ducks, snipe, plover, woodcock, rail, wild pigeons and all other migratory game birds which do not remain permanently within the borders of any State or Territory shall hereafter be deemed to be within the custody and protection of the Government of the United States."

Shiras and his supporters proposed that the Biological Survey take action under this legislation to regulate the hunting of those birds and set a closed season on them. Sportsmen were beginning to realize that spring shooting decimated the flocks of wildfowl which once had seemed inexhaustible. Wild ducks, for instance, pair in the south before starting on their long flight to the northern breeding grounds in spring. If one of the pair is killed on migration, the young birds that they could have been expected to rear during the summer will not be produced. In drawing up his bill, Shiras reflected the sentiment of sportsmen, who called for hunting seasons restricted to the fall and winter, when the young of the year had swelled the total numbers of wildfowl.

"From long experience in various hunting fields [Shiras] knew that this class of birds was inadequately protected under state management," Gilbert Pearson wrote. "In fact, in a number of states no game warden system at that time existed. He did not ask for a committee hearing on his bill but stated that for the present he merely desired to have it printed and circulated for the purpose of arousing discussion among game commissioners, naturalists, the five million sportsmen of the country, and others."

After Shiras's early retirement from Congress, his measure reappeared in much the same form under the sponsorship of Representative John W. Weeks of Massachusetts and Senator George P. McLean of Connecticut. But the legislation dragged on for some years. The states were not yet ready to surrender jurisdiction over migratory wildfowl. Even congressmen friendly to the bill doubted that it was constitutional; game birds, they reasoned, could not by any stretch of the imagination be covered by the Constitution's interstate commerce clause. Besides, though they supported the principle, some members of the bird-protection movement did not believe wholeheartedly in a bill whose chief purpose seemed to be to improve the duck hunters' sport.

The Weeks-McLean Bill was given a vital boost by the so-called Dicky-bird Amendment. Pearson, speaking for the Audubon interests, suggested that *all* migratory birds be covered by the legislation. He argued that the inclusion of songbirds, insectivorous species among them, would attract support from farmers, foresters, and homeowners who could be convinced of those birds' beneficial feeding habits. But many sportsmen continued to be contemptuous of "dicky-birds." It was only when all prospects for the bill's passage seemed lost at the end of 1912 that Hornaday, Grinnell, Burnham, and other prominent conservationists rallied around the Audubon point of view.

Hornaday plunged into the struggle with his usual abandon. He sent out telegrams to influential people, story ideas for newspapers, and a copy of his popular book *Our Vanishing Wildlife* to each member of Congress. He also prepared and distributed a circular entitled "Slaughter of Useful Birds: A Grave Emergency."

"The sockdolager at the end," Hornaday wrote afterward, "was a picture of two glass jars containing the dead bodies of forty-three valuable insectivorous birds that were taken from two Italians in October 1905 in the suburbs of New York City, by field agents of the New York Zoological Society. As pertinent bird pictures we threw in a snipe, killdeer, plover, robin, martin, nighthawk, shrike, and golden-winged woodpecker [flicker]; and believe me, the text was good reading for the farm block."

There was still formidable opposition in Congress. Senator Elihu Root, who had been Theodore Roosevelt's secretary of state, held strong reservations about the bill on constitutional grounds. However, when conservationists took their case to him, he agreed to mute his objections and try instead to shore up the legislation's constitutional support. Toward that end, he later introduced a resolution in the Senate calling for negotiations with Canada that would sanctify the bill's major points in a treaty.

Other congressmen were far more obstinate. The bill's most outspoken foe was Representative Franklin W. Mondell of Wyoming, who presented the case for states' rights.

"This is, in my opinion, the most revolutionary, the most far-reaching legislation, in its possible and probable effect on our system of Government, that has been presented to Congress in the sixteen years during which I have been a member of this body. If this bill should become a law no man who voted for it would ever be justified in raising his voice against any extension, no matter how extreme, of the police authority and control of the Federal government."

Those remarks were delivered, according to Gilbert Pearson, who heard them, with "great vehemence."

Even big business, in the person of Henry Ford, took part in the struggle. Birds had become a chief source of diversion for Ford, as they were for Theodore Roosevelt, and, when he wasn't reading about machinery, he could often be found absorbed in a good book about natural history. Ford especially admired the writings of John Burroughs, so much so that in 1912 he sent the seventy-five-year-old naturalist a new automobile and a man to teach him how to drive it. "John o' Birds" failed to master "the blind desperate thing," which carried him into and through the side of his barn one afternoon, but this did not diminish his respect for Ford, of whom he wrote: "His interest in birds is keen and his knowledge considerable." Ford, in turn, assigned one of his advertising men to Washington to help lobby for what by then was being called the Migratory Bird Bill.

Congress, won over to the cause, passed the bill as a rider on the Agriculture Appropriations Bill in the waning days of the Taft administration, and the President signed it on March 4, 1913. Taft later said that, deluged by last-minute bills and documents, he had been unaware of what the rider contained and otherwise would have vetoed it because he believed it to be unconstitutional. He was not alone, and the act was to face several sharp challenges in the courts within the next year or two. Nonetheless, the Biological Survey immediately banned the hunting of waterfowl in spring and put in motion the machinery to assume responsibility for regulating the hunting of game birds and the outright protection of other migratory species.

"The Audubon Association was much pleased with the regulations, which extended protection to useful non-game birds in those states that had not as yet adopted the Model Audubon Law," Pearson exulted. "Robins were to be protected everywhere, thus finishing one of our special campaigns; and ducks could be killed for only three and one half months each year. Furthermore, sixty-two species of water birds which had been heavily shot, were not to be taken for the next five years."

Almost every hunter had his individual objection to the new regulations, and the Audubon societies held their collective breath while negotiations began to remove the constitutional objections to the act. It was obvious that Elihu Root's suggestion of a treaty with Canada was the only clear-cut solution to the problem, because the terms of a treaty between the United States and a foreign power would take precedence over any laws or regulations put forth by the various states. Even this path seemed doubtful for a while. Great Britain, which would represent Canada (then a Dominion in the British Empire), was soon engulfed in World War I and almost totally preoccupied with preparations for the long struggle.

Pearson, meanwhile, was faced with the other duties of operating a truly national organization. Poachers were still at their bloody work on all the coastlines of the United States. The Audubon Association had not as yet assembled its own network of sanctuaries. (Until after World War I it owned only two small nesting islands: Buzzard Island in South Carolina, and Bird Island, a thirty-five-acre area in Orange Lake, Alachua County, Florida.) Nevertheless, the Association carried on its traditional policy of arranging for wardens at important rookeries and tried to acquire several other pieces of land. For instance, an effort was made to buy No Man's Land, the thirty-acre island on the Maine coast that was the site of a large herring gull colony. When the island was sold instead to a local family, the son of the new owner was appointed warden.

"Later, reports came that the birds were being interfered with, and Arthur H. Norton, our agent in Maine, was asked personally to investigate the situation," *Bird-Lore* told its readers. "He reported there was much evidence to show that the Gulls had been continually robbed of their eggs, and also that foxes had been liberated on the island. He found the colony broken up and the birds all gone. The faithless warden was called to account, and his resignation was accepted."

Florida poachers, an even tougher breed, continued to shoot up rookeries and threaten the lives of Audubon wardens. Pearson appealed for contributions from members to pay for more wardens, especially since a lively little trade had been created by the Seminole Indians of the Everglades and the "poor whites" of the Big Cypress country, who sold plumes for high prices to wealthy winter visitors in Palm Beach and Miami. Pearson lambasted his fellow Floridians.

"I can count on the fingers of one hand the names of all the men and women in that state who contribute a dollar to this work," he grumbled in *Bird-Lore*. "And so we cannot look there for the sinews of war for our Egret campaign in 1916, but, as usual, must turn to the New

England school teacher, the New York businessman, and others of our friends who dwell north of the Potomac River."

But there was no letup in the drive to educate Americans about the value of their birds. Herbert K. Job, the man who a decade earlier had accompanied Guy Bradley into the Everglades and who later became Connecticut's state ornithologist, was hired by the Audubon Association to run an experimental station in Amston, Connecticut. There Job developed techniques for landowners interested in rearing waterfowl and accumulated information about feeding birds around homes and farms. Bird feeding, in fact, was becoming a popular winter pastime, and enthusiasm mounted as various songbirds, now completely protected, began to appear around homes in greater numbers. Backyard birdwatchers were even seeing new species. Historically the evening grosbeak had been a rare visitor east of Wisconsin, but in the winter of 1910–11 a great many of those birds showed up in the eastern states, and the letters column in *Bird-Lore* brimmed with excited reports.

Pearson's attention was continually being drawn westward. In 1916, the income from the Mary Dutcher Memorial Fund was used to buy a new patrol boat for a warden on Klamath Lake in Oregon. Bird protection had made considerable progress in that state under William Finley, Audubon's agent on the West Coast, but now there was reason for disquiet. Local speculators were trying to persuade the state to take title to the huge bird reservation on Malheur Lake that had been set aside by Theodore Roosevelt. A long struggle began for the area, which Pearson, after seeing it in 1915, called the most important single bird reservation in the country, and it would be years before the struggle was resolved.

Close to home, the Audubon cause had brighter prospects. Pearson persuaded the New York State Conservation Commission in 1916 to undertake a "clean-up campaign" against the people still involved in the illegal selling of plumes. With the help of two Audubon agents, who secured the necessary evidence, more than thirty arrests were made, and the plume trade in New York was pushed closer to extinction.

Such triumphs gave the Audubon Association breathing room for less desperate activities. Early in 1917, Walter F. McMahon, who had served as an assistant to E. H. Forbush in the state ornithologist's office in Massachusetts, joined the Audubon Association's staff as chief clerk. McMahon, an enthusiastic birdwatcher, also began leading a series of early morning bird walks in Central Park, a practice that has been carried on by other Audubon staffers down to the present time.

Only a few weeks after McMahon came to New York, the United States went to war on the side of the Allies. McMahon continued with his office duties and bird walks until the beginning of 1918, when he joined the Army. He served with a machine gun squad in France and, on August 28 of that year, he was killed by a sniper.

By an ironic twist, while McMahon was the only Audubon staff member to die in action, three others succumbed to the influenza epidemic that struck New York City late in 1918. No annual meeting was held that year because of the epidemic, and Pearson and Chapman were restricted to communicating with members through the various departments of *Bird-Lore*. The war, it seems, had put a clamp even on the rapid growth of the Junior Audubon clubs, though the final totals for 1918 showed 6,000 active classes with nearly 160,000 children (a decline of 100,000 from the previous year). The dimes for Audubon, it seems, were diverted to the Red Cross and wartime savings stamps.

One incident in wartime showed that the bird-protection movement did not hold old grudges. The Audubon Association threw cold water on someone's patriotic proposal to organize Boy Scouts into bands for the destruction of that perennial nuisance to farmers and gardeners, the English sparrow.

Incredibly, and almost unnoticed, in the clangor of war the struggle for the protection of migratory birds was carried through to a successful conclusion. There had been some uncomfortable and even rancorous moments along the way. Most details of a treaty between the United States and Great Britain (acting on behalf of Canada) had been agreed upon by early 1916, but there was great opposition from many groups of hunters concerning the prohibition on spring waterfowl hunting. This opposition centered in the Midwest, where a group of senators was said to be ready to reject the treaty if it included such a ban. E. W. Nelson of the Biological Survey, long an opponent of spring shooting, nevertheless asked the conservationists to give in on that point because a number of congressmen and senators had threatened to scuttle the treaty and even withhold appropriations for the Biological Survey if it did not change its position. Pearson refused to cave in, and launched his own threat, that of a public attack on the Survey by Audubon groups. He told Nelson that he believed that the Midwestern threat against the Survey was exaggerated and that the Audubon Association "could again engineer a fight for its defense," as it had a decade earlier.

Nelson came to New York and went over Pearson's head to the Association's board of directors. The directors, remembering other congressional attempts to eliminate the only federal agency active in bird-protection work, voted to support Nelson in his stand that he could no longer maintain a February 1 closing of the waterfowl season.

"E. H. Forbush of Boston for years had been a most active anti-spring shooting advocate," Pearson wrote. "Upon learning that the Audubon Association would not further oppose Dr. Nelson's plan for changing the treaty, he at once filed his resignation as our New England representative, raised some money by solicitation from Dr. Hornaday and others, and employed Dr. George W. Field of Boston to go to Missouri and Illinois to find out just how strong was the opposition to the 'February 1st' clause."

Field's investigation confirmed the opinion of Pearson and Forbush that the threat to the Biological Survey had been overstated. To his credit, Nelson attempted to withdraw the amended clause in the treaty, but it was too late. The treaty had been signed by the two countries in July 1916.

"And that is the story," Pearson wrote, "of why it is written in the treaty for the protection of migratory birds of Canada and the United States, that either country, at its pleasure, may permit the shooting of 'ducks, geese and swans' as late in spring as March 10th. But, and this really is the important point, except in a few Canadian Provinces neither country operating under this treaty has permitted the killing of wildfowl later than January 15th."

Although the Migratory Bird Treaty between the United States and Great Britain was quickly ratified by Congress, an enabling act was still needed to authorize a federal agency to be responsible for enforcing its provisions. Almost interminable delays occurred in Congress again, but at last, on July 3, 1918, while the country was still at war, President Wilson signed the Migratory Bird Treaty Act.

The Biological Survey was free from the threat of court action to set regulations for the management of migratory birds. It reiterated the ban on spring hunting and market hunting, limiting the open season on waterfowl to three and a half months and setting daily bag limits of twenty-five ducks and ten geese (a considerable reduction from an earlier day). In a further drastic and courageous step, the Survey placed a ban on the shooting at any time of the shorebird family of sandpipers and plovers (except for woodcock and snipe), a moratorium that is still in effect.

With the passage of the Migratory Bird Treaty Act, the National Association of Audubon Societies was, in Frank Chapman's words, "relieved of the necessity of watching the legislation of every state and of combating the numberless attempts to legalize the destruction of birds for private gain."

# 12

The Texas coast, until the end of World War I, was nearly a *terra incognita* to ornithologists. John James Audubon had made a voyage there in the spring of 1837, but it was not as productive as some of his other expeditions, and the original journal of that trip was lost. After that time, the reports about birdlife in Texas were few and unreliable. It was thus something of a revelation when the untiring Gilbert Pearson visited some of the islands along the Texas coast in 1918 and again in 1920, returning to New York with his copious reports.

The region was, and is, excellent habitat for nesting waterbirds—shallow bays protected by peninsulas and barrier islands, lagoons rimmed by salt marshes, and sand-and-seashell islands covered with grasses, mesquite, yucca, and salt cedar. At South Bird Island, in northern Laguna Madre near Corpus Christi, Pearson reported enormous numbers of birds. He estimated that there were 70,000 royal terns, 18,000 Cabot's (or Sandwich) terns, and more than 20,000 laughing gulls nesting on the island. Among the riot of numbers, there was one shining fact of undoubted importance. Pearson counted sixteen reddish egrets on the island, confirming earlier reports that this bird, which apparently had disappeared as a breeder from Florida, still held on within the boundaries of the United States.

Equally exciting to ornithologists was the discovery by Pearson and his party of nine separate flocks of roseate spoonbills—a total of 179 birds—between Matagorda Bay and Port Isabel near Brownsville. Because spoonbills had nearly been extirpated from Florida and existed in very small numbers in Louisiana, their survival on the Texas coast (probably drawing their numbers from undisturbed colonies in Mexico) was encouraging. Here, in Texas, were populations of large, beautiful birds that had been all but despaired of by American ornithologists.

However remote the Texas islands seemed to be, their nesting birds were still subject to molestation, especially from fishermen who shot up the colonies for food, bait, or fun. Pearson apparently thought the time was right to begin to expand on William Dutcher's original concept of a warden-and-sanctuary system. Freed now from the constant pressure of rushing from state to state to lobby reluctant legislators for bird-protection laws, and with a children's education program recovering from wartime setbacks and thriving once more, the Audubon Association was ready to set in place the foundations of what has become one of the largest privately owned wildlife sanctuary systems in the world.

Pearson was now the Audubon leader in name as well as in fact. William Dutcher had never recovered from the stroke he suffered in 1910. Although unable to speak, he seemed still to be interested in hearing or reading about birds and, walking on a cane, he even attended the annual meeting of the Audubon Association at the American Museum of Natural History in 1915. In the interim, he had moved into a new home in Chevy Chase, Maryland, and he died there at the age of seventy-four on July 1, 1920. The board of directors elected Pearson president of the Association at its annual meeting that fall.

Although most of the founders of the Audubon movement had died or, like Grinnell, turned their main attention to other pursuits, the Association remained in strong hands. Frank Chapman was still extremely active at *Bird-Lore*, and he had added an authoritative voice to his publication in Arthur A. Allen, professor of ornithology at Cornell University, who became editor of the School Department. As the Association began to expand its physical presence around the country—by the creation of Audubon sanctuaries—other competent men and women would join the movement.

A practical man, Pearson realized that there was more to the concept of sanctuaries than seeking out large, glamorous birds and remote islands. As early as 1915 he had urged city dwellers to make use of what were often the most prominent green spaces in their midst—their cemeteries—as bird sanctuaries. He noted that while many birds on migration descended on cemeteries to feed or rest, few of them stayed to breed, and he suggested that civic groups plant shrubs and put out nesting boxes to convert migrants into residents.

"If any place in the world ought to speak of the Resurrection, in whatever form it may come to us, it is the cemeteries of our land," Pearson wrote in one of his educational pamphlets. "In them we should seek inspiring birdsongs, the nesting of birds, the sight of little ones preparing for the world in their flight."

Not long after, in the 1920s, keeping up with America's shift from the spiritual to the secular, Pearson took up golf and detected a new opportunity to advance the Audubon cause. He wrote another pamphlet, entitled "Golf Clubs as Bird Sanctuaries," in which he pointed out that insect-eating birds would be helpful around greens and ornamental shrubs, and he dispensed advice on feeding stations, plantings, and nest-ing boxes. Always enterprising, he went on to organize a Golf Club Bird Sanctuary Committee that included Frank Chapman, Arthur Allen, con-gressman and advertising executive Bruce Barton, the golfing immortal Bobby Jones, and sports writer Grantland Rice.

It was fitting that, even in death, Theodore Roosevelt was responsible for the creation of what is at present the second oldest of all the sanc-tuaries owned by the National Audubon Society. After Roosevelt's death in 1919, crowds flocked to his grave near his old home in Oyster Bay, Long Island. Vendors followed in their wake, setting up shop around the cemetery to sell food, soft drinks, and even bootleg liquor to the pilgrims. Empty whiskey bottles tossed over the fence with the other trash onto the Roosevelt family's estate, as well as rumors that "com-mercial interests" were about to buy the land on three sides of the cemetery to cash in on the crowds, prompted the Roosevelts to look for a solution.

Frank Chapman at the American Museum suggested to Pearson that the Roosevelt property, even in its abused condition, might make a bird sanctuary for the Audubon Association. The suggestion fit neatly into one of Pearson's projects. Immediately after Roosevelt's death, he had proposed to the board of directors that the Association raise money to erect a Roosevelt Memorial Bird Fountain. Letters were sent to prospec-tive donors, and the fund eventually reached $17,700.

An admired sculptor of the day, Bessie Potter Vonnoh, was com-missioned to design the fountain. Working in her Manhattan studio, she created a graceful bronze statue, nine feet high, of two children representing the perpetual youth of Nature; a songbird perched on the hand of a seated boy. Once the statue had been completed, there arose the problem of what to do with it. Various parks in New York and Washington had been suggested as sites, but when the Roosevelts offered the Oyster Bay land for "charitable purposes," Pearson was quick to see not only an opportunity to link the Audubon name with that of the popular former President, but also to provide a home for Mrs. Vonnoh's statue.

After the twelve acres of dry woodland had been transferred by the former President's cousin, Emlen Roosevelt, to Audubon, it became nec-essary to select a sanctuary director who would maintain the property for songbirds as the Roosevelt family wished. Pearson chose a man with a longtime Audubon connection and a devotion to duty that caused the sanctuary to thrive in a most unusual fashion. Eugene Swope had been a dentist in Cincinnati before his immersion in Audubon affairs made him a pioneer in nature education. During the years 1905–15, he had published magazines, one called *Nature and Culture*, and a later one, *Blue-*

*Bird.* In 1912 he had become an Audubon field agent, proving a tireless lecturer and propagandist for that cause and helping to create almost eight thousand Junior Audubon clubs in Ohio.

When Eugene and Mabel Swope moved into a house on the sanctuary at the beginning of 1924, the science of ecology was still in its infancy. The ex-dentist took his assignment to create a songbird refuge absolutely literally, and the little book *Voice of the Woods*, which he wrote about his fourteen years at Oyster Bay and had printed at his own expense, must curl the hair of modern wildlife managers who happen to read it. Any living thing which did not fit Swope's image of a songbird would have done well to give the Theodore Roosevelt Memorial Sanctuary a wide berth.

Even in later years, despite his failing sight and health, Swope was a crack shot with either a .22 rifle or small-bore shotgun. It goes without saying that English sparrows and starlings were quickly dispatched by means of guns and traps. Cowbirds, blue jays, and crows were tolerated in small numbers only long enough to qualify for the list of "resident species" which Swope proudly watched increase during his tenure. Because of his meticulous record-keeping, we know that 147 cats, both pedigreed and alley varieties, fell to his eternal vigilance, as did 360 snakes of at least seven species. (A survey of the sanctuary after his departure failed to turn up a single snake.) A few raccoons were permitted on the sanctuary because Swope believed they helped to control the neighborhood cats, but opossums, gray squirrels, minks, muskrats, weasels, and moles (the latter because they undermined the tender new rootlets of shrubs that Swope had planted to attract songbirds) were all systematically "controlled." Hawks and owls, in particular, generally met a sudden end on the sanctuary. In his book, Swope described the shooting of a pair of screech owls that appropriated a nesting box he had built for flickers.

"Within a month after disposing of the one family, another owl took up residence in the box," Swope wrote. "The next spring a pair attempted to nest in it. Off and on owls chose it for their daylight hideout. It took four years of diligent thinning out of owls before our own birds were normally safe from the murderous claws and beak of this killer that hunts in the night as he drifts on wings as silent as shadows."

Phrases such as "balance of nature" threw Swope into a funk. ("Nature was never balanced," he told a colleague. "Otherwise we'd still have the dinosaurs with us.") But even his detractors must have admitted he was evenhanded, for he believed that serious birdwatchers, or "listers," were almost as great a nuisance on the sanctuary as cats, and he hoped that their pastime was a fad that would soon run its course.

Swope could justly feel satisfied with his work at the Roosevelt Sanctuary. The number of resident songbird species increased from fourteen in 1924 to thirty-six in 1938 when he departed, while the nonnative shrubs proliferated to provide them with food and shelter. James Callaghan, who served as Swope's assistant for a time and then replaced him, recorded the end result of this early venture in sanctuary management.

"Despite all control measures in the years 1924 through 1938 most of the 'pest' avian species have held their own and even increased their kind," Callaghan reported. "Crows, jays and cowbirds are no more and no less abundant. Starlings and English sparrows have certainly increased in numbers, undoubtedly due in large part to the scarcity of natural predators, mainly hawks and owls. To compound the fallacy of the 'controlled' songbird sanctuary, there is the question of finances involved in the highly managed and manipulated plant environment. Many exotic, fruit-bearing trees, shrubs and vines were introduced which, for a few short years, were highly productive in terms of bird attraction qualities, but constant physical management and frequent replacement were essential to the continued success of this program. Plants were introduced which, through lack of constant care, have proven to be highly destructive to natural plant succession. A prime example of this is the English ivy which today has smothered acres of land in the sanctuary, preventing the growth of natural grasses, wild flowers and other ground cover and is actually throttling trees where not checked."

The Theodore Roosevelt Memorial Sanctuary, its ecological balance restored, survived and flourished in our own time with the hard work and imagination of new generations of managers and local Audubon members.

A very different sort of man from Swope was Paul J. Rainey, who may never have heard of the Audubon Association but whose name survives mainly because of his posthumous links with it. He lived the kind of life that ought to be chronicled in the magazines devoted to the blood sports—as in fact, his own life was.

"His list of firsts is amazing," wrote Jim McCafferty in the October 1986 issue of *Outdoor Life.* "He invented the short-lived sport of hunting African lions from horseback with hounds; he led an Arctic expedition farther north than any white hunting party had ever gone before; he shot the first motion pictures of African big game; he lassoed the largest polar bear ever captured alive; he was a member of the first American polo team to defeat the British in international competition. . . . He was Paul Rainey, American playboy."

This blond, robust younger son of a Midwestern coke tycoon had inherited a fortune, though not as large a fortune as it might have been had not his father believed Paul led a profligate life and left most of his money to his other two children. Still, the young man managed to grub along on his twenty million dollars and, while performing his feats of derring-do, acquired considerable holdings in land here and there around the world. One of Rainey's investments was in a land-holding company, in which he was a partner with E. A. McIlhenny, in the marshes of coastal Louisiana.

Rainey earned a great deal of adulation when he led home his polar bear on the end of a rope for deposition in a zoo. But his exploits began to pall a bit when he bragged about the mountain of lions he had slain with the aid of hounds and horses on the African plains; the fact that he had shot nine of those lions within a span of thirty-five minutes seems to have offended even his most ardent admirers at home, and caused consternation among the British colonial authorities in Africa because it was feared he would not leave trophies for anyone else. The authorities restricted his hunting and, after one of his white hunters was fatally mauled by a lion, Rainey packed up and left. Having burned his candle at both ends, he died, apparently of a heart attack, in 1923 at the age of forty-six.

For some years there had been increasing interest in the Gulf Coast marshes among ornithologists because of the region's importance as a wintering home for waterfowl. In 1910, Herbert K. Job and a colleague, W. L. McAtee of the Biological Survey, had disclosed to science (though the fact was already known to the locals) the abundance of blue geese in southern Louisiana during winter. Ornithologists of the time considered the blue goose a distinct species, and a rare one at that. (This bird is now known to be simply a morph, or color phase, of the snow goose.) That thousands of them could be found in the area was welcome news to waterfowl experts.

In 1923, many members of the Audubon Association were jolted by the news that McIlhenny, whose work in preserving egrets at Avery Island had won their admiration, was now proposing to establish a hunting club of not less than two thousand members in the Louisiana marshes. This land, part of it owned by the Vermilion Bay Company, in which he and Paul Rainey had been partners, lay between two extensive state and federal wildlife reservations. Members who gathered at the Association's annual meeting in New York that year asked Gilbert Pearson to make contact with McIlhenny to see if the Association might acquire the property.

Prospects for an agreement of some kind seemed good. McIlhenny said he was willing to give the Association an option on 109,000 acres. Some wealthy friends of Audubon proposed to start a fund for the purchase, and the publisher of *Field & Stream* promised to appeal to that magazine's readers, most of them duck hunters, to contribute to the fund to establish a waterfowl sanctuary. But McIlhenny's price of over a million dollars was thought to be "enormously in excess" of the land's value, and negotiations collapsed, not without some bitterness on both sides.

Pearson, who had visited the area earlier, described it as "a veritable paradise for tens of thousands of wild ducks that come from their summer homes in the Northern states and Canada to spend the winter where the water is always open and food abundant." He was beginning to envision a whole chain of sanctuaries along the Atlantic, Pacific, and Mississippi flyways to preserve the flocks of waterfowl that were still under intense hunting pressure. When he learned that Paul Rainey's sister, Grace Rainey Rogers, had inherited his land holdings in Louisiana, Pearson approached her and, in his direct fundraiser's manner, asked if she would give her share of the Vermilion Bay Company's land to the Audubon Association.

"The thought appealed to her and she tried to buy Mr. McIlhenny's one-third ownership, but he declined to sell," Pearson wrote. "The property, therefore, was divided and Mrs. Rogers deeded to us the 26,161 acres she received as her two-thirds interest. Our contract with her was signed June 18, 1924. She provided for guarding the sanctuary until 1927 when, as originally planned, she gave the Association a special endowment to cover taxes and help in the upkeep. This amounted to $156,786."

At this point, the wily Pearson suggested a stipulation in the deed which, in the light of events a few years later, makes interesting reading, but which proved to be of little solace to him in a struggle to the bitter end with another formidable woman. The stipulation in the deed donating the Vermilion Bay land to the Audubon Association read:

"By 'Sanctuary for Wild Life' is meant a place of refuge wherein the killing, trapping or destruction by any means of wild birds and wild mammals, shall not be permitted; provided, however, that if any form of such life, bird or otherwise, shall at any time be found by the said donee to be obnoxious and injurious and detrimental to other forms of animal life, whether bird or otherwise, (and the donee's decision on this question shall be final and conclusive) the said donee shall in its discretion have the right to eliminate or destroy the form of animal life so found injurious or detrimental, and to this end shall have the right to grant hunting or trapping privileges or otherwise provide for the destruction of the aforesaid animal life. Any income derived from any such grant of hunting or trapping rights shall be applied exclusively for the benefit of the said sanctuary."

In his visit to the area, Pearson had noted the enormous number of muskrats (which are an outsized member of the family of meadow voles) in the marshes. Although he did not plan to carry sanctuary management to the extremes advocated by Eugene Swope, he anticipated that the burgeoning population of plant-eating muskrats might soon, without adequate controls, provide the visiting waterfowl with stiff competition for food—but of that, more later.

Meanwhile, a naturalist named John P. Holman was designated to lead a working party into the marshes that had become the Paul J. Rainey Wildlife Sanctuary. (It is now Audubon's oldest sanctuary.) Holman, in *Bird-Lore*, described the area:

"For untold ages the Mississippi River has been bringing down on its broad bosom minute particles of soil from the Northland and depositing them along the Gulf coast until it has built up a great land area, rich in all the mineral salts which sustain vegetation. The region is checkered with innumerable lakes and lagoons, feathered by tall grasses which isolate them from all but the creatures of the air. Only on the higher land of the 'Chenieres' or live-oak ridges does man make his home; all else lies under the great dome of the sky—a vast and solitary expanse of marsh and water."

Holman and his party penetrated this aqueous land, the breeding ground of rails, egrets, and other marsh birds in spring and the winter home of migrating ducks and geese, to the canal at the entrance to Belle Isle Lake. There they came upon the clubhouse and camps that Rainey had erected for himself and his guests.

"According to a contract executed at the time the assets of the Vermilion Bay Company were divided, these buildings passed to Mrs. Rogers and were in turn transferred to the Audubon Society," Holman continued. "When we arrived at the club house, we discovered that Mr. McIlhenny had removed two of these buildings across the canal to his own property. He had also removed all the furniture from the club house and the permanent fixtures from the bathroom. The locks on all the closets and cupboards had been removed and piles of rubbish lay on the floors of all the rooms. In such manner has that great 'conservationist,' Edward A. McIlhenny, welcomed the advent of a new bird sanctuary on the Louisiana coast. We swept the place and proceeded to establish the headquarters of the National Association of Audubon Societies on the Paul J. Rainey Wild-Life Sanctuary."

Until a permanent manager could be found and appointed at the sanctuary, the federal government agreed to assign a warden to the property, and he moved into the tidied-up clubhouse. Three patrol boats, paid for by Grace Rainey Rogers, were provided for the warden and Audubon officials. Holman and his team, aware that great numbers of ducks congregated in a restricted area will soon exhaust the food supply, began planting widgeon grass, millet, wapato, and wild celery tubers to supplement the forage. It was tedious work, encasing five or six tubers together in balls of clay so that the plants would sink through the water and into the mud and, after the clay disintegrated, take root there. A year later the plants, in contrast to Audubon's relations with the Tabasco tycoon, were flourishing.

"During the months of December, January, and February," Holman reported with obvious satisfaction, "a large quantity of rice-sweepings was fed to the ducks congregated on Belle Isle Lake, and they became very tame and rafted in great numbers around the club house. The hunting grounds of E. A. McIlhenny adjoin the refuge on the west, and every time a shot was fired from one of his blinds a great crowd of ducks would rise and sweep over into Belle Isle Lake and find sanctuary on the refuge. Mr. McIlhenny baited the ducks on his ponds but they were wise enough to feed there only at night when it was too dark to shoot them. This necessitated his hiring a number of men to paddle about the lakes and bayous at night to keep the ducks stirred up so they would come into his ponds after the food in the daytime. They soon learned to stay away altogether and the shooting at the Gulf Coast Club was not very good last year."

The state of Louisiana, taking note of Audubon's success with planting food for waterfowl, began setting out plants on its own refuges nearby, increasing still further the area's value as a wintering ground for wildfowl. Minor nuisance aside, the Louisiana marshes were well in hand. Pearson, meanwhile, had turned his attention farther westward along the Gulf Coast, to the Texas islands, where he had made the exciting observations of reddish egrets and roseate spoonbills at the end of the war. His lobbying skills bore fruit in Texas almost immediately: in 1923, with the legislature's approval, the state's General Land Office gave the Audubon Association a fifty-year lease on 3,871 acres in Laguna Madre, described as Green Island, the group known as Three Islands, North Bird Island, South Bird Island, and the adjacent flats and reefs.

With the foundations of a sanctuary system in place, Pearson was ready to engage a number of wardens who would add excitement and distinction (and, rarely, a discordant note) to the Audubon story in the years ahead.

# 13

"Some time ago I received through the mail a booklet entitled 'Federal Power and Duck Bag Limit Facts,' a study bulletin issued by the National Association of Audubon Societies," wrote Jack Miner, a combatant in the great brouhaha over waterfowl protection in the 1920s and a longtime ally of William Hornaday. "Now I am proud to say that I am a member of this society, yet I am disgustingly surprised to think that such a highly respected organization would issue a bulletin that has a tone upholding state laws privileging any individual to shoot over 2000 ducks and 800 wild geese in one year. . . . Yes, we all know that no sportsman will kill that amount of game in one year. Then why in the name of common sense do we leave that privilege open to those who will?"

Miner's broadside was one of many that were aimed at Gilbert Pearson during the last decade of his tenure as Audubon's leader. Pearson knew what to expect when Hornaday found fault with his conservation policies. But when the attack came from another quarter, with the arrival on the scene of an uncompromising New Yorker named Rosalie Edge, the way was paved for his eventual departure.

Although the Migratory Bird Treaty Act rigidly protected most North American species from hunting and made provisions to regulate the shooting of waterfowl and upland game birds, the changing times had introduced new problems into wildlife conservation. Pearson, devoted to the sanctuary system, was among the first to recognize them. Modern agriculture was draining the marshes and potholes in the northern states which had been the rich breeding grounds of untold millions of waterfowl. Federal regulations now protected ducks to some extent from hunters, but set aside no nesting grounds safe from reclamation projects.

The large-scale preservation of land for various waterfowl and marsh birds had been pretty much restricted to the bird reservations created by President Theodore Roosevelt in 1908. Two of the most important of the refuges lay in the Northwest. The sanctuary at Lower Klamath Lake in southern Oregon and northern California had come about in large part through the efforts of William Finley during the many years he acted on behalf of Audubon on the West Coast. Fifteen miles long and surrounded by extensive tule marshes, this lake flourished as a breeding bird colony after the Audubon Association provided a warden and a patrol boat for its protection. But during World War I, the U.S. Department of the Interior crumbled under pressure from powerful local agricultural groups that wanted the lake and its marshes drained for ranchland. When Pearson, who had seen the colonies of white pelicans, great blue herons, and ducks of many species in the marshes with Finley in 1915, visited the area again in the 1920s, he found that drainage and fire had completed the destruction. "I did not see a ranch, although I was told there were a few somewhere," he reported. "I saw only weeds—miles and miles of thickly growing weeds—and the only living creature we found was a scrawny venomous snake that crossed the road and paused by the wheel track to shake his rattles at the two perspiring men in the car. Farther on we came to open flats over which whirlwinds chased each other like ghosts of the wild life that had departed. In despair, almost in bitterness, I fled."

The same fate befell Malheur Lake (though it was partially reclaimed many years later), northeast of Klamath in Oregon. The struggle to preserve Malheur in 1920 was organized by Finley, who was both president of the Oregon Audubon Society and the western field agent for the Audubon Association. A last-ditch effort to prevent the drainage was made by Finley through a state initiative, for which Pearson had raised funds.

"If the people of the State voted our way the birds could keep their old home," Pearson remembered, "but if we lost the election, the lake was to be destroyed and its dried bed sold for the benefit of the State School Fund. Just before election, the would-be land developers widely distributed a card showing a picture of a little girl and a white pelican, which bore the legend, 'Vote for the Baby.' From all the feathered inhabitants of Malheur, our opponents cleverly chose the pelican on account of the popular prejudice against it as a fish-eating bird. An avalanche of adverse ballots lost us the Initiative election."

Wetlands were disappearing at an accelerating rate throughout the northern states and Canada. Waterfowl populations, after a brief resurgence under the new hunting regulations, began to decline again. There were calls from some conservationists, Hornaday prominent among them, to cut both bag limits and the length of the hunting season. But E. W. Nelson, Chief of the Biological Survey, saw no need to antagonize any further the nation's sportsmen, who already had been asked to accept what they considered to be drastic restrictions on their traditional

E. W. Nelson, Chief of the Bureau of Biological Survey,
and Talbot Denmead, Deputy Chief U.S. Game Warden, with
mounted birds and plumes seized by agents. NAS

hunting privileges. Added restrictions, he felt, might set off a rebellion
in Congress that would undo all of the gains achieved by recent legislation. Lining up behind Nelson were most of the members of the federal advisory board appointed to work with the Biological Survey "as
a liaison group between the government and the public." The group
included Pearson, John Burnham of the American Game Protective
Association, and the latter's unyielding foe, Bill Hornaday. Pearson believed that careful study by the experts, rather than sentimentality, should
guide the nation in making important decisions about wildlife.

"For nearly fifty years there has been an increasing volume of re-
strictive legislation on the killing of wild life," he lectured the readers
of *Bird-Lore* in 1925. "The vast majority of these laws have been of the
utmost importance, but in the minds of some people the idea prevails
that wild life of all kinds is continuing to decrease at an enormous rate,
and to save the so-called 'remnant' it is necessary to go on making more
laws and providing more restrictions. A certain element of our population even goes so far as to desire the total prohibition of killing of all
wild birds and animals. For the man or woman with refined sentiments,
to whom the killing of any bird is abhorrent, we should have the greatest

respect, but certainly it would be most unwise if such people should succeed in translating their feelings into legislative enactment."

Hornaday eventually moved away from Audubon on the waterfowl issue, perhaps largely because of his distrust of Burnham and the American Game Protective Association, which he liked to point out was "created and maintained by the manufacturers of guns, gunpowder and loaded cartridges." He had his own creation in high gear for the battle, funded by such luminaries as Henry Ford, George Eastman, Andrew Carnegie, and Mrs. Russell Sage, and called the Permanent Wild Life Protection Fund. "Societies may come and societies may go, but this Fund will go on forever," the old firebrand bragged.

The conflict, however, apparently helped Pearson to define the Audubon Association's philosophy and function, indeed its very identity, during the 1920s. He was strongly committed to professionalism, as his 1925 "lecture" to Bird-Lore's readers demonstrated; a passion for birds was all well and good, but decisions about whether certain species ought to be harvested for food or sport, and in what numbers, should be left to "those who by their long experience are in position to render expert advice on such subjects." In keeping with this philosophy, the board of directors of the Audubon Association was made up chiefly of men who were outstanding "scientific ornithologists," and the Association's field representatives were drawn from the same group. For instance, in the late 1920s, the board was composed of such names as Grinnell, Chapman, Palmer, Robert Cushman Murphy (the eminent seabird expert of the American Museum of Natural History), and Alexander Wetmore (once antagonistic to Audubon's cause), all well known in ornithological history. One of the few women to serve on the board during those years was Mabel Osgood Wright, herself a prominent writer on ornithology. Even E. H. Forbush rejoined the Audubon fold in 1928 as the Association's paid agent in New England, his grievance forgotten against the board of directors for its refusal to take a strong stand on the spring-shooting issue.

Pearson, although he had come to New York by way of an active state society, had long since ceased to think of the National Association of Audubon Societies as a federation. As the end of the decade approached, there were 125 state and local organizations affiliated by membership with the Association, but the important decisions were made by Pearson and the small group of professionals who sat on the board of directors. The grass-roots contingent was left largely to its own devices. Pearson articulated the Association's policy of centralization in Bird-Lore in 1929.

"In the early days we dreamed of numerous local groups organized into state societies and these all supporting the National office," he wrote. "It was found easy to organize Audubon Societies in almost any community, for in every town and city there were those to whom the subject of wild-life preservation made a strong appeal. It was soon discovered, however, that in those days such groups formed by external stimulus usually could be kept alive only by the same means. We, therefore, abandoned the idea of urging people to form Audubon Societies, and contented ourselves with giving such aid and support as we could to those that came into existence as local undertakings. We felt that our mission could better be developed by building strongly the central organization."

By 1927, the waterfowl crisis was deepening. Vast areas of marshland were being lost to agriculture, while the Biological Survey had almost no money to hire wardens on the areas where ducks still congregated; as ducks and geese crowded into available refuges, they often fell victim to botulism and other diseases. The Biological Survey's E. W. Nelson reported an enormous increase in the illegal sales of wildfowl, a development he attributed to the example of the bootlegging of whiskey under the Volstead Act. "The same men who are bootlegging liquor bootleg ducks," Nelson told a Senate committee.

Nelson and the members of his advisory board, including Pearson and Burnham, soon came to the conclusion that bag limits would have to be reduced, though they also carried on a campaign for a land-acquisition program. But federal agencies and Congress remained indifferent until 1928, when new legislation called the Norbeck-Andresen Bill (after its sponsors, Senator Peter Norbeck of South Dakota and Representative August H. Andresen of Minnesota) began to move through Congress. The bill provided for the purchase of wetlands by the federal government for use as waterfowl refuges. Pearson remained even more active than usual during the next year, rounding up support all over the country among both Audubon members and professional wildlife managers. A valuable ally turned out to be the General Federation of Women's Clubs, which inspired a deluge of letters and telegrams to Congress. The bill was signed into law in 1929 and, shortly afterward, daily bag limits were reduced. Even with a scarcity of funds during the Depression years, the federal government bought more than a million acres of wetlands by 1934.

Hornaday, not satisfied that enough money was being appropriated for wetlands or that bag limits were being reduced fast enough, went on snapping at his fellow conservationists. He leaned too heavily on John Burnham, who sued him for libel in an action that Hornaday was obliged to settle out of court. The ramifications of Pearson's belated acceptance of lower bag limits (and of his disdain for the opinions of amateurs) were to have a more lasting effect.

In 1929, Senator Peter Norbeck of South Dakota (at left)
and Audubon president T. Gilbert Pearson (second from right)
came to the White House to urge President Calvin Coolidge
to sign the Norbeck-Andresen Bill. NAS

Rosalie Edge was once branded publicly by the National Association
of Audubon Societies as a "common scold," and was later called by a
colleague-in-arms "the only honest, unselfish, indomitable hellcat in the
history of conservation." If both parties were able to justify their descriptions of this native New Yorker who had strong ties across the
Atlantic, she did not in the least object. Rosalie Edge sailed almost without warning into the very center of the conservation establishment and
shook it by the scruff of its neck as no one else has before or since. After
forcing, by a series of dramatic confrontations, a change in the Audubon
leadership and almost destroying the organization in the process, she
went on to constructive achievements in the field of habitat conservation
from coast to coast.

Edge's early years might have been patterned on those of the heroine
of a fashionable turn-of-the-century novel. Her father was a first cousin
of Charles Dickens. Growing up in New York society with the obligatory
private school education, she met and married a British consulting engineer. But times were changing, and she with them. She was swept up

in the suffragist movement during World War I and quickly became adept in the techniques of persuasion, publicity, and confrontation.

Rosalie Edge was also a woman with an observant eye for the natural world. She began to watch the birds around her summer home in Rye, New York, and became a life member of the Audubon Association. After separating from her husband, she took a more active interest in conservation, birding in Central Park and scrutinizing Audubon policies. In the latter case, she was not pleased by what she saw.

There were a number of men and women in and around the Audubon movement at the end of the 1920s who would not have qualified, in Gilbert Pearson's eyes, as experts in wildlife matters but nonetheless shared Rosalie Edge's unease. They agreed with Bill Hornaday's assessment of the conservative stand taken by the Audubon Association during the campaign for waterfowl restoration.

"For too long have American bird conservationists been humbly meandering along behind the firing lines, picking up the cripples," Hornaday lamented. "To be sure, they are trying to 'save' them. They gather up the fragments of wildlife, 'band' it for reference purposes or pen it up and try to induce it to lay eggs and breed more gunfodder birds, for more shooting by more sportsmen and more crops of cripples."

Rosalie Edge fell in with a couple of like-minded Audubon members: a journalist named Irving Brant, and Willard Van Name, a scientist at the American Museum of Natural History. Both of them believed Pearson to be guilty of far worse crimes than conservatism, and began spreading abroad their suspicions that Pearson and the Audubon Association were in the pocket of the gun companies. When Edge came across a rather nasty little pamphlet by Van Name entitled "A Crisis in Conservation," in which he suggested that the Association "performed its work with inertia, incompetency and procrastination" because of that sinister entanglement, she joined them in battle and soon became their leader.

Those who met Rosalie Edge for the first time, after having read her broadsides, sometimes remarked that they were astonished to find that she was a "lady." It is said that she spoke in a voice that reminded others of Eleanor Roosevelt's, and *The New Yorker* once described her as dressing "with conservative elegance for office and for society, wearing black satin dresses, and hats with imposing superstructures compounded of things like bristles, fruit, flowers, nets and buckles"—of everything, it might be added, but plumes. She was totally serious about her crusade to preserve wildlife of all sorts, as she was soon to prove. And she was no figurehead for the Hornaday contingent, having the time, money, and above all the unlimited energy to pursue her case to the utmost.

In 1929, she appeared at the Audubon annual meeting, brandishing a copy of Van Name's pamphlet and demanding to know whether the charges in it were true. When she did not receive satisfactory answers she threw the meeting into an open debate, charging mismanagement and dereliction of duty by the Association's leaders. Pearson complained afterward that she "had spoiled the meeting and there was no time to show the motion picture which was to have been the feature of the morning."

In the manner of Hornaday, Edge formed her own organization, the Emergency Conservation Committee, which she operated from a tiny office, turning out pamphlets at a rate that put even her mentor to shame. In one of them, "Compromised Conservation," by Irving Brant, the old charges and some new ones were leveled against the Pearson-led Audubon Association. She fastened on what Pearson took to be a point in his favor, a consistent record of annual surpluses in the budget, and used it against him: why, when there remained many serious problems in bird protection, weren't these surpluses used to buy additional land and hire more wardens?

Pearson, who always prided himself on his conservative fiscal management as well as his fund-raising ability, once remarked that "one of the most pleasant sounds I ever hear is the clink of a life membership fee as it drops into the money box." Now Edge ferreted out tidbits that had never appeared in the Audubon Association's annual financial statements. Pearson, for many years, had not worked on a regular salary scale, but instead had taken a percentage of the Audubon Association's annual income. Carrying her attack to the annual meeting again in 1930, she forced the board of directors to appoint a committee, chaired by Thomas Barbour of the Harvard Museum of Comparative Zoology, to investigate her charges. The committee's eventual report cleared Pearson of any wrongdoing and referred to Edge and her supporters as a "zoophile cult." But, in an addition to the report for the directors' eyes only, the committee recommended that a tighter rein be put on Pearson and that he be paid a fixed wage. In 1931, for the first time, the president's salary showed up in the annual financial report as a part of the general operating statement and was specified as $14,500.

Meanwhile, Edge had asked Pearson for the Audubon Association's mailing list in order to send her various pamphlets to the membership at large. Pearson refused. She hired a lawyer and went to court to force the Association to disgorge it. After a bitter legal dispute, which was well publicized in the press, she walked away with the mailing list.

There was more grist for her mill in the months ahead. Edge shared Hornaday's distaste for the Biological Survey, which she liked to refer to as "the Bureau of Destruction and Extermination." In 1931, she unearthed further proof in Audubon's annual report of what she believed

Rosalie Edge in a moment of repose. COURTESY OF
HAWK MOUNTAIN SANCTUARY

was its collusion with the hated federal agency. Under the income credited to the Paul J. Rainey Fund, she found a line labeled "rentals of
sanctuary," and comparing the item for the years 1929 through 1931, saw
the rather substantial Depression-era sums of $16,234.46; $19,853.42;
and $15,714.40.

One can only imagine her grim satisfaction as the details slowly
unfolded themselves under her relentless questioning. Those innocuous
"rentals" she had noticed proved to be euphemisms masking receipts
paid to the Association by muskrat trappers; and further, the trappers
had plied their trade on the grounds of the Rainey Sanctuary. The figures
represented the Association's share from the sale of pelts of muskrats,
mink, raccoons, and opossums trapped in the sanctuary's marshes.

The whole affair had seemed innocent enough to Pearson and the
board of directors. The Rainey Sanctuary teemed with muskrats that fed
on plants preferred by the blue goose. Officials of the Biological Survey
who served on Audubon's board had recommended that the Association
reduce the muskrats' numbers by allowing local "marsh men" to come
in and trap them. Each man was assigned trapping plots, and Richard
Gordon, the sanctuary's superintendent, received commissions on the

sale of pelts in addition to his salary. The other board members accepted the plan because it promised to solve two nagging problems: there would be no "eat out" of the food supply for the blue goose, as the sanctuary staff feared, and the Association's treasury, already somewhat depleted because of the Depression, would receive a welcome infusion from its share of the proceeds. The decision was to be a costly one.

Rosalie Edge attended the next annual meeting at the American Museum and demanded a stop to the trapping of animals on an area designated as a wildlife sanctuary. She argued that steel traps are a particularly cruel method of dispatching living creatures. Pearson replied that the Audubon Association did not sanction the use of "ordinary" steel traps, but "the most humane device that has thus far been invented for killing animals." Then he produced what he believed to be his trump card, a letter from the sanctuary donor herself, Grace Rainey Rogers.

"I have been much pleased with the manner in which the National Association of Audubon Societies has administered the Paul J. Rainey Wild Life Sanctuary in Louisiana," she had written recently to Pearson. "In giving you this tract as a refuge, especially for wild Ducks and wild Geese, I realized the necessity of protecting the area, not only from human intrusion, but by limiting the numbers of muskrats and predatory animals on the Sanctuary. I am glad that because of a fortunate turn in the market in furs you have not been put to extra expense in controlling these destructive forms of wild life of the region, but have actually received an income from the fur which has made it possible for you adequately to guard the territory and increase the endowment which I was pleased to present to the Association some time after giving you the land."

The stipulation that Pearson had made sure was inserted into the deed for the property seemed now to him to clinch his case. But he had underestimated the powers of Rosalie Edge as a crusader and pamphleteer. The flood of literature from her office increased, distributed with the aid of the mailing list she had extracted from the Association, and with each barrage against the use of traps was included a request for contributions to Edge's Emergency Conservation Committee.

There is no doubt that some of the charges with which her literature bristled turned out to be low blows. For instance, Edge picked up the inaccurate claim by E. A. McIlhenny that Pearson had accepted membership in the gun club that had caused all the trouble a decade earlier in the Louisiana marshes. Pearson was able to prove that McIlhenny had used his and other prominent names without authorization when trying to organize his club; in fact, Pearson had tried to forestall the club's creation by making an offer for the property, and later going to Mrs.

Rogers to ask for a gift of land. Edge's charge that Pearson had used over three thousand dollars of the Association's operating funds to attend an annual meeting of the International Council for Bird Preservation in Switzerland in 1928 was also without foundation. Pearson, who was a founder of the ICBP, traveled on money contributed by people interested in the group's work.

For the next couple of years, Pearson did the best he could to defend himself against the succession of attacks launched by Edge. Although egged on by Hornaday, Brant, Van Name, and other foes of the Audubon leadership, she was very much an independent in action. She later had a falling-out with Van Name (who was the author of the statement quoted earlier about the "hellcat"); and her lawyer, C. D. Williams, withdrew as the Emergency Conservation Committee's counsel when he could no longer verify for himself many of the statements and figures used in its literature.

But Pearson was in trouble. He might argue that his earlier support for higher bag limits for waterfowl was supported by most of the experts on both scientific and political grounds. And he might produce, as he did, old treasurer's reports that showed gun-company contributions to the Audubon Association to have been insignificant. There remained those pamphlets sent out to the Audubon membership by Rosalie Edge, bearing the most unpleasant photographs imaginable of wild animals caught in steel traps of various types. It was the one issue that Pearson, the wildlife professional, could not turn aside. Men and women from all over the country let their memberships lapse; some joined the Emergency Conservation Committee.

Active members who stayed on were slowly changing the makeup of the board of directors. As the older professionals faded away, they were replaced by a new breed of Audubon activist, prominent among them Roger Baldwin of the American Civil Liberties Union and John Baker, an investment banker and ardent birdwatcher. The outspoken Baker was elected chairman of the board in 1933. Disturbed by a precipitous decline in membership since the attacks on Pearson had begun (more than half of the members had left, the number dwindling from about eighty-four hundred in 1929 to thirty-four hundred), and believing that Pearson had lost his effectiveness, Baker urged his dismissal. When Baldwin, Murphy, and even the venerable Frank Chapman sided with Baker, Pearson knew it was time to leave.

# 14

ohn Hopkinson Baker was a man for the times. In an era when many of the nation's conservation leaders were professionals in one or another of the natural sciences, Baker was a throwback in one sense to those earlier men and women for whom the study of the natural world began as a hobby and evolved into something much more. Baker could give the Audubon movement all of the skills of a practical businessman, yet he also knew how to attract as members the people who shared his enthusiasm for finding and identifying birds in the field.

Even in his youth, in the Boston area, he was a student of birdlife and a member of both the Nuttall Ornithological Club of Cambridge and the American Ornithologists' Union. After his graduation from Harvard, Baker flew with the U.S. Army during World War I and eventually became a successful investment counselor in New York. A tall, rugged man, blunt to the point of abrasiveness, he was a tireless field birder who also maintained a large farm in Dutchess County, New York, where he raised Aberdeen-Angus cattle. He was directly recruited for membership on the Audubon Association's board in 1933 after having proved himself a knowledgeable conservationist as president of the Linnaean Society of New York.

Gilbert Pearson's resignation was accepted at the annual meeting of the Audubon Association on October 30, 1934. The board, now dominated by Baker, made a dual choice, electing Kermit Roosevelt as the Association's new president and Baker its executive director. On drafting as their titular leader a son of the man who had championed conservation, and indeed popularized the word itself, during his terms in the White House early in the century, the directors were attempting to restore prestige to the organization's name. Kermit Roosevelt, another Harvard graduate, was a glamorous figure in his own right, having taken part with his father in hazardous expeditions to East Africa and South America and compiled a distinguished military record during World

War I. Since the war, he had made other expeditions to remote places, written several popular books, and been elected to various offices in such organizations as the New York Zoological Society.

But it seems to have been understood from the beginning that even such a personage must take a back seat to Baker in Audubon affairs. Baker, then forty years old, was to direct the organization on a day-to-day basis, being well able to give up his investment business and make do with an Audubon paycheck. The board created a new title, president-emeritus, for Pearson and gave him an office in the cramped quarters at 1974 Broadway. There, the older man (on awful terms with his successor) carried on his work with the International Council for Bird Preservation and began writing his memoirs.

If Pearson went rather quietly, Rosalie Edge did not. Baker ordered an immediate halt to the trapping at Rainey, but the change in leadership which Edge had looked forward to gave rise to new bitterness. It centered on a mountainous area in eastern Pennsylvania which had long been a notorious graveyard for migrating hawks. Each fall, hundreds of gunners took up stations on the rocky outcrops along a spur on the Kittatinny Ridge and fired at the "varmints" as they drifted by almost at eye level. The carcasses were left to rot in the woods nearby.

Edge, learning of the annual slaughter, demanded that the Audubon Association do something about it. When Baker and the Audubon board failed to act promptly, she took an option to buy the key shooting area. Only then did Baker begin to move, hoping to acquire the land as an Audubon sanctuary, but it was too late. Edge raised the necessary funds, bought the land, and established it as one of the most famous of all independent refuges, the Hawk Mountain Sanctuary. Rosalie Edge, triumphant and with her Audubon life membership intact, proceeded to other good causes, which included providing vital funds and propaganda for the creation of Olympic National Park in Washington.

Baker's procrastination in the Hawk Mountain affair was a mistake he did not repeat. Although always businesslike, he acted with great force in seizing for Audubon what he thought would be good for it, even if it meant stepping on the toes of others. He was not as interested in the legislative aspects of conservation as his predecessor, though he was to be effective in that area when he needed to be. Baker believed that a great deal could be accomplished through education, especially of children and schoolteachers, and this program remained a high priority during the twenty-five years in which he led and transformed the Audubon Association. Beyond that, he acted on his belief that birds must be studied as well as protected if they were to survive in the modern world.

Audubon president John Baker (left) touring Florida Bay
with warden Ray Barnes in 1941. NAS

He began building a remarkable staff of educators, researchers, and wildlife wardens—a mix of idiosyncratic talent sometimes bordering on genius—that characterized the Audubon movement for decades to come.

One of those Audubon prototypes was Robert Porter Allen, who gave the research department a vision and, eventually, a home. Almost symbolically, he had been born in 1905, the year the Audubon Association was founded. As a boy in rural Pennsylvania he explored the nearby mountain country, and a reading of Ernest Thompson Seton's *Two Little Savages* at the age of ten confirmed his craving for all things untamed and remote. Birds were his passion. He joined a Junior Audubon Club, described himself as a "Seton Indian," and used his first paycheck from the National Guard to buy himself a pair of binoculars. Allen was somewhat untamed himself. He grew into a stocky, dark-haired man, gentle and humorous, but also one who lived as hard as he worked. It could be said of Allen, as Dr. Johnson had said of the poet Richard Savage, that "at no time of his life was it any part of his character to be the first of his company that desired to separate."

An outdoorsman to the core, Bob Allen fretted under organized scholarship, and his higher education was limited to a couple of brief sojourns at Lafayette College and Cornell. Adventurous young men in the 1920s seemed to choose between the life of a hobo and that of a sailor, and Allen opted for the sea. He sailed on freighters for three years, at one point suffering shipwreck in the Sulu Sea. Back in the United States, he married, then pursued his interest in birds by visiting Audubon's headquarters at 1974 Broadway and talking Gilbert Pearson into giving him a job sorting books and performing other menial chores. Pearson soon made him the Association's librarian. In 1931, Allen visited Maine's offshore islands and surveyed the first known nesting colonies in the United States of the great black-backed gull. As someone once said of Allen, sending him into the field was like "ordering a duck back to water." He displayed both imagination and tenacity in every undertaking that had to do with birds. In 1934, he grew a mustache (to make himself look older, it was rumored) and the board of directors, then led by Baker, was sufficiently impressed to make him director of the Association's sanctuaries.

Audubon's sanctuary system was still in flux. The Maine islands, which had been the focus of Dutcher's interest at the turn of the century, were at the bottom of John Baker's priorities. The gulls, terns, and eiders had made heartening comebacks under bird-protection laws; in the herring gull's case, the comeback was so complete that this opportunistic species had become something of a nuisance, fattening on the wastes at garbage dumps and fish piers, raiding the blueberry fields, and driving common and Arctic terns from the islands where they had traditionally

Robert Porter Allen (left) and Alexander Sprunt, Jr., in an
informal moment on the Maine coast in 1936. NAS

nested. Gradually, Audubon's presence on the Maine islands had been
phased out.

The Texas islands, on the other hand, became the apple of Baker's
eye. Right from the beginning, following the signing of leases with the
state's General Land Office in 1923, the Audubon Association was fortunate in securing the help of a number of able guardians. The first of
them was R. D. Camp, an experienced coastal boatman and "a most
intelligent and enthusiastic field naturalist," according to Pearson. Operating out of his home in Brownsville, Camp checked a number of
colonies along the southern coast, put up warning signs, talked to local
newspaper editors so that people would know what he was up to, and
wrote detailed reports which he sent on to New York.

Green Island, east of Brownsville and the most southerly of the important Texas wading-bird colonies, was the key to the preservation of
the reddish egret. Several thousand adults inhabited the island in the
breeding season. Camp's area, which included various islands in Laguna
Madre and Bahia Grande, as well as the Laguna Muerto (a large island
marsh in Cameron County), contained some of the most vital concen-
trations of birds then nesting in the United States. That year Camp
estimated he was guarding 3,000 Louisiana herons, 600 great blue herons, 180 snowy egrets, and several thousand terns of various species.

Near the end of Camp's report, however, there was an ominous note that the valuable work he had been carrying on for five years was coming to an end.

"Due to a disagreeable attack of rheumatism at the particular part of the season that such work can be carried on," he wrote, "there were no birds banded at any of the reservations this year, as your warden was confined to quarters for something over a month."

Several hundred miles to the north there was a man with the will and the means to carry on Camp's work, and indeed to hold together the bird-protection movement along most of the Texas coast. James J. Carroll was a wealthy lumberman in Houston who became interested in photographing birds and developed a passion for protecting their breeding colonies. He performed his most valuable services during the late 1920s and early 1930s when the Audubon Association's financial and human resources were at a low ebb. Carroll took it upon himself to visit the islands along the coast, pinpointing the most important breeding colonies and recording the shifting around of those colonies in response to the changes in habitat brought about by storms in the shallow bays or man's dredging and draining projects. (These projects have had a tremendous influence on birdlife along the Texas coast in recent decades, the birds often abandoning their natural nesting places to take up new quarters on the spoil islands heaped up by the dredgers, then moving on again as storms and currents wash away the man-made habitat.)

Once he had found a thriving new colony, or one that seemed to be in trouble because of human molestation, Carroll immediately arranged for its protection, choosing reliable local men as wardens and paying their salaries out of his own pocket until the Audubon Association was able to assume the obligation. Commercial fishermen were still a problem, as they robbed the nests of heron squabs with which to bait their crab traps, or even burned the vegetation on the islands to provide large open areas for drying and mending their nets. Occasionally an unregenerate plume hunter picked off a few birds and disposed of the nuptial plumes in Mexican markets. Carroll, a photographer himself, recognized that the new hobby of nature photography presented special problems for bird protection, practitioners often landing on the islands and keeping the adults off the nests while the eggs or helpless young broiled under the sun's glare.

To replace the ailing R. D. Camp, Carroll arranged in 1928 for John O. Larson of Harlingen to serve as the Audubon warden on strategic Green Island. Larson, who had retired from the Navy, was one of the great Audubon wardens, serving on six-acre Green Island, almost at the mouth of the Rio Grande, for many years, living in a shanty with his wife and three children through the intense heat of late spring and summer until the last of the young egrets had fledged. Alexander Sprunt, Jr., who became the director of Audubon's southern sanctuaries in 1935, has described Larson:

"Green Island was reached by a very leaky skiff which possessed an outboard motor which very seldom operated, so it had to be pulled and rowed the quarter of a mile from the mainland to the island. When you landed there, it was without a doubt the most densely grown and thickest island I have ever been on. Now, Larson had a cabin there surmounted by a watch tower, and he with his sons had cut trails through that dense growth that were about two and a half feet wide, curving here and there among these bushes in which the birds nested, and you could not possibly take two steps away from those little narrow trails no matter what you wanted to do. You were just hemmed in.

"I think John would come pretty near being about as dedicated a man as you could very well describe or find in any job. Everything they bought had to be bought ashore, and to pole or jerk that little motorboat across and carry every stitch they had bought in town and over those trails and into the cabin—it was a chore! Even then, when I was a good deal younger, I didn't see how the man would ever make it. And never a complaint and never a 'this is a hell of a life' or anything like that. Everybody down in that section supported him—respected him and left his island alone. Of course, they knew that was the thing to do, because they knew John would never tolerate any infringement of his rules. But he never exceeded his authority. He was a man who knew when to say 'stop that' and not to pile it on."

While Larson's presence on Green Island kept human disturbance at a minimum, it was by no means a certain defense against depredations by other species. The island nesting colonies along the Texas coast are often vulnerable to four-legged predators such as raccoons and coyotes, which easily cross long stretches of shallow bays or make their way from one sandbar to another. Larson had to be alert for these forays. The boat-tailed grackles were a more constant threat, building their nests in the thickets beside those of the various herons and egrets. While such birds as the great blue heron, the great egret, and the black-crowned night heron usually defended their nests, the grackles found Louisiana herons and the snowy and reddish egrets less tenacious. Eyewitnesses tell of watching a grackle land on the nest of one of the smaller egrets, peck at the bird until it left, and then break and eat its eggs.

Larson harassed the grackles with a .22 rifle. In 1934, while Rosalie Edge was pressing her militant campaign to ban the trapping of muskrats on the Rainey sanctuary, Larson received orders from New York to 'stop shooting grackles. Apparently he resumed his war against those predators "unofficially" the next year, however, because Alex Sprunt

Alexander Sprunt dines at Lake Okeechobee, Florida.

PHOTO BY EDWIN WAY TEALE, NAS

wrote to the New York office recommending that the Audubon Association buy a silencer for Larson's old rifle.

"Silencers are not on the market to the ordinary buyer," Sprunt noted, "but should be procurable through the right channels. Gangsters have no trouble in getting them!"

Carroll also arranged for the protection of other breeding sites farther north. The Second Chain of Islands in San Antonio Bay was the home of the largest roseate spoonbill colony in the United States, while on the Vingt-et-un Islands in Galveston Bay there was another important spoonbill refuge. Lydia Ann Island near Port Aransas, on which Carroll found no nesting birds in 1934, had 800 adult reddish egrets in June 1939, as well as 500 Louisiana herons and 3,000 laughing gulls, while 200 spoonbills fed alongside the shorebirds in the island's sloughs and ponds.

Because most of these islands were too small and exposed for human habitation, Carroll arranged for wardens to keep an eye on them from their boats. Louis Rawalt began guarding North Bird and South Bird Islands near Corpus Christi in 1931.

"I was living on Padre Island at the time," Rawalt, a small, wiry, sharp-faced man, once told an Audubon staff member, "and the first couple of years I watched the islands for free, just going out in my sailboat and taking a look. But in 1933 Robert Porter Allen came down from the Audubon office in New York and agreed to pay me fifty dollars for the season as long as I furnished the boat. Later he also got me appointed a federal deputy game warden. I didn't get any salary for that, but it gave me leverage in dealing with people. At first the local people were a little suspicious because they were fishing illegally, but I made a deal with them—I wouldn't tell on them if they left my birds alone."

South Bird Island's treasure was its colony of white pelicans, the only one in the southern United States. According to Rawalt, there were just thirty-one pelicans nesting on the island (which is a half-mile long and 1,500 feet wide) in 1931, but under protection the colony grew to 1,500 birds in a decade. A variety of herons also nested among the treeless island's yucca and prickly pear. Rawalt, believing motors were undependable, used a sailboat in the early days to reach the island. He planted salt cedars and other trees, but none grew, a failure he attributed to the underlying salt water.

By the middle 1930s, Baker, Alex Sprunt, Bob Allen, and others from the Audubon staff were paying frequent visits to the Texas coast. The flourishing colonies of roseate spoonbills and reddish egrets were a constant source of fascination for them, and they kept close check on the birds' progress. The struggling winter colony of whooping cranes, which was mostly confined to the federal refuge at Aransas, was another point of extreme interest in the area.

Not the least of the satisfactions that were part of a trip to Texas were the comforts provided by J. J. Carroll. An Audubon representative was generally whisked by Carroll in his expensive automobile from Houston to Port Lavaca, where he kept his boat. This craft was unlike any other of which the Audubon staff had any experience as they visited bird colonies; their lot was usually to end up in a cramped, leaky boat powered by a tiny motor of uncertain durability, a craft open to storms and whatever noxious insects the region had to offer. Carroll's boat was the *Drifter*, forty-five feet long, powered by twin screws, and cared for by a crew of three. The well-appointed cabin has been described as "luxurious," and was dominated by the painting of a buxom nude. Although in failing health, Carroll remained enthusiastic about the expeditions, and his companions marveled at his dexterity with a large Graflex camera despite a paralyzed right arm.

Carroll died in 1938 at the age of sixty-one. At his request, his ashes were spread from a low-flying plane over the Second Chain of Islands; and in June of that year Baker, Sprunt, Mrs. Carroll, and her three daughters went on the *Drifter* to one of those islands (already named for him) to erect among the phragmites a bronze tablet set in concrete to his memory. The Audubon sanctuaries on the Texas coast had proved a reservoir from which many of the endangered wading birds might return to their former habitats in other parts of the United States.

# 15

From the very first day of his administration, John Baker worked to build an elite staff at headquarters, strengthening the Audubon Association's hand in avian research, nature education, and the protection of nesting colonies. He created, in effect, an in-house youth movement. The newcomers were mainly naturalists in their twenties and thirties, aglow with energy and idealism, and in the words of the man who was to go on from there to become the country's best-known ornithologist, "literally missionaries who worked for almost nothing because they loved it." Both the spirit and the modest cost fitted the demanding Baker perfectly. In pursuing this course, he filled the office, then at 1775 Broadway, with the most extraordinary and idiosyncratic group of bird-conscious young men ever assembled under one roof.

There was an ironic touch to the new order at Audubon headquarters. A complaint of Gilbert Pearson's critics was that, as chief operating officer, he ran a one-man show, surrounding himself in New York mainly with stenographers and office boys. Baker, on his part, filled his limited office space with virtuoso performers, but the operating style did not change; he was far more of an autocrat than Pearson and managed his supporting cast of individualists with an iron hand.

Baker demanded that every decision, even one that might smack of triviality, be made at the top. He minded the store almost around the clock, for he appeared in the office early in the morning and worked late into the evening before walking uptown to his apartment on Fifth Avenue. Audubon office employees must have been among the last in New York to work on Saturdays (until 1:00 P.M.) because Baker insisted that nothing could be accomplished in a five-day week. Some of his employees were afraid of him. He seemed to them cold and aloof, having no small talk and invariably getting right down to brass tacks in his overbearing Boston accent.

Rather pathetically, Pearson was squirreled away in an office on the fringes of what was becoming for him an alien enterprise. Because the Audubon Association had not had a pension plan in his day, the board of directors granted him a stipend and office space so he could carry on his work in international bird protection, though he had to raise money elsewhere for a secretary. Other staff members, not wishing to endanger their own prospects with Baker, tended to avoid the office outcast.

That Baker began to build a prestigious staff did not mean he was throwing money away on salaries; in that respect he remained as parsimonious as Pearson. But he believed, with Rosalie Edge, that people gave money through memberships and contributions to organizations and that it ought to be spent on the purposes for which that organization was founded. "We should spend what we have, and a little more besides," Baker once confided to an aide. "That way we can go out in good conscience and ask for more." He would spend most of it in the field, and if professionals would come and work "for almost nothing," that was an added benefit.

Baker's prize catch was Roger Tory Peterson. This moody but talented young man, who eventually took birdwatching out of the hands of a small group of alleged eccentrics and made it a national pastime, had sharpened his skills in the wilds of New York City's Bronx County. There he ran with a loosely affiliated band of thoroughly absorbed youths who referred to themselves as the Bronx County Bird Club (the BCBC to all involved).

During the late 1920s the Borough of the Bronx, which is to the north and east of Manhattan Island, had not yet been attacked by urban blight. It was largely suburban in aspect, occupied by comfortable apartment houses and well-kept, even luxurious, homes. There were salt marshes, old estates, and abundant parkland, some of the most inviting of which for both birds and birders being Van Cortlandt Park in the northern part of the borough. This park was truly an entity in those days, before four-lane highways carved it into isolated islands, and it had as its centerpiece (now partly obliterated by a golf course) a marsh that was rich in plants and birdlife. John Kieran, the nature writer and radio sage who sometimes joined the BCBC members on their outings, remembered them birding in the park.

"Often I heard and saw them going a-whoopin' and a-hollerin' through the cattail region of the Van Cortlandt marsh, clapping hands loudly at the same time," Kieran wrote. "The din was supposed to— and frequently did—stir up rails that might otherwise be left unseen amid the cattails and marsh grasses."

Nine young men formed the BCBC's core. Among them were Joseph J. Hickey, later professor of wildlife management at the University of Wisconsin and a president of the American Ornithologists' Union, and Allan Cruickshank, who was to become a prominent nature photographer and a popular Audubon lecturer. They spent almost all of their time away from jobs or school in dashing across the city's five boroughs and beyond, tracking down rare birds and rumors thereof, indulging in gamesmanship and the finer points of identification, and in the end revolutionizing the way people go out and look at birds. The individual members and the way they went on to glorify their sport created an atmosphere which attracted thousands of men and women to conservation and ultimately to an Audubon membership.

The BCBC never had a titular leader. But they met regularly at the home of one of the boys near the Harlem River to talk long into the night about birds and question each other sharply about controversial sightings. The one established club to which they belonged was the Linnaean Society of New York.

"The Linnaean meetings were held at the American Museum of Natural History, and that's where we met Roger Peterson when he first came to New York," Joe Hickey once recalled. "He went out with us, and he was always talking about the birds he had seen back in his home town, Jamestown, New York. So we called him Roger Tory Jamestown Peterson. But we let him into our club, anyway."

Although the club members haunted green spaces such as parks, the Bronx Zoo, and the Bronx Botanical Garden, they did not neglect the seamier side of the city.

"We were addicted to the Hunt's Point Dump in the Bronx, and one winter we found four snowy owls feeding there on the rats," Peterson remembered. "But the best place for gulls was a sewer outlet at 92nd Street in Brooklyn. We even found European species such as black-headed and little gulls. You know, the city ruined a lot of good birding places when they cleaned up those dumps and sewers."

Roger Peterson was another product of an "imbuer," a schoolteacher who encouraged his interest in birds and brought him into a Junior Audubon Club. In his case, the teacher was a young woman named Blanche Hornbeck, and the place a seventh-grade classroom in Jamestown, which Peterson had entered as a withdrawn and often rebellious eleven-year-old boy. He had paid his ten cents for membership in the club, received an enameled Audubon pin with a red-winged blackbird's portrait on it, and ten leaflets dealing with common birds. He wasn't much interested at his age in coloring in the outline drawings of birds that came with the material. But when Miss Hornbeck suggested he copy some paintings of birds by Louis Agassiz Fuertes, she stirred his interest more than she had expected to, and he discovered that he had a talent for drawing.

Two of the more colorful figures in Audubon history,
Robert Porter Allen and Roger Tory Peterson.

PHOTO BY DOROTHY DINGLEY, NAS

Behind that talent lay a growing fascination for the birds he had begun to notice everywhere around him.

"Birds seemed to me to reflect some kind of life force," Peterson once said. "Every outstanding ornithologist I know felt much the same way at an early age. After school I was interested in nothing else. The natural world became my *real* world. I remember going to the library and dragging home E. H. Eaton's *Birds of New York* in a little wagon. When I saw a new bird, it was a special day for me. I still know my grandmother's birthday because I saw my first cardinal on that date.

"Birds are associated with almost every event in my life. I suppose you could say I have even acquired my culture through birds. I went to the Acropolis in Athens primarily to see the rock nuthatches there. My memories of Versailles are bound up with a grasshopper warbler I saw near the reflecting pool. I can hear birds anywhere—over the conversation at a cocktail party, or in the midst of traffic in a city."

After leaving high school, Peterson brought both his talent and his passion for birds to New York, where he studied at the Art Students League and, later, at the National Academy of Design. To support himself, he painted little Chinese figures on furniture in a Bronx factory.

Spending his spare time in places where birds congregated, he became acquainted with several other young men who shared his interest. One of them was Robert Porter Allen, who recalled Peterson in the late 1920s as a morose figure, hanging out in a greasy-spoon restaurant in Greenwich Village, joylessly playing a pinball machine until the early hours of the morning. At parties, Peterson rarely spoke unless the conversation came around to birds.

"Roger was being consciously anti-social," Allen wrote to a friend years later, "which meant he was still maturing, still adjusting to a world he felt was all wrong. It was especially difficult for him, because he was farther away from it than most of us are to begin with."

Peterson found real stimulation, and the competition he had always craved, in his outings with the Bronx County Bird Club. "Each one of us tried to outdo the other—in listing the most species, or finding the first spring migrants, or even imitating bird calls," Peterson said. "We bought an old Buick for fifty dollars and drove all over the city and the suburbs to find birds."

Although the BCBC had no officers, its guiding spirit was an older man named Ludlow Griscom. Reputedly the finest birder of his day, Griscom was assistant curator of ornithology at the American Museum when he became acquainted with the BCBC members. They did their best to emulate his wizardry in the field and quickly improve their accuracy under his stern cross-examination.

"Ludlow was our God, and his *Birds of the New York City Region* became our bible," Peterson was later to write of him. "We could recite chapter and verse and even adopted his inflections when we pronounced a bird to be 'unprecedented' or a 'common summer resident.' John Kuerzi, one of our group, even adopted the Griscom hair-do, parting his own hair in the center."

Before Griscom, professional ornithologists did not believe that many of the smaller birds could be distinguished with any certainty in the field. Identification could be clinched only with a shotgun. The bird's presence was established by terminating its existence. Yet, by the 1920s, improved binoculars had enabled experienced field observers like Griscom to sort out even the migrating fall warblers in their drab plumages. All the BCBC crowd had scraped together the money for binoculars, Peterson acquiring a pair of four-power LeMaire glasses for seven dollars after seeing an ad for them in *Bird-Lore.*

Peterson has never disguised his debt to Ludlow Griscom. The older man emphasized field marks to identify birds at a distance—the thickening of a bill, the glint of a wingbar, the flash of color in the tail, the bright patch on throat or rump. Peterson noted Griscom's pointers and, because of his training as an artist, decided to put them down on paper. He made patternistic sketches of the more difficult birds, indicating the diagnostic markings with little arrows, and took them into the field with him for his own use. Those were the drawings that would turn bird-watching into a supersport.

The culmination of each year for the BCBC, the moment of exhilaration for all those youths who relished the game of listing birds, was Audubon's Christmas Bird Count. Before the middle 1920s, most of those counts had been made by small, uncoordinated parties fanning out over the countryside. The Bronx contingent changed the nature of the event, orchestrating the effort as if it were a military campaign. In 1924, the BCBC listed only forty-nine species on the Bronx Count. But the members replotted their count area to include the southern parts of Westchester County, and their totals began to inch upward toward the magic "century mark."

"We took great delight in competing against all the other bird clubs in the region—against the older ornithologists and the businessmen," Hickey remembered. "Those fellows would be at work during the week, but we would get out of classes early and make detailed surveys of the whole area, just as the better count leaders do today. We would stake out certain birds and assign observers to go [to a certain spot] on the appointed day and find them."

In November 1927, when Peterson was out of town, Hickey sent him a note with the latest news.

"The gang is beginning to round up a lot of 'sure things' for the coming Christmas Census," Hickey wrote. "Our 'Old Faithful,' the Arctic Woodpecker, is back in the Hemlocks at the Botanical Gardens, and 3 Goshawks have been seen in the Bronx, and the usual line-up of ducks. [Irving] Kassoy is keeping tabs on Todd's Neck, the Kuerzis [John and Dick] at Kensico, [Richard] Herbert at Rye, and Cruickie [Allan Cruickshank] at Van. The rest of us get out when we can and help fill in the gaps."

On a chilly, misty morning in the winter of 1930, several BCBC members set out in the communal Buick to look for eagles and canvasbacks along the Hudson River. A newcomer to the group was William Vogt, who had written some drama criticism and served as director of the Jones Beach State Bird Sanctuary. Peterson showed Vogt his patternistic sketches.

"Bill was quite excited about them," Peterson recalled later. "He thought they were very helpful, and he urged me to write a bird guide. I didn't take him seriously at first, but he kept after me. Finally, I put my drawings together, and Bill offered to take the guide around to some book editors he knew. Five of them turned it down, so I got it back from Bill and brought it to Houghton Mifflin in Boston."

The Great Depression having put an end to Peterson's courses in art school, he found a job teaching art and natural history at a boys' school in Brookline, Massachusetts. He had become acquainted with one of the editors at Houghton Mifflin, an enthusiastic birder named Francis H. Allen. Allen helped him organize the guide.

"A couple of the other editors there liked the guide well enough, but they didn't have much confidence in it," Peterson has said. "They didn't give me any advance payment, and since making the plates was an added investment for them, they didn't pay me any royalties on the first one thousand copies sold, either. They printed a first edition of two thousand copies."

The first edition of A *Field Guide to the Birds* (it included only those species found in the eastern United States) appeared in April 1934. It sold out within a week. Five thousand additional copies were printed and sold almost as quickly. The success of the guide can be traced to the plates, which characterize what has come to be called "The Peterson System of Identification." Each plate contains a group of related species, two-dimensional birds perched on abbreviated twigs. Slender black pointers indicate the features (patch of color, shape of bill, crest, etc.) by which the bird "tells its name." The text includes basic information on each bird's voice, range, and habitat.

John Baker, an enthusiastic birdwatcher himself, knew of Peterson's abilities as a naturalist and artist (they were both members of the Linnaean Society of New York), and on November 1, 1934, his first day as executive director, he added him to the Audubon Association's staff. Peterson became the Association's educational director, as well as the art director of *Bird-Lore.* From then on, the images of birds that entered the consciousness of a vast number of Americans became those painted by Roger Peterson and reproduced in his succession of field guides, in *Bird-Lore*, or in the leaflets distributed through the Junior Audubon clubs.

Until Peterson's arrival at the Audubon Association, most of the leaflets had been written by William Dutcher or Gilbert Pearson. Now Peterson visited various classrooms and museums in the Northeast to evaluate the impact of the leaflets and the Audubon educational program. Teachers reported that the illustrations were fine, but the text was stodgy and often too difficult for children. After he had talked over his findings with Baker, Peterson redesigned the leaflets (the old Audubon instinct for pamphleteering was still alive!), preparing two editions of each to appeal to separate audiences, one set for children nine and under, the other for older students.

The vigorous new educational program succeeded. Annual junior memberships, which had sagged in recent years, sprang back to pre-Depression levels as over six hundred thousand children signed up in the first four years of the new administration. By the time Peterson left Audubon early in World War II, Baker could boast that more than nine million American children had held membership in the Audubon Junior clubs since their inception in 1910. Many of the former members were already playing major roles in the modern Audubon movement.

# 16

$\mathcal{R}$oger Peterson was soon at work with two other additions to Baker's team on an innovative venture into conservation education. The newcomers were Allan Cruickshank and Carl Buchheister.

Cruickshank, like Peterson and Bob Allen, had been a member of a Junior Audubon Club. While still a high school student in the Bronx, where he grew up, he wrote an article for *Bird-Lore* and received a complimentary letter about it from the world-famous biologist Julian Huxley. A tall, handsome, athletic youngster, he practiced tumbling and gymnastics mainly for the purpose of climbing to hard-to-reach birds' nests. He invested his summer savings in a four-by-five Graflex camera, joined the enthusiastic young men of the Bronx County Bird Club on their expeditions, and soon was recognized as one of the area's outstanding birders.

"Cruickie," as his friends called him, developed an even more recondite skill: he rivaled Frank Chapman in his ability to imitate birds. (The younger man's specialty was an imitation of the American bittern, or "thunder pumper," making love in the marshes.) Combining his skills after moving to Long Island, Cruickshank became a popular lecturer, showing his slides and voicing his variety of whistles, cackles, hoots, and shrieks to delighted audiences. Baker added him to the Audubon staff, where, for much of the year, he lectured in the educational program or came to the office to answer the many letters and phone calls about birds.

"He often gave up to four lectures a day in various schools, and the schools might be some distance apart," his wife, Helen, recalled. "I taught him how to drive a car. He didn't know how to drive, and neither did Roger Peterson or Bob Allen—they all grew up in city situations!"

Aware of a growing opportunity to use such lectures for their promotional and educational value, Baker urged Peterson to make public appearances too. The debut of perhaps the most popular natural-history lecturer of his time was hardly auspicious. Cruickshank had arranged for Peterson to lecture on birds at the Brooklyn Academy of Music, the lecture to be followed by a Douglas Fairbanks movie. Color slides had not yet been developed, and so Peterson hand-colored his glass slides for the program. Unfortunately, he had prepared too much material about the bird he first wanted to talk about—the chestnut-sided warbler.

"Pretty soon I could hear the kids in the audience giggling," Peterson has recalled. "While I was up there talking, the slide was melting in the hot projector because I hadn't used heat-resistant paint to color it. Somehow I got through my slides until the climax of the program, which was a demonstration of bird calls. I was to imitate a bird and Cruickshank, planted in the balcony, would call back to me. We began with a screech owl. Suddenly all the kids began to whistle and yodel too, and the lecture ended in an uproar."

The two men put on more successful programs on Long Island, several of them at the Lawrence School in Hewlett, which had a flourishing natural-history club. This club had been organized by the school's Latin teacher, Carl W. Buchheister. A native of Maryland, Buchheister had studied the classical languages at Johns Hopkins University and later divided his year between teaching at this private school and operating his own summer boys' camp. He had never lost his own youthful fascination for the natural world and led hikes and bird trips whenever he had the opportunity. ("I had a life list of only thirty birds," Buchheister admitted years later, "but I made good use of every one of them.") He was ripe for John Baker's newest plan.


The Audubon name had been associated with the Maine coast since William Dutcher's time. By the 1930s, however, after a series of legislative and enforcement victories had stimulated a remarkable revival of bird colonies there, the ties had loosened. Then, in 1935, Baker was approached by Millicent Todd Bingham, a geographer and author, whose book *Ancestors' Brocades* was an important scholarly study of Emily Dickinson. She was the part owner of Hog Island in Muscongus Bay, Maine. A previous owner had built an inn and a cluster of buildings among rich stands of spruce and balsam on the island's northern peninsula.

"My dream for the island," Mrs. Bingham wrote long afterward, "was that it might be an outside research laboratory where scientific investigations could be carried on to aid man's knowledge of the natural world, and also that might serve to open the eyes of those who had never been aware of the world in which they lived."

She brought her plan to the Audubon Association and met Baker, who responded with enthusiasm. A firm believer in the benefits of going to nature itself for firsthand study, Baker had been searching for a suit-

Allan Cruickshank went to great lengths to
photograph an eagle's nest. NAS

able place for an Audubon camp. Mrs. Bingham leased the island to the Audubon Association for one dollar a year. (In 1960 she presented the island's deed to the National Audubon Society.) A friend of hers (but no relation), Dr. James M. Todd, bought the remainder of Hog Island and gave it outright to the Association. Baker decided to open the first Audubon camp there in the summer of 1936, dedicated to the idea of conservation education for adults, and began a search for a camp director.

Bill Vogt, who had urged Roger Peterson to write a bird guide, now had another suggestion that would have an impact on the Audubon movement. Remembering Carl Buchheister and the nature club that he brought regularly to Jones Beach State Park, Vogt recommended him to Baker. Baker invited Buchheister to his office in New York, interviewed him in his typical direct and searching fashion, and hired him as camp director; Buchheister's salary for the summer was to be $500, a sum which also delivered the services of his wife, Harriet, as camp dietitian.

Baker carefully laid his plans for the camp's opening, announcing it in the fall of 1935 during the Association's first annual dinner and convention in New York. (Before Baker's time, the annual meeting was only the yearly business meeting required of any corporation by New York State law, but now it became a convention lasting several days, with field trips and a banquet.) The new venture in Maine made its debut under the name Audubon Nature Camp, a circumstance that prompted nearby residents of the Maine coast to suppose a nudist colony was being planted in their midst, perhaps because at the time a national "back to nature" (i.e., nudist) movement had received a great deal of exposure in the press. For a while, local workers vied for the opportunity to go to Hog Island on service calls, and a woman registered for the camp under the impression that she would be able to sunbathe in the buff. ("We don't have enough people here to make it an aesthetic experience," Buchheister told her, deadpan.) In later years the name was changed to the Audubon Camp in Maine.

The wily Baker decided that it would be a public relations coup in New England to include in the venture the Massachusetts Audubon Society, then as always the strongest of the state societies. It was also, in effect, a subtle way of trying to extract financial support for the camp from a local Audubon group. Massachusetts Audubon responded cautiously by lending $1,000 to the Association to help finance the project— and Baker responded by paying off the loan in camp scholarships!

The camp was an immediate success. It operated as a series of two-week sessions throughout the summer, each accommodating about sixty men and women who paid forty dollars apiece for the experience. Although many of the campers at first were teachers, others attending

With her donation of
land on Hog Island in 1936,
Millicent Todd Bingham
enabled John Baker
to establish the Audubon
Camp in Maine.
PHOTO BY
SHIRLEY A. BRIGGS, NAS

The office of the Massachusetts Audubon Society at 66 Newbury Street,
Boston, in the 1930s. Winthrop Packard is at far right. NAS

ranged from businessmen and an urban fireman to college students eager to find a place for themselves in conservation education.

Baker provided Buchheister with a strong staff. Roger Peterson and Allan Cruickshank served as instructors in ornithology, and the prominent entomologist Donald J. Borror gave the campers a course in invertebrates. Cruickshank accepted the responsibility for getting people moving in the morning, stationing himself outside each of the buildings in turn and crowing like a rooster or cawing like a crow. (One morning, several people tumbled out of bed an hour early when an authentic crow set up a moonlight ruckus.)

"It was a mistake to let Peterson and Cruickshank room together," Harriet Buchheister said afterward. "They made an 'odd couple.' Allan was always complaining that Roger did not clean up his side of the room."

In general, however, Buchheister ran a tight ship. He expected campers and staff alike to get up, go to bed, and appear at meals and programs punctually. At one point Peterson asked for and was granted permission to keep "some campers" out past ten o'clock at night to go "owling." The exemption lasted until Buchheister discovered that Peterson always limited those expeditions to a party of himself and the comeliest lass in camp.

Later that summer, Baker notified Buchheister that three directors of the Massachusetts Audubon Society were coming to spend several days at the camp. Judge Robert Walcott, Laurence B. Fletcher, and Francis H. Allen (Peterson's first editor at Houghton Mifflin), would be his guests, and "the red carpet must be rolled out" for them. Buchheister did as he was directed, gratifying the directors and apparently ingratiating himself with them in the bargain. Before summer's end, Francis Allen invited Buchheister to come to Boston to be interviewed as a potential successor to the state society's long-term secretary-treasurer and chief executive officer, Winthrop Packard.

By then, Buchheister was sure he wanted to make a permanent career in the Audubon movement. He answered satisfactorily all the questions put to him by the three directors during the interview, the key request being to state his views on hunting. At the time he was unaware that several members of the Massachusetts Audubon board were hunters and that Packard's violently antihunting sentiments had alienated the state's sportsmen. "I have no objection to hunting as long as it is well regulated," Buchheister, a nonhunter, replied, and the job was his.

Just as much in need of a facelift as the old educational leaflets was that flagship of Audubon publications, *Bird-Lore*. Despite Frank Chapman's eminence in the ornithological world and the undoubted importance of the magazine he had long owned and edited to the Audubon movement's success, certain problems had crept in. Chapman's workload was prodigious. He had edited the magazine for thirty-six years while writing fifteen books and more than two hundred technical papers. He had also built the most extensive ornithological collection to be found in any museum in the world.

By the end of 1934, Chapman was seventy years old and increasingly burdened by his many projects. It was said that when he was away on his frequent extended field expeditions to the tropics he turned over all the editorial duties on *Bird-Lore* to his secretary. Gilbert Pearson had complained for some years that conservation matters and the news items from various Audubon societies were too often relegated to small print near the back of the magazine; his offers to have the Audubon Association buy *Bird-Lore* had been rejected several times by Chapman.

But Audubon's vigorous new leader was more insistent. Baker, direct as always, told Chapman that the time had come for the Audubon Association to assume full editorial and publishing responsibility for the magazine, which then had about five thousand readers. (An annual subscription cost only $1.50 for the six issues.) The older man agreed and turned over all rights in the magazine to the Association, which in turn paid him $1,200 a year for the rest of his life.

The changeover was amicable, and when it was announced in the issue of January–February 1935, Chapman looked back on his achievement, asking: "Who can estimate the value to birds, bird-lovers, and bird-lore of *Bird-Lore*'s 14,000 or more pages and nearly 5,000 illustrations?" He had made it a fitting successor to George Bird Grinnell's original *Audubon Magazine*. It had been the voice of the crusade that turned the tide against the slaughter of the egrets and other plume birds, and it spoke powerfully on the dozens of other conservation issues that cropped up during the first third of the twentieth century.

The agreement of sale stipulated that Chapman could stay on as editor as long as he wished. But perhaps the sight of Gilbert Pearson isolated in an office at Audubon suggested to Chapman that, at his age, he would not enjoy working for Baker, and he soon bowed out altogether. Baker already had a successor in the wings. Having birded often on Long Island and met Bill Vogt at Jones Beach, he knew of his prior work as a drama critic and later as an editor for the New York Academy of Sciences. He named Vogt the editor of *Bird-Lore* and ordered him to work with Roger Peterson in giving the magazine a new look.

"The cover of the magazine with its old-fashioned design and Gothic lettering had the look of a religious journal," Peterson wrote many years later in *Audubon*. "It fell to me to design the new cover. I came up with

Robert Cushman Murphy, during his long association with Audubon,
promoted nature education for children. NAS

some new lettering. This facelifting incorporated a painting by myself
of a rough-legged hawk on the wing over a wintry landscape as viewed
from above by another hawk. It came off fairly well and I was wowed
when I received a letter from the legendary Arthur Cleveland Bent of
*Life Histories* fame, stating that it was one of the best bird paintings he
had ever seen. That may have been an overstatement. In contrast, the
next cover, five shovelers springing from the reeds, was a disaster. In
planning covers we were limited to two ink impressions, black and one
color. The color could either be used in the title, on the bird (as the red
on a rose-breasted grosbeak), or as a background tone (green water, blue
sky, etc.)."

Vogt, crippled by polio as a teenager, was a feisty, literate man. He
set his sights beyond the backyard birdwatcher and the sentimental nature writers to the hard issues of science and conservation. He contributed a strong editorial to each issue and commissioned articles from the
leading conservationists of the day, including Aldo Leopold, Robert
Cushman Murphy, Paul Sears, and Paul Errington.

"In a conservation magazine there is always danger of overpessi-
mism, and some subscribers during Vogt's tenure complained of this,

as indeed subscribers do today," Peterson wrote in 1973. "They wanted to be diverted, instructed, and entertained, not preached to. One issue, I recall, was undeniably depressing. There was an essay by Errington about the suicidal tendencies of muskrats under population pressures; another described the difficulties of winter survival of quail; a third dealt with the ecological effects of poisons—the entire issue reeked of death and destruction."

Despite Vogt's success in revitalizing the magazine, he felt Baker kept too tight a rein on him and, indeed, on everyone else on his staff. He considered his boss a "dictator," and tried to foment a rebellion in the office; he suggested a strike of some kind, which he thought would cause the board of directors to lose confidence in Baker and fire him. Although some members of the staff were willing to go along with Vogt, others (notably Peterson) were not. When Baker got wind of the revolt, he took his case to the board, which fired, not Baker, but Vogt.

Vogt's voice in conservation, however, was not one to be stilled, despite temporary exile. Bob Murphy, who admired Vogt's talents though he had sided with Baker, arranged for the deposed editor to undertake a study for the Peruvian Guano Administration on the population dynamics of the birds that nested on the islands off the coast of Peru and whose copious droppings were the basis of an international trade in guano for fertilizers. Vogt, sailing off to his Elba, philosophically remarked that he hoped to "help increase the increment of the excrement." His experience in Latin America produced a different sort of dividend, however, for he became among the first to sound the alarm about the dangers of overpopulation. Later he served on conservation projects for the Pan American Union and Planned Parenthood, and in the 1940s wrote an influential book on the population crisis entitled *Road to Survival*.

Vogt departed from the Audubon Association in 1938. In that same year the archetypal Audubon pamphleteer, George Bird Grinnell, died in his eighty-ninth year at his home in New York.

# 17

In 1932 Captain W. A. Roberts was chief Audubon warden in the Everglades region of Florida. Rumors had reached the New York office that a colony of roseate spoonbills existed somewhere in the Big Cypress country to the north of the Everglades, and Roberts, who had helped to survey that country many years before, was asked to investigate.

Captain Roberts, however, had been in failing health for some time. Feeling too ill to go, he decided to remain aboard the houseboat on which he had been living just off Duck Rock, one of the largest roosts in the Ten Thousand Islands of southwestern Florida (though the rock had long since been covered by muck and mangroves), and sent his son, LeRoy Roberts, instead. Roy, who had served as an assistant warden for several years and had often traveled through the Big Cypress with his father, was a fearless, hard-drinking ex–plume-hunter; men like Roy Roberts often made the best Audubon wardens because they knew all the tricks of the trade.

On a recent evening Roy had come upon three men in a large motorboat shooting egrets at Duck Rock. When he tried to arrest them they sped off, and Roberts pursued. As the larger boat pulled away from him, he opened fire, and one of the plume hunters went down. Roberts soon lost them in the dark, and according to an Audubon report, "Nothing was ever brought to light further than some dead egrets and ibises on the ground at Duck Rock."

Now Roy Roberts set off into the Big Cypress on foot, accompanied by his nephew, Perry Roberts, and carrying enough food and water for several days. A report prepared by the Audubon Sanctuaries Department described the outcome:

"The Cypress country was found to be very dry, and after a couple of days the two men were without water and very little food remained. They finally decided that they would have to give up searching any farther for nesting spoonbills and concentrate on locating a supply of fresh water. They couldn't even find a mudhole! Altogether they were in the Cypress for about six days and had the greatest difficulty in getting out at all. On the last day Roy Roberts had to carry and drag Perry, who was entirely 'beat out'—to use their own expression. At length, their tongues swollen with thirst, they found a small quantity of mud, in which they plunged their faces and tried in some measure to ease the pain of their parched lips and throats."

When they reached the coast the two exhausted men returned by boat to Duck Rock, where tragedy awaited them. The night before, Captain Roberts had suffered a heart attack and toppled into the water alongside the houseboat. His wife and daughter were unable to pull his limp body aboard and finally tied him to the houseboat with a length of rope. The daughter had then set off in a skiff and rowed to a fishing camp several miles down the coast, but by then the old man was beyond help.

Roberts was a name to be reckoned with in the swamps of southwest Florida, where members of that clan left their mark as both plume hunters and wardens. They roamed the Shark River country, using camp sites that had been Indian mounds in the distant past, often the only bits of dry land for many miles around. The very place-names resound with violence and local color. Twister Key, for instance, was one of those dry plots up the Shark River in Hell's Bay, and was a frequent stomping ground (literally) of one of the best of the plume hunters, "Twister" Roberts. His name derived from—but let another man who knew the area later on during his days as an Audubon warden, Charles Brookfield, tell the story.

"Twister used to camp there with some of his friends, also plume hunters," Brookfield said, "and they would get drunk, and this one particular Roberts would get very happy on what they called 'Cape Sable Augerdent.' They made it themselves, of course. Undoubtedly it was the corruption of the Spanish 'aqua ardiente.' But Twister Roberts would get happy on it and he'd have a strong desire to dance, and he would dance and twist around and finally fall down dead drunk, and so this little mound was named Twister Key."

The Roberts family provided only a part of the service and drama that have characterized the significance of Florida in the history of American conservation down to our own time. When John Baker appointed Alexander Sprunt, Jr., director of Southern sanctuaries in 1935 (at a salary of $150 a month), the Florida sanctuaries remained the heart of the Audubon system, as they had been since the days of Guy Bradley. The situation called for a man like Sprunt. He had grown up in South Carolina's low country, knew the wildlife of the South's swamps and forests intimately (he later wrote *The Birds of South Carolina*), and served for a number of years as curator of ornithology at the Charleston Museum.

Florida state law had for a long time vested the ownership of all wild birds and game in the individual counties for the purpose of regulating "their use." The fragmented authority proved to be a disaster for Florida's birdlife. Only in 1927 did the state assert its ownership of all nonmigratory birds and its protection of migratory birds under federal laws. Protection was thus made somewhat easier, though shooting was still a serious problem because an open market for plumes still existed in Cuba. The job of an Audubon warden in Florida remained arduous and dangerous.

In Texas, the society had the benefit of J. J. Carroll's year-round presence, but there was no one comparable elsewhere to keep an eye on the wardens and their unpredictable levels of performance. Sprunt's territory was huge, and much of it barely accessible, but he roamed it by car, by boat, and even by air with unbounded enthusiasm and at very little cost. In April 1935, for instance, he was sent a monthly advance of $100 by the New York office to cover his expenses for office supplies, a lecture in Savannah, several short business trips in the Charleston area, retreading his car's tires, and an eleven-day inspection by auto of the Florida sanctuaries, leaving from and returning to Charleston. At the end of the month Sprunt still had $23.44 on hand. A perusal of his expense sheets may stir longings for the good old days, as illustrated by the following entry for April 26:

> Breakfast, Miami $0.22
> Hotel $1.25
> Lunch, Fort Lauderdale $0.50
> Five gals. gas $1.03
> Supper/tip, Vero Beach $0.70
>
> DAY'S TOTAL $3.70

Some sanctuaries, Sprunt learned, were not in the best of shape or care. One was a rookery near Micanopy in southern Alachua County, which had been guarded since 1912 by a warden named Bouknight. A visit to the area by an Audubon representative in 1932 revealed that Bouknight had hired a couple of farmers named Brown and Mack as deputies, and the rookery itself was practically nonexistent. Part of the trouble can be surmised from the following report sent on by the representative to New York:

"Bouknight is an old man, retired from active work, has heart trouble and a double hernia, lives a considerable distance from the rookery he is supposed to guard, says that he cannot afford to buy gasoline, and does not himself drive a car. No contact was made with Brown and Mack who were out alligator hunting."

Happily, the dismal state of affairs at Micanopy was not typical of most sanctuaries. Arthur O. Eifler guarded a big rookery of white ibises at Lake Washington, which really is a body of water formed by the widening of the St. Johns River. Eifler had been born in Racine, Wisconsin, but ran away from home at the age of thirteen because his father wouldn't buy him a bicycle. After considerable wandering, during which he was a tugboat captain on Puget Sound, a bartender, and a taxi driver, he opened a fishing camp on Lake Washington. He never did own a bicycle.

Eifler guarded the ibis rookery with the help of a tall lookout platform which he built in a grove of palms near his cottage on the eastern shore of the lake. Later he became an Audubon warden in the Ten Thousand Islands, in southwestern Florida. There he was so popular with the other residents that when he had to take two weeks away from his job during the breeding season to escort his wife to a hospital in Miami, a group of local men volunteered to protect his birds for him.

In the Tampa Bay area, Florida had at least a local counterpart of J. J. Carroll in Dr. Herbert Mills, a pathologist who served as an executive of the Florida Aubudon Society. The once-thriving rookeries in the bay had been devastated by the early 1930s, particularly a large colony of white ibises and other wading birds on Green Key. Local people often landed on the island for picnic lunches, the main ingredient of which was a "curlew stew" put together from the scores of baby ibises filched from the nearby nests. In 1934 Mills arranged for a warden to guard the rookeries. The man he selected was a carpenter named Fred W. Schultz. Mills bought him a boat, appropriately named *Audubon*, and provided the material with which he could build a cabin for himself and his wife, Ida, on Whiskey Stump, a small island across from Green Key where moonshiners had once concealed their merchandise in a rotting tree.

A woman who belonged to the Florida Audubon Society has described Schultz: "Tall, lean; hair faded and burnt yellow in spots. Skin burned to a ruddy brown contrasts with blue eyes. He has an air of having learned the secret of excessive silence."

For well over a quarter of a century, Fred and Ida Schultz lived for at least five months of every year among the mangroves, cabbage palms, and sea grapes on Whiskey Stump. The only birds on the three-acre island were the chickens they kept for fresh eggs. When termites consumed the cottage around them, Schultz built a new one. He grew vegetables in the muck heaped in a derelict rowboat and took fish, crabs, and shrimp from the rich waters of the bay.

Under Mills's direction, Schultz doggedly guarded the rookeries from molestation, particularly from picnickers or game dealers who raided the nests for ibis squabs that were later served in Tampa restaurants with yellow rice as "chicken." Although the state had passed laws forbidding the killing of wild birds and the robbing of their nests, it did not forbid people to land on state refuges. Mills noticed that there was often great, if inadvertent, destruction on state refuges in the area. Picnickers, photographers, birdwatchers, Boy Scouts, and other visitors kept the birds off their nests for long periods, causing them to lose their eggs or young. Frightened young birds often scrambled from their nests and became covered with the sandburs that grew on many islands. Mills had obtained permission to post certain islands as "Audubon Sanctuaries," and on these islands he and Fred Schultz enforced the principle of no landing.

Other wardens tend the Tampa Bay islands today, dealing with dredgers, industrial effluents, and oil spills rather than with curlew-stew enthusiasts, but they inherit rookeries whose viability rests on the work done by Mills and Schultz in the 1930s. There are still no nesting birds on Whiskey Stump, the only recent invasion being the botanical one of Brazilian pepper. Among the cabbage palms stands an inscribed monument that holds the ashes of Mills, who died in 1952.

Durability is not restricted to the Tampa Bay sanctuaries. Marvin Chandler inaugurated what is now more than a half-century of one-family warden service in central Florida. He had been born in Basinger and served in the Army during World War I, apprehending draft-dodgers and deserters. After the war he raised cattle on the Kissimmee Prairie and turned down a chance to become a Texas Ranger before starting as an Audubon warden in the early 1930s. He was, according to Sprunt, a taciturn man, "tall, lean, and bronzed as a Seminole."

Marvin Chandler's territory was vast, taking in all of Lake Okeechobee and thousands of acres on the Kissimmee Prairie. To patrol some isolated areas he took a horse in a trailer as far as possible over the rough roads, then completed his tour on horseback. A native of the region, Chandler gained the cooperation of most of his neighbors, particularly in the cattle country, where his presence deterred the small-time rustlers as well as bird hunters. Chandler's neighbors also contributed their bit to underground Audubon lore.

Elliott Coues, the early ornithologist, once wrote of the green heron that "this is a very pretty and engaging heron in spite of the ridiculous nicknames by which it is well known to the great unwashed democracy of America." It is a neglected truth that while the folk names of plants in English tend toward the erotic, those of animals are more often scatological. Coues was delicately referring to this tendency in his description of the green heron, which like other herons and egrets is popularly believed to produce large quantities of excrement almost on demand. In rural areas the residents often combine this characteristic with "poke," an archaic word for bag (as in "pig in a poke"), and refer to any heron as a "shitepoke." The Audubon emblem of a great egret in flight, sewn on Marvin Chandler's sleeve, prompted a lot of chuckling local remarks about "the warden for the Shitepoke Society."

Year in and year out, Marvin Chandler's most difficult struggle was against the egg collectors. Several species of a rather restricted range in the United States—including the caracara, anhinga, chuck-will's-widow, burrowing owl, limpkin, and glossy ibis—nested within his territory, and their eggs were all prized by people who practiced the destructive pastime of collecting. On one occasion Chandler found a spike driven as a marker into almost every cabbage palm where caracaras nested on the Kissimmee Prairie.

Indeed, the collectors of birds' eggs and skins posed special problems for Audubon wardens all over Florida during the 1930s. Richard H. Pough, who carried out various enforcement projects for the society, once happened upon a taxidermist in New Hampshire who had returned from a Florida shooting trip with his son, a trip on which he had collected more than two hundred birds. Pough saw part of this collection in the man's shop. The birds included two roseate spoonbills, three glossy ibises (two of them killed with a single shot), one Audubon's caracara, two Florida sandhill cranes, two snail kites, two great white herons, a bald eagle, a swallow-tailed kite, and a scarlet ibis, the latter having been killed, it was said, on Lake Okeechobee.

These birds, many of them rare, had all been shot legally. Although the man had neither scientific training nor scientific intentions, he had persuaded the New Hampshire fish and game commissioner to exert influence on his Florida counterpart, and so obtained a collecting permit.

"I asked Perkins [the taxidermist] whether they ran into any ivory-billed woodpeckers or Carolina Parakeets," Pough reported, "and he said no, he was quite sure the parakeet was extinct, but that they spent a lot of time hunting for ivorybills, but they always turned out to be the pileated woodpeckers. There is no doubt in my mind but that they would have shot any ivorybills they might have found."

All of southern Florida, the Everglades, Cape Sable, and the Keys, much of which came under special protection when the Everglades National Park was created in 1947, had until then presented a massive bird-protection problem in organization and logistics. The Audubon Sanctuaries Department ran on a total budget of about thirty-five thousand dollars a year during the middle 1930s. Since wardens' salaries, administration, and equipment all came from this sum, it is apparent that a very small pie was being cut into very small pieces, even in the irreplaceable Florida rookeries.

Alex Sprunt made the most of what funds he had. For one season he surveyed remote rookeries from a dirigible made available by the Goodyear Tire and Rubber Company. Later Sprunt found a valuable cooperator in Commander Carl C. vonPaulsen of the United States Coast Guard Station in Miami, who flew him or his wardens over rookeries in southern Florida and Florida Bay.

On one of those flights warden Roy Roberts discovered that several large rookeries of some twenty thousand herons and spoonbills near Immokalee had been wiped out, the birds "killed or run off." Roberts, Sprunt, and a federal agent went to Immokalee, a very tough town, to investigate. Only Roberts' presence averted what Sprunt called "some unpleasantness." Shotgun shells were found at the rookery, and certain information given by the local sheriff led to a hotel in Naples, where some women "of the race-track type" hung out.

According to Sprunt's information, the hotel's owner was said "to secure the favors of those ladies by bestowing plumes on them." At least one of the women made frequent trips to Cuba. The investigation turned up information that the middleman in the operation was a state game warden who had been fired for "shady" practices and then rehired upon the insistence of a local political boss. (No arrests were ever made.)

The Association had better luck elsewhere. The population of the great white heron, which is chiefly confined in the United States to the Florida Keys, was down to less than 150 individuals in 1935. Although the great hurricane of that year was responsible in part for this decline, the herons were regularly harassed by sponge fishermen operating out of Key West, who raided the nests for fresh squabs. Under protection from Audubon wardens, the population rose to 585 by 1938. No small factor in this triumph was the rough treatment handed out to violators of the game laws by a justice of the peace in Tavernier, whose son served for a time as an Audubon warden.

Even the state-supervised Royal Palm Park in the heart of the Everglades remained a trouble spot. While there were stiff state and federal penalties for killing birds or disturbing their nests (up to $500, or six months' imprisonment, or both), there was seldom any government enforcement. It was a popular practice to drive along the canals and other feeding grounds of the birds in Royal Palm Park and shoot them just for the fun of it.

Sprunt hired a warden to help in patrolling this area. Like many other Audubon wardens of the time, Lester Karcher was a retired serviceman, in his case from the Coast Guard, and with his pension he was able to accept the offered salary of seventy-five dollars a month. In addition, Karcher supplied his own car, boat, motor, trailer, and a few other necessities, though the society paid for his gas and oil and soon doubled his salary. Karcher proved to be an excellent warden.

Besides patrolling the roads, he escorted local Indian leaders through the rookeries to give them some idea of the work he was doing. He persuaded the drivers of tourist buses on the Tamiami Trail to stop panicking nesting birds by blowing their horns when they passed a rookery. To keep unauthorized boats away from the important colony of wood storks at Cuthbert Lake he put up "obstructions" in the nearby waterways. (When someone asked if the obstruction of navigable waterways was legal, a local engineer commented that anyone who considered those waterways navigable was "insane.")

Another valuable warden in the area was H. C. Blanchard, a taxidermist and an excellent field naturalist who had also served the society in Texas. Blanchard was installed at Flamingo, today an elaborate settlement in Everglades National Park but before World War II an isolated cluster of fishermen's frame buildings on stilts. The source of Blanchard's water was a Civilian Conservation Corps camp west of the settlement, and he sent out his mail on the fish truck.

The diverse rookeries and conditions of the Florida system seldom ran as smoothly as the Texas sanctuaries, and Alex Sprunt led a busy and sometimes hair-raising existence. Residents chopped up his warning signs for firewood, his boats were always breaking down or in need of a new paint job. A tour of inspection with the unpredictable Roy Roberts, who had succeeded his father as head of Audubon's "Southwest Coast Patrol" in 1932, was not to be looked forward to with any degree of calm. Sprunt once recalled those expeditions with Roberts at the helm, as it were, of a rickety boat, sprawled under the canopy and steering with his toes, roaring in pitch darkness past mangrove islands. Occasionally, there would be a sudden jolt as the boat hit a submerged object.

"Nothin' but one of them sea cows," Roberts would call, and for all Sprunt knew, he was right.

Prolonged drinking bouts brought Roberts' Audubon career to a close. Rehired once, he returned to action briefly only to smash up an Audubon launch on one of his nights off-duty and bring on his final banishment, leaving the wreckage and a string of unpaid bills in his wake.

Unexpected grief came at Sprunt even from New York. It was John Baker's habit to bring various members of the Audubon staff to that city for the Association's annual meetings. One year H. C. Blanchard was among the wardens invited to the meeting. He appeared, smartly and proudly dressed in his Audubon uniform. Baker, who could be very insensitive to others' feelings, looked Blanchard over and then sneered that he looked "like a policeman." Blanchard was crushed.

"It is difficult to believe that a hard-bitten old fellow like him can have much feelings in such a regard," Sprunt wrote to Baker afterward. "However, he had. It was a stiff blow to him. He is under the impression that a lot of people at the meeting thought he really looked very well in the uniform he wore there, and that you were the only one who thought he looked 'like a policeman.' He says he will not wear it again."

# 18

As the 1930s graded into the '40s, the old Audubon Association outwardly recast itself, acquiring a new home, a new name, and an heir apparent to John Baker before confronting a menace that flared, phoenixlike, from the past—the widespread use in commerce of the plumage of wild birds. Fortunately for the birds, Baker was just spoiling for a fight with a worthy opponent.

A new home had been in the cards for a long time. Gilbert Pearson had dreamed of a splendid new headquarters for the organization and bestirred himself as early as 1922 to start a building fund, one of the projects for which Rosalie Edge turned against him because she believed that Audubon money ought not to be squandered on bricks but devoted to sanctuaries. Baker himself preferred modest accommodations for the New York staff, divining that a touch of shabbiness tended to tug at the hearts (and purse strings) of potential contributors. In a note to a member of the board of directors, he remarked that he had inherited a building fund of $90,000, "and a hope on the part of my predecessor that the fund might reach some half a million dollars, and that a Temple of Conservation might be erected which in essence would be a monument to him."

Baker was writing to Guy Emerson, a fellow Bostonian, birder, and Harvard graduate who became a vice president of the Bankers Trust Company in New York. For a number of years he served as a board member and treasurer of the Aubudon Association. Emerson was an archetype of the Audubon board member of the time, an aristocratic northeasterner, charming, impeccably attired, and at times a bit overbearing. He could hold his own with Baker and even Rosalie Edge. When Edge came to annual meetings, often wearing a mink coat, to plead on behalf of furred and feathered creatures, she liked to attack administrative costs.

"We are paying exorbitant salaries, but what are we doing for the birds?" she asked on one occasion.

Emerson stood up, mentioned his long affiliation with the New York Red Cross, of which he was fundraising chairman, and replied, "The Red Cross can't operate without good people, and we have to pay salaries to get them. Everybody at the Audubon Association, from the executive director down, is underpaid. If it were up to me, I would raise *everybody's* salary."

In 1938 Baker won the board's approval to buy a building on the other side of Central Park at 1006 Fifth Avenue, between Eighty-first and Eighty-second streets and directly across from the Metropolitan Museum of Art. The building, dubbed Audubon House, was of six stories, plus a basement. The Audubon Association paid $83,000 for it and, with the help of a mortgage, spent another $20,000 on renovations.

"In this new home, the executive members of the staff will be able to work uninterrupted by typewriters, trolley cars, adding machines, stencil and addressograph machines," *Bird-Lore* trumpeted as the staff prepared to abandon Broadway for uptown elbow room. "The mechanical handling of educational materials on order, the daily volume of which would undoubtedly amaze our members, will be inestimably more efficient because the space provisions will minimize the number of handlings."

Although Gilbert Pearson, like some aging relative, came along with the addressograph machines and was settled in an upstairs office, Baker had by now remade the Audubon Association to his own taste. If Guy Emerson talked to him occasionally like a Dutch uncle, he had a strong but reasonable board of directors that included outstanding scientists such as Frank Chapman, Robert Cushman Murphy, and Aldo Leopold. (Baker was reluctant to go far afield for board members because of the difficulty of gathering a quorum in those days before easy air travel, but the Wisconsin-based Leopold, who was revolutionizing the profession of game management, stood out as an exception.) The board agreed to Baker's philosophy of deficit spending, approving small overruns each year.

But even in dealing with the board, Baker's impulse was to pack off recalcitrant individuals to oblivion. William P. Wharton, who had funded the Junior Audubon clubs generously and established the Association's permanent endowment fund of $200,000 in the '20s (all the while sticking to his fiction that the money was merely funneled through him by an anonymous donor), had never liked Baker. An admirer of Pearson's, he had resented the younger man's bid for control of the Audubon Association in 1934. Baker, on his part, was irritated by Wharton's fiscal conservatism. He mentioned to Emerson that at one time Wharton had contributed as much as $10,000 a year to the children's

Guy Emerson, whose leadership and financial skills helped steer Audubon
through some difficult times in the 1930s and '40s. NAS

program but that, since 1929, "these annual contributions of his have
been considerably smaller," and suggested that the time had come to
"cut the tie." But Emerson balked, pointing out that Wharton's integrity and conservatism were valuable to the board "as a brake on the
majority."

Baker won half a loaf in another vendetta when his businessman's
eye detected cost-cutting possibilities at the Theodore Roosevelt Sanctuary. He had long considered the sanctuary's director, the eccentric Eugene Swope, a troublemaker and referred to him as "one of the relatively
unpleasant personnel problems hanging over from the Old Deal." His
proposed solution was to cut the tie with both Swope and the Roosevelt
Sanctuary, claiming Kermit Roosevelt as an ally in the execution. But
Frank Chapman naturally objected to the plan to abandon the sanctuary,
which he had been primarily responsible for bringing into the Audubon
system, and the only casualty was Swope, who departed to the strains of
a lyrical eulogy written by Pearson for *Bird-Lore*.

If Baker intimidated some of his staff, there were at least two prominent exceptions. Roger Peterson's increasing national fame as the man
who had transformed birdwatching through his field guides gave him a

measure of independence, as well as new visibility for the Audubon name. Baker respected his talents, and Peterson returned the admiration, in later years insisting that Baker was the most effective of all Audubon leaders.

Baker was also very much impressed by Carl Buchheister's performance, both at the Maine camp and at the Massachusetts Audubon Society. By 1938, the summer seasons in Maine were filled to overflowing, and many applicants had to be turned away. Baker also apparently saw in Buchheister a quality he himself lacked and had little interest in cultivating—the ability to get on with a wide variety of people. Buchheister, a good public speaker, was able to light a flame in the men and women he encountered at the Maine camp, and they returned to their homes, offices, and classrooms to spread the glad tidings. In Massachusetts he had even soothed the sportsmen's groups alienated by his predecessor. For instance, he had talked "Mass Audubon's" board into stopping the sale of the cloth No Hunting signs devised by Winthrop Packard in his days as the society's leader, all with the society's name prominently printed on them.

Baker went to his board in New York, argued that if the Audubon Association was to keep growing it needed another able administrator to look after the increasing details, and suggested Buchheister. The board gave its approval for a new position of assistant executive director. It was ironic that in making a move that he thought would strengthen ties between the Audubon Association and its local affiliates around the country, Baker helped to undercut his relations with the strongest of all the state societies.

Judge Robert Walcott, Mass Audubon's chairman of the board, clearly resented what he felt was Baker's raid on an affiliate in depriving it of its administrative chief. He told Baker that he would not stand in Buchheister's way; at the same time, however, he wrote to Buchheister and pointed out some of the pitfalls that might await him in the big city. For one thing, Walcott said, Baker was still a comparatively young man, and Buchheister's chances of ever advancing to the top of the organization were remote; another danger in his relationship to Baker might be Buchheister's strong qualities of honesty and loyalty. Walcott warned, "if John gets into a disagreement with the majority of his Board of Directors . . . you, as his devoted associate, might quite easily lose your place as part of the general turn-over."

Bill Vogt, before his banishment to the guano islands, also tried to talk Buchheister out of accepting the position at the Audubon Association. "If you go to New York, you'll be cutting your own throat," Vogt told him. "Baker will kill you." But, as director of the Maine camp, Buchheister had already worked closely with Baker and believed that he had the even temper to exist on good terms with the Audubon leader. Before deciding "to become a little fish in a big pool," however, he asked Baker to put in writing the scope and responsibilities of the job.

"While final responsibility would continue to be mine," Baker replied in longhand, "I would delegate to you full authority in many matters and would strive to give you that experience which would qualify you to take over my job at any time. I will count on your absolute loyalty not to lend yourself to any scheme with the objective of getting a new executive director!"

It was to Baker's credit that for seventeen years he would stand by the spirit of that agreement, the two working in mutual trust until the older man's retirement, when he turned his office over to Buchheister. Meanwhile, Buchheister inadvertently soured relations between New York and Boston still further when he passed on the position at Mass Audubon. He recommended as his successor a former seed salesman named Russell Mason, who had helped revitalize the Florida Audubon Society. Soon after Mason took the job, Buchheister was dismayed to find a distinct chill emanating from Boston.

Baker, of course, lay at the heart of the problem. The Audubon Association, from the time of Guy Bradley, had been the dominant factor in bird preservation throughout Florida. When Mason, as secretary of the Florida Audubon Society, began to build an effective state organization in the 1930s, he apparently resented Baker's free-wheeling style in selecting wardens and sanctuaries without consulting state leaders. "What the hell's the use of worrying about them? They're going to die anyway," Baker once said, believing that Florida Audubon would go the way of so many other of the old state societies. Mason carried his resentment with him to Boston.

Guy Emerson, both as banker and birder, traveled widely in the United States and always made it a point to talk to local Aubudon members wherever he visited. Invariably he returned from the hinterlands with tales of disaffection caused by Baker's highhandedness. He tried to get Baker to calm the waters both in and outside of New York, in part by communicating more often with the board. He also asked him, in effect, to be a little nicer to Gilbert Pearson. Because Baker refused to speak to the latter, he assigned Buchheister to be a go-between, and from 1940 until the old man retired from Audubon House in 1942 Buchheister would climb the stairs regularly to his little office, explain what was going on below, and in turn listen to Pearson's complaints about Baker.

A good deal more of Buchheister's time was spent traveling around the country in an attempt to keep up the idea of an Audubon family. He found it a "depressing assignment." Many of the smaller societies felt they were never consulted—they simply paid their ten dollars a year as affiliates and in return received a single copy of *Bird-Lore*. Baker, they complained, would write them and ask for money or help on a specific project, but would not respond to *their* appeals for help. In Maine, for instance, the state society told Buchheister of the fate of A. H. Norton, a quiet, modest man whose work in bird preservation had extended back to Dutcher's time. The Audubon Association had paid him a tiny sum, perhaps $100 a year, to be its Maine representative and contribute state news to *Bird-Lore*. Baker fired him. Buchheister would return from such trips to pass on reports of local discontent, but Baker generally shrugged them off. As a hardheaded businessman, he would tell his assistant, he could not condone the loose, weak sort of organization that he found most of the local societies to be.

It would be several years before a satisfactory mechanism was found to bind the Audubon movement once more into a truly national organization. Meanwhile, the first step was a symbolic one. In 1940, the Audubon Association hired as consultants the John Price Jones Corporation of New York to evaluate its operations. The firm made two significant recommendations. The first was that the name *Bird-Lore* had grown antiquated and ought to be changed to *Audubon Magazine*. (It was later shortened simply to *Audubon*.) The magazine first appeared under its new name in January 1941, thus returning full circle to the publication as created by George Bird Grinnell.

The other change applied to the organization itself. The consultants argued that the Audubon Association was no longer really an "association." There were no representatives of the state societies or other local organizations on its board. It represented no one but itself, its own Audubon Society. And so, by vote of the board of directors in 1940, the National Association of Audubon Societies disappeared, to be replaced by the National Audubon Society.

# 19

*R*ichard Hooper Pough stood out even among the star-studded cast of "bird men" who occupied the Audubon office in the years just before World War II. A product of the Massachusetts Institute of Technology and Harvard University, Pough (pronounced "Poe") was an engineer and businessman through formal education, an accomplished ornithologist through practical experience. In the 1930s Pough's documentation of the slaughter of hawks in the Pennsylvania hills led in part to the founding of the Hawk Mountain Sanctuary by Rosalie Edge. After World War II he wrote the series of "Audubon Bird Guides" that complemented Roger Peterson's identification guides with details of nesting and feeding habits; became a founder and president of the Nature Conservancy; and in the opinion of at least one prominent conservationist, "practically invented the land preservation business in this country."

But in 1939 Pough was on the Audubon staff, having been hired three years earlier by Baker to keep an eye on "persecuted species" such as hawks and owls.

"Moira, my wife, came home one day wearing a new feathered hat," he recalled. "I took one look at it and recognized the feather as that of a golden eagle. 'Where did you get that hat?' I asked her. The next day she took me to a Manhattan shop and I looked over the displays and became convinced that most of the plumage on sale came from wild birds."

Pough became a feather detective. He frequented the American Museum, studying its large collection of feathers and learning to identify with considerable precision even those of exotic species. He conducted surveys of department stores and millinery shops and picked out the plumage of at least forty wild birds, most of it imported from abroad. New York, as well as Philadelphia, Chicago, Detroit, and other large cities were glutted with wild bird feathers. The parade of plumed hats on urban sidewalks rivaled that observed by Frank Chapman at the turn of the century.

What had happened to turn back the fashion clock thirty years or more? Pough described the phenomenon and the reasons behind it in an influential pamphlet, "Massacred for Millinery," published by the new National Audubon Society in 1940. The resurgence in the plume trade occurred, as Pough saw it, when loopholes in existing legislation enabled wild bird feathers to flow into the country and prompted milliners to create a new market for them.

One major loophole was the agreement at the time of the Tariff Act of 1913 to permit dealers to go on selling plumes until their stocks already on hand were exhausted; somehow the dealers kept coming up with documents to show that whatever plumes they were selling were of turn-of-the-century origin. Another vehicle for contraband was forged documents from abroad attesting that the imported feathers came from domestic birds. What proved to be the peskiest loophole to close was an amendment to the Tariff Act in 1922, making it legal to import feathers for the manufacture of fishing flies.

"It is a noteworthy and peculiar coincidence that importations of feathers for 'fishing-fly' manufacture took an unusual spurt beginning about three years ago, when feathers first began to come into style again for millinery," Pough wrote. "No corresponding increase in the retail purchase of fishing flies had been reported by any of the dealers."

That some of the feathers were indeed going to the fly-tyers was little consolation, because dealers were promoting the notion that fish preferred to snap at the rarest feathers. One of the leading dealers pressed home the point in his ads:

"Orillard plumes: These plumes are found on the tails of the rare Orillard pheasant, which is found only in a limited area of Asia, and is in fact becoming extinct.

"Roseate spoonbill quills: These are among the rarest feathers in the world. They have beautiful texture.

"Genuine snowy egret skins and plumes: Snowy egret plumes are undoubtedly among the world's most beautiful feathers. Large plumes, 25¢ each."

The company claimed that it had its own hunters scouring the world for the rarer species of wild birds.

Baker began a public relations campaign, bombarding the press with news releases and material for editorials. The newspapers received all the facts every time Pough visited an offending shopkeeper in the company of a conservation officer to issue a summons or a warning. Seizing the high moral ground, Baker and his staff appealed to the consumer's

Richard Pough at
Cape May, New Jersey,
in 1940. NAS

conscience, describing the fate of the chicks of Andean condors or South American rheas when their parents had been shot for their plumage. Baker also organized a permanent public boycott of feathered hats and a drive to plug loopholes in the existing legislation. At the end of 1940, luminaries such as Eleanor Roosevelt and movie star Mary Pickford announced their support for the Audubon cause.

At that point the feather industry caved in. Most of the leading dealers formed an organization known as the Feather Industries of America to deal with the problems arising from the new Audubon plumage campaign and the resulting blow to the millinery industry's public image. This trade group agreed to turn over to the authorities all of its members' stocks in the plumage of rare and endangered species and to produce accurate inventories of the remainder. The dealers also signed an agreement with the National Audubon Society to push for federal and state legislation that would prohibit the future sales of wild bird plumage. Although under the agreement the dealers received another period of grace to dispose of their remaining stocks, Audubon gained a major symbolic victory in the immediate ban on the sale of the feathers of bald and golden eagles in New York.

John Baker had at hand a man to lead the legislative campaign. Thomas C. Desmond, a state senator in New York, was a member of Audubon's board of directors. With Desmond sponsoring the bill in Albany, and Baker and Buchheister successfully exhorting the members of Audubon and affiliated societies to support it, the bill to plug loopholes in existing tariff laws swept through the legislature. It was signed into law by Governor Herbert Lehman in April 1944. The plumage trade, it seemed, was to be restricted in the future to the feathers from less than a dozen kinds of domestic fowl.

Hardly had the ashes of the confiscated plumage cooled when cries of outrage rose from an unexpected quarter. The manufacturers of fishing flies and the sportsmen who tied them charged that Audubon and the Feather Industries of America had conspired to keep them in the dark while rushing through this "un-American" legislation. The attack quickly heated to the boiling point. Much of the rhetoric came from the lowbrow hook-and-bullet press, which compared Audubon leaders to Hitler and Mussolini. One fisherman-journalist, referring to Pough's description of the slaughter of Andean condors for their feathers, called the condor "the worst killer of game birds and animals known to man, [and] furthermore this brutal killer has been known to swoop down out of the air and grab babies in their vicious talons, carry them away to their nest in the lofty cliffs [sic] and tear them to pieces for food for their filthy young."

But among the most outspoken critics of the legislation was an old Audubon ally, the Izaak Walton League. An editorial in the League's publication, *Outdoor America,* called the new plumage law fanatical legislation and suggested that the Audubon Society's ultimate aim was to stop bird-hunting. Kenneth A. Reid, the League's executive secretary, wondered whether the Feather Industries of America had entered into a "shotgun agreement," with Audubon simply because Baker's staff had accumulated damaging evidence about illegal plumage sales by its member dealers.

Baker stood by the basic Audubon belief, held by Grinnell, Dutcher, and Pearson, that the flesh or plumage of wild birds ought never to be put on the market; such a practice led only to the extirpation of many species, and to make an exception in the case of fishing flies opened a loophole that could have disastrous consequences. The fly-tyers, however, opened a drive to amend the hated legislation. Baker offered to agree to an amendment that would allow the importation of certain frequently used feathers from pheasants as long as they had been raised as domestic game.

But the aroused fly-tyers wanted a greater variety of plumage, both imported and domestic. Baker lined up his support, which included a strong stand by the Garden Club of America. Then, to his disgust, Senator Desmond bowed to political pressure and went over to the opposition. The two men, Audubon leader and renegade board member, confronted each other at a meeting held at the New York Conservation Department in New York City early in 1942. Desmond took the offensive, attacking the Audubon and garden clubs' representatives present and adopting the Izaak Walton League's charge that Baker was against bird-hunting.

Desmond argued that his amendment, which provided for a greater variety of imported feathers than Baker wanted, would forestall the outright repeal of the plumage law and, feeling that Baker's refusal to compromise was a betrayal of his supporters in the legislature, called him "dishonorable." Although Baker exercised considerable restraint in restating the Audubon position ("If we have any differences, Tom, let's settle them between ourselves"), Desmond promised to carry his fight to the Audubon board.

At a special meeting of the board of directors called a few days later, Desmond was given an opportunity to confront Baker again and state his case. Baker contended that Desmond's defection had given the public an idea that the National Audubon Society was divided on the issue of commerce in wild bird plumage and encouraged representatives of the Feather Industries of America "to scramble for exemption for themselves." Under questioning by Guy Emerson, Desmond admitted that the fly-tyers had no substantial grounds for complaint, but were irritated because they had not been consulted before the legislature acted on the bill. Emerson suggested that Desmond's position was based purely upon personal expediency and not upon principle.

"Thereupon the Senator gave voice to intemperate accusations directed against Mr. Baker and the directors," according to handwritten minutes of the meeting, "and gave evidence of a high degree of emotional excitement."

Desmond then resigned from the board of directors, asked that he be released "from any financial commitments to the Society," and stormed out of the meeting. The board voted to support Baker's position and the amendment to the plumage law favored by Audubon.

The short-term victory, however, went to Desmond, whose amendment passed the legislature and permitted the fly-tyers to import a variety of plumage for fishing flies. Baker consoled himself with the knowledge that the provisions against the use of wild bird plumage for millinery purposes had not been weakened. Pough and other staff members continued to monitor the commercial use of plumage, calling in state and federal authorities whenever violations were detected. In this campaign, they could even count on support from a familiar gadfly. In 1943, Carl Buchheister sent the following memorandum to Baker:

"Mr. A. C. Lyons, Assistant Treasurer of Lord & Taylor, phoned to say that Mrs. Charles Noel Edge of New York City wrote them that she had been advised by the National Audubon Society that Lord & Taylor was fined for selling hats containing illegal bird plumage. Mr. Lyons stated that he was requested by his boss to ask the Society whether we were sending out communications to our members regarding the selling of these hats by Lord & Taylor."

Buchheister said he explained to Lyons that a story had appeared in *Audubon* magazine about the convictions of several New York firms. Lyons replied that "his buyer purchased the hats in ignorance of the fact that such purchase was illegal," and they wanted to conform with the law.

The fly-tyers' exemption remained a minor irritant to National Audubon until 1952, when Baker formed a coalition of all interested parties, including the Feather Industries of America, the Izaak Walton League, and various fishing-industry and conservation organizations to press for an amendment to the Federal Tariff Act. The amendment (which had been Baker's originally-suggested grounds for compromise) ended the unlimited importation of wild bird plumage for use in the manufacture of fishing flies. The legislation, introduced in Congress by Representative John Dingell of Michigan, provided for the limited importation under license of the plumage of the mandarin duck and various pheasants. A few fishing-fly manufacturers held out, charging National Audubon was run by a clique of fanatics, nearly all of whom were "left wing intellectuals," but Congress passed the amendment.

When New York State passed conforming legislation later the same year, the second great feather fight was history.

# 20

The nomenclature surrounding the Audubon Society's work had tended from the beginning to be all-encompassing, referring mainly to birds in the aggregate—wildlife sanctuaries, model bird laws, plumage birds, migratory-bird treaties, and the like. But beginning in Baker's time the focus was alternately wide-angle and narrow. First, carefully defined groups of birds, and then individual species, were singled out for attention as conditions changed and specialists identified unique problems. Increasingly, the work took place hundreds, even thousands, of miles from Audubon House.

Both hawks and waterfowl absorbed much of Baker's attention at the start of his administration. A report by an Audubon staff member at his first annual meeting noted that more than a million hawks, ninety thousand owls, and seventy thousand eagles had been killed by farmers and sportsmen, many of them for bounties, in the previous two decades. Because most states listed those birds as vermin, they were fair game for anyone who went after them with guns, traps, or poisons. Even such a renowned game protector as William Hornaday enthusiastically joined in the destruction, having compiled his own little blacklist that included horned, barred, and screech owls, goshawks, Cooper's and sharp-shinned hawks, and golden eagles. Of the peregrine falcon, "another hated destroyer of game birds and song birds," he wrote: "Each bird of this species deserves treatment with a choke bore gun. First shoot the male and female, then collect the nest, the young or the eggs, whichever may be present. They all look best in collections." The Roosevelt Sanctuary's Eugene Swope could not have phrased it more compellingly.

Predator control, whether of wolves and grizzlies or of golden eagles and red-tailed hawks, became national policy. State legislators assumed it was their responsibility to sift the "bad" animals from the "good" ones and decree summary justice for the former. Maryland, in the six years between 1925 and 1930, paid bounties on 89,858 hawks. In 1917 the Territory of Alaska's legislature established a two-dollar bounty on the bald eagle, which was felt to be preying excessively on salmon; between that year and 1952, when the bounty was finally lifted, Alaskan bounty hunters collected 128,273 bald eagles.

Aldo Leopold, who joined the Audubon board in 1935, was a leader in formulating what has since become orthodox game-management principles with respect to predatory species.

"When we attempt to say an animal is 'useful,' 'ugly,' or 'cruel,' " he wrote, "we are failing to see it as part of the land. We do not make the same error of calling a carburetor 'greedy.' We see it as part of a functioning motor."

In that transition year, one of Baker's first acts as executive director was to approve a lease on an area near Cape May Point, New Jersey, where the Audubon Association established the Witmer Stone Wild Life Sanctuary (named for an ornithologist who had studied the birds of Cape May for many years). A warden was assigned to the sanctuary to protect hawks and other birds from gunners during the spring migration. Another move by the Audubon Association in 1934 was the publication of the first hardcover book to bear its imprint, *The Hawks of North America* by John B. May, who had worked with E. H. Forbush in Massachusetts and was an expert in economic ornithology. The book, illustrated with Allan Brooks's paintings reproduced in color, focused on the identification of hawks and their food habits, thus emphasizing that, by preying heavily on rodents and other herbivores, most hawks were actually of benefit to farmers and homeowners.

This book's publication had been an opportunity for the Audubon directors to make a "statement of policy" beyond the pages of *Bird-Lore* about hawks and owls. They stated their opposition to the killing of any raptors aside from "individuals known to be damaging property," and went on to condemn all bounties on predatory birds. They concluded by promising to work for laws that gave hawks better protection.

Audubon, in a sense, kept its finger in the dike for another decade or two until favorable propaganda, bolstered by modern wildlife-management principles, brought a change of heart about birds of prey in many parts of the country.

Another of Baker's early priorities had been the drive to reverse the continuing decline in waterfowl. The lower bag limits set by the Biological Survey seemed to have little effect in stopping the decline. Baker called for a closed season in 1935, rallying support for his position and directly appealing to President Franklin D. Roosevelt. Many prominent sportsmen agreed with Baker, as did the Izaak Walton League and other organizations. Naturally, however, there was powerful opposition to closing the hunting season on all ducks, geese, and swans, and Roosevelt decided in favor of the hunters.

"Incredible as it may seem," Baker lamented in *Bird-Lore*, "an executive order issued by the President of the United States, based on advice of the Secretary of Agriculture and the Chief of the Biological Survey, sentences the vanishing American Migratory Duck to sixty consecutive days' barrage in the United States; thirty days each in two zones, north and south; this in the face of the Government's own estimate of only some forty Ducks per hunter remaining to return to the breeding grounds this year."

The campaign, however, led to a permanent ban on the use of such age-old duck-hunting practices as the use of live decoys, baiting, and sink-boxes. It also kindled in Baker an aversion to sportsmen's organizations; he was not against hunting, but he felt that those groups consistently voted against wise conservation measures for selfish or short-sighted reasons. He continued to serve for many years on the Migratory Waterfowl Advisory Committee.

In 1939 the Biological Survey was transferred from the Department of Agriculture to Interior and became the U.S. Fish and Wildlife Service. After Baker's retirement, he was complimented in a 1960 article in *Audubon* by a former director of the Fish and Wildlife Service and a fellow member of the waterfowl committee, Ira N. Gabrielson.

"During the few years when the leadership of the U.S. Department of the Interior seemed to be much more interested in pleasing the hunters than it was in carrying out its major responsibility of maintaining the waterfowl resource," Gabrielson wrote, "John's voice was consistently and clearly heard against this policy. His persistent attention to the declining population of waterfowl and his efforts to get the department to see the importance of preserving and maintaining the resource, had much to do with the final awakening of the high command to the necessity of getting things put back on a more solid basis."

During the 1950s, waterfowl populations were built back to levels that they may never again reach.


For all Audubon's success in protecting most birds, the staff felt helpless as the populations of some of the big "glamor" species went on dwindling. By the late 1930s Baker began to ask insistently, "Why?" The question, he knew, could not be answered without field research, but neither the universities nor government agencies showed any inclination to fund the needed studies. Baker conceived the idea of an Audubon Research Fellowship Plan, then found the money from well-to-do Audubon members and arranged with two universities to carry out thorough studies on endangered birds.

The immediate target species were the ivory-billed woodpecker and the California condor. With the cooperation of Cornell, James Tanner, a recent graduate of the Laboratory of Ornithology at that university, received an Audubon research fellowship to conduct the ivory-bill study beginning in 1937. Tanner and his colleagues slogged through southern swamps, tracking down the remnant population and putting together details of the big woodpecker's life history. The giant trees that the ivory-bill probed for insects and on which it depended for survival were falling to the timbermen, and the study concluded with a sense of foreboding.

Across the continent, Carl Koford, a zoologist and forester, carried out a three-year study on the condor supported by an Audubon grant and by the University of California at Berkeley. The big vulture, which had come down to us from past ages "through the interstices of things ajar," now seemed in a terminal decline. Beginning in 1939, Koford backpacked into the mountains, scaled cliffs, and kept patient vigil near a nest, sometimes living in a cave "not unlike that occupied by the condors a half-mile away." No effective solutions were found for the condor's plight either, and it remained for a later time to make the hard and controversial decisions concerning the terms on which the great bird might avoid extinction.

Both of these studies were published as National Audubon Society Research Reports, with their assembled observations setting a standard for later monographs on individual species. Meanwhile, Bob Allen had sharpened his research skills on a study of nesting black-crowned night herons on Long Island, commuting between home and marsh on a bicycle because at the time he still did not know how to drive a car. Baker now asked him to take on another of the endangered species, the roseate spoonbill.

It was as if Allen had been preparing all his life for this challenge. He made a permanent break with New York, moving with his wife and two children to the little town of Tavernier in the Florida Keys, close to what was then the only nesting colony of spoonbills in Florida. He established the Audubon field research department in Tavernier, and it has stayed there ever since. Baker had asked Allen to find the answer to a single but immensely intricate question: How can the numbers of the roseate spoonbill be increased within the United States?

The spoonbill had been relatively common in Florida in the nineteenth century, and there were several ironies attending its subsequent disappearance. One might have supposed that its gorgeous plumage would be the most coveted of all by the millinery gunners who decimated wading-bird colonies at the end of the century, but that was not the case. The color tended to fade quickly from spoonbill feathers, and the gunners concentrated mainly on white herons and egrets.

Spoonbills are shy, however. Any disturbance in a colony causes them to abandon their eggs or young, and they seldom try to renest in the same year. Their population crashed in the United States, and though most of the other wading-bird species recovered under protective legislation, the spoonbills simply vanished.

"With the advent of the 1920's, it was next to impossible to find so much as a single spoonbill nest in all of Florida," Bob Allen wrote later. "Texas had been deserted as a breeding place for nearly fifty years, and only a few spasmodic nestings were recorded in Louisiana. So far as the United States was concerned, the roseate spoonbill seemed a lost cause."

But around 1920 spoonbills reappeared on the Texas coast and soon were nesting there. Then young, nonbreeding birds were seen in Florida. In 1935 "a pitifully small group," according to Allen, was discovered nesting on Bottlepoint Key in Florida Bay, and it immediately came under the protection of Audubon wardens. This colony, six miles across the bay from Tavernier, became the first object of Allen's research.

Allen never did anything halfway; he spent most of the next three years living almost like a spoonbill. He set up his camp at the edge of a mangrove swamp on Bottlepoint Key, among sand flies, burrowing crabs, and an occasional crocodile. Every ten days or so he would return to Tavernier, an apparition of Robinson Crusoe, to startle the natives as well as his wife and children, have a good meal, and return to his lonely existence.

He lived the life of a hermit, carrying on his studies in the muck and shallow water by day and poring over his notes under a sputtering gasoline lantern in the evenings, often so inattentive to his personal needs that he merely opened a can of beans for supper and ate the contents unheated. Spoonbills nest in late fall around Florida Bay, and when winter storms struck the keys, Audubon wardens could not reach him to deliver new supplies.

Always resourceful, Allen amused himself in his free time by reading, drawing caricatures of himself and the bizarre drifters he encountered in the bay, and dashing off doggerel. One such flight of whimsy began:

> I don't wish to be didactic,
> But there's something enigmatic
> In the little game the Pink Bird plays with time.
> So I've cast my lot with his 'un,
> In this mangrove-studded prison,
> And I'm looking for the reason and the rhyme.

Robert Porter Allen in his lair at Bottlepoint Key, Florida Bay, in 1939.
PHOTO BY ALEXANDER SPRUNT, JR., NAS

Observing spoonbills posed special problems, Bob Allen discovered, as he sought the reason and the rhyme. The small flock was always on the move. As the birds paired off for nesting in October, they became more than ordinarily skittish, and Allen was reluctant to approach them for fear of disrupting the colony. He concentrated then on making an ecological study, trying to learn whether there was some element in their environment—a scarcity of suitable food or an abundance of predators or parasites—that prevented the spoonbills from building up a stable breeding population.

The traditional method of studying a bird's feeding habits was to shoot a few of them and examine the stomach contents. Obviously, this was out of the question with the Florida spoonbill, so Allen frequented the lagoons and other areas where spoonbills habitually fed.

"No snail that crawled, no worm that squirmed, no leaf that grew would escape my ardent attentions," Allen wrote in his book, *The Flame Birds*. "Literally, I would sift out the soft marl and turtle grass and comb the long mounds of shell debris until I was on intimate terms with their animal and vegetable populations. I would have to build dredges for reaching the greater depth of water, even depths beyond the spoonbill's normal interest. For all of these creatures—fishes, crustaceans, insects, mollusks, even the larval forms and the microscopic plankton—are interrelated in one way or another. In composite form they make up the spoonbill's environment, and in their identities and habits and relationships I would look for some of my answers."

The results of his first winter in Florida Bay were disheartening. The colony on Bottlepoint Key produced only nine young spoonbills, and a new colony he discovered on a nearby key was destroyed by a raccoon, which apparently had gone farther afield after a great storm had inundated the mollusk population on which it usually fed.

In April 1940, Allen moved his family and his gear to the Texas coast, where he studied a more robust breeding colony on the Second Chain of Islands, later an Audubon sanctuary. There he found a better vantage point for watching the spoonbills' courtship and nest-building rituals through his thirty-six-power telescope. The descriptions and technical phrases (such as the sudden puzzling takeoffs by the assembled birds that he termed "up-flight") were substantial contributions to ornithological knowledge. Amid all of the minute-to-minute behavioral details, he neither lost his awe of the birds' essential grandeur nor his ability to coin apt expressions for their rituals.

"At this same time the pink birds were seen in another form of behavior that I immediately labeled 'sky-gazing,' " he wrote. "In a Spanish language review of my original description of it, this attitude or posture was referred to as *contemplacion del firmamento,* which is, I think, an improvement on the English."

In Texas Allen learned that the notion of the spoonbill's dependence on mollusks for its food amounted to a false start. His dredging and netting revealed that these birds often fed at night, not because of the security darkness offered but because that was the time when dense shoals of tiny fish—minnows and killifish—poured into shallow water. Most species of these fish, he found, lived in great numbers wherever spoonbills fed, both in Texas and in Florida. The pale killifish, which he found in eight Florida locations, had been previously known to science only from Galveston Bay.

Food, Allen discovered, was not a limiting factor for spoonbills in Texas or Florida. When he returned to New York briefly after nine months in the field to summarize his findings and examine museum specimens, he did not pass up an opportunity to squeeze in a little more field research.

"Although food animals taken by the pink birds are small because they must survive in water habitats of only a few inches in depth, the birds are able to swallow larger objects, as I found out during the New York World's Fair," Allen recalled in *The Flame Birds.* "I spent some time with the roseate spoonbills in the Brazilian exhibit. These birds were regularly fed on pieces of fish, some of which were as large as one's fist. Experimentally I offered them stale buns and bits of chocolate. They swallowed both with apparent pleasure, swinging their bills from side to side as they approached my proffered offerings just as if stale buns and chocolate bars were routine food items to be found at the bottom of every shallow pond in tropical America."

In April 1941, Allen concluded his study by touring Florida Bay in an eighteen-foot open skiff, the *Croc*, outfitted in the bow with a waterproof tarpaulin that he used as his cabin. He lived on this boat, which he described as looking like "a floating rummage sale," for three months, not setting foot on dry land for nine or ten days at a time. Often he had to get out and push the boat across sandbars and mudflats.

His monograph, *The Roseate Spoonbill* (National Audubon Society Research Report No. 2), is a fascinating life history of a fascinating bird. Allen's historical research and field observations indicated that the Texas colonies were replenished in the 1920s by Mexican birds, and the Florida colonies later on by Cuban birds. He suggested conservation measures that have contributed to the spoonbills' increasing population in recent decades.

When World War II broke out, Allen volunteered for service and spent much of the war aboard a minelayer. In leisure moments at sea he wrote the popular book that was later published as *The Flame Birds*. Together with his monograph, it provides a colorful picture of a revolutionary period in ornithological research. On the surface, Allen's spoonbill survey is a painstaking accumulation of trifles, but it is infused with the radiance of a scene sometimes glimpsed and never lost, a leaden bay stained by sunset and a straggle of pink birds beating silently across it.

The whooping crane, in large part through the National Audubon Society's research program, became a nationwide symbol for the struggle to save endangered species. The entire wild population, most of which wintered in Texas and in spring flew off to a northern *terra incognita* to mate and raise its young, reached a low point of twenty-one birds in 1941. (This figure included a few birds in Louisiana that were gone by 1949.) World War II prevented the start of any intensive research into the whooper's problems, though the U.S. Fish and Wildlife Service had set aside an Aransas refuge near Austwell, Texas, for the wintering population and in 1945 established a cooperative undertaking, known as the Whooping Crane Project, with the Audubon Society.

To get the program under way, the Society granted a research fellowship to Olin Sewall Pettingill, Jr., a distinguished ornithologist who was on leave from Carleton College in Minnesota. The most glaring gap in the whooper's dossier was the whereabouts of its nesting grounds. Pettingill, working with Canadian biologists, made extensive trips by air across northern Canada, but there was no sign of the tiny band of scattered whoopers in that vast tangle of lakes, marshes, and stunted forests. In the fall of 1946, Pettingill returned to his teaching duties at Carleton. There was a need for a permanent field researcher.

"Some years before," Bob Allen wrote, "when on the Texas coast working with roseate spoonbills, I'd seen my first whooping cranes and wondered idly what poor, unsuspecting soul would someday be assigned the rugged task of making a full-scale study of them. I hadn't the slightest notion it would be me."

Allen moved his family to Texas again and began his study of the wintering population that fall. The cranes proved even more difficult to approach than spoonbills. Desperate, and willing to try anything, Allen conceived a plan for building a very special sort of blind. Having watched cranes consorting with cattle in the marshes, he fashioned a huge but portable blind in the shape of a bull, stretching a "skin" of heavy red canvas over a light framework of wire and painting on such details as eyes, nose, and even assorted wrinkles. It was, as he afterward admitted, "a bum steer." He abandoned the scheme after a live bull came upon him in the marsh and responded to the intruder with alarming posturings, though later Allen had no qualms about letting the celebrated photographer Andreas Feininger put himself in hazard while trying to take pictures of whoopers from the counterfeit bull.

Allen told the story of his adventures with the big cranes in his book *On the Trail of Vanishing Birds.* He built a tower in the Aransas marshes from which he could observe the birds in safety and noted previously unknown details of their lives. He scouted their migration routes along the North Platte River and through the northern states into Canada. He took part in the arduous and sometimes dangerous search that finally located the whoopers' nesting grounds in 1954 among the eleven million acres of boreal forest and muskeg that compose Wood Buffalo National Park, a tract the Canadian government had set aside in 1922 as a refuge for bison.

One of Allen's supreme gifts was his ability to convert other people to his favorite causes. He was able to go into new localities, make friends almost immediately, and get the residents (farmers, fishermen, business people, and local officials) to understand what he was trying to do. The educational and public relations projects he carried on along the migration route helped to eliminate the shooting of the cranes as they returned from Canada each fall.

Both the roseate spoonbill and the whooping crane had made heartening progress in the struggle for survival by the time of Bob Allen's death in 1963. His name will always be associated with theirs. As the Society's first research director, he established the department's headquarters at Tavernier in the Florida Keys and laid the groundwork for much of the Audubon research that has taken place since.

# 21

"National Association" or "National Audubon Society"—
either designation remained somewhat presumptuous until the mid-
1940s, when a conscious effort by John Baker to reach out beyond the
Northeast finally established a truly national organization.

Most of the old state Audubon societies at the time either were
moribund or stood stubbornly aloof from Baker's operations. But here
and there around the country were vigorous little urban "bird clubs,"
nominally affiliated with the National Audubon Society and professing
to share its conservation interests, but actually devoted mostly to outings
led by local naturalists into woodsy places. Such a one was the St. Louis
(Missouri) Bird Club.

In the late '30s this club boasted of its hundred or so members,
which was indeed a robust number of organized nature enthusiasts in a
city of that size; but no more than a handful could be lured to the
periodic meetings and lectures sponsored by the club. One of the lecturers who gave a program in St. Louis on natural history before a
largely indifferent audience of ten people was a radio news broadcaster
and birdwatcher named Wayne Short. Because he seemed to be a live
wire and had connections with a number of the city's newspaper and
radio people, he was asked to fill the vacant post as club president.
Short, accepting the offer, reasoned that he could build a flourishing
organization only if the club was able to attract the public by a year-
round program.

"I was determined, as club president, never to have a speaker appear
before the club to an audience of only a dozen people again," he recalled. "The consensus of our board was to try to increase membership
by scheduling lecturers with sufficient renown to justify newspaper coverage, but at the same time, offering 'bird walks' in Forest Park, thereby
continuing the curiosity."

Short lived up to his reputation as a live wire. He organized bird
walks that attracted anywhere from fifty to three hundred men, women,

and children. The other part of Short's plan to stimulate membership succeeded in part because of a major technological breakthrough. Color motion-picture film had been improved just before World War II and was becoming available to independent photographers at a reasonable cost. Many of the country's leading naturalists rushed to take advantage of the new technology. They carried their movie cameras into the woods, fields, marshes, and other of their favorite haunts and began to produce the first films that captured the natural world in all of its astonishing color. As word of these films reached St. Louis, Short began to approach the filmmakers and, combining his considerable persuasive arts with the modest sums he had raised for the venture, he built an attractive series of film lectures for the winter months. Among the nature photographers he attracted to St. Louis were Roger Tory Peterson, Karl Maslowski, John Storer, George Miksch Sutton, and Olin Sewall Pettingill, Jr.

Pettingill was typical of the ornithologists who became prominent film-lecturers. After leaving the Laboratory of Ornithology at Cornell, he had ridden out the last years of the great Depression on a meager salary, teaching biology at Carleton College and picking up a few extra dollars by giving lectures illustrated by slides which he had laboriously hand-colored. He had, as we have seen, carried out the first whooping crane surveys for National Audubon. A new day dawned for him with the purchase of a Ciné Kodak Special, a camera with which he made several motion pictures about wildlife in the northern states. Having produced "rather elaborate brochures extolling their highlights," Pettingill accepted lecture invitations on weekends and during school vacations. At length he came to Short's notice and was invited to lecture in St. Louis.

Within a couple of years the membership of the St. Louis Bird Club had expanded to more than seven hundred, and an average of a thousand people attended each of the lectures. Short, by now, was thoroughly absorbed in his project and convinced cinema was the way to open the natural world to thousands of people in the cities and suburbs. Other urban bird clubs, he was sure, could make use of the same kind of carefully planned, dependable film program to swell their own membership lists. He began to envision a nationwide film-lecture program, directed from a single location and matching lecturers with specific cities. What better organization to coordinate such a venture than the National Audubon Society?

The United States entered World War II at the end of 1941, but with imagination and tenacity, Short went on producing successful lectures in St. Louis. Baker, beset with wartime problems that cut into some of his own programs, was reluctant to undertake another one. But he kept hearing about the success of the St. Louis programs from Pettingill, John

Olin Sewall Pettingill, Jr., was one of the noted ornithologists who played important roles in building the Audubon Screen Tours. NAS

Storer, and the other lecturers with whom he was acquainted. Baker finally accepted Short's invitation to St. Louis in the summer of 1943, arriving in one of the DC-3 planes that were then beginning to link American cities by regularly scheduled commercial flights. The two men settled on a program in which five lecturers would visit ten Midwestern cities during the winter of 1943–44. Short was to line up the sponsors in each of the cities, asking them to pay an amount sufficient to compensate the speakers and to support, at least in part, the lecture department that Short would direct. He also extracted from Baker an agreement that he be permitted to operate the department from St. Louis.

The program, called the Audubon Screen Tours, was a rousing success almost at once. More than a thousand people crowded the Rackham Auditorium in Detroit that fall for the first of the new department's programs, a color film on the wildlife of Florida presented by John Storer and sponsored by the Detroit Bird Club. Within a year or two, more than fifty cities from New England to California were in the program.

"From the very beginning, my major duty was to travel to every state in the Union and all of the provinces of Canada, returning again and again in some cases, in order to meet with potential sponsors and set up series," Short wrote. "The DC-3 has often been touted as America's safest airplane, and the most uncomfortable; so slow that, with many stops, it took 16 hours to cross the United States."

New speakers and filmmakers joined the tour as other cities were added. (Within a decade, Short had twenty-nine speakers available to active sponsors in more than two hundred cities.) Some of the lecturers made use of the omnipresent DC-3s, without which the program might never have succeeded. Others, such as Pettingill, who often traveled with his wife, Eleanor, preferred to drive from city to city, their film, projectors, and personal luggage piled in the back.

Conditions and audiences varied tremendously. Equipment breakdowns, minor illnesses, and the occasional unresponsive audience had to be surmounted. Pettingill dreaded the programs given in churches, where the odor of sanctity hung heavy and even the lively film he had made of penguins in the Falkland Islands failed to arouse the faintest ripple of amusement. But often the programs went well from the start. Even an introduction given by a nervous local "entertainment chairman" could set the proper light tone.

"One introducer said, 'I am sure Dr. Pettingill has enjoyed taking the pictures much more than you will enjoy seeing them,' " Pettingill wrote in an unpublished history of his screen-tour adventures. "Another introducer declared, 'This man has written guides to all the birds.' Whereupon Eleanor, sitting by the projector in the audience, heard a lady nearby gleefully remark to her companion, 'Why, that's Roger Peterson!' My favorite introduction, which included some factual information, concluded with, 'Now I am happy to introduce Dr. Penguin.' This broke up the house and put me in just the right mood for my narration."

The Audubon Screen Tours were to have two lasting effects, one of which was to enable the Society to reach a new, potentially responsive audience for the conservation message. The other was the creation of a means by which the Audubon movement could become, in truth, a national association of Audubon societies; until then, only the Junior Audubon clubs maintained a genuinely national network. Carl Buchheister, Wayne Short, and others on his staff had persuaded Baker to see the advantages of bringing the various local organizations sponsoring the Audubon Screen Tours into a closer relationship with the National Audubon Society as dues-sharing branches.

"It would take a colossal effort, particularly in getting the groups to change their precious names from bird clubs, naturalist clubs, and the like to Audubon societies," Short wrote. "I've always thought, rightly or wrongly, that Baker was well aware that his jug-a-rum voice and establishment demeanor did not lend themselves to some situations requiring a lot of finesse. His conservation stories about 'negras' were not in the best of taste. Carl Buchheister had the necessary ingredients. Again Baker was faced with how best to use the time of his staff, in this case his own [chief assistant]. It took some doing, but he was finally convinced that the way to begin the branch plan was to have [our staff] produce a film which Buchheister would present on the circuit. [Buchheister's film, centered on the wildlife he had become familiar with as director of the Maine camp, also provided splendid propaganda for National Audubon.] A condition of his doing so was that he should be scheduled so as to allow him two days with each sponsor in order to sell the idea of their becoming a branch."

In 1943 Baker suggested that Short persuade the leaders of the St. Louis Bird Club to change its name to the St. Louis Audubon Society and become a branch of National Audubon. Short encountered the expected opposition from those members who did not want to change the club's name or share dues with National Audubon. But he succeeded in his mission, and the new St. Louis Audubon Society became the first Audubon branch, with its members from then on holding joint membership in both the local and national organizations. Buchheister's coast-to-coast film and arm-twisting tour was also a success, and soon dozens of other local organizations entered the fold. The "branch system" was the origin of the network that, with a change of nomenclature, grew to more than five hundred Audubon chapters in the next forty years.

Baker's achievement in acquiring a truly national status for the Society was remarkable for its timing. Most nonprofit organizations were barely holding their own or were lapsing into a kind of hibernation in wartime America. Even enthusiastic birdwatchers found difficulties as they pursued their favorite avocation, being barred from certain familiar birding sites that had been taken over by the military or arousing the suspicions of the police when they tramped onto remote beaches or marshes with their binoculars. After the Japanese attack on Pearl Harbor, the Honolulu Audubon Society canceled its Christmas Bird Count because of travel restrictions. Participants in the 1941 Christmas Count in the San Diego region were stopped five times by military personnel on the lookout for "saboteurs or spies," and were warned away from many large areas along the coast. The Bausch and Lomb Company bought ads in *Audubon Magazine*, announcing that all its production would be going to the military for some time to come and urging civilians to mail their own binoculars to the Naval Observatory in Washington, D.C.

Death took some familiar Audubon figures in 1943. Gilbert Pearson died just short of his seventieth birthday. National Audubon's board of directors eulogized him in *Audubon Magazine*, emphasizing the ground-breaking legislative battles in which he played the leading role.

"He must be considered the chief builder of the Audubon work in this country," the directors said. "It was he, again, who began large-scale nature education among children and under his guidance the Audubon Junior Clubs molded the nature interests of more than five million American school children. In [another] field, that of international bird protection, he was a pioneer among those who realized that no one country could fight alone the battle for the birds."

Kermit Roosevelt, who had served as Audubon president directly after Pearson (1935–37), had died only a few months earlier while on active service as a major with the United States Army in Alaska. (Two of his brothers also died on active service: Quentin in World War I and Theodore, Jr., in World War II.) Alaska was also the scene of the death of James Moffitt, who had been an Audubon director and a Curator of Birds at the California Academy of Sciences and who lost his life in the crash of a Navy plane. And finally, in 1943, Audubon lost Lester Karcher, who had become the supervising warden of its south Florida sanctuaries. A note in *Audubon Magazine* suggests this popular warden's dedication:

"In February, 1942, as a result of over-exertion in the maintenance of the Society's equipment, he suffered a cerebral hemorrhage from which he never fully recovered. In July of that year, he was recalled to war service as a Coast Guard recruiting officer. Beset by numerous physical complications throughout the following year, his spirit never flagged. In December, he was assigned to boat inspection service in the Seventh Naval District, and died suddenly, in late June."

Against these losses and restrictions, Baker pushed to broaden Audubon's national base. Aside from the early activity of William L. Finley as warden, lobbyist, and slide lecturer, the Society had been slow to make its presence felt on the West Coast. Transportation difficulties in the days before dependable commercial flights were one obvious reason for the failure to seize fertile conservation territory. Another was the belief that privately owned sanctuaries were not needed as badly in much of the West as in, for instance, the East Coast and Gulf states; the federal government owned a large percentage of the land in the West, and colonial birds usually nested in its refuges, national parks and monuments, and national forests.

But as early as 1939, Baker became aware that a surging population was altering the landscape in California. He met that year with the officers of various Audubon societies and other groups loosely affiliated with the national organization to consider suitable sites for sanctuaries in southern California. Largely through the efforts of Alma Stultz, a naturalist who headed a sanctuary committee for the purpose, National

Audubon bought nine acres and leased over three hundred more in bottomland at El Monte, near the San Gabriel River.

The new sanctuary, only twelve miles from Los Angeles, became the center for a number of children's programs in natural history. The "jungle-like" growth on the sanctuary also served as the backdrop for some of the Tarzan films, and visiting nature lovers grew accustomed to coming upon a docile elephant chained among the grapevines. Eventually, with Alma Stultz as director, the Audubon Center of Southern California arose on the site.

Baker's knack for attracting imaginative (and sometimes eccentric) staff members carried over to California. Charles Albert "Bert" Harwell came out of that mold. His prime credentials for the job as National Audubon's "Western Representative" were his experiences and reputation as chief naturalist at Yosemite National Park, where his nature walks had become a popular attraction. But his value to Audubon as a public relations man and pacifier of hard feelings was based on his skills as an entertainer. He was a lecturer, piano player, and photographer who stood out as a favorite with audiences for the Audubon Screen Tours. Moreover, he carried his peculiar genius for imitating the calls of birds even beyond the achievements in that line of Frank Chapman and Allan Cruickshank.

"I have whistled my way out of most of my troubles and into many of the best things in my life," he once said, adding that he inherited his talent from his mother, an Arkansas farm girl who had learned to whistle like a red-tailed hawk to teach her chicks to scurry for cover.

By the time he was twelve years old, Harwell could imitate the songs of fifty California birds. He attended a whistling school in Los Angeles (from which another graduate went on to supply the birdsong for the score of *Snow White*). While teaching in a more conventional school, Harwell began whistling on the radio and became known as the Birdman. One day, however, he abandoned teaching, enrolled in a school for ranger naturalists at Yosemite, and began building the reputation that finally came to Baker's attention. The bird calls remained part of all his programs, indoors and out. Donald Culross Peattie, writing in *Audubon Magazine*, has left us a brief picture of Harwell in action.

"If you are wise," Peattie wrote, "you'll go far just to be out there in front when Bert steps up to the piano, cocks his head, cocks his eye like a bird, and, pursing his lips, lets out of the cage of his memory all the songs, all the springtime, stored there from his years afield."

Harwell toured California in a station wagon with the words "National Audubon Society" painted on its doors, giving programs in schools, promoting Audubon Wildlife Tours to the most fertile birding places (an idea introduced by Baker in Florida a year or two earlier),

Charles A. "Bert" Harwell, a long-time Audubon leader
in California, with his camera in Yosemite in 1943.
PHOTO BY R. H. ANDERSON, NAS

and urging local people to form new Audubon societies. At his urging, societies sprang up in Sacramento, Stockton, and other areas around the state in the early 1940s. California was on its way to becoming a strong Audubon outpost.

An often overlooked aspect of Baker's personality gave impetus to National Audubon's wartime growth. Aloof and even highhanded as he was in many of his relationships with staff members and other conservationists, he was an extraordinary salesman and publicist. In addition, his business acumen was admired by Guy Emerson and the other members of the board who had banking and Wall Street experience. In those areas of action Baker was often a one-man show, dealing successfully on the personal level with potential financial contributors and donors of land and (as in the case of the 1940s plumage campaign) writing the Society's press releases himself.

"It never bothered me that there was not any news item to hang a release on," he told one of his staff members. "I just created the news, or sent a release that had no news angle. Many of them were, nevertheless, printed. I think it takes a little ingenuity and imagination."

Buchheister and others who knew Baker in those days liked to point out that he was not invariably the aloof sour-puss who too often came across to those outside his tight circle. He was a charming if dignified salesman for Audubon in large gatherings, and his top staff knew he could be a convivial companion after a long day in the field. Buchheister liked to recall a particularly uproarious evening at Hog Island, Maine, when Baker, with an undetermined number of his favorite martinis under his ample belt, wobbled off the dock and was quickly sobered in the icy water of Muscongus Bay.

If the Society owned land, Baker demanded that it be as productive as possible, either as a refuge for wildlife or as a site for educational projects, to which he sometimes added the stipulation that it pay its own way through its natural resources. When Rosalie Edge quashed the trapping scheme at the Rainey Sanctuary in Louisiana, Baker quickly seized on another potential income-producer. He signed a lease with an oil company during the war to explore the petroleum resources on that sanctuary, under carefully monitored conditions. The oil rights at Rainey were to become an important source of income for Audubon in the years ahead.

Baker was always on the alert for land acquisition. One of National Audubon's most valuable properties came to it in 1942 when Eleanor Steele Reese and H. Hall Clovis donated to the Society 281 acres in the Round Hill section of Greenwich, Connecticut, for a wildlife sanctuary.

Here was a rich and diverse landscape of forest and swamp, field and orchard, lake and stream, set in the midst of one of the world's

Roger Tory Peterson and Guy Emerson were frequent
birding companions in the 1930s and '40s. NAS

wealthiest neighborhoods and within easy distance of New York City.
Baker, with the help of local residents, set about building the Audubon
Center in Greenwich as a flagship for the Society's programs in urban
and suburban nature education. To Greenwich would come, every summer, teachers from urban schools for courses in natural history and
conservation. Returning to their classrooms, the teachers would help to
pass on the Audubon message to new generations. It was ironic that the
Greenwich program was nearly steamrollered at the start by the new
United Nations Organization. A report by a special UN committee in
1946 recommended that consideration as a site for its new headquarters
be given to an area near the Connecticut–New York border which included the Audubon Center! The owners of some adjacent properties
protested, but National Audubon decided to sit tight and ride out the
storm. As all the world knows, the UN finally decided to make its home
in New York City.

As Baker paid visits to potential contributors, both corporations and
private individuals, his self-confidence needed but one added prop: a
loftier title. The post of executive director had sounded fine to him a
decade earlier when he was dealing mainly with problems in his own

shop or within the conservation movement; but now, approaching leaders in business and finance and members of the upper crust generally, he felt that the title of president would more adequately reflect his decision-making role in National Audubon. He went before the board of directors in 1944 and suggested he be given a title with added impact. Accordingly, Emerson stepped down as titular president, the board abolished the post of executive director, and Baker assumed the title of president. The board also named Buchheister as his vice president and elected that legendary birder Ludlow Griscom as chairman.

The war years, with their giant step forward in technological innovation, offered Baker one more opportunity to act with foresight, and he seized it before any of his contemporaries. The United States Armed Forces, searching for an insecticide to protect its troops against malaria, yellow fever, and the other insect-borne diseases that had plagued armies for centuries, happened upon a chemical compound developed by a Swiss firm and called dichloro-diphenyl-trichloroethane. DDT, as the product became popularly known, worked wonders as a louse powder. It is not nearly so acutely toxic in small quantities to human beings as most other insecticides are, and applied to the bodies and clothing of soldiers and civilians in the Mediterranean theater of war, DDT smothered a potentially disastrous typhoid epidemic. Later, DDT proved dramatically effective when it was mixed with kerosene or other solutions and sprayed over the breeding grounds of malarial mosquitoes.

Word of DDT's wartime miracles spread quickly, and a large public was awaiting its production for nonmilitary markets. The world's insect problems seemed to be solved. But Baker, aware of some disquietude among scientists he had talked to, sensed the threat to wildlife of distributing widely in the environment a chemical designed to kill living things. Near the end of the war, he involved National Audubon with the U.S. Fish and Wildlife Service in several experiments that were designed to test DDT's effects on birds. Dick Pough, sent by Baker to observe studies sponsored by the two organizations near Moscow, Pennsylvania, became alarmed. He saw that entire areas of the forest lost their birds when DDT was applied at the then-recommended dosage of five pounds per acre, and that there were significant changes in the bird population at much lower dosages. Pough tried to counteract the growing enthusiasm for the chemical among agricultural and forestry groups.

"A spray like DDT makes people think of a continent arranged like a manicured garden, but you can't kick nature around that way," he was quoted by *The New Yorker* in its issue of May 26, 1945. "If DDT should ever be used widely and without care, we would have a country without freshwater fish, serpents, frogs, and most of the birds we have now. Mind you, we don't object to its use to save lives now. What we are afraid of is what might happen when peace comes."

Baker adopted the same tone in his column in *Audubon Magazine*, warning that the current unrestrained optimism might very well lead to an irreversible environmental catastrophe. The message was in keeping with the new responsibilities of a national conservation organization on the threshold of an era that was to be dominated by a runaway technology.

# 22

$\mathcal{S}$wamps, storks, and cypress trees formed a dramatic backdrop for John Baker's final decade at Audubon. Those dwindling wild treasures became the objects of benefactions that flowed from diverse sources—among them southern lumbermen, local Audubon societies, garden clubs, and (in an early episode of what was to become a long relationship for National Audubon) the Rockefeller family.

Baker's boundless energy, coupled with his skill at persuading other people to make land available in one way or another to the Society, went on to develop new programs in the postwar years. The success of the Audubon Camp of Maine and the new camp in Greenwich (later enhanced by the addition of the 125-acre Fairchild Wildflower Garden nearby) encouraged him to establish nature camps in other parts of the country. In 1948 he arranged to lease the Sugar Bowl Lodge at Norden, California. There, among mountain meadows splashed with wildflowers and with snowcapped peaks in the distance, he established the Audubon Camp of California (later named the Audubon Camp of the West). Teachers and other men and women eager to immerse themselves in a crash course in the natural history of the region put themselves body and soul in the hands of a succession of camp directors, perhaps the most notable of whom was William Goodall. Goodall, a short, brisk man with a fund of wisecracks and comic stories, eventually replaced Bert Harwell as the Society's western representative.

At the same time that Baker was organizing a camp in California, he was at work in Texas on a similar project. With the help of Magnolia Greene, a resident of Austin who was prominent in garden clubs and various conservation groups, he founded the Texas Audubon Camp at the Schriner Institute. A junior college associated with the Presbyterian Church, the Institute leased to Audubon its campus in Kerrville during the summer months. Again, Baker had chosen a lovely setting, this one on the Guadalupe River, a clear-running stream bordered by big cypresses, near the edge of the Edwards Plateau. A favorite trip for the campers was to a neighboring ranch in the limestone country, the site of an enormous bat cave.

"There were said to be between twenty and thirty million Mexican free-tailed bats in New Cave," recalled Alex Sprunt's son, Sandy, who was on the camp's staff. "The bats started to come out before sundown and there were hawks that fed on this stream of bats—peregrines, red-tailed and sharp-shinned hawks. Three groups of hawks, in fact—falcons, buteos, and accipiters—all feeding on this same bat stream."

Unfortunately, the camp lasted only five years, closing after the 1952 season. The Texas Board of Education put a stiff requirement on its teachers at the time, requiring many of them to earn advanced degrees during the summer months, while apparently many non-Texans did not think of the state as a summer haven.

Wisconsin, like Maine, was free of that handicap as a place for a summer camp. Carl Buchheister, in fact, opened the way for the Audubon Camp of Wisconsin in the days when he was still spending his summers at Hog Island. Velma "Dixie" Larkin of Milwaukee had been an enthusiastic Audubon camper in both California and Maine. While at Hog Island, she spoke to Buchheister about the possibility of establishing an Audubon camp in Wisconsin. He described the kind of site and funding needed.

Upon returning home, Dixie Larkin organized a drive to locate both of the necessities. The site materialized with the contribution by Frances Andrews of Minneapolis of the summer farm that she and her father owned in northern Wisconsin, near the town of Sarona. Dixie Larkin and her friend raised $68,000 to erect the required buildings among the farm's lakes and grand old trees. In 1955, the camp opened. On its staff was Dorothy Treat, one of the leading natural-history instructors of her time, who was to help devise the programs at nearly all the Audubon camps (she had been on the staff of the Texas camp, too) and would be remembered fondly by a generation of natural-history students.

Meanwhile, Baker was spreading the conservation message and promoting the Society's camps, Screen Tours, and other projects with the help of a succession of editors at *Audubon Magazine*. After Bill Vogt's abrupt departure, the magazine was run for a time by Margaret Brooks, who had been an assistant to Vogt. But eventually she married Joe Hickey, that indefatigable point-man of the Bronx County Bird Club, and moved with him to the University of Wisconsin, where he taught for many years.

Baker looked around for a new editor at cut-rate prices. Dick Pough had a candidate in mind, a young writer and editor of scientific publications at the United States Bureau of Fisheries (later absorbed by the Fish and Wildlife Service). Her name was Rachel Carson. Baker ignored the suggestion and, as everyone knows, she went on to write a series of best-selling books including that environmental classic of the postwar era, *Silent Spring*. Baker settled on another woman as editor of *Audubon Magazine*, one who had both a deep interest in conservation and a lively sense of humor—Eleanor Anthony King. (A great kidder, she liked to correspond with her authors about their stories, posing as an ex-chorus girl named McSnoyd.)

After becoming editor in 1942, King took the revolutionary step of paying certain authors in an attempt to upgrade the magazine's literary quality. The writers received fees based on their recognition index. For instance, in 1948, Alexander Skutch, who was tucked away in the wilds of Central America, received twenty-five dollars for an article, and Louise de Kiriline Lawrence, similarly obscured in the north country, received thirty-five. Edwin Way Teale was worth $100 to King, while a big gun like Donald Culross Peattie commanded $200. Photographers received ten dollars for cover photos, which in those days were always published in black and white. King must have used her wiles to bury these payments in the magazine's budget, for Baker later told one of her successors, John Terres, that "I did not know it."

King, suffering from cancer, nevertheless went on working until a week before her death in 1949. Ken Morrison, assisted and later succeeded by Terres, edited the magazine during the remainder of Baker's administration. Terres himself became a power in the nature field. During the 1930s he had served as a wildlife specialist in the U.S. Department of Agriculture, where he spent most of his time in the field, recording the feeding habits of birds and compiling many of the dozens of volumes of field notebooks on which his subsequent writings were based.

Several of the dramatic articles Terres wrote while at *Audubon Magazine* triggered campaigns to save wild areas from development, among them Island Beach State Park, New Jersey, which became an important station for the banding of migratory birds. In 1956, Terres became aware of the tremendous loss of birdlife in Manhattan every fall when thousands of migrants struck the Empire State Building. He visited the building's managers and convinced them that the problem was the dazzling 25-million-candlepower fixed-beam light on top of what was then the tallest building in the world. Management conceded, turning off the fixed-beam light and depending on the rotating warning lights during migration, and the birds have had easier passage over Thirty-fourth Street ever since.

As Baker worked to reshape the Society, in both soul and body, to his own specifications, he supervised a couple of significant changes in 1953. In that year National Audubon adopted the flying great egret as

Audubon House, at Fifth Avenue and Ninety-fourth Street. NAS

its emblem. A likeness of the big white bird has appeared since then on the arm patch of all uniformed staff members, as well as on much of the Society's stationery, its publications, and its sanctuary signs.

The Society also acquired a new Audubon House. It was a four-story Georgian-style mansion of red brick, built about 1915 for a wealthy New Yorker, Willard Straight, at 1130 Fifth Avenue on the corner of Ninety-fourth Street. Arrangements to buy the property from its current owner, Mrs. Harrison Williams, were concluded in July 1952, the building at 1006 Fifth Avenue was sold, and the staff moved into its new headquarters shortly after the first of the year.

Baker, tireless as always, was soon engrossed in negotiations to acquire an even grander property some fifteen hundred miles to the south.

The Florida landscape had become familiar ground to Baker, as it has for every National Audubon president. In the years immediately after World War II he had flown over much of the southern part of the state in a "puddle-jumper" with his old friend Commander Carl C. von-Paulsen of the Coast Guard Air Station in Coconut Grove. At first, his interest was mainly in the rookeries guarded by Audubon wardens, especially those of the great white heron, whose range and population were both small. Later he played a leading role in bringing together the local conservationists, politicians, and government agencies for the establishment of Everglades National Park.

Baker had been especially effective in dealing with Florida Governor Spessard Holland and his successor, Millard Caldwell, inviting them on a trip by boat with warden Arthur Eifler to tour sections of the Everglades they had never seen. En route across Florida Bay, around Cape Sable, and up through the Ten Thousand Islands to Everglades City, Baker talked about ways in which Holland could fulfill his campaign pledge to promote the idea of a national park in southern Florida. Baker urged Holland to appoint a new Everglades National Park Commission and even suggested the names of several influential people who might serve on it. Conservationists close to the negotiations pointed to Baker's crucial role when the national park was established in 1947.

The experience alerted Baker to the fact that National Audubon, aside from its wardens, was weakly represented in the state. On Commander vonPaulsen's recommendation he hired a former Coast Guardsman, Charles Brookfield, first as a warden at the Shark River Rookery and later as National Audubon's "South Florida Representative." Brookfield thought the title a little too trivial.

"I said let's call it Tropical Florida representative and Baker agreed to that," Brookfield recalled. "I found out later there were only twenty-nine members of the National Audubon Society in South Florida, including Miami, and one of them promptly died on me. Baker wanted me to lead national tours into the Everglades, at first to drum up support for the national park and later to promote National Audubon in that area. I organized eleven branches for the Society, and in the next sixteen years I took sixteen thousand people into the park and various rookeries. One of the people I took in was Rosalie Edge. She told me, 'I do not approve of John Baker.' "

One of the areas where Brookfield led tours, even before the national park opened, was Cuthbert Lake, to which Guy Bradley had taken Herbert K. Job and Arthur C. Bent more than forty years earlier. The lake had retained its original wildness.

"It was a marvelous sight," Brookfield said. "It was truly a hidden creek in there. The first year, we had to clear away the mangrove limbs along the creek to get our boats in there."

There were other important rookeries to the north that had not been included in the new national park. Gilbert Pearson had employed wardens as early as 1912 to guard the big egret rookeries in the cypress swamps. Alongside the egrets in that area nested wood storks, a species which is North America's only true stork. It is a big bird, three and a half feet tall, white with black feathers, and the bare, wrinkled, gray skin on its head prompted the backcountry name, "flinthead." Because the storks' plumage had little value, the local people seldom shot them, except for the pot, and their rookeries remained largely intact in the Big Cypress country. There the storks, which in the Everglades often nest in mangroves, gathered in the magnificent bald cypress trees that grow in "strands" along the course of ancient depressions. These are among the oldest trees in eastern North America, some of them 400 years old with a girth of nearly twenty-five feet.

The wood stork, which had weathered the plume-hunting era, was one of the birds whose very existence became threatened by conditions in the second half of the twentieth century. The Big Cypress country was on its way to destruction, and at this time was the heart of the stork's restricted range. Lumber companies were cutting their way with incredible speed through the stands of those valuable trees, while agricultural companies drained the underlying wetlands for their truck farms; and poised to come in behind them were the developers, who intensified the practice of cutting trees and draining the land. By 1953, the last significant strand of bald cypress remained in the Corkscrew Swamp (named for the twisting creek that flowed out of it) in Collier County, twenty-five miles inland from the Gulf of Mexico. This strand, which old-timers in the area remembered as being twenty-five miles long, had been reduced to three miles by lumbermen and occasional fires, and the remainder seemed to be doomed.

There was a swelling tide of sentiment around the state to save the Corkscrew Swamp. Baker went to Tampa in March 1954 to meet a number of people interested in saving the trees. There he reported on the meetings he had already held with officials of the two companies that owned the cypress strand: J. Arthur Currey of the Lee Tidewater Cypress Company, and Miles Collier of Collier Enterprises. (Lee Tidewater was already cutting in the swamp.) The two officials, Baker reported, seemed to want to find a solution; apparently they had no stomach for being responsible for felling the last of the big cypress. The conservationists then assembled in Tampa formed the Corkscrew Cypress Rookery Association and elected Baker finance chairman. There was now a fresh urgency to the campaign. Conservationists said that eight or ten thousand pairs of storks nested at Corkscrew, by far the largest concentration of those birds anywhere in the state.

Baker, curiously, did not plan to add Corkscrew to National Audubon's roster of sanctuaries. He told the Rookery Association that the Society was prepared to accept title to the land, maintain it, and provide wardens and interpretive personnel. But the money needed to purchase the land, as well as build the needed facilities for the visitor center and staff, would have to be raised by other organizations. Perhaps Baker believed that National Audubon, with so many other projects under way, could not afford to buy and maintain a sanctuary of more than ten thousand acres in modern Florida. He expected Corkscrew to be taken over eventually by another agency such as the Florida Board of Parks.

The Lee Tidewater Cypress Company asked mainly that the purchase price cover the value of the cypress trees still standing. Nevertheless, that cost, added to a modest building program once the land had been bought as a sanctuary, would bring the sale price to more than $200,000. The money had to be raised quickly, because Currey was eager to close the company's mill. A part of the money was raised in Florida, Marjorie Smith, the president of the Florida Federation of Garden Clubs, successfully approaching the individual clubs, and Charlie Brookfield, working out of Miami, finding some generous contributors among businessmen and industrialists.

At this point Dick Pough came into the picture. Pough, who was always essentially an entrepreneur and seemed uncomfortable working for anyone else, had naturally existed on prickly terms with Baker. Having left National Audubon to chair a department of conservation and ecology at the American Museum of Natural History, he was brought into the Corkscrew campaign through O. Earle Frye, Jr., assistant director of the Florida Game and Fresh Water Fish Commission. Pough offered to help Baker, who implied that the Rookery Association would have to settle for half a loaf.

"I asked if he'd mind if I tried to raise the rest of the money," Pough said, "and he laughed in a funny way he had, suggesting that if I was fool enough to try, it was okay with him."

Pough, who was on his way to becoming conservation's leading fundraiser, obtained part of the money from philanthropists and foundations but was still about $90,000 short of the needed total. He went to his friend Horace Albright, a former chief of the National Park Service who was an adviser to John D. Rockefeller, Jr., on conservation matters. Although Albright told Pough that he had made it a practice not to ask Rockefeller for money, he agreed to make an exception in this case. After lunching with Rockefeller, he telephoned Pough to say that Rockefeller would make up the sum needed to purchase the trees from Lee Tidewater Cypress.

"I called Baker and asked him to get in touch with Currey and tell him that Audubon had the money and to call off the loggers," Pough said. "I well remember his reply. He said he needed it in writing before he could commit the Society! I said, 'Well, John, if you want to ask Mr. Rockefeller for it in writing, go ahead. His word is good enough for me.' This had the desired effect and Baker called Currey."

Then, in a rare gesture of good will, the company gave National

Audubon a "Christmas present" of 640 additional acres. At the same time, Collier Enterprises leased 3,200 acres of cutover land to the Society for one dollar a year, and the purchase price of $25,000 was raised later in a comparatively leisurely campaign. Baker, with more than 6,000 acres in hand and paid for, decided to maintain Corkscrew Swamp permanently as an Audubon sanctuary. (In 1968, National Audubon, with the help of a matching grant from the Ford Foundation, bought additional land, bringing the total to nearly 11,000 acres.)

To establish National Audubon's presence at Corkscrew, Baker assigned one of his best wardens, Henry "Hank" Bennett, to the new sanctuary as "protective representative." Bennett, fearless and devoted, was a natural for the position. He had belonged to a Junior Audubon Club as a child. While serving as the Audubon warden at Duck Rock, he had lived on a small boat from March until September and had once been assaulted by poachers shooting up a white ibis rookery in the area. (They were later convicted and fined at Key West, though the judge suspended their jail term.) In winter, Bennett led Audubon Wildlife Tours into the Everglades. Now he settled into a one-room cabin with a screened porch hastily built for him by a local hunter named Sam Whidden. This retreat, without phone or electricity and accessible only by jeep, was to Bennett's taste.

But Bennett's paradise was short-lived. National Audubon made the decision to open this gem of its sanctuary system to visitors, disturbing as little as possible the resident wildlife community.

"How to do it?" Alex Sprunt once wrote. "Even if it were desirable, few would care to investigate the fantastic beauty of the swamp by 'bogging it out,' or wading hip-deep through sourgrass, arrowhead, and water-lettuce as did a party of distinguished guests in 1955. The obvious answer was a boardwalk which would take the visitor to the heart of the area dryshod."

Sprunt's son, Sandy, who later succeeded Bob Allen as Audubon's director of research, came to Corkscrew in the fall of 1955 to help Bennett build the boardwalk. Sam Whidden and several of his brothers were also drafted into the labor force. The construction was an arduous undertaking, with the workers slogging into the muck and sometimes wading chest-high in swamp water. One section of the original boardwalk was set down that fall, and another the following year, to bring its total length to 5,600 feet. The water in one of the lettuce lakes was exceptionally deep.

"Poor Hank, who was a rather short person, was up to his chin a lot of the time crossing that water, whereas the rest of us had a little more altitude," Sandy Sprunt recalled. "That was the only place we ever ran afoul of an alligator, too. There was a big female that lived in there and we kept a wary eye out for her. But Hank and I always felt that the alligator was at a distinct disadvantage in attacking a Whidden because the Whiddens had lived off the swamp and trapped and taken furs and alligator hides for all of their lives, and we figured it was unequal difficulties for the alligator. We stumbled over her one day, and she made no particular demur about the situation."

Sandy's father led many of the early tours into the sanctuary. Because there were no living or dining accommodations in the area, the visitors had to establish their base at Clewiston on Lake Okeechobee, seventy miles away, until about 1960 when the new highway between Naples and Immokalee brought civilization a little closer. Visitors, at one dollar a head, began coming to the sanctuary in increasing numbers to gain access to what once had been a hidden world to all but the most intrepid. All this was too much for Hank Bennett. Believing that the flow of visitors would change the wilderness character of the swamp, he resigned in disgust. Baker sent James Callaghan, director of the Roosevelt Sanctuary at Oyster Bay, to take over temporarily at Corkscrew, and the resourceful Callaghan designed many of the improvements that are evident on the sanctuary today.

There were many kinds of curiosities, of course, among the human visitors as well as among the native flora and fauna. Sandy Sprunt, who conducted some of the tours, had been warned by his father about the impending arrival of an unusually naive tourist who bothered the other members of the tour with pointless questions. Sandy was prepared.

At one point on the boardwalk, the tourist leaned over the railing, gaped at the dark water, and came up with a question: "How many dead bodies were found floating in the swamp when they were building this thing?"

"Oh, not very many," Sandy Sprunt replied.

Which seemed to satisfy the visitor's curiosity.

# 23

The Buchheister years (1959–1967) represent the *Pax Romana* of the Audubon movement. Although they coincided with perhaps the most intense series of legislative struggles in the modern conservation era, there was harmony at Audubon House and an unusual degree of unity among the major organizations. Even Rosalie Edge, reconciled if unrepentant, returned to the Audubon fold on the eve of her death.

A comparatively new pension system at the National Audubon Society provided that an employee retire at the age of sixty-five unless granted a waiver by the board of directors. In 1959, the board asked Baker if he wanted to stay on as president, but he declined.

"It would set a bad precedent," he told Carl Buchheister. "It should be sixty-five for everybody."

Baker had made it plain from the beginning that he had hired Buchheister to be his successor, and the younger man, diplomatic yet almost old-fashioned in his adherence to principle, never gave him reason to change his mind. Paul B. Sears, a noted ecologist at Yale University and at the time Audubon's chairman of the board, came to Buchheister and asked him to be president. Buchheister, who wanted to be president very much, nevertheless acted as a kind of devil's advocate on the offer, pointing out that Baker ran such a one-man show that he, Buchheister, had had little experience in certain areas of administration; he remained primarily an educator. But Sears quickly brushed aside the demur.

"You've been close to Baker and you know the Society," he said. 'You've got seven or eight more years before you have to retire. Take it."

Then Sears asked Buchheister if he would object to a suggestion to put Baker back on the board of directors.

"I certainly would," Buchheister replied. "He has been my boss for all these years, and if he goes on the board he will still be my boss. If I am going to take on this job, I want a free hand."

He had no objection, however, to the board's plan to install Baker in an office at Audubon House, with a secretary, travel expenses, and a modest consulting fee, to carry on his work in fundraising and land acquisition. That Baker never again brought in substantial amounts of either money or land was not the reason Buchheister came to regret his presence on the scene. The older man's reluctance to drop the reins of power (an understandable impulse related to "founder's syndrome") remained a minor irritant to Buchheister for the next several years, though using tact and firmness he carried out his programs without any sort of an uproar. His only reference to the situation was a mild offhand comment to a colleague: "It would have been better if John had not stayed."

Still, no one understood or admired Baker's achievements more than Buchheister. Like Roger Peterson, he always considered Baker the finest of Audubon leaders—the most gifted, the most energetic, and the most clear-eyed when advancing the Society's interest. Under his leadership, membership had increased from thirty-five hundred in 1934 to thirty-one thousand at his retirement. He had built a full-time staff of seventy-five employees, servicing the camps, sanctuaries, educational centers, and three hundred branches around the country. The Audubon Screen Tours annually reached half a million people in over two hundred cities. Enrollment in the Junior Audubon clubs had passed ten million children. The Society paid tribute to Baker at a banquet during its annual convention at the Hotel Roosevelt on November 10, 1959, with past and current board members presenting him with a large painting of nesting whooping cranes they had commissioned for the event from Roger Peterson.

Certainly one of Baker's legacies to Buchheister was the belief that he would need a strong and trustworthy assistant to support him in his own administration. Buchheister's search for an aide began even before he took over from Baker. He realized that, in the modern era, bird protection must be tied to wider environmental battles, many of which were already shaping up in Washington. Working with lawmakers would not be as simple as it had been in Gilbert Pearson's day. Legislation by Congress had imposed severe restrictions on nonprofit organizations, jeopardizing their rights to receive tax-deductible contributions if they devoted any "substantial" effort to influencing legislation. The Internal Revenue Service was inclined to stick to the letter of the law. As a result of this, Baker had shied away from close encounters with Congress, and there was no one on the Society's staff really skilled at sophisticated lobbying within the limits of the law.

As the first step in recruiting a conservationist who would be able to meet the new challenges, Buchheister asked the advice of some of his friends in Washington. The man who came most highly recommended

Charles H. Callison, who
made Audubon a
powerful presence in the
nation's capital. NAS

was Charles H. Callison. Callison had been born in Alberta, Canada, where his parents, both natives of Missouri, homesteaded for a time when they were first married. Returning with his family to Missouri while still an infant, Callison grew up on a farm, became a newspaperman, and later studied public administration in the Graduate School of the U.S. Department of Agriculture. He had been on the staff of the National Wildlife Federation, which he served as secretary and conservation director, since 1951. Callison and Buchheister had met while the former was chairman of the Natural Resources Council of America, a coordinating group to which about forty national conservation organizations and scientific societies belonged.

"I got to know Buchheister because we each represented our organization at meetings of the Natural Resources Council," Callison recalled. "During the annual meeting in 1959, when I was council president, Carl began hanging around me. I didn't know he was looking me over. At the end of the meeting, my wife Amy and I invited everyone in for a party. Carl always loved parties, and that I could put one on with some grace probably convinced him that I was his man."

Buchheister's task was to persuade this "country boy" to move to New York. But the two men liked each other from the start and, when Callison, who was not happy at the National Wildlife Federation, was offered a raise by National Audubon, he accepted Buchheister's offer.

"Carl and Harriet Buchheister had a large apartment on the upper East Side in Manhattan and they invited me to move in with them," Callison said. "I saw that Carl was the same kind of gentleman, with an attachment to old-fashioned manners, that he appeared to be in public. He would never even come to breakfast in the apartment until he had put on a jacket and tie. I commuted between Washington and New York until we sold our home and the whole family moved to a New York suburb."

The Buchheister years were under way. There had been some changes in staff. Roger Peterson had long since gone his own way to write his bird guides and other books, birding and lecturing in far places, while John Terres had more recently taken the same course. A new editor, John Vosburgh, had come from a Miami newspaper to take over the magazine, for which the book reviews were written by a woman who was on the way to becoming a distinguished American poet, Amy Clampitt. Shirley Miller continued in charge of the Junior Audubon clubs as she had for many years, but Wayne Short had been banished by Baker because, as stubborn as his boss, he refused to move the Screen Tours headquarters to New York.

Buchheister installed Callison in an office next to him. ("We worked like two peas in a pod," Buchheister once said. "If I needed anything I just hollered across the hall to him.") Callison began instructing his new chief in the ways of Washington, giving him résumés on the legislators and their staffs and teaching him how to make presentations before Congressional committees. He would have Buchheister read a statement on a current issue, then ask him the sort of tough questions a congressman might ask.

Although the Audubon branches in the hinterlands had proliferated impressively in recent years, Buchheister felt that communication was poor between them and Audubon House. He wanted Audubon in all its components to speak with one voice. Turning to Callison, he asked him to start a newsletter which would go out to the branches on a regular basis, alerting them to legislative developments and the action (or lack of it) being taken by federal agencies. The result was the *Audubon Leaders' Conservation Guide*, which was sent from New York regularly to the officers of Audubon branches.

A project for which John Baker felt some irritation toward his successor was the annual convention. Buchheister believed that one of the steps toward keeping the Society "National" was to take the conventions out of New York and hold them in various parts of the country. But Baker argued that taking the conventions on the road was a prescription for losing money. (He had tried it only once, in 1949.) The new president stuck to his guns and, in 1961, held the convention at one of the sprawling old hotels on the boardwalk at Atlantic City. The convention attracted a large turnout and made money. Baker was nearly apoplectic the next fall when Buchheister scheduled the convention for Corpus

Christi, Texas. Again, there was a large attendance, more than twelve hundred people making it the most successful annual convention the Society had ever held. The participants enjoyed tours of the Aransas National Wildlife Refuge to see whooping cranes, the mammoth King Ranch to inspect semidesert wildlife habitat, and other birding "hotspots" with Roger Peterson, Allan Cruickshank, and Sewall Pettingill.

On the evening before the convention banquet, Cruickshank rushed into Buchheister's room, and said, "Who do you think is here, Carl? Guess who is here!"

Buchheister, startled, gave up.

"Rosalie Edge," Cruickshank announced, and feigned a fainting spell.

Edge, of course, had once been a fixture at annual meetings but had not concerned herself with the trappings of field trips and banquets. She was by then a very old woman and, though still active in the organizations she had founded, the Emergency Conservation Committee and the Hawk Mountain Sanctuary Association, had gradually retreated from the Audubon scene.

"She is sitting downstairs in the lobby, and she told me she came here to see what was going on," Cruickshank said. "She registered for the convention today."

Later that evening, during a meeting to plan the seating at the dais, Buchheister came to a decision.

"Rosalie Edge hates us and we hate her, but she is the officer of two national conservation organizations," he said. "We will ask her to sit on the dais as an honored guest."

Cruickshank was dispatched to extend the invitation to her. He came back to the room after a few minutes, looking a little dazed, and told Buchheister, "God almighty, she accepted it."

The next day Buchheister sent Edge a handwritten invitation to attend the prebanquet reception at which the notables gathered, among them the governor of the state, a United States senator, and the chiefs of several federal agencies. Edge was the center of attention at the reception. When the banquet began, she entered the ballroom on Buchheister's arm. A few minutes later, during the introduction, this fiercest of Audubon foes received from the membership a standing ovation.

Rosalie Edge flew back to New York after the convention and told her son Peter, "I have made peace with the National Audubon Society." Three weeks later she died at the age of eighty-five.

The convention schedule was simply one example of Buchheister's determination to establish the Audubon presence in all parts of the country. There were still only two field representatives at the beginning of his administration, Charlie Brookfield in Florida and Bill Goodall in California. Both men were tireless workers, leading tours into the prime wildlife habitats in their regions and charming potential members or contributors with their fund of stories. Brookfield played a leading role in the establishment of the National Key Deer Wildlife Refuge in 1963, thereby preserving that collie-sized race of the white-tailed deer when it seemed on the edge of extinction. Goodall, working out of his office in San Francisco, recruited people of all ages for the Audubon Camp of the West at Norden and, when a replacement was needed, found a new site in Wyoming.

Buchheister and Callison spent a great deal of time trying to strengthen National Audubon's ties with state and local societies. Baker's contention that many of these groups had little direction or effectiveness may have been true to some extent, but he had tended to aggravate old wounds rather than heal them. To the Massachusetts Audubon Society, which wanted to be dealt with not as a chapter but as an equal, he suggested that dues from its members be sent directly to National Audubon, which would then return a portion of the money to the state society. The breach widened.

Buchheister encouraged the development of strong local leaders. About 1950, for instance, a group of Audubon members in southern New Jersey had become disenchanted with the state society. They set up a South Jersey Audubon Society with headquarters in an old house at Cape May Courthouse. Personalities clashed, and the two groups ran competing programs and birding tours, until the New Jersey groups were reunited under the able Frank McLaughlin.

Conditions varied considerably from state to state. For instance, the Michigan Audubon Society became a National Audubon chapter after long negotiations between the Detroit and Michigan societies to determine how they would divide members in that area. The Massachusetts Audubon Society had continued to grow in the postwar era under Russell Mason, then received a significant lift when Louise Hatheway, who was interested in environmental education, left the society $1.5 million to endow its new headquarters at Drumlin Farm in Lincoln. A major part of Mass Audubon's increasing influence was the creation of the Hatheway School of Conservation Education at Drumlin Farm. There, on winter evenings, William H. Drury, Jr., a biologist at Harvard University, came to teach courses for adults in science and natural history.

"I remember hearing people at the time complain that 'science has no business in a conservation organization,' " Drury has said. "I was especially interested in conducting teacher workshops after I went to work at the Hatheway School. The graduates of teaching schools all came with the abominable science and natural history background then pre-

Audubon members make a field trip to Montauk Point, Long Island,
during the 1947 convention. NAS

vailing. It was even difficult to get many conservation leaders themselves
to recognize that programs ought to be motivated by science and not
by policy. Russ Mason had a lot of missionary zeal. But, like any
fundamentalist, he never found it helpful to get other people's ideas."

When Mason left, Mass Audubon moved ahead even more vigorously under its new executive vice president, Allen Morgan. The addition of Morgan and Drury (who became director of the Hatheway School)
turned this state society into one of the most advanced conservation
organizations in the country.

"Morgan went head-to-head with National Audubon, trying to grab
local affiliates throughout New England and align them with Mass Audubon," Charlie Callison has recalled. "In fact, we learned of a plan to
form a new federation of state societies that would eclipse National
Audubon and put it out of business."

To combat the grab for power in New England, Buchheister hired
a young man named Stanley Quickmire to establish a New England
office and work to hold local chapters for National Audubon. He met
with mixed success. To this day, National Audubon does not have a
single chapter in Massachusetts, New Hampshire, or Rhode Island.
Strong chapters grew in Vermont, Connecticut, and Maine, however,

coexisting in the latter two states with independent state societies, a source of much confusion among local residents unversed in the byzantine politics of conservation. An attempt by Quickmire to lure the Maine Audubon Society into the national fold failed when he allied himself with an executive director who had lost local support and was facing imminent ouster.

Buchheister himself took an active and successful interest in the Florida situation because of his friendship with the president of the Florida Audubon Society, John Storer. Storer, a photographer and ecologist who had shown his films for years on the Audubon Screen Tours, believed that National Audubon should not have chapters in Florida, because they competed for dues-paying members with the state society. (Adding to the complications was Storer's choice of Russell Mason, Buchheister's successor and antagonist at Mass Audubon, to take the position of executive director at Florida Audubon.) A meeting was arranged at Florida Audubon's headquarters in Maitland, with Buchheister, Charlie Brookfield, and Alex Sprunt sitting down with Storer and Mason to try to forge an agreement between them. Mason brought up past grievances, but Buchheister replied, "We're not here to talk about the past."

From that meeting came a complex scenario in which all National Audubon chapters in the state would be designated chapters of Florida Audubon, too; members would receive *Audubon* (the word *Magazine* having by that time been dropped from the publication's title) and dues were split three ways among the chapter and the national and state societies. Back in New York, John Baker wondered what his old society was coming to, but Buchheister was determined to return the apostate affiliates to National Audubon.

# 24

To complement the local work of the growing number of Audubon chapters around the country, Carl Buchheister redoubled the longtime attempt to involve children in conservation and natural history. Thus, when he was approached in 1961 by an Audubon board member named Erard A. Matthiessen with a proposition to form a merger with another organization, he was immediately interested.

The other organization, Nature Centers for Young America, was headed by an environmental educator and onetime protégé of William Hornaday named John Ripley Forbes. The rather grandiose aims of this small organization were "to aid American communities in setting aside areas of natural land, establishing living museums, exhibits and natural science workshops, and developing dynamic outdoor educational programs for the youth of America, their families, and the generations to come." Forbes was a go-getter, a man with big ideas and the energy to see them sometimes become a reality. He had attracted to his board a number of prominent men in business and finance, among them Matthiessen and an executive of the Rockefeller Brothers Fund, Gene Setzer, who occasionally worked with Laurance S. Rockefeller on conservation projects. Setzer's appearance on Forbes's board indicated that the Rockefellers had contributed to the organization and, as was their custom, were keeping an eye on the course of events there.

Nature Centers for Young America was not creating quite the impact some of its board members had hoped for. It was Matthiessen's idea that, if the organization merged with another widely known for its work in conservation education, it might begin reaching some of its lofty goals faster. Naturally, as a member of National Audubon's board too, he thought of Audubon first and suggested the merger to Buchheister. The two boards duly approved the transaction, and National Audubon swallowed the smaller entity, which became one of its divisions.

John Ripley Forbes joined National Audubon to supervise the new division. An entrepreneur, he was accordingly not very happy to work under the conservative Buchheister; nor did Buchheister admire the other man's style, and Forbes soon departed. A more lasting association came about because National Audubon absorbed some of the now-defunct organization's board members, most notably Gene Setzer. With Setzer's presence on the Audubon board, the Rockefellers became important contributors to the Society. Apparently encouraged by Laurance Rockefeller, Setzer agreed to become chairman of Audubon's board of directors, lending the Rockefeller prestige to that position for a decade.

The acquisition of a nature-center division made sense for National Audubon at the time. The goal of such a division was to interest community leaders in planning such facilities as a focus on local nature education. National Audubon already had successful nature centers in regions as distinct from each other as Connecticut and California. (The El Monte Nature Center attracted more than ten thousand children annually and was later turned over to Los Angeles County.) These centers provided both experimental programs and model structures from which planners in other areas might draw both inspiration and expertise. A third Audubon Nature Center which Buchheister's administration had inherited was in Dayton, Ohio. The story of how it came about illustrates the kind of commitment for which both Baker and Buchheister wanted National Audubon to be known.

Marie Aull was the widow of a prominent Dayton businessman. Around their old house on the outskirts of the city she had nurtured a sea of wildflowers as an integral part of the deciduous forest; her property, "Aullwood," became nationally known among horticulturists. Inspired by her husband's love of the land and his belief that it "is ours only to hold in trust, to pass on to the next generation as beautiful as it was given to us," she became concerned about what the future held for the area. World War II had changed Dayton forever, bringing in heavy industry and sweeping away the farms that had characterized the rolling countryside. Open space was dwindling. Having been a member of the National Audubon Society for many years, she wrote to John Baker and told him that she wanted her land to be preserved as an Audubon sanctuary after her death.

Baker arrived in Dayton shortly afterward and toured Marie Aull's gardens and woodlands. A persuasive salesman and propagandist, Baker was aware that both the uniqueness and the strength of the Audubon movement had as a basis its tangible holdings—the network of wildlife sanctuaries, nature centers, and summer camps throughout the country. He saw at once that the Aull property did not meet the traditional requirements for an Audubon sanctuary (such as critical breeding or wintering grounds for threatened species). But the Midwest had no phys-

Marie Aull created "Aullwood," one of the nation's most famous gardens,
adjacent to the Audubon center in Dayton, Ohio. © 1985 RICHARD FRANK

ical installation capable of fitting into Audubon's year-round educational
programs.

"We would like to have the land for a nature center," he told Marie
Aull. "And why wait until after you are gone? Why not give the land
now so that you can have the fun of seeing people enjoying all its benefits?"

Baker suggested that she donate seventy of her hundred acres to the
Society, keeping the house with its gardens and fringe of woodlands for
herself. But first, Baker wanted her to become familiar with other of the
Society's educational facilities and programs.

During the coming months Marie Aull threw herself with characteristic enthusiasm into the job of learning more about nature education.
She visited the Audubon nature centers in Connecticut and California.
Then, in the summer of 1956, she went as a student to the Audubon
camp in Wisconsin. There she met a woman who was to have a profound effect on her outlook.

Dorothy Treat was a longtime Audubon staff member, a professional
biologist, and a specialist in nature education who was for a while in
charge of the Audubon Junior Program. She was a believer in dramatic

presentation, putting across a message to children with the help of artistic materials and theatrical techniques. She wrote many of the original "Audubon Nature Bulletins" and "Audubon Aids," telling a story with an obvious moral (about a child who used magic spectacles to discover all of the natural materials that go into the making of common household objects, or the farmer who brought down a rodent plague on his land by shooting all the hawks and owls).

It was John Baker's policy to send Dorothy Treat to new Audubon camps to organize their educational programs. She was at the Wisconsin camp when Marie Aull met her.

"I was enormously impressed with the way Dorothy could transfer her enthusiasm for natural things even to older people," Aull said. "I began to see how a nature program could really work. By the time I got home I had made up my mind to give my property to the Society right away. When I told my financial adviser how Dorothy Treat's work had inspired me to make this agreement, he said, 'If anyone can put stars in your eyes like that, go ahead and do it.' "

Before the end of 1956 she had given the seventy acres to the National Audubon Society, adding a substantial endowment for the proposed nature center. The site chosen for the center was the heart of the old farm. The headquarters building went up on the foundations of the barn, and Treat, appropriately, moved into the renovated brick farmhouse as the nature center's first director.

The two women laid out trails and planned the rapid growth of a facility that would soon serve thousands of children (and often their families as well) in the Dayton area. As Baker had suggested, Aull earned the immediate satisfaction of seeing the center's impact on her city. But there was another unexpected satisfaction. Well-to-do people in the past had often been patrons to scholars and artists who came to live with them and enriched their cultural life. But here Aull had found a treasure of a different sort, a woman close at hand to increase her understanding of the natural world.

"As you can see, all along I have been the one to benefit from what has taken place here," she said.

Within a year of the nature center's dedication in 1957, Marie Aull realized that she had made only a start. There were indications that a large farm adjoining the nature center was to be broken up and sold. Treat pointed out some of the ecological dangers to the center if the nearby forest should be leveled.

Aull decided to convert the adjoining property into an educational farm especially for children. As a child, she recalled, she had always been excited to visit a farm, to walk into a barn and see the calves and foals and watch the cows being milked, and then go into the henhouse and find the newly laid eggs. She remembered the sights and sounds of the barnyard and loved it all. She wanted the children of contemporary Dayton to experience what she had lived and loved.

She spoke of her hopes to Carl Buchheister, by then installed as Audubon president. He took the idea to the board of directors, but at first most of them failed to see the connection between a farm and the National Audubon Society. However, after Buchheister explained that here was an opportunity to teach the conservation of soil and water, and that the farm would stress the importance of those elements in a healthy community, the board voted to accept Marie Aull's offer.

In 1960 the old working farm was bought and eventually combined with the center, a total of two hundred acres, to form the Aullwood Audubon Center and Farm. The children of Dayton, either bused in from their schools or visiting on weekends with their families, have been the beneficiaries.

"Dorothy Treat lived to see us add the working farm to the center and give children a sense of a way of life that was becoming an anachronism around Dayton," Marie Aull remembered. "But by 1964 Dorothy was terminally ill with cancer. She got a great deal of pleasure when people like Carl Buchheister and Sewall Pettingill, whom she had known for years in the Audubon Society, would make detours to Dayton on their travels to visit her. The staff at Aullwood once smuggled a screech owl into the hospital so she could see one for the last time."

# 25

"I would suggest that you send Sandy [Sprunt] to the meeting to represent our Research Department and to give a paper on the wood stork," Robert Porter Allen had written to the New York office in 1960, referring to the approaching annual meeting of the American Ornithologists' Union. "I wouldn't go under any conditions. Hopelessly allergic to meetings."

Although Allen was about to retire as the Society's research director, he refused to the end to change his spots. The Florida Keys remained his paradise, and Alexander "Sandy" Sprunt IV (by then Allen's assistant) shared his feelings. When the younger Sprunt succeeded to Allen's title, he opted for Florida Bay's tall birds and mangrove swamps over New York's East Side and the lecture halls of modern campuses. The Audubon field research department has stayed firmly anchored, despite occasional attempts to dislodge it, at Tavernier in the Keys.

Sandy Sprunt was the original "Audubon brat." As a boy, gangling, freckled, and redheaded, he had spent several summers with his father at the Audubon Camp of Maine and had grown up on familiar terms with all the big Audubon names, Baker and Buchheister, Peterson and Cruickshank and Allen. Born in Charleston, he had earned degrees in biology at Davidson College and Virginia Polytechnic Institute, worked at various Audubon camps and sanctuaries, and found a permanent niche when he went to work for his idol in the research department. Like Allen, he wanted to be in the swamps, working with big birds. Of all those birds, perhaps the closest to his heart is the flamingo, the study of which allowed him to carry on the research and protection projects, tinged with the romance of the past, begun by Frank Chapman, Gilbert Pearson, and Bob Allen.

Of all the birds on the North American Checklist, none carries with it such an air of unreality as the greater (or American) flamingo. It is a much more wonderful bird than the pelican, for, as precocious school-children like to point out, it is the only vertebrate that feeds with its head upside down while it is standing right side up. Or, as a verbally agile naturalist once wrote of flamingos, "By pedal elevation and oral depression they are able to exist dry and comfortable in a world of splashing liquid."

Our continent's most spectacular bird, in fact, hardly ever comes naturally to the U.S. mainland anymore, as it used to in large numbers. These days when a stroller out in the Florida marshes spots a flamingo it's probably a truant from the Hialeah Racetrack, and if the "flamingo" is on the Texas coast it's almost surely a roseate spoonbill. Even John James Audubon, after trying frantically for years to get somebody to ship him one from Florida so that he could paint it for his folio, finally settled for a Cuban specimen. The flamingo thus remains an excellent, and by far the most important, reason for National Audubon's presence in the West Indies.

This presence, though it may surprise many Audubon members, is apparently well known to certain segments of the West Indian populace. On one of his research trips, Sprunt passed a couple of ragged little boys on a street in Matthew Town on the Bahamian island of Great Inagua.

"Who dot is?" Sprunt heard one of the urchins ask.

"You don't know who dot is?" the other replied incredulously. "Who dot is is de fillymingo mon!"

Audubon's involvement with West Indian birds was also known to the creator of Her Majesty's matchless secret servant, 007. Ian Fleming, who spent much time in the Caribbean, usually kept with him a copy of *Birds of the West Indies,* the standard guide for the region, which was written by James Bond, a prominent ornithologist long associated with the Philadelphia Academy of Natural Sciences. When he was casting about for a suitable name for the shadowy hero of his first spy thriller, Fleming decided that the one ready-made on the jacket of his bird guide neatly combined the qualities he was looking for—he found it crisp, masculine, and "the dullest name I ever heard"—and cold-bloodedly filched the genuine ornithologist's identity. In *Doctor No,* one of his better-known thrillers, Fleming set the scene on a Caribbean island that alleg-edly was an Audubon sanctuary. His island's topography, its sights and sounds, and the two bird wardens with their primitive little camp in the interior, smack strongly of the National Audubon Society's real-life re-search project on Great Inagua.

"It was some people in America called the Audubon Society," ex-plained the ersatz James Bond's chief of staff as he pinpointed the source of complaints about Doctor No, the Yellow Peril incarnate, who had

Young Sandy Sprunt with his father, Alex, on the Dry Tortugas in 1946.
PHOTO BY LAURIE DEWEESE, NAS

been zapping spoonbills and Audubon wardens with a flamethrower. "They protect rare birds from extinction or something like that. Got on to our ambassador in Washington, and the F.O. passed the buck to the Colonial Office. They shoved it on to us. Seems these bird people are pretty powerful in America."

The flamingos are a very ancient group, most closely related among living birds, perhaps, to the storks. Modern ornithologists recognize six species or subspecies of flamingos which inhabit parts of the Americas, Europe, Asia and Africa. The American flamingo, which includes a small population in the Galapagos Islands, is considered a race of the greater flamingo of Eurasia and Africa. There is no evidence that they ever nested in what is now the United States during historical times, but until the early nineteenth century flocks used to spend the winter along both coasts of Florida, and until about 1903 in Florida Bay.

What happened to the flocks in Florida can be summed up in a description written by Gustavus Würdemann, who collected birds in Florida before the Civil War. In 1857 he accompanied a man who captured flamingos at a time when they were molting and relatively defenseless. The man took them by canoe to Key West, where they were sold for about five dollars a pair.

"There were more than one hundred of these unfortunate birds packed away in the little canoe, without regard to their comfort or their lives," Würdemann wrote. "We were so laden down that the sail could not be used. [The birds] were struggling, flapping their wings, and covering everything with their blood; scarcely one of them escaped injury."

Occasional flamingos were seen (or shot) in Florida during the first decades of the twentieth century, but it was generally recognized that the birds were gone from our shores. Then, in 1931, a couple of dozen flamingos were imported by the management of the Hialeah Racetrack to ornament the infield. Others were brought over in the following years until a sizable captive flock was built up, and these birds produced chicks of their own. Although many of the flamingos were never pinioned, most of them were partial to Hialeah's room and board and have remained on the grounds, but periodically one flies the coop. These are the "wild" stragglers sometimes sighted in Florida Bay.

Why didn't flocks begin to return from the Caribbean to Florida Bay once effective bird-protection laws had been passed in the United States? Ornithologists began to suspect that flamingos were being handled more roughly in the islands than on the mainland. The first of these men to gain substantial evidence was Frank Chapman, who visited Andros Island in 1902 and 1904. He made some of the first detailed studies of the nesting colonies but was appalled by the slaughter of flamingos. Andros, close to Florida, had probably been the nesting place of Florida's wintering flocks.

In January 1905, when the National Association of Audubon Societies was created, Chapman took his case to the first meeting of its board of directors. He presented a resolution, which was unanimously adopted, asking the governor and the Assembly of the Bahamas to grant legal protection to the flamingos. The Society's connection with this species thus goes back to its very beginnings.

The Bahamas passed a bird-protection act in 1905, and in 1922 set aside a flamingo reserve on Andros Island. A year later the Audubon Association bought a patrol boat for the Andros wardens. Protection remained difficult. Native people still raided the colonies for squabs, while a series of severe hurricanes during the late 1920s wiped out several years' production of young. Somehow the colonies survived on Andros until World War II. Ironically, the final blow was given them by Royal Air Force pilots, who took to buzzing the colonies for fun.

After the war, John Baker decided that the Society should continue to work for the flamingos' protection. Were there any colonies left in the Bahamas? If so, where? Baker asked Paul Zahl, a biologist with experience in the Caribbean, to look for them on South Andros Island. Zahl slogged around and found a few birds, but he also learned that the local people were still killing them. Baker ordered a full-scale survey of flamingos in the Caribbean and assigned the job to Bob Allen.

Allen began his flamingo survey in the spring of 1950, flying to Yucatan on the coast of Mexico and tracking down part of the little-known resident flocks. The following May he sailed from Nassau to South Andros to look for remnants of the great flamingo cities described by Chapman, but he found only some decaying nest mounds and "twelve rather sad-looking flamingos." In addition to having confirmed the worst fears about the Andros flamingos, he nearly lost his life when an off-season hurricane raged through the Tongue of the Ocean between Andros and Nassau during his return voyage.

Bob Allen went on to search all of the places where flamingos were rumored to nest in the Caribbean. He found colonies that were small yet still holding their own on Great Abaco Island in the Bahamas and in the Dominican Republic. Haiti, so mired in poverty that any large bird suitable for the pot seemed a gift from the gods, was hopeless. In Cuba, he visited the old National Flamingo Refuge, where he watched three men skin, cook, and eat a flamingo they had just shot.

Allen returned to Cuba in 1952 to try to confirm the existence of a flourishing colony he had heard about in Oriente Province. Guided to the site by several boys, he found the remains of two thousand nest mounds no more than a year old. There were no birds in sight. Instead, Allen saw old fishing nets stretched between tree trunks or poles that had been pounded into the soft mud.

"In one, scarcely recognizable, was what remained of the body of a young, half-grown flamingo," Allen wrote in his book *On the Trail of Vanishing Birds.* "These nets, the boys readily explained, were used to capture the young birds before they were large enough to fly. Oh yes, they had helped in this capture. Each year the flamingos nested here and each year, when the young were the right size, the nets were spread and several hundred birds driven into them and caught. Some alive, some dead, all to be sold or eaten. Not many—four hundred, five hundred perhaps. A good haul was made last year. Strange that none had nested this season. It was mid-May and ordinarily they should have hatched most of their chicks by now. What could have happened?

"I thought I knew what had happened. There had been one raid too many. I had found my Cuban flamingo colony—one year too late!"

Basing his calculations on both his travels and his search of old records, Allen reported that fifteen colonies had been abandoned in the Caribbean during the previous thirty-five years. Everywhere the flamingos were being crowded out by increasing human populations. But stories still persisted about a great colony in the inhospitable wilds of Great Inagua. That colony had been vividly described by Gilbert Klingel, a writer and naturalist who had been shipwrecked on the island in the early 1930s.

"The flamingos of Inagua Island are one of the world's truly grand and inexpressibly lovely spectacles," Klingel wrote in his book *The Ocean Island (Inagua)*. "If the great flock of this island were readily available to the people of the Earth so that it might be reached without having to endure sun and thirst and the sting of salty water, it would be a mecca for hundreds of thousands. But that will never be, for when civilization comes the flamingos depart forever; this most marvelous of all avian sights will remain the privilege of the few, a half-dozen naturalists and inquisitives who have tucked in their bodies an unquenchable thirst for the unbelievably exquisite, the ultimate of loveliness."

Klingel believed that Inagua's flamingos were doomed. Bob Allen inevitably approached Inagua with trepidation, but on his arrival in the spring of 1952 he was put in touch with a burly native, Sam Nixon, as a man highly qualified to serve as his guide in the island's interior, and matters went well from the very beginning. The two men—both sturdy, resourceful, and adventurous—hit it off. Nixon took Allen in a shallow-bottomed boat to the Upper Lakes, where the long chain of disappointments finally ended. They found more than a thousand flamingos "commulating," as Nixon had promised they would, the birds massed in that riotous courtship ritual of head-turning, wing-flicking, and exaggerated strutting that Allen called "the flamingo quadrille."

Here, Allen realized, was a breeding population flourishing in isolation and from which long-abandoned colonies elsewhere in the Caribbean might one day be replenished. Partly on the initiative of John Baker, an organization called the Society for the Protection of the Flamingo in the Bahamas was formed, made up of a number of American and Bahamian conservationists. Allen saw to it that the new society appointed Sam Nixon the first flamingo warden on Great Inagua, with the National Audubon Society providing money for his salary and equipment. Later in 1952, Nixon's brother Jimmy became his assistant. Allen designed and built a little camp on Long Cay and named it for Arthur Vernay, the first president of the new society. It became the Nixons' up-country home during the nesting season and Allen's headquarters on each of his many trips to Great Inagua.

Great Inagua, approached from the air, fulfills no one's preconception of a Bahamian island. In fact, it seems to bear an affinity to one of the outer rings of Dante's Inferno, or a landscape of terror existing only in the mind of a spy thriller's creator. It is an island about forty-five miles long, eighteen miles across at its widest point, its western end stamped with the peculiar desolation that can be produced only by nature and mankind working in concert. Here the island appears to be a vast, disheveled salt flat, blistered with outcrops of blighted vegetation. Everywhere—rimming the lakes and lagoons, in great mounds at the shore, overlaying what once might have been grass and shrubs—lies salt. A long concrete dock stretches into the ocean, and alongside it a ship waits to take the salt to the United States for processing.

The island's only permanent settlement, Matthew Town, stands nearby. Named for an early governor of the islands, it was until World War I a port of at least some consequence, standing at the entrance to the Windward Passage and furnishing a reservoir of stevedores which northern European vessels took on to help unload cargo once they reached larger ports to the west and south. The war diverted the German vessels that were the chief source of local income. Workers drifted away to more active ports, and until 1954 the remnant population supported itself mainly on a few small farms and solar salt works. In that year the operation was bought by Morton Bahamas Ltd., a subsidiary of the giant American salt company. Today Great Inagua's 1,100 residents are confined almost wholly to Matthew Town and are dependent for their subsistence in one way or another on Morton.

The upper lakes region may be described simply as an expanse of muck, mangroves, and shallow water, though such a picture misses the complex mix of elements that has created a landscape so stark to human eyes yet so hospitable to those of flamingos. In profile, the island is shaped like a giant saucer. The interior is a broad depression, lying mostly at sea level itself. The underlying rock is limestone, honeycombed with various sinks and caverns through which seawater flows to well up here and there far inland. Heavy rains mingle with the seawater in this saucer, especially in early spring, and form a series of lakes among the winding ridges or "cays" that are also a feature of the land.

But these lakes are almost as fleeting as spring pools in New England. Persistent easterly trade winds and a relentless sun carry on the process of evaporation. As the lakes begin to dry up, the water grows saltier, becoming twice (and sometimes four times) as saline as the sea. A rind of snowy crystals forms at the edge of the lakes as water levels drop. Life teems in this briny, evanescent world. The sun's energy combines with the rich residue of minerals in the dwindling lakes to support the small fish, brine shrimp, mollusks, and the seeds of salt-tolerant plants on which flamingos subsist.

The omnipresent taste of salt on the visitor's lips may result partly from the power of suggestion, but these shallow salinas and brine flats touch other human senses even more forcibly. Anaerobic bacteria help to decompose the organic matter, producing odors characteristic of hydrogen sulfide and in places tinting the water a pale pink.

Mangroves, typically trees of the shoreline, grow here many miles inland with no apparent link to the sea. But the link is indeed present, in the underground caverns that bring salt water, and perhaps the great Caribbean storms carry mangrove seeds from the coast over the low intervening ridges to the Upper Lakes where they find congenial conditions for germination. Red mangroves grow mainly over the ocean holes where the salinity (incongruously) is comparatively low because of the constant infusion of salt water, while black mangroves predominate on the extremely saline periphery (where evaporation concentrates salt) because they are able to exude salt through their leaves. Even the black mangroves die when the salinity exceeds levels of ninety parts per thousand.

During the nesting season, flamingos, singly or in long undulating chains, seem constantly in the air over the Upper Lakes. A flamingo in flight is one of the natural wonders of the world, its body pulsing throughout all that incredible distance from beak to toes as if in response to recurrent waves of rapture, its short wings producing a high sweet hum like a chorus of small sparrows. Their nests, often found on the flats away from the mangroves, are shaped like the cones of little volcanoes, about eight inches high, put together from broken shells mixed with sand and clay. The birds sit under the glaring sun, legs tucked under their bodies, brooding the single big white egg.

Out of Bob Allen's many trips to the island came the monograph (1956) that is the basis of much of our present knowledge of the "Caribbean" flamingo's natural history. Allen's research in the field also stimulated conservationists to provide for the species' protection. By an odd twist of fate, it was not direct human persecution that became a major threat to Great Inagua's flamingos, but the marauding wild pigs that were introduced by early settlers and began to feed on the birds' eggs and young. The Nixons' constant vigilance (as well as their hankering for roast pork) did much to neutralize that threat.

Another positive step was the creation of the Bahamas National Trust by acts of the Assembly in 1959 and 1961. As the official organization responsible for wildlife protection and conservation in the Bahamas, the Trust took over the work of the old Society for the Protection of the Flamingo. By working closely with the salt company, various government agencies, and the National Audubon Society, the Trust helped the resident flamingo population grow from several thousand birds in 1952 to almost thirty thousand birds a couple of decades later.

Bob Allen served as Audubon's first representative on the Trust's council until failing health caused him to resign. Sandy Sprunt took over for him in 1962 and has since devoted much of his time to flamingos. Part of his work has been as a biologist, part as an emissary.

"Back in the early 1960s the Trust was trying to get a lease from the government on the land that the flamingos use here," Sprunt has recalled. "It amounted to two hundred eighty-seven square miles in the center of the island. The Trust members are really volunteers, and none of them had the time to go through all the red tape involved in getting the lease. I volunteered to do the job if the Bahamians would tell me what steps to take. I came over to Nassau and spent ten days going from office to office, just walking the papers through.

"The final hurdle was to get an exact map of the area to be leased. I learned that the Crown Lands officer in the Bahamas, R. E. Z. Sweetnam, had been a surveyor. I told him just what sort of lands we needed, and he worked it out on precise lines. The ninety-nine-year lease was approved, and Rudy Sweetnam later became president of the Trust."

Sprunt also carried out a banding study on the flamingos for a number of years. Using some of the techniques of the old pothunters, he designed small corrals made of poles and yellow nylon fishnet, with two net-draped wings leading away from the corral's mouth at angles of about forty-five degrees. The older birds desert the chicks when they are about three weeks old. Sprunt and his helpers drove the gray, flightless, chicken-sized young flamingos toward the funnel-shaped entrance formed by the wings and into the corral, where they fitted them with colored plastic bands on the left leg and numbered aluminum bands on the right leg. As a result of banding, ornithologists have learned more about the rate of mortality among flamingos after they have fledged, the composition of populations by age, and the movement of the birds throughout the Caribbean. Sprunt learned, for instance, that there is now a lot of shuttling of flamingos back and forth between Great Inagua and Cuba.

The stability of the colonies on Great Inagua reflects in large part the ties between the National Audubon Society and conservationists in the Bahamas.

# 26

In November 1961, the extreme right-wing political columnist Westbrook Pegler gave his favorite target, Eleanor Roosevelt, a moment's respite and donned the trappings of a naturalist to write an article in *Sports Afield.* The distortions and intemperate language that Pegler's readers had grown accustomed to were much in evidence, but the object of his vitriol on this occasion was the bald eagle.

In his article, "The Eagle," Pegler belittled the eagle's status as America's national bird, charged that it was a killer of "grown deer or antelope," and a "demon . . . which can crack the back of a sheep with one blow of its beak." The bald eagle of Pegler's imagination was, moreover, a glutton of such proportions that it was unable to lift itself off the ground after dining on a lamb, and when a properly outraged stockman accorded the bird its just deserts and yanked off its head, lamb hearts came tumbling out.

Pegler's tirade was not simply an isolated aberration. His was simply a colorful expression of sentiments widely held throughout the West, especially among ranchers and the government trappers who thrived on the exaggerations that were popular in the folklore of predation. Pegler, in fact, seems to have based his article on the reports of men whose business it was to kill eagles, mountain lions, bobcats, and other predatory animals on western ranchlands.

The golden eagle was usually a chief victim of antipredator campaigns. Branded a varmint and unprotected by law, the golden eagle was shot, trapped, and poisoned almost everywhere in the campaign to make the West safe for sheep and cattle. But the bald eagle, primarily a feeder on fish and carrion, came in for its share of persecution despite the fact that it had been protected by federal law since 1940; it was condemned because of guilt by association with its relative, or because most people in the business of killing predators were unable to distinguish its young from the similarly dark-plumaged golden eagle.

The National Audubon Society in the early 1960s threw itself aggressively into the struggle to secure adequate protection for both species of eagle. Eagle populations were declining at an alarming rate in the lower forty-eight states. The campaign directed by Carl Buchheister to reverse the decline took on the characteristics that he perfected during his years as Audubon president. All sectors of the Society would be drawn into the effort. The fight for the eagles was to be carried on by intensive lobbying in Washington, publicity and public relations, basic field research, and action on the local level.

As a part of the campaign, there were articles in *Audubon,* including a strong reply to Pegler by the California cattleman and conservationist Ian McMillan. Referring to Pegler's "wild piece of nature faking," McMillan condemned the federal predator-control programs and pointed to overgrazing and other ecological sins as lying at the root of ranchers' troubles. At the same time, Charlie Callison reached the public through a series of press releases on wildlife problems and alerted local activists through the Society's publication, the *Audubon Leaders' Conservation Guide.* Buchheister himself made a number of talks on the subject, one of them at the national convention of the Fraternal Order of Eagles, which gave him an enthusiastic reception and promised to support Audubon's eagle project.

The Society also embarked on an ambitious research program to fill in the gaps in the current dossier on the natural history of both bald and golden eagles. In the past, because of its skimpy staff, the Society often had to go to outside organizations (such as the American Museum of Natural History or federal agencies) for help in assembling or collecting material on subjects in which it was vitally interested. Now Audubon had shored up its own staff and supplemented it with the work of consultants on contract. The New York office had a staff biologist, Roland C. Clement, who had arrived in the last year of the Baker administration after eight years as the executive secretary of the Rhode Island Audubon Society.

Clement was a contrast in appearance and style to Sprunt, with whom he was not always on the best of terms: short and compact, with graying hair, he was an administrator and spokesman rather than a field researcher. But his analytical mind and direct, even crusty, prose style were valuable weapons for the Society against the often flabby pronouncements of politicians and apologists for polluting industries. Clement set the scientific tone of the Society's public statements during the environmental battles of the decade ahead.

Beginning in 1960, Sandy Sprunt launched the Continental Bald Eagle Project, which was designed to investigate the numbers and distribution of bald eagles in the lower forty-eight states, measure their reproduction, and then determine the causes of the sharp population decline reported by scattered observers. As the coordinating organization for most of the bald eagle research in the United States during the 1960s, the Audubon research department gathered information by mail from both professionals and volunteers, and sponsored conferences devoted to the problems of eagles and other raptors.

"This project was instrumental," Sprunt wrote later, "in showing that DDT had a large part to play in the pollution of the environment and in the decline of several raptor species, including the bald eagle."

Meanwhile, the Society pressed its drive to gain better protection for all eagles. Help came from an unlikely direction when the government of Mexico proposed that the golden eagle, which migrates from Canada to Mexico and is the latter country's national bird, be included among the species protected under the migratory-bird treaty between Mexico and the United States.

The slaughter of eagles on ranchlands, particularly in Texas and New Mexico, was growing in intensity. (The killing of as many as twenty-five golden eagles in a single day, over a thousand during one winter, and over twelve thousand in twenty years was credited to one bounty hunter in Alpine, Texas.) Yet, because of Internal Revenue Service restrictions on lobbying by tax-exempt organizations, the Society was forced to disguise its leading role in the attempt to amend the Bald Eagle Act of 1940 to extend its provisions to the golden eagle. As a means of supplying information to biologists and conservationists better able to sway legislators, the Society commissioned Walter R. Spofford of Syracuse University to study the relationship between eagles and the sheep and goat industry in Texas.

"Dr. Spofford was highly biased in favor of eagles," Charlie Callison commented dryly, "and he came up with a report that was beneficial to our case."

Nevertheless, Spofford's report was the first of many that put in perspective the predation by eagles on live lambs and kids. It showed that, as a rule, such predation is of minor consequence to sheep and goat ranchers in relation to losses caused by disease, malnutrition, and overgrazing. The increasing scientific evidence that established the golden eagle as, on balance, a healthy factor in the West's environment won the struggle in Congress. The desired amendment was passed by both houses in 1962 (though poaching and loopholes in the law remained a problem), and the golden eagle at last received a substantial measure of federal protection.

The drive to protect the golden eagle was another indication of National Audubon's growing involvement in the Far West. From the beginning of his career in conservation, Charlie Callison had taken a special interest in the quality of public lands, most of which lay in the western states. During the early 1960s, he headed Audubon's contingent in support of the Wilderness Bill, which was perhaps the most laborious legislative struggle over the environment in that decade. Callison worked closely with Howard Zahniser, the executive secretary of the Wilderness Society, who was generally credited by his colleagues with being their spark plug in the eight-year struggle to make the wilderness preservation of certain remote areas on public lands a statutory directive from Congress to the managing agency. (The National Park Service, for instance, would then be relieved of excessive political pressure to build roads, reservoirs, or resort hotels in the backwoods regions of its domain.) Despite bitter opposition from the ranching, mining, and forest industries, and occasional signs of weariness among the conservation forces, the bill was finally passed by Congress in 1964.

On the other side of the ledger was the gloomy prognosis for a western species that had soared on great wings over the plains and sinks where mastodons and saber-toothed tigers were dying, a bird in which Audubon had been vitally interested for decades—the California condor. Since the Society had sponsored Carl Koford's research report, the big bird had drifted closer to extinction. There was speculation that the condor, a vulture whose nine-foot wingspread was the largest of any land bird in the United States (a foot or two wider than the bald eagle's, though a little less than the trumpeter swan's), had reached the end of its natural span, that it was a relict of past ages already in its final decline even before human beings had invaded its ancient stronghold.

Whether or not the condor was doomed, National Audubon took the position that human interference during the past century had greatly speeded its fall. It had not responded to modern prescriptions for recovery. Perhaps the effort had begun too late. In any case, the Society sponsored a new study of the species, which was financed by the National Geographic Society and conducted by three prominent California naturalists and conservationists, Alden H. Miller, Ian I. McMillan, and his brother, Eben McMillan. The researchers documented the disaster already feared by conservationists, reporting that a population estimated at sixty birds two decades earlier had dwindled to about forty in 1964. They attributed the decline not to any diminution in the condor's reproductive capacity but to illegal shooting, powerful poisons set out for rodent control, and constant disturbance from human activity in the condor's mountain strongholds.

The researchers came up with several suggestions to help the condor, including better law enforcement, increased public education, a ban on poisons within the condor's principal range, and the addition of buffer lands around the important Sespe Condor Refuge. One of the recom-

Roland Clement (in hat) and John Borneman in the Mexican desert.

mendations on which Buchheister could act immediately was for the appointment of an Audubon warden in the area. His choice for the position was a happy one, putting on the scene in 1965 a man who, by disposition and talents, was suited to win friends for a vulture in hostile territory.

The new man on the condor beat was John Borneman. Like many other Audubon wardens, Borneman came to his calling by a roundabout route. He began as a musician, and for some years toured the country as a singer and comedian with Fred Waring's "Pennsylvanians." To lighten the tedium of travel Borneman began to watch birds. ("The first bald eagles I ever saw were those I spotted through the windows of the Waring bus," Borneman has said.) He collected books about nature and ecology, prompting the card players in the back of the bus used to refer to the section where he sat as "the library."

In 1959, Borneman left the road show and joined a barbershop quartet called the Dapper Dans of Disneyland. But nature was his chief interest by then. He found a job at Audubon's nature center in El Monte. Buchheister detected what he liked to call the true Audubon spirit in this lively young man and, acting upon the condor report, hired him to help guard the birds' nesting and roosting areas.

"In this kind of work you come across some pretty crazy people," Borneman once said. "Guy Bradley was a warden, and he got killed. I decided not to adopt that title and I called myself a condor naturalist."

Touring the ranches and mountain forests where the condors soared, Borneman kept an eye on them and established a protective presence. Later he was to help provide food for them by talking ranchers into leaving the carcasses of cattle and deer in the open, or collecting road kills and trucking them into the birds' feeding areas; he referred to these gifts as "condor popsicles." But perhaps his greatest service in the struggle to stave off the condor's extinction was in the area of public relations, touring the Southern California backcountry, talking to the local people, and trying to get them to change the way they thought about those "forty dirty birds."

"You'd be surprised at the number of people who asked me how I can admire a bird that 'eats dead things,'" Borneman said. "Well, I always look straight at a person like that and I ask, 'Tell me, sir—do you eat *live* things?'"

Despite Borneman's disarming way, however, on the issue of condors there was a bitter struggle just ahead.


During the Buchheister years no single scientific issue was more closely identified with the National Audubon Society, either by its members or the public at large, than the national campaign for a sane pesticide policy. This special interest on Audubon's part was inevitable. DDT was one of the strands in that menacing web of contamination that seemed to have enmeshed all life on earth. John Baker, Dick Pough, and other Audubon spokesmen had already warned against the indiscriminate spread of this new generation of persistent chemicals in the environment. Not only the chemical industry but also large numbers of commercial growers, legislators, government technocrats, and even academic scientists were caught up in the euphoria brought on by what was advertised as a panacea for the world's insect problems. In an article at that time, the ecologist Frank E. Egler observed that the public had become bewildered by, and was at the mercy of, "the flow of sound and unsound scientific knowledge."

It took the work of a remarkable woman to jolt the world into the recognition that there was a serious problem. Rachel Carson was a marine biologist working for the federal government as a researcher and editor until her book, *The Sea Around Us,* became a worldwide best seller in 1951. An intensely private person, she had a deep interest in the natural world. (She had been a birding companion of Roger Tory Peterson and other prominent ornithologists when they were stationed in

Washington, D.C., during World War II and the Audubon Naturalist Society of the Central Atlantic States experienced a renaissance.) Carson wanted nothing better than to spend the rest of her days writing about the life of the oceans. But, like many other biologists, she became aware of the ominous reports about DDT and its effects on the chain of life.

"So it seems time that someone wrote of life in the light of the truth as it now appears to us," Carson said in a letter to Marie Rodell. "I still feel there is a case to be made for my old belief that as man approaches the 'new heaven and the new earth'—or the space-age universe, if you will, he must do so with humility rather than with arrogance. And along with humility, I think there is still a place for wonder."

After four years of work and pain, sorting through immense amounts of scientific material and battling the cancer that soon would kill her, Carson finally published her momentous book in 1962. *Silent Spring,* which became an enormous best seller immediately, broke the information barrier. In her book, she pointed out that one of the qualities that had attracted chemists to DDT and its new sister poisons was their persistence. And yet this persistence—the capacity to accumulate and endure in living tissues—was also the quality that made it a threat not only to the target insect but also to all living things. Chapter by chapter and case by case, she recounted the way in which humans (including the experts) had poured a withering rain of pesticides into the environment, and the paths by which these complex toxins contaminated the earth.

*Silent Spring* touched off a furious controversy. The chemical and agriculture industries answered Carson not with technological reform but with a public relations barrage. One chemical company official said that Carson had written not "as a scientist but as a fanatic defender of the cult of the balance of nature." Others called *Silent Spring* a "hoax," and its author a "mystic." Some national magazines, as well as the industry press, picked up the attack.

The National Audubon Society took the lead in Carson's defense. The reform of pesticide use, both through legislation and public education, became one of its foremost priorities. Perhaps the Society's most effective spokesman, both in his articles and in his statements at public hearings, was staff biologist Roland Clement. He pulled no punches. He compared the United States Department of Agriculture's insect "eradication" programs to the overkill policies demonstrated by the military in the stockpiling of nuclear weapons.

"When combined with the chemical industry's productive overcapacity and the hustling salesmanship of a free enterprise system," Clement wrote, "this commitment threatens to poison the landscape and to make the farmer increasingly dependent and the consumer well nigh helpless."

Rachel Carson receives the Audubon Medal from Society president
Carl W. Buchheister at the annual dinner in New York in 1963. NAS

At the time, the word "ecology" (first written "oecology") had been around for nearly a century without entering the general vocabulary. Rachel Carson's contribution was that she made plain to people who had little biology and less chemistry the complex "web of nature" that ecologists study. Her subject, the control of "pests" by either chemical or biological methods, lent itself ideally to tracing the pathways along which chemicals pass among plants and animals; the buildup of poisons as they are passed up from plants to lower animals and finally to the higher animals through food chains helped the public grasp at last the principles of ecology.

After Carson's death in 1964, Buchheister and Clement were approached by a prominent California conservationist, Margaret Owings, who suggested the creation of a fund in the author's memory. From their discussions came the Rachel Carson Memorial Fund, to be administered by the National Audubon Society with the advice of a Rachel Carson Council of prominent scientists and conservationists. (This council was distinct from the Rachel Carson Trust for the Living Environment, founded in Washington, D.C., at about the same time.) The memorial fund made several important contributions to the struggle for pesticide reform. Through Clement, money was made available to a new organization of scientists called the Environmental Defense Fund to press effective legal action against the use of DDT, first on Long Island and later in Michigan and Wisconsin. The eventual result was a virtual ban on that chemical in the United States. Money from the memorial fund also supported a series of articles in *Audubon* in 1967 on pesticide legislation and regulation in the years following the publication of *Silent Spring.*

The choice of *Audubon* to publicize the struggle for pesticide reform was no longer simply a matter of make-do. The Society's publication had suddenly blossomed in the middle 1960s into a national force, widely read by scientists and conservationists and influencing public opinion in a way that would have astonished even that sprightly publicist, George Bird Grinnell. The Society suddenly had an effective medium for sending its message on science and conservation to many thousands of people.

The remaking of the magazine began in 1965, when Buchheister secured a grant for National Audubon from the Old Dominion Foundation (a predecessor of the A. W. Mellon Foundation) of $300,000. *Audubon* would be able to make use of fine color reproduction on high-quality paper and begin to pay writers, illustrators, and photographers fees that were competitive with those of many leading general-interest magazines. At the same time, Buchheister was having policy differences with *Audubon*'s editor, John Vosburgh, and the latter's days at Audubon House were numbered.

Charlie Callison, who was in close touch with local Audubon societies around the country and regularly read their newsletters and bulletins, noticed that the Michigan Audubon Society published an exceptionally good newsletter. On a trip to Michigan, he met its editor who, as he suspected, was a professional. Les Line was at the time the outdoors editor and chief photographer of the *Midland Daily News*. He was also, as Callison discovered, an active conservationist, a director of the Michigan Audubon Society, and a talented wildlife photographer. (His photograph of a Kirtland's warbler had already appeared on a cover of *Audubon*.)

Callison offered Line a job as an assistant editor of the magazine, which Line accepted, and he and his wife Lois moved to New York. The subordinate role was only temporary. In the fall of 1966, Line assumed control of *Audubon* and began to develop a handsome, well-written publication that brought the Society's members and branches into the mainstream of the modern environmental movement.

John "Frosty" Anderson
led the Audubon
sanctuary program during
some of its critical years.
WARREN RUMSEY, 1968

The recasting of *Audubon*, like the publication of *Silent Spring*, signaled a new and (for many men and women who had fought the lonely battles of the past) an unsettling era in the conservation movement. Concerns about personal health and the quality of their lives were attracting a vastly wider public to the movement, including people who did not know the difference between a bluebird and a blue jay but who felt that the world was somehow out of control and were looking for innovative solutions. Like penitents flocking to a church in times of pestilence, the newcomers were welcome, but graybeards among the faithful realized that the congregation would inevitably undergo drastic changes in tone and leadership.

For National Audubon, change was already taking place. A major step forward was the adoption by the Society of modern methods of recruitment and fundraising. Buchheister and board chairman Gene Setzer worked out a test mailing for what proved to be the Society's first large-scale membership promotion campaign. With the help of a "rich list" partly supplied by other board members and using the attractive magazine as a lure, membership soared from 36,000 in 1965 to 46,000 at the beginning of 1967, and 60,000 only twelve months later.

One of Buchheister's best and brightest legacies to the Society during his last year or two as president was the appointment of a classic "Audubon type" as director of the growing sanctuary system. John "Frosty" Anderson, like Bob Allen, was an experienced hand with wildlife in the field and a convivial companion with whom to while away all the long hours after darkness fell.

A product of the game-management program at Ohio State University before World War II, Anderson often worked as a freelance biologist for the U.S. Fish and Wildlife Service and various state agencies. He became a specialist in waterfowl. From 1950 until 1966 he was the manager of the Winous Point Shooting Club on Lake Erie, the oldest waterfowl hunting club in the United States (chartered in 1856), where he carried out studies on vegetation, muskrats, and waterfowl food habits. Active in various conservation organizations, he got to know men like John Baker, Charlie Callison, and Carl Buchheister. The latter, with his knack for matching the right professional to the job, asked Anderson to come to Audubon as full-time sanctuary director.

The offer was tempting to Anderson, but not tempting enough to make him agree to sit in a cage, however gilded, in the heart of Manhattan. Fortunately, the Society had just acquired the Miles Wildlife Sanctuary, seven hundred acres of forest, swamp, and beaver ponds a few miles from the Sharon Audubon Center in northwestern Connecticut. Buchheister had tried to lure Sandy Sprunt into making his field research headquarters at Miles, which is a great deal closer to New York than Tavernier, Florida, but that native of the Deep South refused to budge. Because a northern winter held no terrors for Anderson, his interest quickened at Buchheister's mention of the Miles Sanctuary and, when he finally accepted the job, he staked out the territory as headquarters of the Sanctuary department. (Seeing Anderson and Sprunt together at a meeting with Anderson's assistant and eventual successor, Frank "Dusty" Dunstan, a wag remarked: "Frosty . . . Sandy . . . Dusty—it sounds as if Snow White has added to her entourage!")

Now Buchheister, as John Baker had before him, was stepping down at the age of sixty-five and, as Baker had, he recommended to the board of directors that his assistant be named his successor. (Baker, in a chilling reminder of William Dutcher's fate, suffered an incapacitating illness in 1967; he died six years later.) But these were different times, and this a different board of directors. When Buchheister retired early in 1967, the board declined to name a successor from within the Society. Instead, it began a nationwide search for a new president, naming Callison in the interim as executive vice president and chief administrator.

"I supported Carl's recommendation that Callison succeed him as president," Setzer said years later. "But a majority of the board wanted more of a 'name,' someone who might attract people outside the conservation movement who had never heard of Charlie Callison, or even of a whooping crane, for that matter."

Buchheister was disappointed and angry. He felt that the decision was motivated by New York "snobbery," a charge that was also sometimes made by board members from the Midwest and South who found themselves in the minority. (At the time, nineteen of the thirty-six Audubon board members were from New York or Connecticut.) Callison, however, would remain in a position of leadership for another decade, and would exert considerable influence on the Society for at least twice that length of time. He summed up the Buchheister years.

"Carl Buchheister made four major contributions as Audubon's president," Callison has said. "He really consolidated the Society nationally by healing old wounds and making friends with state leaders. He directed the upgrading of the magazine. He led the staff into increasing its participation in national issues. And he began the expansion of the field staff, which led directly to the tremendous growth in Audubon membership."

Buchheister, as he grew older, looked back increasingly on his Audubon beginnings at the camp in Maine—and his work with the Junior Audubon clubs and nature centers.

"The kind of enthusiastic teaching done in the camps and centers," Roger Tory Peterson once wrote, "the kind that evokes in the student an equally excited interest in the wonderful systems of nature we call ecology—that is Carl Buchheister's kind of teaching. His influence can be observed wherever we find naturalists working with people out-of-doors."

Carl Buchheister preferred to be remembered as a teacher.

# 27

*T*he Audubon interregnum, with Charlie Callison administering the Society, lasted for nearly two years. Having worked so closely with Buchheister, he carried on operations so that there was no break in the Baker-Buchheister continuum.

The Society kept growing both in membership and real estate. One of the more significant advances in that time, further "opening the West," so to speak, was the decision to build a new western regional office on a two-and-a-half-acre site in Sacramento. Callison also worked out a plan to strengthen the grass-roots movement within the Society, changing the name of the local units from branches to chapters and giving them a share of the dues paid by members recruited in their individual territories. The chapters now had a financial stake in National Audubon, with money from New York flowing back into their treasuries for use in local projects.

During this time, Callison and Roland Clement (who was elected a vice president at the time of Buchheister's departure) helped to make the Environmental Defense Fund an important ally in the pesticide struggle. Formed by a group of activist scientists and a brash, imaginative young lawyer named Victor Yannacone (whose "Sue the bastards!" became an environmental rallying cry of the time), EDF could carry the fight to the enemy using the most aggressive means, while Audubon worked behind the scenes in its characteristic pose as the "gray lady" of the conservation movement. Clement served on EDF's board of directors, and until the new organization conformed to IRS standards as a tax-exempt organization, National Audubon handled its funds, primarily a startup grant from the Ford Foundation.

How conservative National Audubon's board could be at the time was shown by its reluctance to go on record against the use of DDT. Staff members since John Baker's day had been in the forefront of those clamoring to have the chemical banned, yet the board held back an official resolution for fear of offending certain well-to-do contributors who had interests in finance, industry, and agriculture and did not want to be part of what they considered a direct assault on corporate profits.

That was changed at the annual meeting held during the convention at Atlantic City in the fall of 1967. Clement conspired with Yannacone and other EDF members to have a resolution for the board's consideration brought up on the floor. On cue, another Audubon staff member asked Clement, as staff biologist, to comment on the effects of DDT in the open environment. Clement's condemnation of the chemical stirred the audience (which was one of the largest at an annual meeting since the heyday of Rosalie Edge) so that the board was unable to table the issue.

The National Audubon Society had finally gone on record against the use of DDT. The foundations of the organization did not fall, but Crawford Greenewalt, an Audubon life member and a longtime executive of DuPont (his book of photographs of hummingbirds is an ornithological classic), resigned from the Society in protest.

Through the Buchheister years, Callison had functioned as Audubon's "man in Washington," shuttling back and forth between New York and the capital to confer with federal officials, make statements before Congressional committees, and in general keep an eye on what the government was up to in conservation matters. But for a long time he had felt the need of a resident observer in Washington. He made inquiries among his friends there and learned that, with the approaching end of President Lyndon Johnson's administration, a capable young woman named Cynthia Wilson, who had worked for Lady Bird Johnson, would be out of a job.

Wilson, a native of New York State, had majored in journalism at the University of Texas. After earning her degree there in 1964, she received a surprise letter from the White House: Liz Carpenter, an aide to the First Lady, had heard about Wilson from friends at the University of Texas and offered her a job answering Mrs. Johnson's mail. Eventually, she became a public relations specialist, working on the passage of the Highway Beautification Act and the other environmental projects in which Lady Bird Johnson was interested. Wilson accepted Callison's assignment to establish an Audubon office in Washington, but delayed taking her new job until early in 1969, when she finished helping Liz Carpenter on a book she was writing.

"I took a lease on a one-room office on the top floor of a shabby building off Connecticut Avenue," Wilson remembered. "In those days, the IRS was making it hard on non-profit organizations when they did much lobbying, so I spent most of my time keeping a low profile in Congress and working through the federal agencies on conservation problems."

Elvis T. Stahr became
the first nationally
known figure
to lead Audubon when
he was chosen as
the Society's president
in 1968. NAS

By the time the Washington office opened, National Audubon had a new president. The hiring of Elvis Stahr seemed a quirky decision at first, especially to old-line conservationists and perhaps even to some members of Audubon's board of directors. The board, in fact, at first approached Stewart L. Udall, who had been President Johnson's Secretary of the Interior and a popular figure with conservationists. But Udall, after considering the offer for a time, decided not to be tied down after eight strenuous years in Washington. Audubon's second choice, Russell E. Train of the Conservation Foundation, was reluctant to leave the Washington area and also declined. The board of directors then threw the problem into the lap of a "headhunting" firm, Cresap, McCormick and Paget, management consultants adept at finding suitable executives for corporations and other organizations.

"This firm came up with Elvis Stahr," Gene Setzer said. "He didn't know much about birds—in fact, I showed Elvis his first belted kingfisher. But he had the qualities that the board was looking for. He had a national name, a good background in education, and a reputation as being well connected in Washington."

Stahr came to Audubon by an unlikely route. Born in western Kentucky near the Tennessee border, he was the son of a state senator and circuit judge who was the original Elvis in more ways than one.

"Elvis Presley's mother was from Tiptonville, just over the border in Tennessee," Stahr said. "Like most other people in the region, she knew about my father, and so she named her son after him. She wanted an unusual name, I guess."

The young Stahr earned a Phi Beta Kappa key at the University of Kentucky and went on to Oxford University in England as a Rhodes Scholar. There he studied law and received three additional degrees. On his return to the United States, he practiced law in New York City and served as an infantry officer in World War II. He rose to the rank of lieutenant colonel, spending much of his time in China, and was decorated by both the United States and Chinese governments.

Stahr's return to civilian life was only partial, because he was torn between law and the army and was soon careening from one responsible position to another.

"I've never stayed in one place very long," he once said to a friend. "I don't like routine—and I've generally managed to avoid it."

He moved from law practice in New York to the post of dean of the University of Kentucky College of Law, and later provost of the university, and then to a series of assignments as a special assistant to the Secretary of the Army during the Korean War. In 1956 Stahr went back to Washington, where he served as executive director of President Eisenhower's Committee on Education Beyond High School. There followed, in quick succession, calls to the University of Pittsburgh as vice chancellor and to West Virginia University as president.

"I was in West Virginia in 1961 when another call came, this one from Robert McNamara, who had just been appointed Secretary of Defense by President Kennedy," Stahr said. "He asked me to come to Washington right away. I thought he was simply looking for some advice on Army matters, but he told me he wanted me to be Secretary of the Army."

Stahr, who believes in the delegation of authority, did not find it easy working under the compulsive, autocratic McNamara and, after a little more than a year at the Pentagon, welcomed a return to academia. This time he accepted the position as president of the University of Indiana. But there were many days then when he longed for the comparative placidity of life under McNamara, for the 1960s were hell on university presidents. Campuses all over the United States were in a state of upheaval. Protests, proclamations, and takeovers were everyday events. Particularly distressing to Stahr were the disruptions during public lectures, which he called "really an attack on academic freedom." By 1968, he was, by his own admission, "a burnt-out case."

After a brief vacation, Stahr began to look around again for a challenging job. He did not want to go back to teaching law, nor did the corporate offers he received sound very interesting.

"But the headhunters came looking for me," he remembered. "One day I got a call from them asking me how I would like to be president of the National Audubon Society. I had heard of it, of course, but I didn't really know anything about it. Anyway, it sounded interesting to me, so I went to New York in the late summer of 1968 and met with Gene Setzer and other members of the board. After going to a board meeting at the Yale Club, I went home and played some tennis and thought some more about it. And I finally decided to accept the job."

Stahr began work on October 21, 1968, and was almost immediately pressed into service to counter an attempt to put a dam in Kentucky's Red River Gorge. It was a perfect showcase for Stahr to demonstrate his talents in his debut as an environmental leader. There were high emotions involved, as an agency then cast as a prime environmental villain, the U.S. Army Corps of Engineers, threatened to submerge a natural gem under the waters of a reservoir created by its dam. Stahr took advantage of one of his former posts; as Secretary of the Army he had been boss of the Corps of Engineers.

"I went right to some of my old acquaintances," Stahr said, "and I told them, 'Now look here, I don't want to embarrass you fellows. We don't need this boondoggle.' Then I talked to Senator John Sherman Cooper of Kentucky because I had known him for a long time and, since the Corps was no longer stirring things up, Cooper was able to make sure the project didn't get any funding. And so it was dead."

A struggle of much greater magnitude at the beginning of Stahr's administration, fittingly, renewed a theme sounded again and again throughout the Audubon movement's history—the determination to preserve the land and wild things of the Everglades. The movement had been forged in the passionate crusade to save the big wading birds that had retreated to the tip of Florida. John Baker and Charlie Brookfield had played critical roles in the creation of Everglades National Park, and now, in the late 1960s, the Everglades itself was threatened with destruction.

A mammoth jetport scheduled to be built just north of the park would almost certainly restrict and pollute the flow of fresh water from central Florida that is the 'Glades' lifeblood. Joe Browder, who had replaced Brookfield as Audubon's representative in south Florida, was working closely with Gary Soucie, then the Sierra Club's man in the area, to defeat the jetport proposal. Soon after Stahr moved into Audubon House, he heard from Browder and Soucie.

"We don't have the stature to fight this thing successfully, but we think that you do," they told him.

Stahr called a meeting with other leading environmentalists in Washington and suggested that they form a coalition to protect the Everglades in the present crisis. The coalition, carrying the prestige of a number of national organizations, was formed with Stahr and Anthony Wayne Smith of the National Parks Association serving as co-chairmen.

Glen Chandler in retirement. He was succeeded in his duties as an
Audubon warden by his brother Rod. © 1985 RICHARD FRANK

The campaign was bitter. "A new city is going to rise up in the
middle of Florida," crowed the director of the Dade County Port Authority about the proposed complex. "You are going to have one [a
jetport] whether you like it or not." And the Miami area's manager for
the Federal Aviation Administration discounted adverse effects on the
Everglades by remarking: "Nobody will be close enough to complain—
except, possibly, alligators."

The National Audubon Society led the complainers. Stahr, using
Southern charm and all the influence of his Army and government connections, carried the fight to Washington's highest offices. On the scene,
Browder and other Audubon staff members painstakingly collected the
facts to feed the widespread public opposition to the proposed jetport.
The coalition ultimately won a dramatic victory. The federal government
responded to the ecological evidence by halting work on the project.

Stahr's impact on water projects in Florida remained powerful. Later,
the Florida Barge Canal, fought for years by conservationists as a waste
of money, was ripe for final approval by President Nixon. *Audubon*
planned a major article on the subject with color photographs depicting
the grandeur of the landscape and the ugly reality of an already completed portion of the canal. Stahr secured an appointment at the White

House with John Carroll Whitaker, the Cabinet Secretary for President Nixon (and later an Audubon board member!), who was preparing a paper on the project for the President's study.

"I took an advance copy of the magazine to Whitaker and asked him to show it to the President," Stahr recalled. "The next day, Nixon announced his opposition to the canal, and that effectively killed it."

Earth Day, organized by environmental activists on April 22, 1970, was a remarkable public relations stroke that alerted many Americans to both the degradation and the remaining glories of their natural heritage. National Audubon was well positioned to take advantage of the public sentiment to renew those values. The membership had just exceeded 100,000 (a figure, Stahr liked to point out, which could realistically be increased to 140,000 if family memberships were counted as two people). The number of chapters was growing with the memberships. Charlie Callison was building a strong national staff; about the time of Earth Day, he hired Ron Klataske, who had been an editor of the Wyoming Game and Fish Commission's publication, as regional representative for the West Central states. The Society also added an assistant to Paul Howard, who had succeeded Bill Goodall as western representative. The newcomer was Robert K. Turner, a civil engineer and former conservation chairman of the Sacramento Audubon Society, and he soon took over National Audubon's new office in the Rocky Mountains. Callison had fulfilled his objective of establishing regional representatives in each of nine major regions of the country. (Alaska was still handled by Paul Howard out of the Sacramento office.)

Turner's new region provided an illuminating example of the growth and vitality of the chapter system. Until 1970, the Audubon presence in the Rocky Mountain states would have been difficult to detect unless one knew where to look. There were only five scattered chapters with about fifteen hundred members in the region, but those figures were to grow in the next decade or so to more than forty chapters and eighteen thousand members.

Even more important than the growth in the West was the region's activism. In 1971, the Murie Audubon Society at Casper, Wyoming, made headlines across the country when its members discovered a graveyard of eagles in Jackson Canyon, where ranchers had dumped the birds after they had been illegally poisoned. A prominent sheepman pleaded no contest and paid a fine for violating state law in the poisoning episode. The discovery also led to a federal ban on the use of thallium sulfate and restrictions on several other powerful toxins set out to kill predators. Later, in cooperation with The Nature Conservancy, Murie

Audubon persuaded the Bureau of Land Management to designate Jackson Canyon as an Area of Critical Environmental Concern and convert it, in effect, from a graveyard to a sanctuary for wintering bald and golden eagles.

Murie Audubon also took over the operation of a sanctuary on the Platte River. Tucson Audubon acquired two sanctuaries as well as its Desert Institute of Ecology; Denver Audubon created the Grasslands Institute in the Pawnee National Grasslands; Utah Audubon began a series of Basin and Range Seminars; Golden Eagle Audubon in Boise has educated the public as well as its members in annual raptor workshops; and the Arkansas Valley chapter at Pueblo, Colorado, established the River Trails Audubon Center. Many chapters in the region plunged into conservation battles on their own initiative, blocking dams that would destroy wild rivers and endanger wildlife or persuading power companies to redesign their transmission towers to avoid electrocuting eagles. Others worked with federal agencies in land-use planning or on curbing overgrazing on government lands. More than two dozen chapters in the West "adopted" national wildlife refuges, helping the local managers solve potentially destructive problems.

Each region of the country provided its own examples of chapters that carried their environmental concerns far beyond the logistics of a Sunday morning bird walk. In 1972, the Columbus (Georgia) Audubon Society took on the United States Department of Agriculture, which tried to persuade the Columbus city council to alter its stiff ordinance prohibiting aerial spraying without permission. USDA had planned to apply a new chemical, mirex, over a wide area to control fire ants. Rachel Carson was the first to expose USDA's fire ant program in the South, an attempt at eradication that eventually turned into an environmental disaster, killing untold numbers of wild animals while the fire ants continued to expand their range dramatically. Columbus Audubon's newsletter described how it turned the tide against the use of mirex, which was known to have undesirable side effects:

"The campaign was carried out properly—we got our facts and lots of them, we organized almost overnight, we communicated to and educated the public and the councils, we followed up our words with enthusiastic action and when the gentlemen from the Department of Agriculture appeared before the council, their inability to answer the intelligent questions of the councilmen defeated them more than did all our testimony combined."

But the chapter's meticulous preparation had put those questions in the councilmen's minds. The council defeated the request and prohibited the spraying.

If National Audubon and its chapters generally fought under one banner, they did not always see eye to eye on the best means to achieve victory. During the late 1960s, when there was a concerted drive by conservationists in California to create a Redwood National Park, National Audubon joined the National Park Service in advocating a compromise proposal, believing it was the best they could do in the face of fierce timber industry opposition. Several California chapters, however, sided with the Sierra Club and advocated the inclusion of additional land in the proposal. The chapters' proposal finally succeeded.

The New York staff was growing to keep up with the membership. Audubon House, the fine old building at Fifth Avenue and Ninety-fourth Street in Manhattan, was no longer large enough to hold all the personnel required to operate a national conservation organization in the aftermath of Earth Day. Office space, for instance, had been rented in a nearby building for the Nature Centers Division, which was doing a booming business and eventually helped more than three hundred communities in acquiring their own nature-education centers. The search was on for a new headquarters building.

The search proved even more complex than that for the new president. At first there was some sentiment among the board of directors to move the Society to Washington, D.C., where National Audubon would be able to work more closely with the other major organizations which had their headquarters there. Marie Aull felt that if space in Washington proved too expensive, the Society ought to move to the new community of Reston, Virginia, nearby. But that argument was doomed to rejection, not only because so many of the board members lived in the New York area, but also because New York City had always been the source of major funding. In addition, the magazine's increasing role in the Society's success, it was argued, made it advisable to keep it in the center of the publishing industry, with its bottomless supply of technical and artistic talent.

The board considered several suburban sites. A property was available in New Rochelle, and there were sound economic reasons for building on the Society's own land at the Audubon Center in Greenwich. There was even a strong possibility that the Rockefellers would make a gift of property from their own extensive holdings some thirty miles north of New York City.

But in the end the ancient hold of the city proved too strong. Robert Goelet, a powerful board member who was in the real estate business, suggested a site on Third Avenue at Fifty-seventh Street, in one of the city's new huge glass boxes for which the owners needed immediate tenants. Rents were expensive, as usual, in Manhattan, but the proponents of the move argued that the lease could turn out to be favorable in a rising real estate market. After a lively debate, the board chose the Third Avenue site by a single vote. (A story that has come down from that meeting is that one of the opponents of the move was in the bathroom when the critical vote was taken.) Although many staff members were horrified by this impersonal new Audubon House, Stahr supported the board's decision and the Society moved to 950 Third Avenue in 1971.

Despite the Society's happy position, riding a wave of national support for environmental causes with many legislators eager to board the bandwagon, there remained a major roadblock to even greater success. Stahr, as a lawyer, knew where the chief obstacle lay. Tax laws placed conservation organizations, museums, symphony orchestras, colleges, YMCAs, Scout groups, fundraising societies such as those for cancer and heart disease, and some other nonprofit groups, none of which was founded primarily to influence legislation, in a special classification known as 501 (c) (3). Contributions to groups covered by this clause were ruled tax deductible, unless a "substantial" part of a recipient group's activities consisted of attempts to influence legislation. The Internal Revenue Service did not define "substantial," but there were indications that outlays on legislative activity ought not to exceed five percent of an organization's total expenditures.

In 1966, the IRS had dealt the Sierra Club a stunning blow by ruling that it had spent too much money on lobbying and revoking its special status. The warning to other groups was clear: go easy on lobbying. Conservation groups remained at a tremendous disadvantage in their attempts to impose legislative curbs on polluting industries, which operated under no such restrictions. Perhaps Elvis Stahr's most lasting contribution to the conservation movement was his leadership in persuading Congress to alter this discriminatory law.

"As more and more of national life became affected by the federal government," he pointed out, "it became more and more important to private organizations to be able to influence the development of public programs affecting their particular areas of concern."

One weekend afternoon soon after he became Audubon president, Stahr was playing tennis with friends. His partner was James Alfred Moore, who had been his classmate at the University of Kentucky and was then specializing in tax law in Philadelphia.

"Does the Audubon Society do much lobbying in Washington?" Moore asked Stahr.

"No," Stahr replied. "We just can't do much to help ourselves there, but we'd like to."

Moore happened to be representing a large private foundation which was beginning to feel severely restricted in its operations and in the way it was able to fund nonprofit groups. Several powerful congressmen of the day had moved to hamstring all foundations, sometimes precisely because these groups might become extremely effective in influencing legislation. Others believed most national problems had become too large for the private sector and must be handled by government. Moore offered to work with Stahr to ease the problem.

"When donees get hurt, donors get hurt, too," Moore remarked.

Stahr and Moore worked out a strategy and secured the backing of the American Bar Association. Years of struggle followed, chiefly because of the Treasury Department's hostility toward such a change in the tax laws. The Nixon administration had given lukewarm support to tax reform by 1972. But, according to Stahr, a high Treasury official named Edwin S. Cohen sabotaged the bill in closed session with the House Ways and Means Committee.

"Cohen went in there and asked the committee if it wanted to subsidize pressure groups and have those 'billions' of dollars turned loose on them," Stahr recalled. "He painted the picture of a tidal wave of wild-eyed, long-haired zealots descending on them. He just scared the hell out of those congressmen."

Stahr organized and chaired the "Coalition of Concerned Charities," composed of some sixty national 501 (c) (3) organizations. ("The only so-called local organization was the New York Zoological Society," Stahr said. "I wanted to be able to say we had groups from A to Z—Arts to Zoo.") The coalition's sole objective was to persuade Congress to clarify and liberalize the law constraining legislative activity by such organizations. While Stahr and others testified in favor of reform, the coalition also employed Moore to lobby for it. (Although Moore's firm received some fees, mostly from National Audubon, much of the work was carried on *pro bono.*) Stahr asked Gene Setzer if he could get the Rockefellers to help, an astute step which resulted in Nelson Rockefeller's introducing Stahr to an upstate New York congressman named Barber Conable, who agreed to push the remedial legislation in Congress.

"During one session, Conable had it all set with Wilbur Mills, the chairman of the Ways and Means Committee, to get the bill through," Stahr said. "But Mills forgot to call Conable to speak during the crucial debate. In the last minute confusion the bill died."

Conable persisted, however, and his leadership and organizing ability were decisive. The 1976 Tax Reform Act as passed by Congress included many of Conable's proposals, which allowed environmental organizations considerably increased latitude in attempting to influence legislation. The term "substantial" was defined in terms of dollars. The act stipulated that qualifying organizations be permitted to spend up to twenty percent of the first half-million dollars of their total annual budget on lobbying, the percentage to decline as the total budget increased. The act set an absolute maximum of $1 million in any one year for lobbying expenditures. Organizations need not count the time of volunteers as an expenditure, however, and money spent lobbying executive agencies is not charged against the allowance.

Environmental organizations, with the help of the Conable Act, could now approach legislators on comparatively even terms with their ideological adversaries.

# 28

$\mathcal{A}$mid the conflicting claims of science, politics, and public relations, conservation organizations in the 1970s found it increasingly difficult to set policy.

National Audubon, by agreement with Albert Willcox at its incorporation in 1905, had stated that its primary objective was to be the protection of birds and "other animals." Over the years it had occasionally campaigned with other organizations to protect large mammals in the West and, at least since Rosalie Edge's protest, it had kept a watchful eye on all of the wildlife on its sanctuaries. Early in Elvis Stahr's administration, the Society took an aggressive stand on banning the killing of alligators for the leather trade; the principles of opposing the use of endangered wildlife for human adornment in this case were the same as those which motivated the stand on plume birds.

In broadening its membership base, National Audubon came under increasing pressure from within to step up its defense of a wide variety of living things, from butterflies and mountain lions to redwoods and Furbish's lousewort. This extension of the protective umbrella was, of course, another expression of the attempt to nurture entire ecosystems. In keeping with concerns that were strong even in Gilbert Pearson's day, the Society did not restrict its work to the boundaries of the United States. Not even the plume birds and whooping cranes, Audubon found in the early 1970s, could inspire as much sympathy and support as the great whales.

By then, the international whaling industry had brought five of the world's eight species of great whales (including the blue whale, the largest animal that has ever lived on earth) perilously close to extinction. A worldwide trade in whale products had sprung up, including the processing of whale parts into lipstick, margarine, pet food, and other products for which alternative ingredients existed. The United States had taken a leading role on the International Whaling Commission in trying to impose limitations on the killing. In 1972, Elvis Stahr was a member of the United States delegation—the only representative of a private organization—at the United Nations Conference on the Human Environment in Stockholm, where he helped to draft a resolution calling for a ten-year moratorium on the killing of whales. The resolution was adopted by fifty-three nations present without a dissenting vote.

But within the International Whaling Commission both Japan and the Soviet Union continued to resist the calls for substantial reform in the industry. Those two countries, in fact, accounted for about eighty percent of all the great whales taken, and they repudiated the quotas set by the commission in 1973. Several conservation groups had already organized a boycott of Japanese and Russian products, hoping to force those countries into agreeing to the ten-year moratorium. National Audubon held back at first, preferring to rely on direct negotiations with the offending governments. Stahr made personal appeals to the heads of state in both Japan and Russia, calling on them to agree to the quotas set by other nations, but they did not respond.

Finally, in the spring of 1974, the Society urged its members (which had grown in number to 300,000) and the general public to boycott goods made in Japan and the Soviet Union until they "cease their needless slaughtering of whales." Audubon's board of directors showed how seriously it took the issue by ordering the magazine not to accept advertisements for any Japanese and Russian products. This was a serious blow to the magazine, which had helped to fund its increasing size and quality through ads for cameras and binoculars, a substantial proportion of which were made in Japan. It was later estimated that over the course of the boycott the magazine lost about a quarter of a million dollars in advertising revenue.

This action, the first boycott of its kind ever urged on its members by the Society, was not adopted without some misgivings. Many business leaders are philosophically opposed to boycotts for obvious reasons; yet whatever reservations individual board members held they were overridden by evidence about the plight of the whales and the arrogance with which the offenders had circumvented even the modest restrictions put on the whaling fleets by the commission. Stahr also recognized the hypocrisy in the Americans' moral stance. Americans had been pioneers in the invasion of the great whales' stronghold in the southern oceans. The tolerance displayed by the federal government to the Eskimos' bowhead hunt off Alaska was notorious; five times the number of bowheads taken every year were lost beneath the ice because of inefficient hunting techniques. The record in the American tuna industry was even more appalling, for thousands of those smaller whales, the porpoises, were killed each year as part of the "incidental catch."

It was generally the conservationist position that the use of whale meat as food for humans had become only marginal in recent years. It was used as food mainly by the Russians to fatten mink and other animals for the fur trade, while its other uses seemed trivial in comparison to the lives of those remarkable sea mammals. National Audubon continued its boycott until 1977.

"We have been concerned during the past several months that the effectiveness of the boycott is tailing off, and that continued participation in it may be counter-productive," Allen Morgan of the Massachusetts Audubon Society wrote to Stahr early that spring. "Recent publicity—an important feature of any boycott—has been slight; both the Japanese and the Russians have been abiding by the decisions of the International Whaling Commission and it is unclear to many just what the goals of the boycott are. . . . We are not eager to [lift the boycott unilaterally] as we view our concerted action with our sister organizations as important."

Stahr organized a meeting with whale experts and federal officials at which he became satisfied that the Japanese and Russians had made progress in conforming to the commission's quotas in recent years. Although several of the organizations decided to pursue the boycott, and there was some grumbling about the withdrawal among several Audubon chapters, Stahr recommended to the board that Audubon drop the boycott. He reminded the board that Audubon's participation had limited objectives to begin with.

"We are convinced that the boycott by the National Audubon Society and other conservation organizations was influential in bringing about major progress toward the preservation of the world's remaining populations of whales," Stahr said in suspending the boycott. "In effect, our boycott simply expired because it had achieved its stated purpose."

The cooperation between the National and Massachusetts Audubon societies in the whale boycott reflected a détente between the two organizations during the 1970s. Its basis was a plan cooked up by Roland Clement and William Drury to organize a joint scientific staff which would work on problems of common concern to the two organizations. ("If National Audubon even thought that Allen Morgan had anything to do with the idea, they would have turned it down," Drury said.) The plan was a sound one, stemming from the belief held by Clement and Drury that the policy of their respective societies ought to be based on good science, and not the other way around.

The venture was a success, with Drury and his assistant, Ian C. T. Nisbet, supplying a strong scientific team that more than held its own with National Audubon's. The addition to the joint staff of a nuclear physicist as well as a natural-resources economist (to gather data to determine the real costs to the country of strip mining, stream channelization, and water pollution) showed a desire on the part of both societies to enter the "big leagues" of original research.

Some excellent results came out of the collaboration, particularly on the effects of pesticides in the open environment. For instance, Clement and Nisbet produced a provocative report, *The Suburban Woodland: Trees and Insects in the Human Environment,* which explored forest dynamics in the heavily populated Northeast. Also, out of the collaboration came ideas that prompted National Audubon to support the captive propagation of peregrine falcons by Tom J. Cade at Cornell's Laboratory of Ornithology after the species' breeding population had been exterminated in the northeastern United States by DDT and other persistent insecticides.

"Too often bad science has been used to denigrate *all science,"* Drury said afterward. "In National Audubon's case, this showed up in their reluctance for a long time to support a plan for the captive breeding of whooping cranes because of some sloppy work that had been done earlier in a zoo. What was learned in the 1970s, however, showed all of us that programs like Cade's at Cornell could be vitally important in bringing back a species. Later, National Audubon was able to give its blessing to the U.S. Fish and Wildlife Service's program of taking eggs on the crane's nesting grounds to create a second flock as insurance."

Despite such successes, science did not always win the day. Drury left Mass Audubon later on to go back to teaching because he felt that its leadership continued to consider public relations over science in making policy. One such point of conflict occurred at Plymouth Beach, where great horned owls and black-crowned night herons disturbed the tern colony. Drury's studies indicated that the site was too difficult to defend against predation and that the terns should be allowed to abandon Plymouth Beach for more suitable nesting places in the area. The sentiment at Mass Audubon, however, was that every effort must be made to maintain the highly visible colony at Plymouth Beach because of its public relations value.

Clement certainly thought that policy at Audubon House came from sources other than the scientists. There the medium was, in fact, a big part of the message. Les Line, prodigious of girth and often disdainful of niceties, had eased himself into a power vacuum, moving the magazine out in front of the rest of the Society, in effect making policy with articles on a variety of environmental issues.

In keeping with the trend among universities, museums, and other nonprofit organizations, the duties of Audubon's president had shifted more and more toward fundraising. Thus Stahr was frequently on the road, cultivating potential contributors, while Callison occupied himself in Washington with government regulations, or in the hinterlands where the Society was expanding at an astonishing rate. Audubon's former staples were losing momentum; the Junior Audubon clubs faded as most school districts came to frown on the practice of teachers' collecting money from the children for dues and bird charts; the Screen Tours (in later years called Audubon Wildlife Films) were running into increasing competition from television; there was no longer a Roger Tory Peterson in house to produce attractive new educational leaflets.

The magazine, on the other hand, was clearly attracting thousands of new members, a hard fact that Line, a great editor by any standard, used effectively to build his budget. *The New York Times* called *Audubon* "the most beautiful magazine in the world." In successive years (1975 and 1976) it took the National Magazine Award for Excellence in Reporting, and Line won the prestigious Gold Medal of the Rhode Island School of Design. Some staff members in other departments (particularly science and sanctuaries) felt that Line treated them cavalierly when they asked him to print articles about their pet projects, the kind of material that would have appeared as a matter of course in *Bird-Lore* or the early *Audubon Magazine*. They had failed to realize that Les Line's *Audubon* was not published as a house organ but as a national, award-winning magazine. And sometimes a corporate advertisement or even an article in the magazine seemed to undercut a position taken by a chapter.

Line, raised to a senior vice president of the Society and put in charge of all its publications, was also for a time responsible for its scientific magazine, *American Birds*. This publication, which increasingly linked serious amateur birdwatchers and career ornithologists, could trace its origins all the way back to 1900 when a series on birds and seasons first appeared in *Bird-Lore*. Volunteer editors compiled reports of birds seen by observers in their regions of the country and submitted them to *Bird-Lore* at the end of each season. The Christmas Bird Count became a part of the annual reporting cycle after Frank Chapman dreamed it up later that year.

The seasonal reports at first were restricted to three or four pages in *Bird-Lore*. As interest in birds grew, so did "The Season," until in 1939 it was mailed with the parent magazine as a separate supplement. In 1947 this feature was renamed *Audubon Field Notes* and issued by National Audubon as a publication in its own right, with its own staff and subscription list. It became *American Birds* under a new editor, Robert Arbib, in 1971. With Line and Arbib redesigning the publication, it grew from a circulation of thirty-five hundred to thirteen thousand in the late '70s, and evolved into a showcase for substantial articles on migration, distribution, identification, behavior, habitat, and population studies.

One of the issues on which Roland Clement clashed with Line and Arbib was falconry. Clement had taken a special interest in the birds of prey ever since coming to National Audubon and had edited its research reports on the golden eagle and the California condor. When the peregrine falcon's population crashed, he followed the situation closely and in 1968 asked fish and game departments in the coastal states to declare a moratorium on the taking of migrating peregrines for use in falconry. But Clement's research soon convinced him that DDT, not the falconers, was the cause of the species' population disaster. He felt that falconers such as Tom Cade, who had devised techniques for breeding the birds in captivity and releasing them into the wild to rebuild the population, were the peregrine's best hope. He saw the falconers as a conservation ally and wanted an Audubon policy that would support falconry under careful regulations.

"Responsible falconry never has been, and is not now, a hazard to raptors," Clement wrote in a memo in 1973 to provide a more sympathetic view of falconry within the Society. "Let us therefore allow only responsible falconry by sound State regulation and enforcement. We can then benefit from the falconer's know-how in saving the finest raptor of all—the Peregrine Falcon. It is unlikely to survive without this help."

Clement's attempt to produce from his office a unified and conciliatory Audubon policy on falconry was doomed to failure, at least in the short run. There were strong feelings against capturing wild and, in some cases, rare birds to use for sport, feelings not only among members but also at Audubon headquarters. Charlie Callison, Les Line, and Bob Arbib all held antifalconry positions. In 1971, Line published an article in *Audubon,* "The Falconer's Paradox" by George Laycock, that was critical of the sport. Clement objected to the article in manuscript but was told that Line had "overruled" him.

Three years later Arbib wrote a strong editorial in *American Birds,* calling for a ban on falconry. Still later, after Callison declined to distribute to Audubon chapters a copy of Clement's sympathetic memo on falconry, he irritated Clement again by giving "wide circulation" to a vigorous attack on falconry by Robert Witzeman of the Maricopa Audubon Society in Phoenix, Arizona. Clement shot off another memo.

"Mr. Callison has conducted an anti-falconry campaign in the guise of informing our members, both by repressing any discussion of contrary views, and by feeding our members a party line," Clement complained.

It was Clement's view that Audubon members, instead of being given a scientific evaluation of complex problems to weigh for themselves, were receiving a point of view based on personal opinion which the members then "spout back . . . as though it were a grassroots demand."

But Clement was writing as if he were a part of the ideal scientific institution. The National Audubon Society was, as Drury recognized at Mass Audubon, a membership organization composed of different viewpoints that, particularly in reference to animals, are not based always on science; the emotions that draw many people to animals in the first place remain with them after they join an organization established to protect those animals.

From its beginnings, National Audubon has been a blend of hunters and antihunters, and some of the sentiments implied in that division spilled over into the dispute on falconry. Callison, Line, and Arbib were not simply manufacturing a grass-roots uproar. They were expressing a point of view already held by many members.

National Audubon, over the years, has maintained the stand that the focus of its protection work is directed toward the species level. This focus has allowed the Society to co-exist with hunters, just as it was able to make its peace with the falconers. The Society does not disapprove of those sports as long as they are carried on under careful regulation that preserves the species. When politics, public relations, or just plain sentiment intrudes, however, the hard edges of policy are often blurred, and the give-and-take begins.

# 29

In 1969 there died in California one of those shadowy figures whom newspapers invariably refer to as "an eccentric millionaire." In this case the shoe seemed to fit. "Captain" George Whittell, Jr., was a man who went his own way, often exercised exotic tastes in philosophy, animals, and affairs of the heart, and ended up confounding his survivors and, perhaps, his own cherished designs.

The Los Angeles *Times* has described him:

"In his day, Whittell was called 'the king-sized playboy.' He was a big man—6 feet 5 five inches, 240 pounds. Think of the most romantic adventures that a man could pack into a lifetime, and Whittell experienced them. He ran off with the Barnum and Bailey Circus when he was twenty. He went on safaris with famed animal trainer Frank (Bring 'Em Back Alive) Buck and was a close friend of pioneer aviator Wiley Post. Whittell also was married to a showgirl for a short time just after the turn of the century. He drove and collected expensive Duesenberg cars, flew with the Lafayette Escadrille in France, and built a castle at Lake Tahoe, where he had major landholdings on the Nevada side."

Whittell had inherited a small fortune. In the 1930s, when he discovered Lake Tahoe, he apparently made up his mind to acquire it as he might any desirable bauble and finally bought 40,000 acres, including sixteen miles of the Nevada shore, for about twenty-five dollars an acre. It is no exaggeration to say that the land eventually sent his fortune spiraling.

He also owned a fifty-acre estate at Woodside, California, which he stocked with a menagerie that included an elephant, a lion, a bear, cheetahs, and other large animals.

"But the animals didn't do very well," Kenneth J. Ashcraft, Whittell's friend and later an executor of his estate, has said. "Some of them died, and others got sick and had to be given to zoos. This weighed on his conscience. It began to turn his thoughts toward the suffering of animals and explains what he did later on."

If animals generally rose in Whittell's estimation, he became increasingly disenchanted with other members of his own species and was heard to remark that he expected to be reincarnated as an elephant. Lawyers ranked especially low in his regard.

"I used to have long talks with Captain Whittell," Ashcraft said. "It's a funny thing to say, but I can't really tell you how he got the title 'captain.' He owned a yacht, and he went around the world on it once, and I think that's when people began calling him Captain Whittell. Anyway, when he was going into the hospital I asked about his will. He didn't have one, but he wouldn't get in touch with a lawyer. Finally he asked me to get him some forms, and he used them to make out his own will."

It turned out to be an untidy way to wind up his affairs. After his death at the age of eighty-six, his executors discovered that he had left a fortune of $50 million, most of which was to "relieve pain and suffering among animal, bird, and fish life, and to preserve, improve, and perpetuate animal, bird, and fish life." According to Whittell the money was to go to three organizations: the Defenders of Wildlife, "the Society for the Prevention of Cruelty to Animals (local or national)," and the National Audubon Society "of Washington, D.C." Each of these organizations was to receive about twenty-five percent of Whittell's estate after taxes and other fees, and eventually the remainder was to go to one or more of those same organizations to be selected by the executors.

Alas, the tax collectors and the hated lawyers fared nearly as well at Whittell's hands as the animals, birds, and fish, in part because of inattention to detail. While the Defenders of Wildlife had a clear claim to its share of the estate, the executors learned that there is no single Society for the Prevention of Cruelty to Animals, but merely dozens of unaffiliated organizations of that (or similar) name scattered across the country. So many of them laid claim to a share of the money that, when legal proceedings began, the presiding judge ordered the forty or more lawyers who showed up in court to pin numbered placards on their suits and dresses so that he could identify them.

One man asked for $20,000 to take his talking dog on a nationwide tour of schools. (A reporter who called long distance to interview the dog was told that it was tied up and could not come to the phone.) After some bizarre testimony about both Captain Whittell and the humane societies, the judge directed the estate's executors to select the most deserving societies, and they settled on twenty-nine of the claimants.

When the executors notified officials of the National Audubon Society that it seemed to be in line for at least twenty-five percent of the estate, excitement was mingled with puzzlement. Who was George Whittell? A hurried search of the files revealed that Whittell had become a life member of the Society in the 1920s when the fee was $100. Further research turned up the fact that when the Society was struggling to pay its bills during the late 1930s, one of its representatives was sent to California, armed with a list of life members, and had talked to Whittell but had come away empty-handed.

Whittell's vagueness was also the source of consternation at Audubon House in New York. Elvis Stahr learned that the mistake in identifying National Audubon as a Washington-based organization came from an Internal Revenue Service booklet listing tax-exempt organizations, one edition of which had incorrectly reported the Society's address. Stahr rushed to Baltimore to secure an affidavit from the editor who had prepared that edition but found she had recently died. After some legal maneuvering, the Society managed to establish its claim, with a settlement to the Audubon Naturalist Society of the Central Atlantic States, which has its headquarters just outside the District of Columbia.

The Society eventually received more than twelve million dollars from the Whittell estate. Much of this money went to the sanctuaries, where it played a large part in acquiring new areas or in supporting construction and research on existing sanctuaries. For instance, the Society used Whittell funds to buy important wildfowl feeding grounds in San Francisco Bay and in the nearby Richardson Bay Sanctuary, and gave more than seventy-five thousand dollars in matching funds to the Audubon Canyon Ranch (which is operated by several of the Society's chapters in northern California) to buy some of the superb bird habitat around Bolinas Lagoon and Tomales Bay. With Defenders of Wildlife, the Society bought 640 acres on the east slope of the Sierra Nevada to be operated as the Whittell Audubon Center by the Lahontan Audubon Society of Nevada.

Whittell's bequest is still sending vital ripples through the sanctuary system. The magnificent cypress–black-gum forest in South Carolina's Four Holes Swamp was bought in part with these funds and is now a showcase as the 5,400-acre Francis Beidler Forest Sanctuary. As at Corkscrew, a boardwalk leads visitors into the great, vaulted forest.

In Texas, the Society matched an Exxon USA grant with Whittell funds to buy part of the land for the Sabal Palm Grove Sanctuary near Brownsville. There, among the only remaining wild groves of these palms in the United States, the speckled racer snake and several beetles also find their only home in this country. Ebony trees, the coral bean, and lantana grow while birdwatchers add chachalacas, buff-bellied hummingbirds, green jays, pauraques, and golden-fronted woodpeckers to their life lists.

This sanctuary was once owned by a commercial nursery, which used the sabal palms to shade its exotic plants, and early Tarzan movies were

Audubon warden Susan Bailey at Sydnes Island, Texas, in 1975. NAS

filmed there among the introduced banana and papaya trees. The staff began rooting out the exotics to make possible a study of the interaction between plants and animals in a wild sabal palm grove.

Stahr and Frosty Anderson liked to point out that the Audubon sanctuaries are not wilderness areas. They are to be kept as natural as possible, but as they are beset on all sides by the residues of mankind's "busyness," certain wildlife-management techniques must be introduced to keep fragile ecosystems intact.

"The sanctuaries are managed to protect and perpetuate plant and animal species," Stahr said. "But they are also there to educate human beings about the natural world. We have to manage those areas, or we'll lose them."

Fortunately, Whittell funds were not restricted to capital investments. Audubon diverted part of the money outside the sanctuaries to support programs on behalf of the whooping crane, brown pelican, mountain lion, wood stork, and California condor. Other Whittell money has gone to projects helping the alligator, wild sheep, and colonial nesting birds. And so, in the long run, the untidy will of a dying man perpetuated the good he dreamed of doing.

# 30

*E*lvis Stahr's tenure at National Audubon belied the image of a capricious leader that he sometimes, in his "good ol' boy" style, tried to palm off on his listeners. Despite his inclination to delegate administrative detail, and even authority, to his staff, he spent long hours on the job. He wooed potential contributors on the road with the same persistence with which he kept an eye on minutiae of policy or legislation in the office. He remained at Audubon as president for more than ten years and, when he decided it was time to retire, he offered to lend a hand to the Society's Washington office for an additional year or two.

News of impending change spread through the Society in June 1978, when Stahr told Edward H. Harte, chairman of the board of directors, that he was ready to step down as president and that a search for his successor should begin; as he was sixty-three years old, he would like to go on serving the Society in some other position until his sixty-fifth birthday. In a report to the membership later that year, Stahr reviewed some of the gains of the past decade:

"In 1968 the Society had only about 88,000 members. We now have more than 388,000 members. . . . Despite the striking growth in total membership of 340 percent, our total *staff* has grown in ten years by only 29 percent (from 164 to 212). . . .

"During the same period the Society's 'net worth' (total endowment-type funds, excluding properties) grew from $8.1 million to over $18.5 million, and the unrestricted portion rose from $1.4 million to over $7.7 million—all that, despite growth in annual operating expenditures from $2.5 million to $10.1 million!

"National Audubon owns many millions of dollars' worth of real estate, but because Audubon sanctuaries and centers are *not* for sale, we carry them on our books at a combined value of exactly one dollar. They are, nonetheless, tremendous assets for our missions of conservation action, wildlife and ecosystem research, and environmental education."

There were areas of "unfinished business" in which Stahr remained keenly interested. Among them was the political struggle in Washington to pass an Alaska National Interest Lands Conservation Act. This legislation, which was designed to give permanent protection to all those scenic lands and wildlife habitats given temporary relief from exploitation by the Alaska Native Claims Settlement Act of 1971, was strenuously opposed by many business interests and developers, as well as by that state's congressional delegation. The new protective act was passed by the House of Representatives in 1978, but the Senate failed to act before adjournment. The critical lands were thus left prey to private interests, as the protective provision in the earlier legislation expired that year. Audubon would fight again another year.

Stahr, who had thrown part of the Society's resources into the Alaska battle, was partly mollified by gains within Audubon's own sanctuary system. For instance, in the summer of his final year as president, he accepted for the Society a two-mile stretch of wild ocean beach and dunes, as well as hundreds of acres of marshland, on North Carolina's Outer Banks. The donor was a Winston-Salem businessman, Earl Slick. The gift, which resulted in the Pine Island Sanctuary, is a vital link in the succession of private, state, and federal reserves that protect the Outer Banks between the Back Bay National Wildlife Refuge in Virginia and the Cape Hatteras National Seashore in North Carolina.

This time the search for a new Audubon president focused on a rather obvious candidate. Russell W. Peterson was no stranger to the Audubon board and membership, for in the fall of 1977 he had been awarded the Audubon Medal at the Society's annual dinner. (The Medal, created in 1947 when it was given to Hugh H. Bennett of the Soil Conservation Service for outstanding service to conservation, had quickly become one of the more prestigious honors in the field.) Peterson, a native of Wisconsin, had come to the conservation movement in a roundabout fashion. After earning a Ph.D. in chemistry at the University of Wisconsin in 1942, he joined the DuPont Company and, during the next twenty-six years, climbed the corporate ladder through assignments in research, production, and sales to become director of DuPont's research and development division.

Meanwhile, having made his home near the DuPont headquarters in Delaware, Peterson became a prominent figure in the local Republican party. He was elected governor of the state and, during his four years in office (1969–73), he cultivated a mild interest in birdwatching into a broad command of environmental issues that coincided with the general enthusiasm created by Earth Day. Although Peterson worked for reforms in state administration and criminal justice, none of his other achievements as governor brought him as much favorable recognition as his campaign to protect the state's shoreline. The passage of the Delaware Coastal Zone Act under his leadership gave an important lift to conservationists all over the country at a time when there was great public concern about the loss of coastal wetlands to development.

After leaving the governor's office, Peterson went on to Washington with a reputation as an environmentalist and, during the Richard Nixon–Gerald Ford years, served as chairman of the President's Council on Environmental Quality. There his outlook on world environmental problems broadened considerably: he was appointed vice chairman of the U.S. Delegation to the United Nations World Population Conference in Bucharest in 1974 and, two years later, vice chairman of the U.S. Delegation to the United Nations World Conference on Human Settlements at Vancouver. Those and several similar experiences shaped his views in the years to come.

In 1978, while serving as director of the Office of Technology Assessment for Congress, Peterson was approached by Audubon's board of directors and interviewed as a possible successor to Elvis Stahr. He had the high-level experience and national reputation which the board considered vital to the job. Moreover, during his interviews, he impressed the board's members as a man having both unbounded energy and a vision that transcended even the Society's reasonably extensive concerns. Peterson expressed surprise as well as pleasure to friends when Audubon's board offered him (then just past his sixty-second birthday) a seven-year contract; he gave up his congressional appointment (amid the grumbling of some congressmen, who felt he had not been there long enough to warm his chair) and became National Audubon's chief executive officer on April 1, 1979.

The new president, who asked staff members to address him simply as "Russ," smoothed his entry into a difficult position by bringing with him from Delaware an administrative assistant, Mary Joy Breton, whose skills had first impressed him when she served as a volunteer during his campaign for governor. (Breton became a vice president at Audubon and stayed on after Peterson's departure to serve his successor in a similar capacity.)

But Peterson received a number of inheritances from his predecessor that made his entry anything but smooth. One was a trend, begun about 1976, toward larger operating deficits that as yet had caused no serious alarm. Another was a cluster of conservation struggles over Alaska, endangered species, and pork-barrel water projects in the West. A third was the comparatively new top-level management team of Paul M. Howard, Jr., and Robert O. Binnewies, who had succeeded Charlie Callison and Roland Clement after both took early retirements. Under the same classification might be considered Elvis Stahr himself, whose offer to stay on in some capacity until the age of sixty-five had been accepted by the board and which resulted in some of the same unhappiness experienced by earlier Audubon presidents in their relationships with their predecessors.

It was apparent from the beginning that Audubon was undergoing an abrupt change in style. Stahr, a master of the relaxed, informal administration, had been succeeded by an idea man who kept the staff in continual ferment. Peterson had a vision for the Society, and it went far beyond the image of an assemblage of birdwatchers and sanctuary wardens which had persisted in the public's mind. He wanted to lead the Audubon movement under the slogan "Think Globally, Act Locally."

"Environmental degradation knows no borders," he once wrote. "American acid rain is killing Canadian lakes. Soil erosion in one state affects food supplies in another. Our exported pesticides come back to us in our beans, beef and coffee. One nation's radioactive waste dumped in the ocean may end up in another country's tuna sandwiches. The birds at your feeder in the fall may find their winter habitat destroyed when they arrive in South America."

He called on Audubon members to be aware of, and to care about, "the downwind and downstream effects of locally-produced pollutants," to join in the search for ways to avert nuclear war, and to realize that each human being is part of the "cumulative impact" on the Earth resulting from runaway populations. Peterson was never quite able to haul the Society with him into the upper reaches of global issues. There was always the problem of where the money was to come from to finance a truly international program that would be effective in dealing with the great issues of nuclear war and population explosions; and beyond the problems of insufficient funding lay the disquietude of some Audubon board members, staff professionals, and individual members who considered the Society's mission to be historically that of wildlife protection. These people were concerned primarily with policy rather than with global politics.

But Russ Peterson was the proverbial political animal. He never gave up the attempt to introduce the Audubon name into the global issues of the day, even if the only way to do it was to take a personal role in international societies and conferences. As his curriculum vitae phrased it, he "was a prime mover in the creation of the Global Tomorrow Coalition, The Center on the Consequences of Nuclear War and the Better World Society." He also actively campaigned for and was elected to the presidency of that organization founded a half-century earlier by Gilbert Pearson, the International Council for Bird Preservation.

On the national scene, events quickly impelled Russ Peterson into becoming the most politically engaged of all Audubon leaders. His years of corporate and political experience in Delaware and the intervening succession of appointments in Washington had fixed his orientation on the national capital. The first year of his Audubon administration saw the Society's Washington office begin to take on added importance when Elvis Stahr agreed to serve out his remaining Audubon time as "senior counselor" attached to the Society's now bulging set of rooms near the White House.

"I'm not here to be a boss, but rather to be supportive to this staff," Stahr said at the time. "A lot of people know me in this town. I get around quite a bit, visiting congressmen or administration officials, attending meetings with other environmental groups, and this helps to let people know that Audubon is here. And sometimes I can open doors for our other staff members."

Cynthia Wilson, who had first staffed Audubon's Washington office, moved back into the federal government, this time as a special assistant to Cecil Andrus while he served as Jimmy Carter's Secretary of the Interior. But by Russ Peterson's time the capital staff had grown to more than a dozen men and women working on such issues as Alaska wildlands, predator control, and various pollution and energy problems. Lobbying, because of the legislation advocated by Stahr to relieve the Internal Revenue Service restrictions on nonprofit organizations, was becoming an increasingly important function of conservation organizations. With this added importance came new sophistication.

"An area of government we environmentalists have generally neglected is appropriations," one of the Audubon staff said. "We can lobby into existence the best legislation and regulations in the world, and even go to court to have them enforced, but if our programs don't get the proper funding they are doomed from the beginning."

Volunteers familiar with the intricacies of the federal budget worked with staff members to show them how the President and his White House aides put a budget together, how the various agencies participate, how the essential documents are produced, and how congressional appropriations committees function. The message was that the person who controls the money, in Congress or in a federal agency, controls the program. That person must be a prime target of the lobbyists.

"Some conservation organizations spend most of their time lobbying liberals, who are supposed to be more friendly to their concerns," another Audubon staff member said. "But we don't write off anybody. We feel that most legislators are interested in wildlife, and we try to figure out the best ways to reach them with relevant material."

Wildlife is a particularly volatile subject in Washington. Aggressive lobbyists, ranging from hunters to the animal-rights groups, roam the halls of Congress and the Department of the Interior, pushing their own points of view and trying to root out heretical notions within the conservation movement itself. Over the years, the National Audubon Society has sometimes run afoul of some of its sister organizations because of its willingness to work out compromise legislation on extremely difficult issues. Although the Society has been twitted by some of its accustomed allies as the "gray lady of the conservation movement," and accused of being soft on certain issues, the Audubon leaders always believed they were working from a knowledge of practical politics, keeping doors open which had been closed to more militant groups. In the late 1970s, for instance, Audubon played an effective team role in the Alaska Coalition, which was made up of a number of organizations that finally lobbied the Alaska lands bill to passage by Congress. At the same time, Audubon's Washington staff was criticized by other conservationists for accepting what most of them believed to be a weakening amendment to the legislation renewing the Endangered Species Act.

"Those other groups didn't read the political climate correctly," Stahr argued. "We took a position only after our head count showed that the 'no compromise' approach had only about twenty votes at best in the Senate. The entire act was being jeopardized by the hard-line groups. Senator John Culver of Iowa was the legislation's floor manager, and we realized that our best chance for passage was to work with him on the compromise legislation he had proposed. A year later those other groups came around to our point of view and joined with us to get the legislation through."

Stahr's working philosophy, "Stick to policies and principles, and stay away from politics and personalities," generally reflected the practice of generations of Audubon leaders. He had been a frequent visitor to the White House under Presidents Nixon, Ford, and Carter. But now, at the beginning of the 1980s, that option was denied to Russ Peterson. The election of Ronald Reagan brought in an administration whose leaders were more hostile to conservation principles than any other since the heyday of natural-resource exploitation in the nineteenth century. Under ordinary circumstances, the arrival of a Republican administration at the time when a prominent Republican politician was molding the Society to his own vision would have brought on a period of at least nominal good will between the White House and Audubon House.

But from the first it was apparent that the policy of Reagan's chief spokesman on the environment, Secretary of the Interior James Watt, was to roll back most of the environmental regulations and legislation of recent decades. Public lands and natural resources, especially in the West, went up for grabs. Peterson protested the new administration's policies, then attacked the offending bureaucrats in both the Interior

Department and the Environmental Protection Agency. He, as well as his staff, became *persona non grata* at the White House and later at the Interior Department. Even a formerly influential Republican and Audubon board member, Nathaniel P. Reed (who had been an Assistant Secretary of the Interior in the Nixon and Ford administrations), was lumped with the "radical environmentalists" by the new administration. On the other hand, eleven of the top sixteen officials in Watt's Interior Department had worked for the five major industries regulated by that agency.

The closest that Peterson was to come to a dialogue with the Reagan administration was at a meeting arranged in the White House in January 1982, with Edwin Meese III, counselor to the President. The meeting included the leaders of two other major conservation organizations, Jay D. Hair of the National Wildlife Federation and J. Michael McCloskey of the Sierra Club. Meese tried to put the best possible face on matters, calling Reagan a "good environmentalist" and blaming the concerns of conservationists on "misperceptions."

Peterson replied that his concerns were based not on perceptions, but on facts such as the dismissal of scientists and enforcement personnel and the crippling budget reductions at the Environmental Protection Agency. (A year later, EPA director Anne Gorsuch Burford and twenty other officials there were forced to resign amid charges of mismanagement and misconduct.) Peterson also brought up the administration's rush to lease much of the country's publicly owned coal, oil, forests, and grasslands at bargain prices and its plan (later abandoned) to sell federal lands. Meese, on the other hand, described nuclear power as the safest and most economical source of energy; he also defended the administration's reversal of President Nixon's ban on predator poisons on public lands by arguing that sheep ranchers had not been treated fairly. The meeting ended in an impasse.

"If we needed any confirmation of the complete lack of respect the President and his team have for what we in the conservation movement stand for, we got it at this meeting," Peterson said afterward. "We are going to keep trying to get our message across but the probability of any meaningful dialogue with this administration is low indeed."

Meanwhile, Peterson was shaping the Audubon staff to his plans. Neither of his two top vice presidents lasted very long in New York. Paul Howard, a deeply religious man who had proved to be an extremely effective Western representative for the Society while working in Sacramento, was not able to accommodate himself to the Peterson style in New York and soon left the Society for good. Bob Binnewies, who had served with the National Park Service and worked for a time with a Rockefeller-funded land-preservation organization in Maine, likewise was

Russell W. Peterson came to Audubon as president in 1979
after a long career in industry and government. NAS

uncomfortable with life in New York; when an opportunity came to return to the National Park Service, he accepted it.

Peterson made two major appointments in New York. One was M. Rupert Cutler (a former kitchen helper as a youngster at the Audubon Camp of Maine), who had been Assistant Secretary of Agriculture for Natural Resources and Environment under President Carter and became a senior vice president of the National Audubon Society in 1980. The other high-ranking staff member was Glenn Paulson, whom Peterson appointed vice president for science. Paulson reflected the Society's new emphasis on expanding its environmental concerns. He was a biochemist with a deep interest in combating environmental contamination but with little practical experience in wildlife management. This appointment and the new emphasis it implied made some of the field staff uneasy for a time (for instance, Audubon lost its primacy in bald eagle research to the National Wildlife Federation during this period), but eventually they came to appreciate Paulson's professionalism. He was a very able administrator, adept at securing grants from major foundations and was able to fund a variety of Audubon science projects throughout the Peterson years.

Later, Peterson added another specialist, Jan Beyea, to the science staff; Beyea produced a detailed proposal for a national energy plan designed to influence both academic and governmental thinking in that field in the years ahead. Meanwhile, Elvis Stahr, whose prominent presence in the Washington office seemed to make Peterson uncomfortable, left to enter private law practice. He continued to serve the Society from his law office, however, supervising the later periodic contributions to Audubon from the Whittell bequest.

Peterson, believing that Washington would be a more logical place of business than New York for a national conservation organization, made a strenuous effort to move Audubon's headquarters there during the 1980s. New staff members were hired with that in mind. (Several of them, understandably reluctant to find permanent homes in the New York area when a move to Washington was imminent, were lodged for a time in facilities at the Audubon Center in Greenwich, where the decor was described by a wag as "reform school modern.") Peterson hoped to help finance the move by selling the remainder of the lease on the New York headquarters back to the landlord, a feasible idea at the time because Manhattan rents had skyrocketed since Audubon had signed the original lease. The plan was to use that money to help buy and renovate a building somewhere in the Washington area. An adjunct to the plan was to revive the attempt, begun under Stahr, to unify National Audubon with the successor of the original District of Columbia Audubon

Society, now called the Audubon Naturalist Society of the Central Atlantic States.

But those projects eventually failed. Prices were rising in Washington too, and a suitable headquarters building was never found. The local Audubon society, having grown prosperous itself, refused Peterson's overture. National Audubon's own financial picture was causing further concern for the board of directors. Although the Society was growing rapidly toward half a million members, Peterson's expanding programs were forcing him to juggle his budget year after year to gain board approval for new projects. The deficit in expenses, as opposed to support and revenues for the fiscal year ending June 30, 1982, was $300,000, but the figure a year later exceeded $1.5 million. While contributions, bequests, and other capital additions to the endowment funds showed a barely negligible deficit on paper, the operating budget obviously was not going to please many board members.

Russ Peterson, however, was both imaginative and resourceful, and National Audubon continued for a time to function in high gear.

# 31

In May 1979, *Audubon* published the first of a series of five articles that was designed to take a fair and penetrating look at all aspects of sport hunting in America. The series, written by *Audubon* field editor John G. Mitchell and entitled "Bitter Harvest," set off an immediate storm within the Society. The response to Mitchell's articles may have revealed something about attitudes in an increasingly urbanized country, and it surely said much about the makeup of the modern National Audubon Society.

Even before the first article appeared, mail on the subject began pouring in from people who had merely read an announcement of its impending publication. Members wrote to advise the editor that if they had wanted to know *anything* about hunting they would have subscribed to one of the rod-and-gun magazines. A number of them announced that they were tearing up their membership cards. One antihunter wrote that the only way to be "fair" to hunters was to "pursue, terrorize, trap, torture and shoot them with their own bows and arrows. Then leave them to hobble wounded until they die."

Mail on the subject increased in volume once the series began to appear:

"One more of your blood-and-guts, pro-hunting issues and I drop my ten-year membership," wrote a woman in Santa Rosa, California.

"After reading 'Bitter Harvest,' I felt the gorge coming up in my throat," claimed a man in Petoskey, Michigan. "If ever I have read a slanted, anti-hunting article, this is it."

"I must end my support of the National Audubon Society," wrote a man in Vicksburg, Mississippi. "I am an avid environmentalist. I am also one of those cold-hearted individuals who enjoys hunting. . . . I don't feel we must defend our views. *Audubon* should have avoided this touchy issue."

"Ideologues, of whatever stripe are much the same when it comes to close mindedness and you are going to take a lot of flak," concluded a reader in Marine-on-St. Croix, Minnesota. "But hang in there! We need some sanity in this discussion, and *Audubon* is the likeliest place to get it."

Ever since Earth Day and the Society's tremendous growth in membership, National Audubon had begun to look less like a cult of single-minded enthusiasts and more like a vast ecclesiastical or political body that sheltered people of diverse viewpoints and from many walks of life. Some members had joined to support a wide assortment of conservation goals. Others applied for membership because of the Society's long identification with birds, still others because it complemented the aims of another specialized fraternity such as hunting or fishing, to which they also belonged. And perhaps the highest percentage signed up mainly to receive the opulent magazine.

Because a minority of those members, certainly no more than twenty percent, were consistently active in local Audubon chapters, the one conduit open to the majority for receiving information and expressing their opinions remained the magazine. The opportunity for debate in the magazine was increased by editor Les Line's freedom of action and his willingness to pursue controversial subjects in its pages. One colleague likened his policy to a Darwinian process of natural selection, in which the unfit readers were winnowed out by the controversial nature of the subject matter.

There was no doubt that Mitchell's series, though it was remarkably evenhanded in approach, caused the Society to lose some members who held passionate positions on either side of the hunting issue; an even-handed presentation was exactly what those people did not want to see. Another aspect of the controversy, treated later (July 1982) in some detail by the same author, was trapping and the use of the steel leghold trap. (Mitchell came down rather hard on the ultimate issue there, that of the humaneness of the trap and of the trade in furs.) Many animal-rights advocates, including some Audubon members, have compared the trapping of animals for their fur with the shooting of egrets for the plume trade, and wondered why National Audubon has not taken a more vigorous stand against the former.

Here the rationale of the Society's policy stems from the differing biological standings of the two cases. The herons, egrets, and terns were attacked on their crowded colonies during the breeding season when their nuptial plumes were at their grandest and the birds at their most vulnerable. Thus concentrated, they could be shot in large numbers and their breeding cycle hopelessly broken. The plume trade decimated and eventually threatened the very existence of those populations. The trapping of fur-bearing animals is carried out on a spot basis, without interfering substantially with an entire population's breeding cycle,

Les Line, creator of "the most beautiful magazine in the world."

and has no appreciable effect on the population's survival. In game-management terms, the trapper is simply "harvesting the surplus."

National Audubon's policy on trapping has grown out of its approach to hunting: as a conservation organization rather than a humane society, Audubon exists to protect populations of animals and intervenes only against policies and practices that scientific evidence suggests may threaten those populations.

In the case of the leghold trap, Audubon has recommended a search for the most humane instruments of trapping, but in the absence of effective alternatives, it has not fought against its use. Indeed, National Audubon has in the past sometimes resorted to the use of leghold traps in the protection of threatened or endangered species. Despite the Rosalie Edge uproar, the Society's board of directors has occasionally authorized the trapping of nutria, an exotic fur-bearing animal that was introduced to Louisiana and is often considered a "pest" at the Rainey Wildlife Sanctuary and other marshes. Under the conditions by which Grace Rainey Rogers donated the property, National Audubon is responsible for maintaining it for the benefit of the blue goose and other wintering waterfowl, and the nutria has replaced the muskrat there as a major competitor for the available food. The Society also approved the use of leghold traps to remove raccoons on Squam Lake in New Hampshire, where they were preying heavily on common loons, and on beaches and the offshore islands of Florida and Georgia, where they threatened the nests of endangered marine turtles.

If the vehemence of the response to "Bitter Harvest" astonished most staff members, they were better prepared for the backlash from an *Audubon* article on dove-hunting. Some members of the Society, particularly in the Midwest, had campaigned for a long time to have mourning doves placed on the list of songbirds in their states, thus giving them protection from hunting. Again, National Audubon has never taken a position for or against dove-hunting. Because field studies show that hunting has no significant effect on dove populations, the Society maintains that hunting can be opposed "only on aesthetic, not biological, grounds, and that this matter is one for each state to decide through democratic processes."

When Les Line published an article on mourning doves, it appeared at a time when several chapters in Indiana had just lost a battle to stop the state from holding a dove-hunting season. The article not only took the opposite stand, but also suggested that the opponents of the hunting season were sentimental and unscientific. There was an understandable cry of betrayal from the involved chapters. Audubon members, it is apparent, seldom speak with one voice.

Similar signs of unrest have arrived in the New York office when advertisements in *Audubon* seem to undercut a chapter's position. Russ Peterson was faced with an incident of this sort almost immediately after he took office. The Tahoma Audubon Society in Tacoma, Washington, had been fighting hard for more government forests to be set aside as wilderness before the loggers reached them. To their pained surprise, an advertisement placed by one of the giants of the logging industry appeared in *Audubon* at the end of 1978, bearing the questionable message: "Setting aside unrealistically increased areas for wilderness diminishes any chance of meeting America's growing need for forest products."

Peterson addressed the complaints about *Audubon*'s advertising policies at a meeting with Les Line and other staff members in June 1979. The magazine's position under Line until then had been that it would be an abridgement of free speech to deny opponents an opportunity to state their views, as long as those views were clearly labeled as a paid advertisement and did not contain false or purposely misleading statements. Peterson argued, however, that *Audubon* was not a commercial publication; it was intended to be an advocate of the Audubon cause, and if certain ads offended members, the Society would be hurt.

From this meeting emerged a statement of policy: *Audubon* will not accept advertisements which directly advocate stands on legal and public issues. Another policy of more restricted scope, one felt by some staff members to be shortsighted, was also adopted: *"Audubon* will refuse to accept advertisements seeking membership and contributions for conservation organizations which are in direct competition with the National Audubon Society for funds and members."

One of the major conservation projects that Peterson had inherited from his predecessor soon wobbled out of control and into a nasty little inhouse squabble. The Garrison Diversion Unit, planned by the federal government's Bureau of Reclamation and authorized by Congress in 1965, had grown into an environmental nightmare. Its design called for some three thousand miles of canals, pipelines, drains, and regulating reservoirs. These, at a cost of well over a billion dollars, would move water from the Missouri River to irrigate farms (perhaps as many as thirteen hundred, perhaps fewer than three hundred) in North Dakota. It was a classic boondoggle. Cecil Andrus, a former Secretary of the Interior, once remarked that "some water projects are good, some are poor, but the Garrison project is the dog of all."

The project encountered protests from many directions. Both conservationists and many local farmers protested that Garrison would destroy thousands of acres of some of the best inland marsh and prairie pothole country left in North America; wildlife refuges, native grasslands and range, even more than four thousand acres of woodlands, would be lost to the region. The government of Canada protested on the grounds that water, pushed back over the international boundary, would transfer fish parasites and diseases from the Missouri River to the Hudson Bay watershed. Taxpayers protested when it became apparent that the project would cost as much as $700,000 for every farm it benefited!

Yet, as a matter of local politics, Garrison took on a life of its own; North Dakota was somehow "owed" a major irrigation project, though the obligation was based on Dust Bowl conditions that had prevailed in the 1930s. The National Audubon Society mobilized opposition to the project from a broad spectrum of conservation organizations. During the 1970s, the Society hired as its regional vice president for the North Midwest Region a local activist named Richard Madson, who had already organized opposition to Garrison among farmers and other residents. Although Congress kept funding the project, and a canal was cutting a great gash across the prairie, Madson developed a personal following. An intense, religiously motivated young man, he won increasing support in North Dakota for the drive to kill Garrison. In 1981, the House of Representatives in Washington voted to do just that, and the Society seemed on the verge of winning one of its most dramatic postwar victories.

Then, unaccountably, the principals in the Audubon effort managed to throw away their advantage. Grumbling arose among a couple of board members and some Audubon activists in the North Midwest Region that Madson was giving short shrift to other aspects of his job. There was more to the region, they argued, than North Dakota. Vice president Rupert Cutler visited Madson and ordered him to move his headquarters from Jamestown, North Dakota, to Minneapolis to better serve the entire region. Madson, totally involved in Garrison, balked at the order.

What happened next is a matter of some confusion. Madson flew to New York in December 1981, to talk over the situation with Peterson and Cutler, since Cutler had wanted to fire him for insubordination. At this meeting, Madson apparently agreed to move the regional office to Minneapolis. Back in Jamestown, he received a "Merry Christmas" call from Peterson, reaffirming his support for keeping him on the Audubon staff. Then, after the first of the year, Madson phoned Cutler to argue that there was growing resentment about the proposed move in North Dakota and that the Garrison campaign, among other local issues, might be damaged. Cutler fired him. Madson later contended that he was simply arguing against the move, not rejecting it.

The chapters in North Dakota rushed to Madson's defense. A Committee for the Preservation of Audubon Ethics was quickly formed, and the dispute between Madson and his former bosses in New York received prominent coverage in the local newspapers. Proponents of the Garrison Unit were delighted, its opponents chagrined. Dr. Clayton E. Jensen, coordinator of the Committee for the Preservation of Audubon Ethics, petitioned the board of directors to have Madson reinstated and the office in Jamestown kept open to complement the work of the proposed Minneapolis office. Local funding for the latter office was offered.

"We understand that a factor behind the firing of Regional Vice-President Richard Madson," Jensen wrote to other chapter officers in the region, "and the subsequent resignation of Regional Representative Steve Hiniker involved a series of complaints by NAS Board Member Wallace Dayton, and some unidentified NAS members to the effect that staff were not available often enough for chapter or issue activity. . . . We share the desire for more staff help on various Audubon activities. Put yourself in their position—which often involved work of more than 70 hours per week, and many days on the road responding to our various requests. Could you have done any better, had you been in their shoes? . . . The publicity being received by the National Audubon Society in this region as a result of the firing and resignation does not make Audubon a fair and professional organization. In that respect the publicity is accurate on this issue, for the actions taken by NAS senior staff were neither fair nor professional."

Peterson was caught in the crossfire between board member Wallace Dayton of Minneapolis and vice president Rupert Cutler on the one hand, and chapter leaders in North Dakota on the other. As the uproar continued, he was asked by board chairman Thomas W. Keesee, Jr., to fly to North Dakota and respond in person to the chapter leaders' concerns about the firing of Madson. Peterson later described these meetings to Keesee as "traumatic."

"Early in the two meetings nasty comments from the audience about NAS leadership were applauded," he told Keesee. "One person accused me of having been bought off by the Garrison interests. Another said she would forgive me just like Jesus had forgiven Judas. As the meetings went on, however, one could see the audience becoming disillusioned with Rich [Madson]."

Madson, who attended the meetings along with about eighty chapter members, seems to have overplayed his hand. Peterson reported that he had intended, not to rehire Madson, but to offer him a contract to represent National Audubon on Garrison matters in North Dakota. But when Madson staged a press conference of his own, outlining his grievances and upstaging Peterson's own press conference on Garrison, the break between the two men was final. Peterson outlined for chapter members what he said were Madson's deficiencies in his job, including "antagonizing confrontations" with other Audubon staff members and chapter leaders, and said he would have nothing more to do with him under any circumstances.

Although some of the local chapter people remained estranged because of the way the matter had been handled, others thanked Peterson for his frankness and agreed to work with him in the future. Clayton Jensen told Peterson that the Committee for the Preservation of Audubon Ethics had been Madson's idea, and that he, Jensen, was now sorry he had gone along with it. But the squabble remained a public relations fiasco, and Audubon lost part of its support in North Dakota.

Rupert Cutler did not long outlast Madson in what had become a revolving door for vice presidents in the volatile Peterson era. Meanwhile, the Garrison project lived on, in a somewhat reduced version, as its proponents continued to play on the average congressman's penchant for logrolling. Audubon's Washington office has gone on fighting the boondoggles.

# 32

*A*more enduring struggle even than that over the Garrison Unit was going on in California, where National Audubon continued to monitor the condor's decline. There, amid politics and power plays, science and sentiment, a desperate attempt was made to salvage a wisp of hope from one of the most disturbing environmental calamities of our time.

As early as the 1960s, proposals had surfaced here and there in the conservation movement to bring in from the wild some of the condors, noted for the slow pace of their reproduction, and begin a captive propagation program. National Audubon had vigorously opposed captive propagation in the case of the whooping crane, influenced in large part by the botched attempts to get that species to reproduce in zoos. Better to leave the birds to fend for themselves in the wild, was the Society's conclusion. And the hands-off approach had been gratifyingly successful, as the wild crane flocks slowly built back their numbers from the edge of the abyss.

But times had changed. Propagation techniques were spectacularly improved, and the peregrine falcon program at Cornell was putting dozens of birds back into the wild. As the condor population sank, the Society's biologists, including Roland Clement and Sandy Sprunt, were ready to explore their options. The Endangered Species Act of 1973 authorized the Fish and Wildlife Service to prepare recovery programs for selected species whose populations had sunk to critical levels. The condor received high priority, and the Fish and Wildlife Service assigned a biologist, Fred Sibley, to work on the problem in southern California.

Carl Koford, who had written the original monograph on the species for National Audubon, became convinced that the only way to save the condor was to isolate it from humans and strenuously objected to Sibley's visits to nest sites. When Sibley opposed a water-development project in the condor's range, pressure was brought on the Fish and Wildlife Service by local boosters to order him to back off, and he finally withdrew from the condor program. His successor, Sanford Wilbur, came to the conclusion that the condor could not reproduce itself in the wild and suggested captive propagation.

The Fish and Wildlife Service at its higher levels had come to a conclusion of its own, however, namely that the species could not be saved under any conditions. The agency leaders were content to make a show of support for the beleaguered bird but did not want to squander a large amount of money on a lost cause. Efforts by National Audubon to push the agency into action on the condor came to nothing. Finally, in the late 1970s, Clement and his assistant Richard Plunkett proposed the formation of an external review committee to explore an active means of aiding the condor. They persuaded the American Ornithologists' Union to appoint members (including some of the best-qualified raptor specialists) to the committee. This select group came up with a review of the condor's plight and a series of recommendations which boiled down to asking the Fish and Wildlife Service to make a more aggressive research effort in the field while also beginning a program of captive propagation.

That agency's leaders resisted the attempts to get them to do anything at all throughout 1978 and part of 1979. Then, pushed to a point at which a response became necessary, the Fish and Wildlife Service said to Audubon, in effect, "Put your money where your mouth is." Audubon complied, contributing $300,000 as an opening gesture of support and then lobbying Congress for the funds that would permit the Fish and Wildlife Service to take an active part in a recovery program for the condor. According to the contract signed between National Audubon and the Fish and Wildlife Service, these two "lead" agencies would head the recovery team and share responsibilities for the joint program.

National Audubon chose one of its most experienced biologists, John Ogden, to direct its part of the program. A native of Tennessee, Ogden had come to Tavernier from the National Park Service and had carried out extensive studies on wood storks and crocodiles, while at the same time gaining a great deal of experience in the handling of birds of prey. He agreed to move from Florida to California to get the program under way. Once there, he began work with his counterpart from the Fish and Wildlife Service, another biologist with considerable experience in the handling of endangered species, Noel Snyder.

"In one sense, I was very naive about the political situation," Ogden said later. "I had been told it would take me two or three years to do the job, but it took two years to even get permission to trap condors, and I ended up spending five years there. Also, no one in 1980 realized the depth of the opposition in California to the trapping of condors."

The political situation was treacherous. Charles Fullerton, the director of the California Fish and Game Department, had been battling the U.S. Fish and Wildlife Service for years over who ultimately had control of wildlife in California. Because only his department could give permits to trap wild condors (a nonmigratory species), Fullerton saw this program as an opportunity to put the federal agency in its place. Even without the state-federal rivalry, Fullerton would have been inclined to move slowly because of the wide public sentiment against tinkering with a wild and "noble" animal.

And the sentiment against biological tinkering was intense. The announced objectives of the recovery program involved the trapping of condors with large nets fired by "cannons" when the birds came to an animal carcass set out as bait. The biologists planned to put small radios on the wings of some of the trapped condors in order to keep track of their movements after their release; others would be taken for use in the captive-propagation program.

The state's conservation establishment opposed this program. At a series of hearings on the matter held by the Fish and Game Department, members of the Sierra Club suggested that the program focus on protecting the condor's habitat and leave the birds themselves alone. David R. Brower, the "Archdruid" of the movement and by then president of Friends of the Earth, rose to say that "the condor is not an electric toy to play with, rough up, manipulate, blindfold, manhandle, peer into, wire for sound, tinker with the great wings of, double-clutch, or put on crutches or behind bars." He went on to insist that "the wilderness within the condor and the wilderness essential to it have rights. We deplore the overcuriosity of biologists who would invade that privacy."

Some of the strongest opposition to the recovery plan came from Audubon members in California. The Golden Gate chapter already had a tradition of disagreeing with National Audubon in public, being one of the chapters that some years before had sided with the Sierra Club against the New York office in a dispute over the proposed boundaries of Redwood National Park. Now it was joined by at least half of the other chapters in the state in its opposition to trapping condors. Golden Gate talked of joining Friends of the Earth in a court case against National Audubon and the Fish and Wildlife Service.

Ogden began to spend much of his time away from the field in explaining the program to Audubon chapters or attending public hearings on applications to state officials for various permits. Some of the chapters softened their opposition (Los Angeles Audubon even giving money to the program), though most of those in the Bay Area remained hostile. According to Ogden one of the greatest handicaps to winning public approval for the program was the death of Carl Koford shortly before the recovery team organized in California in 1979.

"The opposition—or the 'grass-roots movement,' as it was called—could be traced to Koford," Ogden said. "His report on the condor was the 'Bible' for a lot of people. They would show up at hearings and meetings, all wearing the same kind of beat-up plaid shirt he used to wear—it was a uniform, almost—and they would pull out a copy of Koford's monograph and read from it like it was Scripture, and say 'Koford would never do anything like this.'

"The problem was that we knew that Koford's ideas about isolating the condor, fencing it off, were not right any more. The condor had been declining ever since Koford's work, but nobody knew how much it had declined because nobody was monitoring it. We had been told when we came out here that there were twenty-five to thirty-five left, but in reality the total was in the low twenties. The condor was dying off in isolation. Koford may have been right about some of the problems in the 1930s, but wrong about the 1980s. If he was still alive, we could have worked with him, maybe got him to admit where he was wrong, or at least we could have discredited his later theories. But, dead, Koford was a symbol."

The recovery team, which had established itself at the Condor Research Center in Ventura in 1980, planned to acquire as much up-to-date information as possible on the birds' physical condition, diet, and movements. Occasional visits to the nest, tracking the birds with radios, and spot observations would, the biologists believed, help to pinpoint the species' problems and perhaps indicate solutions. Earlier, there had been speculation that poor reproduction and insufficient habitat accounted for the condor's decline. Another part of the plan was to try "double-clutching," a practice in which the first egg hatched by a breeding female (which normally lays only one egg) would be taken and the chick hatched and raised in captivity; the female would then lay again; that chick would grow up in the wild.

There was a continued demand by local conservationists that the biologists back away from the birds and focus on saving habitat. But the recovery team's observations soon cast doubt on some of the earlier speculation. Five pairs were beginning to nest, a healthy proportion of the remaining adults, and they were not having trouble finding food for their young.

"There's no evidence yet that habitat was the main problem either," Ogden said early in the program. "Condor habitat has been lost in recent years but not at nearly the rate the population has declined. There seems to be plenty of habitat and food out there to support the small number of birds. The people who are proposing we start saving the habitat before we really learn something about the condors are being premature."

Ogden argued that it was unreasonable to petition the state and federal governments to set aside critical condor habitat before it had been precisely identified. The only way to monitor the birds' movements through their habitat with any accuracy was by telemetry, or radio tracking. But Ogden and Snyder, the team leaders, were delayed time and again in getting the necessary permits from the state's Fish and Wildlife Department. Charles Fullerton, its director, carefully surveyed the political winds before taking each step, and progress was painfully slow.

The program almost received a fatal blow in the fall of 1980. The team had just received permission to visit a nest site and examine the chick's physical condition, photograph, weigh, and measure it, and collect the remaining eggshell material and the molted feathers from the adults for chemical analysis. While Ogden and Snyder watched from a distance, a team of expert climbers descended the steep cliff to the nest ledge and began making their observations. To everyone's horror, the chick suddenly began to wobble and, within thirty seconds, fell over dead.

An immense uproar followed. Several state officials panicked and at first denied permission had been given to visit the nest. Newspaper reports indicated that the team member handling the chick was not a trained biologist. Neither statement was true, but the program's opponents had a field day, and the research plans were set back for nearly a year.

"It was one of those inexplicable incidents," Ogden recalled. "All of us had handled perhaps thousands of chicks without having anything like this happen before. But we knew in advance that there were risks, and this chick suffered some kind of unusual stress."

Slowly, confidence was restored, and the team began to accumulate information again by observations and visits to nests. But Fullerton continued to stall on the matter of permitting condors to be trapped. Ogden, frustrated, suggested to Russ Peterson that National Audubon withdraw from the program. In a final attempt to hold the recovery team together, Peterson arranged to meet Fullerton in a conference room at O'Hare Airport in Chicago in the late summer of 1982. The two men talked over the problems, and Fullerton agreed secretly to concessions. In the fall, the recovery team received its permits, and condors began to be trapped for radio telemetry or captive propagation. Soon Ogden, who was in charge of the telemetry work (Noel Snyder concentrated on

John Ogden (right) and Peter Bloom with a young California condor,
one of the last remaining members of the species in the wild. NAS

the propagation aspects), was collecting the first detailed information on
condor movements.

By the fall of 1984, just after the team had trapped five birds in
seven days, the program seemed outwardly a success. The biologists
believed they could, with a little luck, stabilize the condor population in
the wild. Indications were coming in that a major problem for the birds
was lead poisoning, picked up from the carcasses of deer and other
animals that had been shot.

"The hunting of mule deer is a major sport in Southern California,"
Ogden noted. "There are estimates that between forty and fifty percent
of the wounded deer get away and die later on. There is also a regular
program of predator control on the bigger ranches. When the state or
federal trappers catch a coyote in a trap, they simply put a bullet in it
and toss the carcass in a ditch. Most of the wild condors had elevated
lead levels in their bodies, and we knew of two that had died of lead
poisoning in recent years."

One of the solutions called for the recovery team to put out "clean
carcasses" in condor habitat. Technically, progress was being made. But
behind the scenes problems were cropping up. The ease with which

Audubon biologists had once been able to work with their federal counterparts had greatly diminished.

"Increasingly, Audubon had to work in this program under the Federal Code of Regulations, and Audubon philosophy was taking a back seat to those regulations," Ogden said afterward. "We had to do things the Fish and Wildlife Service way. For instance, if county officials in the condor range were talking about issuing a permit to subdivide a ranch, we thought it logical to go to the public hearing on it. 'No,' we'd be told, 'the federal government doesn't work that way.' "

One source of disagreement was Snyder's desire to take as many birds as possible into captivity, whereas Ogden wanted to keep more of them in the field to gather data on their behavior and the possible environmental hazards. The pendulum, however, was swinging the other way. The recovery team had already signed a contract with the San Diego Wild Animal Park to handle the captive-propagation program. This zoo was to take chicks or even adults with the objective of eventually inducing them to mate and produce chicks which, in the future, would be released into the wild.

But the propagation program became intensely political. The San Diego Zoo had achieved a worldwide reputation for excellence, far beyond that of the Los Angeles Zoo just up the coast. In the 1980s, the Los Angeles Zoo's supporters were making a determined effort to come out from under the shadow of San Diego. The president of the Greater Los Angeles Zoological Association was Marcia Hobbs, a leading contributor to the Republican party in California and, not so incidentally, Ronald Reagan's goddaughter. After Hobbs visited the White House and the Interior Department, the Los Angeles Zoo soon had a contract to share in the condor-propagation program.

Ogden, after five years on the job, asked to be transferred "back home" to Tavernier so that he could continue his work on wading birds, though he would remain on the condor-recovery team and make frequent trips to California. Just after he left, disaster struck the program. Five or six of the condors surviving in the wild simply disappeared. Top officials of the Fish and Wildlife Service, prodded by the zoos and perhaps weary of the whole collapsing venture, came to a decision. Although decisions by the recovery team had always before been made by consensus, the Fish and Wildlife Service called a press conference and announced that they were bringing in all of the remaining birds from the wild. At the end of the announcement, Marcia Hobbs glanced over at the Audubon contingent, grinned, and asked, "What are you going to do now—sue us?"

Audubon did. The Society went to court in 1985 to get an injunction to keep the remaining birds in the wild. It was true that the wild population was now doomed. Only one of the birds that had disappeared had been radioed and, aside from a single condor found dead of lead poisoning, there was no indication of exactly what had happened. One adult from each of the remaining five nesting pairs had been lost. But Audubon argued that some condors ought to be kept in the wild, in part to make sure that developers did not use the birds' absence as an excuse to exploit land in the condor range. Also, it was argued, a few ought to be left as "guide birds" for the time when young condors were released from the zoos.

"Behind our lawsuit was an attempt to keep the Fish and Wildlife Service from going too far off the track, to maintain what we thought of as the original style and purpose of the program," Ogden said afterward. "We had to make sure that we went on discussing all the options. We had learned, for instance, where the condors spent most of their time feeding and roosting, and we wanted to pressure the Fish and Wildlife Service into buying land in that habitat. We also wanted to make sure the zoos began releasing birds as soon as possible. We wanted the condor back in its natural habitat again."

But the inevitable moment arrived on the morning of April 20, 1987. The injunction won by National Audubon to keep the last condors in the wild had been overturned the year before by the U.S. District Court in Washington, D.C. The Fish and Wildlife Service, contending that it could not protect the three remaining adult birds "out there," and that they were needed to increase the genetic base of the captive population and thus help to prevent inbreeding, prepared for the last dramatic steps in this phase of the attempt to save the species. At a cost of nearly four million dollars, the federal government bought the eleven-thousand-acre Hudson Ranch and a thirteen-hundred-acre parcel nearby in the heart of the condor range. The National Audubon team, which included the most experienced condor trappers in the country, had no choice but to take part in the roundup. Two of the birds were snared.

A team of condor handlers headed by Audubon biologist Gregory Sanders assembled on the Hudson Ranch, now named the Bitter Creek National Wildlife Refuge, forty miles southwest of Bakersfield. Carcasses of a calf and a goat were laid out on the ground, within reach of the big net coiled in its firing device. Hidden nearby in blinds and a pit covered by straw were the team members, not very confident that the last wild condor, an adult male they had named AC 9 (for "adult condor") would come within reach. They had trailed the bird for months, on an assignment none of them wanted, but the bird had remained aloof. It was the condor breeding season, and the fugitive bird wandered widely, searching its accustomed haunts for a wild mate that did not exist.

Then, in midmorning, the condor appeared. It circled the carcasses, extremely wary or, as someone put it, expressing a "mystical" reluctance to come to the bait. The arrival of several ravens and golden eagles on the carcasses emboldened the condor. It dropped to feed, and at 10:15, Audubon biologist Peter Bloom triggered the cannon.

AC 9, comforted and quieted by team members, was eased into a big cage and taken to the San Diego Wild Animal Park to join the twenty-six other adults and chicks then in captivity. On their success in producing new generations behind bars (several chicks have already hatched by 1990) would lie the prospects for the species' future in what is left of wilderness in California.

# 33

$\mathcal{U}$pheaval and stability, progress and a tug backward toward traditional concerns, marked the closing years of Russell Peterson's tenure at National Audubon. And the Society, under Peterson, entered the age of television.

Peterson, scrambling for the money to put into practice the programs that would fulfill the promise of his "Think Globally, Act Locally" theme, also looked for areas in which he could make savings. The New York office was already in extreme flux. Vice presidents during the Peterson years came and went with confusing speed, so that departments such as development (fundraising), chapter relations, and education lacked the continuity to perform at peak effectiveness. Only Les Line flourished among the staff leaders in New York, a circumstance that gave him the leverage to bargain for a hefty share of the budget. The magazine, continuing to reap prizes and accolades, was also helping to change the nature of the membership; many of the new members lured into joining the Society because of the magazine's appeal were not deep-dyed conservationists. Thus the turnover in membership approached twenty-five percent a year, a gap in the ranks that had to be constantly plugged by expensive magazine- and membership-promotion campaigns.

One of the areas that had generally fallen into disrepair (a condition that had antedated Peterson's time, to be sure) was the mix of programs that could be lumped rather loosely under the umbrella of "education." The Junior Audubon clubs had collapsed, as noted earlier, when schools began to frown on the practice of collecting money from children, even for such educational materials as those provided by National Audubon. Standard Audubon publications such as the leaflets and nature bulletins that had been available to teachers, Scout leaders, and other educators since the Society's beginnings were hurt, ironically, by their own success; as they became more in demand, commercial publishers leaped into the field and flooded the market with their own nature materials.

"My impression is that the Audubon education effort reached a nadir in about 1982 and 1983," reported Scott Reed, a lawyer in Coeur d'Alene, Idaho, who later became chairman of the Education Committee on the board of directors. "The not very successful programs had been eliminated. The Audubon centers were largely localized. . . . The camps were seasonal. There was nothing going on in the National Audubon education effort."

The Nature Centers Planning Division also disappeared. Its achievements in planning and establishing nature centers throughout the country had been considerable, but again success proved fatal, as the division's pioneering work was assumed by local governments and private organizations (including some Audubon chapters), which in turn began to finance their own nature centers. The division was finally abolished under Peterson.

Through all this disarray, the film-lecture series limped on, at a deficit but one which in previous years had seemed worth the cost because of the publicity and good will it brought the Society. Russ Peterson was no longer willing to make up the deficit. In the summer of 1982, the lecturers under contract to Audubon gathered for one of their periodical conferences at the Audubon Center in Greenwich to swap information and experiences. Peterson, addressing the conference, dropped a bombshell when he told the lecturers that the Society would no longer fund the program, but instead farm it out to a private group. A search was already on for an organization willing to take over the coming season's schedule.

Karl Maslowski, one of the veteran film-lecturers, put in a call to the program's founder, Wayne Short. Short, who had broken with John Baker years before, was still involved through his own company in presenting film and lecture programs, and agreed to fly to New York to talk to the lecturers themselves. Most of them rallied around Short and asked Peterson to subcontract the program to him.

"I spent a good part of the summer in New York, hammering out an agreement with Peterson's various vice presidents," Short recalled. "I asked for sixty thousand dollars to fund the program for the first year. We finally came to an agreement. When I got home I called Roger Tory Peterson, Sewall Pettingill, and other longtime stars of the tour, and everybody was excited. Then I got a call from one of Peterson's vice presidents telling me the deal was off. Somehow they had *overlooked* the stipulation for sixty thousand dollars, and Peterson had decided not to sign."

Peterson, in fact, had concluded that the film-lecture series was a dying proposition, a once-dynamic program whose function in bringing nature films to the public had been taken over by national television.

He was trying to move the Society in that direction and already wondering how to pay for it. There he would need substantial help.

National Audubon's annual operating budget was now approaching, in the mid-1980s, $25 million. Although membership was over half a million in five hundred chapters, the Society was paying out more than it was taking in and dipping into reserves to make up the difference. More and more, Peterson was asking programs to pay for themselves. The Science Department, under Glenn Paulson, was doing well by tapping various outside research grants, while its sanctuaries were to some extent endowed through the bequests of members.

Other departments were struggling; even Les Line was soon faced with budget problems in his area. Line supervised more than just the magazine. There was the *Audubon Leader,* a four-page publication sent twice a month to chapter leaders to keep them up to date on legislative actions and other Society interests. There was a new publication, *Audubon Action,* a tabloid-sized newspaper published six times a year in the months between *Audubon* issues, that carried timely articles on conservation matters of immediate interest to the Society. All three were successful.

But other of Line's responsibilities faced serious money shortages. There was a move to close the Audubon Library, which had been a valuable source of information to outside researchers and staff members ever since it had been put together by Gilbert Pearson and Robert Porter Allen in about 1930. Only a strong protest by staff members and some influential chapter activists kept the collection (which includes one of John James Audubon's double elephant folios) largely intact, though it was eventually closed to outside use.

Another trouble spot was *American Birds.* Because of this publication's special appeal to serious birders, it had always had a limited circulation; this continued to be so despite attempts by Line to make it more attractive, with glossy paper and striking color photographs, to not-so-serious birdwatchers. Circulation, in fact, had somewhat declined to about nine thousand readers. According to Russ Peterson, by 1985 *American Birds* was running at an annual deficit of $135,000, amounting to a subsidy of about $15 for each of its subscribers. Rumors began to fly. Among those spreading the word that Peterson planned to scuttle the publication was Robert Arbib, its former editor and a feisty infighter who took to a row like one of his beloved ducks to water. The birding fraternity, many of whom were convinced that their pastime was National Audubon's prime reason for existence, immediately dispatched appeals to Peterson to rescue the magazine.

"*American Birds* is a unique publication," wrote Greg W. Lasley, a sergeant on the Austin, Texas, police force and a nonsalaried regional editor who compiled detailed reports on his area's birdlife for every issue. "It is the only data base for seasonal distribution of bird species that covers the entire United States each season. The information in *AB* is absolutely essential for almost any future research on U.S. avian topics. A glance through almost any ornithological publication will show you how often *AB* is cited in scientific studies years after the seasonal report in *AB* was written. . . . *AB* is a publication aimed at someone other than 'armchair naturalists'; it is for the field observers, for the active birders of this country."

Peterson denied the magazine was going to be eliminated and, with the spirited help of Audubon biologists and board members, found ways to keep it afloat. Under the editorship of Arbib's longtime assistant, Susan Roney Drennan, *American Birds* found a new lease on life. (Eventually, it was moved to the Science Department.)

That Peterson occasionally failed to come up with the money for desired projects was not for want of trying, and at one point his energetic search led the Society into a bizarre episode. It began with a telephone call in 1982 to one of Peterson's vice presidents in the New York office. The caller was Ronald W. Norman, the Mayor of Sarasota, Florida, who, with another local man, was representing a group of treasure hunters.

The story, as Norman told it, was that this group had been trying to trace an enormous hoard of coins and jewelry that had belonged to one Carlos, a chieftain of the Calusa Indians just before the settlement of Florida by Europeans. The Indians, according to the story, had gathered the hoard mainly from galleons shipwrecked in that region while en route to Spain. Now the treasure-seeking group was certain that all of the maps and other clues to the treasure's location pointed to Rookery Bay on the Gulf Coast—to an island in the Rookery Bay Sanctuary owned by the National Audubon Society!

"It was like a bomb scare," someone said at Audubon House afterward. "Even though you may think it's a hoax, you can't ignore it."

Russ Peterson certainly did not ignore the call. He summoned Sandy Sprunt from Tavernier to acquaint him with the news and establish a plan. Nathaniel P. Reed, chairman of the Audubon board of directors' executive committee, who lived in Florida, was brought in to advise Peterson, Sprunt, and other staff members on possible complications in the state. A New York lawyer was engaged to study state and federal laws and precedents pertaining to the ownership of buried treasure on private land.

Staff members, sworn to secrecy, conferred with Mayor Norman and an Orlando lawyer representing the treasure hunters, who were asking for seventy-five percent of the hoard. They also visited Tallahassee to review old records in the archives that mentioned Carlos' cache and the reports of a Spaniard to whom it had been shown in an excavation located in a sand dune in south Florida.

"The reports described the chest as six feet by six feet by four feet, packed solid with treasure," Sprunt recalled. "We did some computations and came up with eye-opening figures—if the treasure was gold, it would weigh sixteen tons and be worth as much as sixty-four million dollars. Russ was already thinking of ways to spend it!"

Negotiations continued between the two parties. A complex scale of sharing the profits was drawn up, granting the "licensees" their requested seventy-five percent as a starter but shifting past fifty-fifty in the Society's favor as the trove's value increased, and finally awarding National Audubon seventy-five percent if the total value reached the magic number of $64 million. Audubon lawyers drew up a contract for the two parties' signatures, rivaling in complexity that for a sales agreement on an East Side Manhattan skyscraper. Meanwhile, three Audubon wardens were relieved of their regular duties to stand guard, in shifts and fully armed, on the designated islet.

One of the treasure hunters, an electronics specialist, had built a mysterious black box with which it was said he had once located a buried gold bar near Fort Pierce, Florida. Final plans for the excavation were made. National Audubon, which had leased this island to the state of Florida to be managed as part of the Rookery Bay National Estuarine Sanctuary, was given permission by state officials, as managers of the sanctuary, to conduct "scientific archaeological research" on the dune.

And so, on the appointed day, nineteen men and women, including the treasure hunters, Audubon staff members, and Russ Peterson himself, were transported through the mangroves and out to the little island. Mosquitoes were abundant, though the man with the black box was the center of attention. The party advanced on a little hill in the center of the island.

"The treasure hunters had thought it was an Indian mound built up of shells, but I could tell that once you got down a couple of inches it was mostly a sand dune," Sprunt said. "The electronics expert set up his black box, some kind of magnetometer that was operated with a battery and connected to a pipe, and began to go through a series of triangulations to get some bearings on whatever was down there. Russ was standing by with a shovel—a big shovel—ready to pitch in. Ed Carlson, the manager of our Corkscrew Swamp Sanctuary, was there with a core-borer. He started boring. He got down to twenty-two feet—and hit water."

Smiles faded. The gear was repacked, and the party was ferried back to the mainland. A dozen or more Audubon staff members had spent six weeks and about twenty-five thousand dollars on what became known as "the King Carlos Caper."

But, as the man had asked, how could anyone ignore the call?

It may be that Russ Peterson's most lasting contribution to the Society was its introduction to the world of television.

He had been trying for several years to effect an entry, but without success. He could come up with neither the format nor the source of funding that would enable National Audubon to produce, as the National Geographic Society had already done, a series of high-quality television films. An unlikely collaboration brought his quest to a successful conclusion.

Christopher Palmer, who worked on energy policy in Audubon's Washington office, had served as a senior staff officer at the Environmental Protection Agency during the Carter Administration. He joined the Audubon staff in 1980 and, at one point, set out to make a film about energy conservation.

"I really had no experience in film making," Palmer has said, "but about this time I heard that Ted Turner, who had his own cable television system, was interested in conservation. I took a chance and wrote a proposal for him."

Ted Turner was known as a man of many interests. His sponsorship of America's Cup yachts, his ownership of the Atlanta Braves baseball team, and his creation of the Turner Broadcasting System had brought him national prominence. His response to the proposal was encouraging; no doubt the idea of an alliance between his young network and an organization like the National Audubon Society appealed to his sense of showmanship.

Russ Peterson and Turner came to a quick understanding. Out of their meeting evolved a television series about people working to protect wildlife and the environment. *The World of Audubon,* for which both Turner and Chris Palmer helped to raise the needed funding, made its debut in the fall of 1984. Palmer, whom Peterson appointed Audubon's vice president for television programming, soon was totally involved in bringing the Audubon message to the American public by way of cable and public television. Among narrators of the early Audubon television films were the actors Robert Redford, Cliff Robertson, and Richard Chamberlain. *The World of Audubon,* over which Audubon retained editorial control, won much critical acclaim.

Palmer's television programs led to other Audubon initiatives. Computer software, home video, and even short, inexpensive videocassettes featuring members of the Society's staff and designed for the use of chapter activists, soon followed.

The success of *The World of Audubon* had brought a needed lift to the Society's educational program. Although there had been little direction from New York for a number of years, the Society had acquired a strong staff of educators who were scattered among its camps and nature centers. Under its director, Philip Schaeffer, the Greenwich Center provided a base from which to introduce environmental education to teachers in urban schools. The staff at Aullwood in a Dayton suburb brought young families into its woods and fields to experience a new identification with nature. The Richardson Bay Sanctuary in Tiburon, California, provided Bay Area children with a splendid new nature center, partly through the Whittell bequest. The Schlitz Center in Milwaukee prospered with local funding, and the Northeast Audubon Center, in Sharon, Connecticut, gave Audubon a strong regional presence. (The Randall Davey Nature Center in Sante Fe was soon to come on line.) And, in an offbeat project, the Audubon Expedition Institute formed a kind of nature caravan which took older students for a full year into wild places all over America.

Yet some of the old guard in the Society, a group including Carl Buchheister, Roger Tory Peterson, Sewall Pettingill, and Charlie Callison, bemoaned the extinction of the Junior Audubon clubs, the nationwide project that had propelled so many young people into the conservation movement. At board meetings, at regional conferences, and at annual dinners, they campaigned for a revival of that program. The Society, they urged, ought to reach out once more into the classrooms of America to put itself in touch with the future.

The message got through to the board of directors, which issued a directive to the staff to re-create a national children's program. "Keep it simple," became the motto. "Make it happen." In December 1983, Richard Martyr, who had succeeded Rupert Cutler as senior vice president for programs, brought staff members with expertise in education from all over the country to a meeting at the Audubon Center in Greenwich. His mission was to have this group devise a vehicle for getting the Society back into children's education.

The result was a four-page newspaper, *Audubon Adventures,* which would be produced through a revitalized Education Department presided over by a former regional representative, Marshal Case. The newspaper and an accompanying leader's (or teacher's) guide would be sent into classrooms six times a year. Drawing on the resources of the Audubon membership, the Society would ask the individual chapters to be the means of introducing the paper to the classrooms in their own localities. Through a mixture of informative text and sprightly, detailed illustrations, the Audubon message would be broadcast to youngsters as it was in the days of Pearson, Baker, and Buchheister.

The board of directors supported the *Adventures* project from the beginning. Because one of the original stipulations was to keep the price modest, the Society (despite a series of spartan budgets for other programs) subsidized the paper and guide until outside grants and contributions could put it on a sustaining basis. Meanwhile, with many chapters adopting *Audubon Adventures* as their chief educational project, more than fifty thousand children began to receive the paper and other materials during the first year of publication.

When Russ Peterson, a man of great ambition and driving force, came to New York, he saw an opportunity to transform not only the National Audubon Society but also, in a sense, the world. His interests lay chiefly in some of the overriding issues of our time—the threats to the global environment posed by nuclear arms, human population growth, the lack of strong national energy policies, and pollution from toxic materials. But his years at Audubon coincided almost exactly with the dominance of a national administration that was often indifferent or even hostile to finding solutions to those threats.

It was a frustrating experience for Peterson. Cut off by his own outspokenness from a dialogue with the politicians and agencies that he might have expected to be his allies, Peterson was unable to reach his potential as a national spokesman on environmental issues. Rather than gaining the leverage, or finding the means, needed to pull the Society after him on the path from local concerns to "global action," he was forced to spend much of his energy in keeping James Watt, Anne Burford, and their ideological bedfellows from rolling back the environmental advances of past administrations.

On June 30, 1984, Peterson announced that he would remain as the Society's president for only one more year, in effect cutting short his seven-year contract, which would not expire until 1986. He wanted, he said, the freedom to become a "more effective 'one-world' activist." He would spend his "next career" writing and speaking, "catalyzing action toward reducing threats to all plant and animal life."

His achievements at Audubon were substantial. Often impetuous, he was nevertheless willing to take chances. Under him, the Society had begun to make use of television on a large scale and returned to its early emphasis on children's environmental education. Perhaps most important, as board chairman Donal C. O'Brien, Jr., suggested, was that under Russ Peterson the Society had grown in the goals it set for itself.

# 34

*P*eter A. A. Berle became National Audubon's president in the summer of 1985 because, in his own words, "I wanted to be an instrument of change." In a discouraging turn of events, however, he spent a large part of his first two years on the job wrestling the Society back on course, dealing first with a painful financial crisis and then with the most tumultuous insurrection within the membership since the swashbuckling era of Rosalie Edge.

Berle was the product of a tradition of professional service. His father, Adolph A. Berle, a graduate of Harvard University and Harvard Law School, was a practicing lawyer in New York and a teacher at both Harvard and Columbia. During the New Deal era he served successively as a member of Franklin D. Roosevelt's "Brain Trust," financial adviser to the Cuban government, Assistant Secretary of State, and United States Ambassador to Brazil. Peter's mother, Beatrice Bishop Berle, rebelling against the restrictions put on her by her wealthy parents, performed social work in Newfoundland and, after her marriage, earned a degree in medicine; at one time she helped bring primary medical services to disadvantaged people through store-front facilities in East Harlem.

The search committee established by Audubon's board to recommend a successor to Russ Peterson put Peter Berle high on its list from the very beginning. Like his father, he was a graduate of Harvard University and Harvard Law School. He had skied in competition, served as a paratrooper, and operated a farm with his wife, Lila, in the Berkshire Hills of Massachusetts. After joining a law firm in New York, he served three terms (1968–74) as a Democratic state assemblyman representing a district on Manhattan's Upper East Side.

During his time in Albany, Berle led the floor fight that created the legislation for the Adirondack Park Agency, which was then the most comprehensive program for land-use controls in the nation. From 1976 until 1979, he was director of the New York State Department of Environmental Conservation. He and his staff discovered and confronted the environmental disaster caused by contaminants leaking from a land-fill at Love Canal (a housing development near Niagara Falls, New York), and he launched one of the first serious efforts by any state to deal with toxic wastes. Because of his unusual diligence on the job, Berle was eased out of that position by Governor Hugh Carey, a lukewarm environmentalist at best, and he returned to his New York law firm.

Even though he was out of public service, Berle continued to exert an influence on the state's environmental affairs. His firm, which earlier had won a landmark victory by preventing the Consolidated Edison Company from building an electric plant on the top of Storm King Mountain, now took on other lawsuits, including a major class action on behalf of homeowners against the Union Carbide Company for the pollution of groundwater with pesticides on Long Island.

In the spring of 1985, as he was preparing for a new court case, Berle received a telephone call from a onetime schoolmate who was then working for a "headhunting" firm. Could he come and talk to Berle about the Audubon job? The two men later explored it in his office, but Berle said that he was "absolutely not interested."

His friend persisted, however, and asked Berle if he would attend a meeting with Audubon's board chairman, Donal C. O'Brien, Jr. O'Brien, who was a lawyer for the Rockefeller family, had his office in Rockefeller Center, close to Berle's law firm.

"If his office had been two blocks away from mine, I would have just said I didn't have the time to go," Berle said later, "but it was only one block, so I went."

The meeting, which was attended by several other members of the board's search committee, was not particularly successful from Berle's point of view. He sat with his back to a bank of windows, with a warm spring sun flooding in over his shoulder and into the eyes of his inter-rogators. They squinted uncomfortably at him, while one or two heads began to nod. Two months passed after that meeting, and Berle began to forget about the opening. Then his friend called to say that the search had narrowed to two candidates, Berle being one of them, and asked him to pay O'Brien another visit.

For the first time, Berle began to think seriously about accepting an offer to lead Audubon. He had heard through the conservation grape-vine of the Society's large budget deficits and of how some of the board's committees had already intervened to straighten out problems in several of its departments. Berle talked over the situation frankly with O'Brien and extracted the chairman's assurance that the new president would have full authority over all departments. When the board asked him to be president, Berle accepted.

"I hope the board wanted action," he said immediately afterward.

Peter A. A. Berle led the Society safely through the financial crisis
and the subsequent membership controversy in the late 1980s.
© 1985 SUSAN ORISTAGLIO, NAS

"If not, they picked the wrong guy. I had come to see the job as a chance
to make a difference in an area of great importance."

Berle moved slowly through his first months in office. For one thing,
both he and the board of directors were only then beginning to realize
the full extent of the Society's financial troubles. The practice in recent
years of juggling budget items and of trying to pay for certain programs
with money not yet in hand had begun to take its toll. Television and
the annual *Audubon Wildlife Report,* for instance, were "off-budget" items,
taken on without any real idea of where the money to pay for them
would be found; sometimes it wasn't, and the Society was forced to dip
into its unrestricted reserves. The income from the Society's endowment
of more than thirty-five million dollars was largely restricted to the areas
such as sanctuaries or scientific research as specified by its original donors and could not be diverted to general operating expenses.

But all of the problems were hardly leftovers from the past. Just at
the time that Peter Berle began struggling to bring expenses in line with
income, contemporary events conspired to deal the Society a series of

almost crippling blows. The world's oil glut in the mid-1980s undermined the industry's prosperity in Louisiana and Texas, eliminating the handsome royalties of a quarter of a million dollars or so a year that Audubon had become accustomed to earning from its wells on the Rainey Sanctuary. The doubling and tripling of liability-insurance premiums caused another drain on finances, especially in view of the Society's far-flung system of physical properties such as sanctuaries, summer camps, and nature centers. Finally, substantial increases in the costs of paper and postage struck hard at an organization that was committed to spreading the conservation message through its various publications while depending heavily on repeated mailings for new memberships, contributions, and subscriptions. The total losses brought on by those developments came to over a million dollars, almost exactly the amount of the budget shortfall that appeared on the Society's books in 1986.

Berle weighed his selections carefully as he began to put together his own leadership team. The resignation of Glenn Paulson prior to Peterson's departure had left the Science Department without a chief. Here Berle turned to traditional concerns and brought in an experienced ornithologist as vice president for science. J. P. "Pete" Myers, who was on the staff of the Academy of Natural Sciences of Philadelphia, had established a sound reputation for his research on migratory shorebirds; a large area of concern for him was the conservation problem that had arisen because of the international nature of those birds' flight patterns, extending from the subarctic to remote parts of Central and South America. Myers' addition to the staff in New York immediately entrenched Audubon once more in specific international wildlife projects, such as the preservation of feeding and resting areas on the migration routes. Upon Frosty Anderson's retirement, Frank "Dusty" Dunstan took charge of the Sanctuary Department under Myers.

The chapters, now more than five hundred of them, had become a vibrant force of their own. Flexing their muscles, some of the leaders even began to believe the Society could jettison the expensive magazine (which by then cost more than $2.5 million annually to produce) and use the money for chapter programs, more active lobbying campaigns on all political levels, and the like; in this regard, they discounted the view of the New York office that *Audubon* was the "premium" attracting the large if passive proportion of the membership that gave the active twenty percent or so the heft to impress legislators.

On a more positive note, the chapters took on some of the functions formerly handled by the professional staff. The "Adopt-a-Refuge" program brought members into working arrangements with the managers of federal refuges around the country, each involved chapter acting to shield its "adopted" refuge from political pressure that might damage its integrity, while providing volunteers to help in the field when extra hands were needed. Other chapters adopted private sanctuaries.

The *Audubon Adventures* program was designed by Marshal Case, now vice president for education, to be uniquely dependent on the chapters' initiative. (Largely developed and written by Ada Graham, an author of prize-winning children's books, the newspaper was supplemented from its beginnings by a leader's guide prepared by Jean Porter, a specialist in environmental education at the Audubon Center in Greenwich.) The chapter leaders set out to find local contributors who would add to National Audubon's subsidy of *Adventures* and then persuaded teachers and school systems to make the paper and leader's guide a part of each term's curriculum. At the end of five years of publication, *Adventures* was reaching nearly a quarter of a million children.

"The flowering of the *Audubon Adventures* must be the single most exciting new development that has occurred in Audubon in the last five years," Scott Reed, chairman of the education committee of the board of directors, wrote in a special report in 1988. One fortunate result of *Adventures* was that it enabled Audubon to reach minority children in the cities. This audience had so far been largely closed to national conservation organizations, but now Audubon set its sights on trying to build for a truly democratic future by increasing minority representation (including Native Americans) to twenty percent in the *Adventures* program.

# 35

*H*ard work and imagination still characterized the Audubon staff in the field. In an era when so much of the news from the natural world tended to make depressing reading—the swift demise of rain forests, the poaching of the big cats for their pelts, the last of the California condors staring out at the world from their cages—one Audubon biologist was carrying on a project that could only be described as "upbeat." The "puffin transplant" had, for a number of years, been providing the Society with invaluable publicity.

The idea had come to Stephen W. Kress in the early 1970s after he joined the staff of the Audubon Camp in Maine. The Atlantic puffin, barely a foot long, is one of the "glamor birds" for the American public. Enthralled observers have devoted entire books to the singular image and specialized life of *Fratercula arctica* (meaning "little brother of the Arctic"). Biologists may disapprove in their technical primness of the way some writers lapse into anthropomorphic notions when they summon up the puffin for our admiration—the "comical gait," the "clown's nose," the "Pickwickian curiosity and meddlesomeness"—but only a flinty heart can keep from rhapsodizing just a little. Kress, a rhapsodist as well as a biologist, lamented the depredations of the fishermen who had exterminated those little seabirds from the vicinity of Hog Island in Muscongus Bay nearly a century before.

Kress wondered if puffins could somehow be induced to return to Eastern Egg Rock at the mouth of the bay, where they used to nest. He developed a proposal to work with the Canadian Wildlife Service, importing chicks from a large Newfoundland colony and rearing them on Eastern Egg Rock, which, conveniently, National Audubon leased from the state of Maine and was to dedicate in 1976 as the Allan D. Cruickshank Wildlife Sanctuary. Kress's theory was that, if the chicks were brought to Egg Rock early enough in life, they would remember it as their "natal island" and return later to breed.

Steve Kress raised puffin chicks on the Maine coast. NAS

The chances of success seemed to be small. The Atlantic puffin nested then on only one island south of Canada—a couple of hundred pairs on Matinicus Rock, off Rockland, Maine. (The species also nests nearby on Machias Seal Island, a remote fragment of land off Cutler, Maine, on which Canada maintains a lighthouse.) Would puffin chicks raised on Eastern Egg Rock, when they reached sexual maturity at about five years of age, simply opt for the large Canadian colonies where most of their companions would head in the breeding season? Kress was entering uncharted territory.

But, with the Society's approval in hand, he established his plan. After a small-scale experimental program in 1973, he brought a hundred or more chicks to Maine each summer from the big Newfoundland colony at Witless Bay. (The chicks traveled in a private jet on loan to the project from a "friend of Audubon.") Taken by small boat from the mainland to Eastern Egg Rock, the "pufflings" (ten days to two weeks old) were put in burrows especially prepared for them by Kress. Chicken wire, clamped over the openings to keep the chicks in and predatory gulls out, was removed several times a day by the staff when they dropped in the smelt on which pufflings thrive.

"We kept in touch with Hog Island by CB radio," Kress said. "The lobstermen in the bay could listen in on their radios. With all the talk about 'ice' and 'chicks,' they may have gotten the wrong impression about what we were doing out there."

Late each summer, fattened by smelt and released from their artificial nesting burrows, the little puffins made their way over the rocks to the shore and paddled off into the mists of the North Atlantic. Each wore a metal band whose color indicated its year of "matriculation." For the first several years, nothing more was seen of Kress's puffins. Then, in 1977, some of the banded subadult puffins began to appear around the island, proving they were imprinted on those seven acres of rocks and turf at the edge of the Atlantic.

No one knew where the puffins had been in the long interval, but each summer they increased in number around Egg Rock. Donal O'Brien, recently added to the board of directors and an enthusiastic decoy carver, produced models of little wooden puffins that helped to lure the prospecting birds to the rocks. (Some touring yachtsmen, scanning Egg Rock with their binoculars, are said to have added O'Brien's decoys to their birding life lists!) Finally, in 1981, five pairs of puffins bred and reared their young among the tumbled boulders. Eastern Egg Rock was a puffin colony once more.

Ironically, there was a curmudgeonly complaint about Kress's project once it had begun to receive national publicity through newspapers, magazines, and television. Ralph Palmer, the author of *Maine Birds,* a classic monograph on the occurrence and distribution of birds in the state, grumbled to Roland Clement that, because the Atlantic puffin was not an endangered species, the puffin transplant was being accorded too much publicity (and funding) for its value as a conservation project. Clement, who had approved Kress's proposal when he was with National Audubon, had since assembled a number of complaints of his own about the Society's policies and delighted in making them known.

"It has now become a major PR project with a life of its own," he wrote to Glenn Paulson about the puffin project, "and people feel that it is not contributing substantively."

It was Kress's, and the Society's, point that the puffin transplant was already a substantive conservation project because it had brought seabirds and their little-known problems to the attention of a wide public (a prime reason for the readiness with which David Nettleship, a seabird specialist with the Canadian Wildlife Service, had agreed to let Kress take Canadian chicks). Moreover, Kress's work was largely supported by outside grants and contributions. It had developed new techniques to help transplant seabird species should their nesting sites be destroyed or seriously threatened in the future. By 1987, those techniques were already being put to use by Kress to reintroduce terns (already in trouble along the New England coast) and petrels to safe breeding sites.

. . .

As the Egg Rock puffin colony stabilized at eighteen breeding pairs in 1987 the project was judged to have completed its research stage and moved into the area of "monitoring and management"—a primary concern of the sanctuary system. No one aspect of that operation demonstrates its sophistication more neatly than Audubon's Ecosystems Research Unit, headed by Michael Duever at the Corkscrew Swamp Sanctuary.

"Doctor Do-Over," as he is known among his staff for his persistence in getting things *right,* is a zoologist and hydrologist whose object is to maintain the Society's natural areas as healthy, functioning ecosystems. His detailed studies of climate and water fluctuations have helped to avoid—or undo—serious management mistakes on the sanctuaries.

"We avoid managing a sanctuary for just one or two species," Duever has said. "For instance, if you were trying to create a wading-bird rookery you might be tempted to ensure that there is a lot of water under the trees or bushes in which the birds nest—which may provide optimum conditions for the birds—but you would eventually destroy the rookery by killing the trees and bushes."

Before Duever arrived at Corkscrew, the Society had installed (at considerable expense and on the advice of engineers) a dike to prevent a nearby residential development from draining off water thought to be vital to the survival of the sanctuary's cypress trees and swamp creatures. Duever devised a complex system of shallow wells, gauges, and evaporation pans to measure the precipitation and the flow of surface water. He discovered that Corkscrew, in fact, was receiving too much water.

Water levels, he insists, are less important to marsh and other plant communities than *how long* the sites are inundated. With the dike in place, willows and other shrubs had encroached on the open marsh more rapidly than anyone had previously expected. The marsh was staying wet too long, preventing the occasional fires that turn back the advancing shrubs.

"A cypress forest also needs dry periods," Duever pointed out. "The seeds, because of their size, are dispersed by water, not air, and they must soak from one to three months so that water permeates the thick seed coat. But the seeds will not germinate underwater. By keeping too much water in the Corkscrew sanctuary, we were inhibiting their germination."

Corkscrew's dike, now fitted with boards in its culverts, can be used by the sanctuary staff only when a need is discovered to manipulate the local water levels.

From Duever's work at Corkscrew and other sanctuaries have come both the principles and techniques to manage sanctuaries continually beset by problems occurring "on the other side of the fence." Sometimes wildlife managers, because of changing conditions in the surrounding countryside, may have to manipulate habitats within a sanctuary to preserve rare plant and animal communities. But, if the manipulation is carried out without enough information, the entire ecosystem may be thrown out of balance.

"Don't make irretrievable commitments, either politically or environmentally," Mike Duever has argued.

Commitments of any kind in the sanctuaries have seldom been made in recent years until "Doctor Do-Over" has made a house call.


George Powell, working in Bob Allen's old backyard in Tavernier, imaginatively used a single population of birds to make a rapid and accurate diagnosis of an entire ecosystem—Florida Bay. In doing so, Powell brought to light "the case of the panhandling herons."

Few birds have been associated with the Audubon name longer than the great white heron. John James Audubon himself discovered and named the bird in the Florida Keys, and until recent years it was generally considered a full species. Investigation, however, proved it to be simply a white color morph, or phase, of the great blue heron, with which it often mates.

Nevertheless, National Audubon has traditionally fought for the population's integrity. Long after most of the other plume birds were on the road to recovery, the great white heron was struggling for survival, its numbers down to a couple of hundred birds under constant pressure from pothunters during the Great Depression. The terrible hurricane that swept the Keys over Labor Day 1935 almost exterminated the population there. Through John Baker's efforts, however, President Franklin D. Roosevelt established a Great White Heron Refuge two years later, and the bird began its modest comeback. Biologists estimated its population in southern Florida at about two thousand individuals in 1988, with a somewhat lesser number scattered throughout the Caribbean.

Shortly after George Powell left the U.S. Fish and Wildlife Service to join the Audubon research staff at Tavernier in the early 1980s, he discovered that a great white heron "came with" the house he had rented along a canal at the edge of Florida Bay. The bird patrolled that stretch of the canal, where it took handouts from the human residents, and it defended this feeding territory with a tumultuous squawking and flap-

George Powell studies wading birds in Florida Bay. NAS

ping of wings against all other avian intruders. Powell soon saw that most other canals and stretches of inhabited shoreline had their own resident (and fiercely possessive) adult herons.

Once he had become settled in his new surroundings, Powell seized this opportunity to conduct original research. There had been indications, not yet scientifically confirmed, that the enormous influx of human beings was seriously affecting the environmental quality of Florida Bay. Could the great white heron be used as an "indicator species" to get at the truth? Only a percentage of the heron population was exploiting the new "resource" (handouts from humans). If those birds were faring significantly better than their nonpanhandling counterparts, Powell would have an important piece of evidence.

His research turned up the fact that Ernest G. Holt, who had managed Audubon sanctuaries under Gilbert Pearson, had studied the great whites of Florida Bay in 1923. Although they were badly persecuted by humans, the birds replaced their losses with a healthy rate of reproduction, fledging 2.6 young per nest. In Holt's time, the herons, which fed almost wholly at night, were getting sufficient food to fatten their chicks.

Today's herons also feed at night on small fish in the bay's shallows. But, as Powell observed, some of them haunted residential neighborhoods in the Keys by day. One heron presented itself at its human benefactor's house every morning as soon as it heard the television news snapped on. Another, if its usual host lingered in bed, "developed the habit of running its bill across an opened jalousie window and making a horrible rattle." Still others followed returning sport-fishing boats up the canals and begged for fish (sometimes with the species' mating call) once the owners began to sort the catch.

Powell devised a battery-powered trap that snared the panhandlers as they fed on lawns and walks. He marked each bird before releasing it, then arranged for the human residents to report the amounts of fish they daily offered their "personal" herons. By more traditional methods, Powell and his helpers marked nests and kept track of both panhandlers and "wild" herons in the colonies nearby.

The results of Powell's three-year study were striking—and sobering. The panhandlers were laying eggs (3.6 per nest) and raising young (2.5 per nest) at almost the same rate as that discovered by Ernest Holt six decades earlier. The birds that eschewed welfare, on the other hand, were faring poorly; they fledged only 1.5 young per nest, apparently not enough to maintain the population. Those fledged were often undersized, with decreased chances of survival. The evidence suggested there was not enough food to go around in the bay.

"Our studies have alerted us to a potentially serious disturbance in the complicated food chain of Florida Bay," George Powell and his co-workers wrote in 1988. "We have now begun an intensive ecological study of the area. Thanks to the panhandlers, we know that we must guard the quality of this important estuarine habitat."


In Peter Berle's administration, as in that of William Dutcher, the keystone of bird protection is the Audubon warden. There is no overtime in the lives of those men and women, and, in the case of the Chandlers of central Florida's Kissimmee Prairie, the job of protecting the resident cranes, ibises, egrets, and crested caracaras amounts to a family saga.

Roderick Chandler, as he set out in his Bronco to patrol the prairie in 1987, was fulfilling a responsibility first taken up by his uncle, Marvin Chandler, nearly sixty years earlier. Rod's brother, Glen, served as warden there after World War II and since his retirement lives in a little cabin deep in the wet prairie. Rod himself has patrolled a hundred square miles of prairie and the marshes around Lake Okeechobee just to the south since the 1960s. Now his son, Noel, keeps an eye on the handful of snail kites and other scarce birds that survive in the breeding colonies around the lake. Both Rod and Noel wear Audubon's emblem, the flying great egret, on their sleeves while on patrol, but they have never worn the badges often given to earlier Audubon wardens deputized by state or federal wildlife agencies.

"My Uncle Marvin always had a pretty good-size badge from the Department of the Interior that he wore on his belt," Rod told a visitor he took into the prairie one day. "After he died, Glen took over the job and wore the same badge. But I've never carried a badge or a gun. Noel and I try to work this thing a little different. We like to work with the people—a lot of them we grew up with—not to get them afraid of us but have them on our side, trying to do the same thing we're doing. Of course, we can give them a warning, or swear out a warrant if we have to. Wearing a damn gun just gets you in trouble. If they know you're not wearing a gun, nobody around here's going to shoot you."

The basis of Rod Chandler's success as a warden is his sense of fellowship with local people. Game wardens are often branded as the enemy in rural areas. Rod sees himself as just another Cracker who prepared for his Audubon assignment by learning about the land and its wildlife during his earlier years as a hunter and trapper. He was just better at it than his neighbors and acquired what can only be described as an earthy admiration for the wild creatures that are the focus of his world.

Chandler is everybody's idea of a backwoodsman, lean, brown, and sharp-faced, with not much hair remaining under the ever-present Stet-

Rod Chandler, member of a family of Audubon wardens
on the Kissimmee Prairie. © 1985 RICHARD FRANK

son, and an eye undimmed by his seventy years on Kissimmee Prairie.
He was born there, in the farming community of Basinger, in 1916. As
a boy, he shot alligators and trapped raccoons and gigged (or hooked)
frogs.

"Today I try to get these local boys to use a camera instead of a
gun," Rod said. "They say, 'Why, Rod, you've shot more damn deer
than anybody around this part of the country.'

" 'Yeah, but I'm not doing it any more.'

"They say, 'But you're being *paid* not to do it.'

"I have to laugh at that but, you know, they don't give me much
trouble here. I guess it takes a damn outlaw to know another one."

Despite the longtime Audubon presence on the Kissimmee Prairie,
there was no true sanctuary there until 1980. Before then, the basis of
protection was simply the Society's agreements with various ranchers in
the region and the Chandlers' relationship with the people. The Chandlers were able to hold the web of local interests together, but outside
forces threatened to overwhelm them. The U.S. Army Corps of Engineers channelized the Kissimmee River, turning it into what Rod called
"a damn sewer ditch" and depriving the region of much of its natural
overflow. Shoreline wildlife habitat dwindled. Developers began buying

up the land, draining it through a series of broad, unsightly canals, and dividing it into small plots. Suburban sprawl picked up momentum from its source around Orlando and Disney World just to the north.

The staff and board of directors of the National Audubon Society realized that ownership of vital nesting habitat was a necessary step if some of the key species were to remain a part of the prairie. Negotiations began around 1970 and dragged on for a decade. The breakthrough occurred in 1980 when Audubon made its first major land purchase on the prairie. The Society made additional purchases in 1981 and 1984 to assemble 7,294 acres in the new Ordway-Whittell Kissimmee Prairie Sanctuary, about thirty miles north of the city of Okeechobee. Agreements with ranchers have brought the total prairie land watched over by Rod Chandler to about sixty thousand acres.

"Just a while ago I found a little red paperback book with not many pages in it that was put out way back in Uncle Marvin's day by the Audubon Society," Rod Chandler once told a visitor to the prairie. "It tells all about their sanctuaries. Well, I've had this book a pretty good while and the reason I kept it was because Uncle Marvin's picture is in it. The way he's pictured there makes me homesick for him, because he had on those high, lace-up boots—he was a long-legged rascal—that he'd wear when he figured on working out in the water and he had to protect himself from the snakes and ticks and insects that you get out there. This book pictures him on a boardwalk and it says, 'A warden is essential to any refuge.' "

# 36

*T*he entire Audubon edifice seemed to totter for four painful months during the late spring and summer of 1987.

The explosion, when it came, caught nearly everyone off-guard, including Peter Berle and board chairman Donal O'Brien, who triggered it with an astonishing letter to chapter leaders. Indeed, the men and women most active in chapter affairs generally had the impression that the board was moving to resolve differences with the membership, repairing the defects in communication between New York and the hinterlands, and putting the Society back on track. Complaints about the board's high-handedness were diminishing.

Only the previous year, a new chapter policy had been worked out. Section III affirmed that "When there are proposed changes in issues that directly affect chapters, National will solicit and carefully consider chapter views, primarily through regional offices." A percentage of each member's dues continued to be allotted to the chapter in that member's area, regardless of whether he or she took part in chapter programs.

Also in 1986, the board had approved a budget that accepted a $1 million deficit on the premise that Berle needed a year to unravel the financial problems thrust upon him. But the problems persisted as income lagged behind expenses. The board concluded during its meeting of May 14–17, 1987, that "if we were to continue existing programs next year with no change in revenue, it would cost $2.5 million more to run the Society than we will take in." It was already apparent that by June 30, the end of the fiscal year, the unrestricted reserves would be used up and the National Audubon Society would be, in Peter Berle's words, "technically broke."

A day after the board meeting, Berle and Donal O'Brien sent an eight-page letter to the chapter leaders outlining the crisis and their response to it: the board had passed a balanced budget for the coming year and, to make this possible, would "restructure" the Society's regional operations. In effect, the present system was to be dismantled,

with most of the regional offices closed or shorn of much of their capacity to function. There were plans to reduce the chapters' share of
membership dues. A couple of dozen staff members would disappear in
the restructuring, as would the Wisconsin Summer Camp and the bimonthly newspaper *Audubon Action* (recently itself "restructured" and
named the *NAS News-Journal*). Budgets of several programs, including
the magazine, were sharply cut.

A particular shock to most staff members was the firing, without
any credible explanation, of two of Audubon's best-known biologists,
John Ogden and David Blankinship; it seemed as if the Society were
jettisoning the whooping crane, the wood stork, and the California condor with those two dedicated scientists who had worked so long on their
behalf. Isolated on their sanctuaries and research stations, members of
the field staff could only speculate by telephone about "conspiracies"
and wonder where the next blow would fall.

The backlash to Audubon's "night of the long knives" immediately
hit New York. Letters and phone calls of passionate, and sometimes
vitriolic, intensity poured in. (Donal O'Brien, an enthusiastic sportsman
as well as an environmentalist, recalled later that one Audubon activist
addressed him as a "grouse-shooting pig.") It soon became clear to Berle
and the board members that what they had on their hands was not
simply an angry outburst by scattered members in the hinterlands but
an organized uprising.

Chapter leaders all over the country were in touch with each other
by mail and phone. The new generation of activists was joined in protest
by some of the great Audubon names of the past—Roger Tory Peterson,
Sewall Pettingill, Helen Cruickshank, Harriet Buchheister, and (in a
behind-the-scenes financial contribution) Marie Aull. Much of the uprising began to coalesce almost instinctively around Charlie Callison, then
in semiretirement in Missouri.

"What we need," Harriet Buchheister, only recently widowed, said
to Callison over the phone one day in her scratchy little voice, "is another Rosalie Edge."

Callison, in his matter-of-fact way, assumed the role. He put together
a proxy movement to break the pattern of selection and recruitment
from within an inner circle that had characterized Audubon's board
membership for years; the new movement's object was to find other men
and women who were seen by chapter activists as more sensitive to
grass-roots concerns.

In response to what was now a full-fledged uprising, Berle flew to
half a dozen cities to confer with chapter leaders, explaining the board's
action and assuring them that the Society was cutting costs in New York
and Washington as well as at the local level. But Callison and others felt

that Berle and the board continued to be "hard-nosed" about the "draconian measures." Chapters in Texas threatened to withdraw from National Audubon and establish an independent state society, akin to those in Massachusetts and Florida.

Meanwhile, chapter leaders in several regions suggested that they raise money to keep the local offices open until the Society was back on its feet. Berle pointed out that at least nine board members had past experience as Audubon activists at the local level. (For instance, Bruce Howard, the chairman of the board's Chapter Relations Committee and one of those working most strenuously to calm the waters, had been an officer of the Golden Gate Audubon Society in California.) Berle also reminded protesters that the *Audubon Activist,* a bimonthly newspaper addressed to chapter concerns, had been created to replace the defunct *Audubon Action,* though it was mailed only to those who bought subscriptions.

With the uprising still in high gear, Donal O'Brien called a special meeting of the board at the end of July to deal with it. In his call, however, he made several remarks that further inflamed the rebels. He expressed his concern that the chapter leaders were not really representative of the membership as a whole and that they would frighten away potential contributors to the Society.

"Most major financial supporters of conservation organizations—be they individuals, foundations or corporations—do not choose to support citizen activism," O'Brien wrote. "These supporters, most especially foundations and corporations, tend to shy away, for either legal or policy reasons, from supporting controversial political or legislative activities. This is something which is well known and understood by some of our sister organizations, such as The Nature Conservancy and Ducks Unlimited."

Callison, when a copy of the letter fell into his hands, addressed a letter in response to all board members in which he accused them of treating the chapters as "foreign principalities," and not as integral parts of the Society. He challenged O'Brien's supposition that chapter activists would frighten away large donors.

"He even suggests NAS should perhaps emulate the examples of The Nature Conservancy and Ducks Unlimited, both well known as issue neuters," Callison wrote. "The Audubon Society has been an activist organization through nearly a century of history, never shrinking from controversy, and while it has had lean times it has never lacked for wealthy and generous supporters.

"Another high officer of the Society recently expressed Mr. O'Brien's fear in more candid terms. Should they succeed in a proxy campaign, the officer said, the Chapter 'agitators' would likely elect directors who wouldn't fit in socially with the rest of the Board, and whose manners could prove embarrassing in the presence of foundation executives and corporate officers. I have talked to a number of leaders who have been contemplating a proxy campaign and I can assure you, my friends, that they will not nominate any 'red-necks.' All their nominees will be gentlemen and gentlewomen."

The call for a special meeting of the board was a tacit admission by Berle and O'Brien that they had erred in trying to push the restructuring of the Society's regional system without consulting chapter leaders. Berle now felt a little better about the financial situation. To give the Society a fresh start in the new fiscal year, he had arranged for the Audubon pension fund to be restructured to give the unrestricted reserves an infusion of $3 million on July 1. Then, after reviewing current fiscal problems with his staff, Berle decided to ask O'Brien to "democratize" the board, following suggestions often made in recent years to allow the chapters themselves to nominate a certain proportion of its members.

"I was pleasantly surprised when Don O'Brien not only agreed with me, but went further than I had been willing to suggest up to that point," Berle has said. "O'Brien laid out the plan that was adopted later that summer."

Both men were apprehensive about what might happen at the Society's biennial convention, scheduled for Bellingham, Washington, in late August. They expected a horde of angry activists to be on hand to precipitate a confrontation. If matters were settled beforehand, they believed, an unruly demonstration could be averted. Thus Berle and O'Brien put together (with the help of a special committee of the board) proposals that would keep most of the regional offices open (some with local funding), and they devised a formula for bringing chapter activists onto the board of directors. The special board meeting approved the new proposals on July 27.

"Then we invited a broad spectrum of chapter leaders to meet with some of us in Washington and review the proposals," Berle has said. "We invited some of our most outspoken opponents, but I purposely excluded Charlie Callison and one or two others who were most involved with the proxy campaign. I admire all that Callison has done for the Society, but now I felt he was representing a return to the past, the way things were once done, and I didn't want to go in that direction."

The meeting in Washington took place as planned. There were some uncomfortable moments, and several times the opposing sides "caucused" in hallways to consider specific points. But, in the end, there was a feeling that the chapters would go along with the new proposals. Only one of the regional offices was to be closed (Richard Madson's old bailiwick, the North Midwest Region, was swallowed by the West Central

Region). In contrast, the Society's Southwest office, under regional vice president Dede Armentrout, worked closely with the restive activists in Texas to find the money that ensured its continued operation; Walt Pomeroy in the Middle Atlantic Region was another who kept the office functioning with local support. Meanwhile, nine of the Society's current board of thirty-six members were asked to step aside for those nominated by the chapters. And any plans to reduce the chapters' share of membership dues was postponed at least until the new board took shape.

Nevertheless, Callison and his followers refused to drop the proxy campaign. They believed that the Washington meeting had been "rigged" in favor of the board, and in turn put up their own slate of twelve nominees. In a letter to a former supporter who had agreed to the board's proposals, Callison argued that it was only the proxy threat that had forced Berle and O'Brien to back down, and only the proxy threat would force them to carry out the new proposals.

"I hope that you will not repeat the hyperbole that a proxy contest 'could seriously damage or destroy the Society,' " Callison wrote. "Nothing could destroy the Audubon Society; it is too firmly entrenched in the American consciousness. A spirited proxy contest will revitalize the Society; it won't 'damage' it. No one involved in the proxy campaign has acted out of any motive other than total loyalty to the National Audubon Society."

The proxy campaign, however, was now carried on mainly to make a point. Although Roger Peterson, Sewall Pettingill, John Gallagher of the Ohio Audubo.. Council, and others of the old guard continued to support it, Berle and the board of directors had drawn the sting from the uprising by their concessions at the meeting in early August. Those concessions had the effect of averting a confrontation during the convention at Bellingham later that month. Callison stayed mainly behind the scenes there, delivering no statements and asking no questions during the open forums on chapter policy, huddling a few times with disaffected activists in side rooms, and leaving Bellingham early to return to Missouri for meetings on a local conservation issue. Berle survived a few testy remarks made by chapter leaders during their meetings, but left a good impression on them with his forthright answers to their questions.

The chapters agreed to a procedure, hastily constructed, to provide for the election of nine new members to the board. Callison, as he had promised, continued to solicit proxy ballots for his group's slate of twelve nominees, several of which were also put forward by the chapters under the "establishment's" new procedures. (Callison himself was not a nominee.) The New York Office, which in past years had distributed its own proxy form by bulk mail or by stuffing it into the magazine, now organized a first-class mail campaign (at a cost of $200,000 for postage, business-reply forms, paper, printing, and handling) to make certain the membership received its message. Callison complained of "overkill," while Berle charged Callison with putting the struggling Society to great expense.

The ballots were counted that December at the Society's annual meeting. Callison and John Gallagher had carted two suitcases bulging with their proxies to the New York hotel where more than a hundred people jammed the small conference room for the showdown. One look at the stacked cartons wheeled in as the fruit of Berle's proxy effort prompted Callison to concede without an official tabulation. (The final score, based on the combatants' own counts, was 106,529 signed proxies for the official slate, 5,111 for Callison's side.) Yet, in defeat, Callison and his followers had forced far-reaching changes on the Society, more substantial perhaps than even those brought about by Rosalie Edge.

"How lasting the change will be depends on whether the nine Regionally-elected Directors can make themselves heard on the Board," Callison and Gallagher told their followers. "Much more will depend on whether the chapters themselves continue to insist on being heard in New York. They must not tolerate the point-of-view that they are merely expensive and non-essential appendages of an organization made up of a national Board of Directors, a national staff, and a body of magazine subscribers."

But a new sense of mission was already reviving among chapters and staff. Harold E. Woodsum, Jr., chairman of the finance committee (and later O'Brien's successor as the chairman of the board), worked with the vice president for finance, James A. Cunningham, to explore every aspect of the Society's financial structure and provide solutions for the weak spots they uncovered. Within six months of the close of the proxy battle, Berle and O'Brien were able to point to a dramatic turn-around in the Society's fiscal position. A combination of tightened expenditures and aggressive fundraising had converted red ink to black and, on June 30, 1988, with a responsible annual budget of over thirty-two million dollars in place, the nagging deficit had disappeared for the first time in memory.

The National Audubon Society was once more free to go about its real business—which is, as stated in its original charter and now requiring an all-out assault on a broad spectrum of environmental ills, "the Protection of Wild Birds and Animals."

# *Epilogue*

The Audubon Society was born more than a century ago with a messianic sense of mission. There was the pamphleteer's logical, if sometimes cranky, note of urgency in the air, as well as the street-corner revivalist's appeal to "Repent!"—though the target was often enough simply a small boy with a slingshot or a stylish lady in a plumed hat. But the message endured for reasons that until lately have been unclear to all save the chosen few.

The Audubon message was, and is, really about biology. It presupposes close links between humans and the natural world, links that grew murky to the eye as industrial civilization developed and went on expanding. But nowhere was there an official or an otherwise powerful sanction for that view. We the people are defined by government as political animals, by the churches as spiritual beings, and by society as cogs in the economic structure. As biological organisms we became *persona non grata*.

The founders and influential members of the Audubon societies cared deeply about wild nature. They were hunters, gardeners, naturalists, or simply people who liked to go out at night and look up at the stars. They sensed that their well-being depended on a various and functioning natural world. They had learned to say *yes* to all life.

Later converts to the conservation movement too often flocked in out of a sense of fear. Environmental disasters—from Dust Bowl conditions to killer smogs, poisoned wells, foods tainted by toxic chemicals, signs of the greenhouse effect, or holes in the ozone layer, even declining property values caused by urban blight—shocked them into seeing that the good life cannot be bought at the expense of humanity's ties to natural processes. What's bad for birds is usually awful for human beings.

The history of the National Audubon Society is, ultimately, the story of how one group of people organized to get others looking at the wild world, not with indifference or even with fear, but with *love*. The child who has a lively interest in plants and animals, and who wants to learn more about them, will surely grow into a more steadfast champion of Earth's welfare than one who comes to that persuasion out of fear of getting environmental cancers. The latter tends to lose interest as soon as the government sounds the all-clear sirens.

It is plain from a reading of conservation history that government, on either the federal or local level, is no bulwark against environmental degradation. In fact, most of the major environmental problems of our time, from pesticide contamination, acid rain, toxic dumps, water-project boondoggles, energy waste, and wetland losses to (specifically) the invasion on a large scale of fragile wildlife refuges by the oil drillers, can be traced not only to government inaction but often to its outright encouragement. Government officials need, some of them seem to crave, pressures to cave in to. Here is where the private conservation organization comes in, as a counterweight to the pressures exerted on bureaucrats and legislators by those who would exploit natural resources to the point of exhaustion.

Is an organization created a century ago to protect plume birds adequately positioned to take a leading role in battling for a healthy environment—and thus a better life for all Americans—today? This history suggests that, from the initial impulse to speak out for life, the National Audubon Society has grown to meet the challenges that sprang up successively because of that commitment.

No other organization of its kind is so well equipped, on so many fronts, to meet the enormous environmental challenges facing us at the end of the twentieth century. There is an experienced government-relations staff of fifteen professionals to deal with Congress and federal agencies in Washington; an increasingly sophisticated and far-flung group of scientists to find solutions to pressing problems in energy policy, environmental contamination, and wildlife protection; an education department once more reaching out with timely, attractive materials for America's children; and a magazine and other publications in the forefront of environmental reporting that draw thousands of new members while keeping informed those already in the fold.

The Society's greatest treasure remains its quarter-million acres in more than eighty individual sanctuaries, staffed by the kind of wardens whom William Dutcher knew must stand as a barrier between wildlife and the "harmful class of selfish people." In the years ahead, the sanctuaries will become an even more important part of the Society. Are they to remain chiefly as refuges and research areas? Or will almost all of them be made more accessible as they have been at Corkscrew Swamp and at Beidler Forest Sanctuary in South Carolina, to educate an increasingly interested public and promote the Audubon cause?

The membership, now at an all-time high of over 550,000 men and women, gives the Society high visibility and much political leverage from coast to coast. This "grass-roots" element will take a more aggressive role in making decisions and in carrying out Audubon programs. If there are great strides to be made in the near future, they must come in this area by expanding both the numbers and the social makeup of the membership.

In Great Britain, the Royal Society for the Protection of Birds has a membership equal to National Audubon's, but in a population only a quarter of that of the United States. Numbers imply power in a democracy. But, even more, increased numbers in this case would imply reaching into new sectors of America to bring in people who have been notoriously under-represented in conservation organizations. *Audubon, Audubon Adventures,* television specials, and other of the Society's programs are already making some inroads on that front. Can people on all income levels be convinced that it is desirable, even *responsible,* to contribute to a cause that is working effectively for a better life for all of us?

But those are matters for Audubon leaders of the present and the future to pursue. The task here has been to bring into perspective the hopes and deeds that brought National Audubon to this point. The Audubon past has had a glory of its own.

# A Note on the Sources

Because of the scattered nature of the Society's files and (as was mentioned in my Preface) the disappearance of many of them, the most comprehensive source of information is the succession of magazines that have served as its official publication. The succession begins with George Bird Grinnell's *Audubon Magazine* (1886–88), continues with Frank M. Chapman's *Bird-Lore* (1899–1940), changes again to *Audubon Magazine* in 1941, and evolves into the modern *Audubon* (1953). Another invaluable source of information on the Audubon movement's early years is T. Gilbert Pearson's *Adventures in Bird Protection* (New York, Appleton-Century, 1937).

CHAPTER ONE: A highly readable introduction to Grinnell's life is John G. Mitchell's "A Man Called Bird" (*Audubon*, March 1987, pp. 81–104). Grinnell's own magazine, *Forest and Stream*, remains one of the most rewarding sources of information on natural history, conservation, and game policy during the later nineteenth century and early twentieth century.

Helpful for an understanding of the plight of birds in nineteenth-century America are John James Audubon's *Ornithological Biography* (available in several editions); Robert Henry Walker's *Birds and Men: American Birds in Science, Art and Literature, and Conservation, 1800–1900* (Cambridge, Harvard University Press, 1955); and Peter Matthiessen's *Wildlife in America* (New York, Viking Press, 1959).

CHAPTER TWO: A contribution to early conservation history is Richard K. Walton's *Massachusetts Audubon Society: The First Twenty-five Years 1896–1921* (to be published in connection with that society's centennial). Two brief looks at the early Audubon movement are found in "Vignettes of Early Days of the Audubon Society of the District of Columbia," by J. E. Wade (*Atlantic Naturalist*, April 1956) and Irston R. Barnes's column, "Perspectives" (*Audubon Naturalist*, January and April 1957).

Other sources for this chapter include Pearson's *Adventures in Bird Protection*, correspondence now in the National Audubon Society Collection of the New York Public Library, Rare Books and Manuscripts Division, and contemporary issues of *The Auk* (the publication of the American Ornithologists' Union).

CHAPTER THREE: Primary sources here are the file on William Dutcher and his work, including the letters, in the National Audubon Society Collection at the New York Public Library, and the files collected by Carl W. Buchheister and now in possession of the Society. Background for this chapter can also be found in *Feather Fashions and Bird Preservation* by Robin W. Doughty (Berkeley, University of California Press, 1975) and two of my own books, *Man's Dominion: The Story of Conservation in America* (New York, M. Evans, 1971) and *Gulls: A Social History* (New York, Random House, 1975).

CHAPTER FOUR: Sources for this chapter, besides *The Auk* and *Bird-Lore*, include "Frank Michler Chapman, 1864–1945," by Robert Cushman Murphy in *The Auk*, July 1950, "Boy Meets Bullfinch," by Geoffrey Hellman in *The New Yorker*, March 4, 1939, and Chapman's *Camps and Cruises of an Ornithologist* (New York, D. Appleton, 1908). A fascinating look at early American ornithology can be found in *Elliott Coues: Naturalist and Frontier Historian* by Paul Russell Cutright and Michael J. Brodhead (Urbana, University of Illinois Press, 1981).

CHAPTER FIVE: The correspondence of Dutcher in the Audubon Society Collection at the New York Public Library provides primary source material for this chapter, as does Pearson's *Adventures in Bird Protection*. See also the issues of *Bird-Lore* for those years.

CHAPTER SIX: A first-hand description of the young Guy Bradley and his world, as well as the plume-hunter Lechevalier, is found in "The Cruise of the Bonton," by Charles William Pierce (*Tequesta*, the Journal of the Historical Association of Southern Florida, XXII, 1962), and "Who Was the Frenchman of Frenchman's Creek?" by Walter P. Fuller (ibid., XXIX, pp. 45–59, 1969). See also Robert Porter Allen's *The Roseate Spoonbill* (New York, National Audubon Society, 1942); Herbert K. Job's *Wild Wings* (Boston and New York, Houghton Mifflin, 1905); Charlton W. Tebeau's *Man in the Everglades* (Coral Gables, University of Miami Press, 1968); and Frank M. Chapman's *Camps and Cruises of an Ornithologist* (op. cit.). *Bird-Lore* also records important details.

CHAPTERS SEVEN, EIGHT, AND NINE: Pearson, who never hid his own light under a bushel basket, is the prime source for the Audubon struggle during these years. *Bird-Lore* supplies most of the gaps he left. I told the Hornaday story in somewhat greater detail in *Man's Dominion* (op. cit.), where I drew heavily on the published and unpublished writings of Hornaday which were in the possession of John Ripley Forbes at his offices in New Canaan, Connecticut. See especially Hornaday's *Our Vanishing Wildlife* (New York Zoological Society, 1914). Senator Reed's remarks can be found in the *Congressional Record*, 63rd Cong., 1st sess., 16 Aug., 1913, 3426.

CHAPTER TEN: Pearson again is a leading primary source here, as is *Bird-Lore* and various leaflets produced by the Society. In regard to Hornaday and

Burnham, see *Crusade for Wildlife* by James B. Trefethan (Harrisburg, Pa., the Stockpole Company, and New York, the Boone and Crockett Club, 1961).

CHAPTER ELEVEN: Pearson and *Bird-Lore* provide a wealth of detail on the events of those years, as does Hornaday's *Thirty Years' War for Wildlife* (New York, Scribner's, 1931). An excellent summary of the complex wildlife legislation of the time is found in *The Evolution of National Wildlife Law,* prepared for the Council on Environmental Quality by Michael J. Bean and the Environmental Law Institute (Washington, D.C., U.S. Government Printing Office, 1977). This publication also discusses the discrimination against alien hunters as reflected in the actions of state legislatures and courts of the time. (See especially pages 44ff.)

CHAPTER TWELVE: Once more, Pearson and *Bird-Lore* provide a framework for these events. See also Eugene Swope's *Voice of the Woods* (New York, Paebar Co., 1946). There is a glimpse of the dashing aspect of Paul J. Rainey in *Outdoor Life,* October 6, 1986. James Callaghan's reports in the files of the Theodore Roosevelt Wildlife Sanctuary are an effective antidote to Swope's euphoric prose.

CHAPTER THIRTEEN: Pearson and *Bird-Lore* provide sedate coverage of this chapter's events compared to the colorful prose found in the Hornaday material collected by John Ripley Forbes (op. cit.) and the Rosalie Edge files at the Hawk Mountain Sanctuary. Also see the minutes of various National Audubon Society board meetings and the collection of Edge's correspondence and publications in the Denver Public Library.

CHAPTER FOURTEEN: Here *Bird-Lore* is amply supplemented by various wardens' reports in the files of the Society's Field Research Department in Tavernier, Florida. I interviewed Louis Rawalt at Corpus Christi in 1977. See also my history of the Society's Sanctuary System, "The Audubon Ark" (*Audubon,* January 1978, pp. 2–172).

CHAPTER FIFTEEN: This account is based partly on the recollections of Carl Buchheister, as well as on my interviews at various places over several years with Roger Tory Peterson and Joseph J. Hickey. See also my article in *Audubon* ("A-Birding in the Bronx," May 1982, pp. 10–16).

CHAPTER SIXTEEN: Buchheister interviewed Helen Cruickshank in June 1976. My interviews with Carl and Harriet Buchheister, Roger Tory Peterson, and William Vogt, as well as material in Carl Buchheister's files, are the chief sources here. See also Peterson's "The Evolution of a Magazine" (*Audubon,* January 1973, pp. 46–51).

CHAPTER SEVENTEEN: Reports and letters of Audubon wardens, as well as those of Alexander Sprunt, Jr., in the files of the Field Research Department at Tavernier, provide much of the background for this chapter. See also my articles

"The Audubon Ark" (op. cit.) and "A Warden's Story" (*Audubon*, March 1987, pp. 105–20). A close look at Fred Schultz is found in "King of Whiskey Stump" by James J. Cox (*Audubon*, November 1954, pp. 268–71).

CHAPTER EIGHTEEN: Baker's letters in the Audubon Society Collection in the New York Public Library, as well as Buchheister's files and recollections, form the basis of this chapter.

CHAPTER NINETEEN: My interviews with Richard Pough—see my article "Conservation's Ultimate Entrepreneur" (*Audubon*, November 1984, pp. 102–11)—in addition to the files on the "Second Great Plumage War" collected by Buchheister and now in the Society's possession, form the basis of this chapter. See also the minutes of various board meetings of the Society during those years.

CHAPTER TWENTY: See *The Hawks of North America* by John B. May (New York, National Association of Audubon Societies, 1935), *The Ivory-billed Woodpecker* by James T. Tanner (Research Report No. 1, New York, National Audubon Society, 1942), and *The Roseate Spoonbill* by Robert Porter Allen (op. cit.). Two books that Allen wrote for the general reader, *The Flame Birds* (New York, Dodd, Mead, 1947) and *On the Trail of Vanishing Birds* (New York, McGraw-Hill, 1957), are lively accounts of his experiences with spoonbills and other glamorous species. Also see *A Sand County Almanac* by Aldo Leopold (New York, Oxford University Press, 1966).

CHAPTER TWENTY-ONE: Parts of this chapter are based on two unpublished histories of the Audubon Screen Tours, one by Wayne Short, the other by O. S. Pettingill, Jr. Buchheister's recollections and various articles in *Audubon* tell other parts of the story.

CHAPTER TWENTY-TWO: My interviews with Alexander Sprunt IV and Richard Pough, plus material in the files of Buchheister and the Field Research Department, are the major sources here.

CHAPTER TWENTY-THREE: Buchheister's files and recollections, in addition to my interviews with Charles H. Callison and William H. Drury, Jr., form the basis of this chapter.

CHAPTER TWENTY-FOUR: Buchheister's recollections and my interviews with Gene Setzer and Marie Aull provided most of the background here. See my article, "Marie Aull and the Flowering of Aullwood" (*Audubon*, May 1986, pp. 66–75).

CHAPTER TWENTY-FIVE: My trip to Great Inagua, supplemented by the files of the Field Research Department, are the basis for this chapter. See my article "De Fillymingo Mon!" (*Audubon*, January 1983, pp. 50–65). For details of G. A. Würdeman's experience, see Robert Porter Allen's *The Flamingos: Their Life and Survival* (Research Report No. 5, New York, National Audubon Society, 1956).

CHAPTER TWENTY-SIX: Files in the Society's Science Department in addition to my interviews with Callison, Setzer, John Borneman, and John M. Anderson provide background for much of this chapter. Buchheister's recollections are also important. See also my book *Since Silent Spring* (Boston, Houghton Mifflin, 1970).

CHAPTER TWENTY-SEVEN: My interviews with Callison, Cynthia Wilson, Elvis Stahr, and Gary Soucie form the basis of this chapter.

CHAPTER TWENTY-EIGHT: My interviews with Stahr and Drury, in addition to files of the Society's Science Department, provide the background here.

CHAPTER TWENTY-NINE: My interviews with Stahr and Kenneth Ashcraft, in addition to material that Stahr provided, form the basis of this chapter.

CHAPTER THIRTY: My interview with Stahr, material supplied by Mary Joy Breton, and my own experience with the Society during these years provide the background.

CHAPTER THIRTY-ONE: Articles in *Audubon*, in addition to the files of the Society's Science Department and the president's office, are vital sources here.

CHAPTER THIRTY-TWO: My interviews with John Ogden form the basis of this chapter. I also consulted files in the Science Department. See also *In Condor Country* by David Darlington (Boston, Houghton Mifflin, 1987).

CHAPTER THIRTY-THREE: Besides recalling my own involvement in the Society during this time, I have drawn on a number of sources: material sent me by Scott Reed, Wayne Short, and Greg Lasley, my interviews with Sandy Sprunt, Frank Dunstan, and Christopher Palmer, and the files of the Field Research Department in Tavernier.

CHAPTER THIRTY-FOUR: My interviews with Peter Berle are central to this chapter. See also *A Life in Two Worlds: An Autobiography* by Beatrice Bishop Berle (New York, Walker, 1983).

CHAPTER THIRTY-FIVE: This chapter is based primarily on my research for various articles in *Audubon*. See especially "Seabirds Under Siege" (*Audubon*, November 1976, pp. 52–73); "Biology with Poetry" (*Audubon*, September 1983, pp. 102–21); "How Fare the Audubon Birds a Century Later?" (*Audubon*, March 1987, pp. 14–18); and "A Warden's Story" (op. cit.)

CHAPTER THIRTY-SIX: This chapter is based on my interviews with Peter Berle and Charles Callison, and on the materials that each of them supplied to me. I was also present at the meetings in Bellingham, Washington, and New York.

# Index

Note: *References to illustrations are in italics.*

## A Note About the Author

Frank Graham, Jr., was born in New York City in 1925. Graduated from Columbia College, Mr. Graham has been since 1958 a free-lance writer specializing in nature and conservation. He has written more than a dozen books, among them *Since Silent Spring* (1970), *Where the Place Called Morning Lies* (1973), and *The Adirondack Park* (1978). He and his wife, Ada, have also collaborated on a number of books for young readers in the fields of natural history and the environment. Since 1968 he has been a field editor for *Audubon* magazine. In 1976 Mr. Graham received an honorary Doctorate in Humane Letters from Colby College. The Grahams live in Milbridge, Maine.

A NOTE ON THE TYPE

The text of this book was set in a digitized version of
Garamond No. 3, a modern rendering of the type first cut
by Claude Garamond (c. 1480-1561). Garamond was a pupil
of Geoffroy Tory and is believed to have based his letters on
the Venetian models, although he introduced a number of
important differences, and it is to him we owe the letter
known as "old style." He gave to his letters a certain elegance and a feeling of movement that won for their creator
an immediate reputation and the patronage of Francis I
of France.

Composed by Creative Graphics, Inc.,
Allentown, Pennsylvania

Design by Dorothy S. Baker